FOUNDATIONS

A STATEMENT OF CHRISTIAN BELIEF
IN TERMS OF MODERN THOUGHT

FOUNDATIONS

A STATEMENT OF CHRISTIAN
BELIEF IN TERMS OF MODERN
THOUGHT: BY SEVEN OXFORD MEN

B. H. STREETER

R. BROOK   A. E. J. RAWLINSON
W. H. MOBERLY   N. S. TALBOT
R. G. PARSONS   W. TEMPLE

Essay Index Reprint Series

 BOOKS FOR LIBRARIES PRESS
FREEPORT, NEW YORK

First Published 1912
Reprinted 1971

INTERNATIONAL STANDARD BOOK NUMBER:
0-8369-2189-5

LIBRARY OF CONGRESS CATALOG CARD NUMBER:
77-152171

PRINTED IN THE UNITED STATES OF AMERICA

CONTENTS

INTRODUCTION

I. THE MODERN SITUATION

By *the* Rev. N. S. TALBOT, M.A., *Fellow, Tutor and*
Chaplain of Balliol College I

PAGE

II. THE BIBLE

By *the* Rev. R. BROOK, M.A., *Fellow and Tutor of*
Merton College, Lecturer in Theology at Merton and
Oriel Colleges, Examining Chaplain to the Bishop
of Wakefield 25

III. THE HISTORIC CHRIST

By *the* Rev. B. H. STREETER, M.A., *Fellow and Dean*
of Queen's College, Oxford; Lecturer in Theology at
Queen's and Hertford Colleges, Formerly Fellow of
Pembroke College, Oxford 73

IV. THE INTERPRETATION OF THE CHRIST IN THE NEW TESTAMENT

By *the* Rev. A. E. J. RAWLINSON, M.A., *Tutor of Keble*
College, and the Rev. R. G. PARSONS, M.A.,
Principal of Wells Theological College, and Pre-
bendary of Wells Cathedral, Examining Chaplain to
the Bishop of Winchester, Formerly Fellow and
Praelector in Theology of University College, Oxford 147

V. THE DIVINITY OF CHRIST

PAGE

By the Rev. W. TEMPLE, M.A., *Headmaster of Repton,
Chaplain to the Archbishop of Canterbury, Formerly
Fellow and Lecturer in Philosophy, Queen's College,
Oxford* 211

VI. THE ATONEMENT

By W. H. MOBERLY, M.A., *Fellow and Lecturer in
Philosophy of Lincoln College, Formerly Fellow of
Merton College* 265

VII. THE CHURCH

By the Rev. W. TEMPLE 337

VIII. THE PRINCIPLE OF AUTHORITY

AUTHORITY AND TRUTH; AUTHORITY AND CHURCH
ORDER; AUTHORITY AND REUNION. APPENDIX,
The Historical Origins of the Christian Ministry.
By the Rev. A. E. J. RAWLINSON . . . 361

IX. GOD AND THE ABSOLUTE

By W. H. MOBERLY 423

EPILOGUE . . . 525

INDEX 529

INTRODUCTION

THE modern world is asking questions. Christianity and its traditional theology have come down to us from an age very different from our own, an age when the sun and the stars moved round the earth, when the meaning of natural law and evolution was only dimly apprehended, when the psychology of religion, the historical method and the critical study of ancient documents were yet unborn. These things touch the foundations of the old beliefs, and it is about the foundations that the world is asking.

The world is calling for religion; but it cannot accept a religion if its theology is out of harmony with science, philosophy, and scholarship. Religion, if it is to dominate life, must satisfy both the head and the heart, a thing which neither obscurantism nor rationalism can do. At such a time it seems most necessary that those who believe that Christianity is no mere picturesque survival of a romantic past, but a real religion with a real message for the present and the future, should set themselves to a careful re-examination, and if need be re-statement, of the foundations of their belief in the light of the knowledge and thought of the day.

The present volume, the outcome of an Oxford friendship, is due to the conviction that such a task might be more successfully attempted by a corporate effort than by the labours of separate individuals. The majority of us on many occasions, and all of us more than once, have been able to meet together in conference for mutual criticism of the essays previously circulated in draft form. Four times these conferences have been of the nature of a retreat continued during three or four days, and each essay has been thus discussed at more than one stage before it assumed its present form.

We came to the study of the subject from points of view which differed widely with our differing temperaments, interests, and ecclesiastical associations, but from our various conferences there has resulted a far greater measure of agreement than we had originally anticipated. Differences, some of opinion, others rather of emphasis, of course remain. It is neither possible nor desirable that seven minds should think exactly alike on so many complex problems. In a few cases the differences concern points which some of us would regard as of the first importance. But nevertheless the book is put forward not as a collection of detached studies but as a single whole, and as, in the main, the expression of a corporate mind ; and the essays are intended to read as a connected series in the order and context in which they stand.

Throughout our discussions we have kept in view the fact that the problems we are attacking are felt keenly as such far beyond the circle of professed theo-

logians. Hence we have made a special effort by the
avoidance, so far as possible, of technical terminology,
to present our conclusions in such a way as to be
of interest to the educated layman, or to the cleric who
makes no claim to be a theological specialist. We
hope, however, that we have not fallen into the error
of being " popular " in the bad sense, and that some of
the things we have written may be considered not
unworthy of perusal even by theologians.

A word may be added as to the principle which has
determined the arrangement of the essays in the book.

The fundamental question for religion, and one of
which our own age is by no means inclined to take an
answer for granted, is that of the existence of God. But
the idea of God, in the sense in which the Christian speaks
of God, was not given to mankind all at once, nor was
it arrived at by processes of pure philosophy or abstract
reasoning. It came through the direct spiritual apprehension of the Hebrew prophets, the explicit teaching
of our Lord Himself, and the interpretation of the
Person of Christ by the inspired writers of the New
Testament and in the long history of the Church. It
would seem, then, that an examination of these sources
of the belief in the light of modern knowledge should
precede an examination into the validity of the belief
itself. And it is this consideration which has determined the order in which the various subjects have
been treated.

In every department of thought advance is only
made when men will make experiments and put forward

suggestions, some of which after due consideration may win their way to acceptance while others will be rejected. In theology this task must always be the special duty of the younger generation. The men whose position in the Church is such that they cannot speak at all except with authority can rarely venture on experiments outside the sphere of practice. It is otherwise with us. We fully recognise the obligations of loyalty to the traditions of the Church to which we belong, we make no claim to irresponsibility; but we are young men, and our responsibility is of a different kind. It is the responsibility of making experiments.

At the Reformation, the last great crisis in the history of the Church, the principle deliberately adopted by the Church of England was to "keep the mean between the two extremes of too much stiffness in refusing and of too much easiness in admitting variation." The principle of combining continuity and progress is one which underlies all sound development, and we write in the hope that what we have to say may be found to be an application of this principle to the needs of the present situation.

We do not profess to have covered the whole field, and some important problems we have left untouched. We have confined ourselves to those which seemed to us the most fundamental, or those on which we felt we had something to offer. Still less do we profess to offer a final Theology. A final Theology means a complete account of the ways of God in relation to the universe and to man. It will not be reached till Nature has

yielded up her last secret to science, till the philosopher
has attained his goal and " contemplates all time and
all existence," and till the kingdom of God is come.
What we have written is put forward, not as the
solution, but as a contribution towards the solution of
the problems we have approached, not as a last word
even for our own generation or our own immediate
circle, but as a word that has come to us and one which
we believe we ought to speak. Whatever in it is of
value will be absorbed into the common heritage of
Christian thought, whatever is crude, misleading, or
erroneous will be soon forgotten.

B. H. S.

August 1912.

I

THE MODERN SITUATION

BY

NEVILLE S. TALBOT

SYNOPSIS

PAGE

I. This generation is modern in the sense that its members are not "Victorian." In early and middle nineteenth century the majority of liberal thinkers confidently relied on elementary assumptions in religion, or at least in morality. This confidence contributed towards their enthusiasm for emancipation, for escape from dogma, for education, etc. The political and economic theories of the Manchester School implied the assumption of the benevolence of nature to the individual   4

Darwin the sexton to Victorian assumptions. His teaching contemporary with popularization of agnostic science and radical Bible criticism   6

Victorian optimism has been sapped by a "cosmic" uneasiness, by a philosophy of relativity, by realization of the indifference of nature to the individual, by the sickness of an industrial order built on a false political economy, by increased sensitiveness to evil and cruelty in the world   7

The average man and church-goer have still to realize the situation. They are bound to suffer in a measure the convulsions already undergone by a minority   10

II. Who can heal "the hurt of the daughter of My people"? .   11

Not moral philosophy by itself, unless reasoned convictions take the place of assumptions in its presuppositions . .   11

Not Christian morality by itself: for it seems to be bound up with an other-worldly philosophy with which the mind of to-day (dominated by commerce and competition) is acutely at variance .   13

What, then, is the position of the Christian preacher? He cannot renounce, but must face the world and its facts. His hold on a supernatural Gospel may be weak. But if there is a crisis in the Christian faith there is a worse one in any other .   15

III. Hence to-day is a day of new hope for the Christian religion. It is a day of Jesus Christ. Men are again feeling the need which He came to satisfy—the need of God. This is best realized by a study of the mind of the original disciples in face of the "day of the Lord"   18

Jesus appealed to Jewish faith in God : He found it alive in a few : He raised it to its highest power in bringing them to acknowledge Him as Messiah. This faith was broken by the Cross as recapitulating all that had ever made Jewish faith in God waver. It was remade by the Resurrection and Pentecost . . .   19

The essence of Christianity was the *truth of God* put to final proof. Its disclosure was the supreme disclosure . . .   22

But the truth of God became a foundation, buried out of sight and built upon. The disclosure became an assumption and convention. The results of this. To-day the original conditions return; the questions to which the Gospel was an answer are again being asked, and Christianity as the truth of God will live again in living men   22

I

THE MODERN SITUATION

PROBABLY every generation of men has called itself modern, and more than that, has held its modernism to be more radical, genuine, and interesting than that of any previous time. Certainly this generation—and by that is meant people of about thirty years of age— is tempted to do·so. A temptation implies a possible fault : here the fault lies in that form of snobbery which assumes, as a matter of course, that to-day is better than yesterday ; that what is latest in time is also highest in value, and that all change must be for the better.

One course is open to those who, whether snobs or not, cannot rid themselves of the consciousness of being modern. It is to attempt to describe the change between to-day and yesterday. Prior to the question whether the mere passage of time must involve progress, is the question, what has it involved ? What changes have occurred ? In short, in what sense are self-styled modern men modern ?

This essay represents such an attempt. It has staggered with difficulty to its goal, for on the way it has found itself entangled in the hazards which attend upon generalization. As it is, it is likely to furnish another instance of the inexactness of general impressions. But to refrain for that reason from trying to generalize, would be to yield to a rumour that there are lions in the street.[1] Generalizations serve as lines of communication between generations, and, if necessary, risks must be run in order to keep the lines open.

I

This generation in Great Britain is modern in the sense that it is not Victorian. Its members were born whilst Queen Victoria was still alive, but they never knew—they were not themselves moulded by—the times before the "sixties." They were not born, as their parents were, into the atmosphere of pre-"critical" and pre-Darwinian religion. Their education did not begin with the statement "Creation of the world, 4004," nor are their minds governed by the assumptions it implies.

In fact, the change from genuinely Victorian times to to-day is a change from the reliance upon, to the criticism of, assumptions.

This is true whether, as we look back, we consider conservative or liberal, orthodox or agnostic thought. The mind of the early and middle nineteenth century was held together in an union which differences strained but did not break. Yet the differences were violent enough. On the one hand, neither insularity nor reaction could keep out of England the movements which had their source and inspiration in the French Revolution. A passion for liberty and reform was a note of the century which had such a beginning. On the other hand, the religious world in England in early Victorian days was as an island within an island. Little of the radicalism and scepticism which did cross the Channel percolated into a world of immemorial tradition revitalized by two revivals. Nevertheless, the gulf between free-thinking, reforming intellectuals and good Evangelicals or Tractarians was not so deep, but that they had moral and even religious assumptions in

[1] Proverbs xxvi. 13 : The sluggard saith, There is a lion in the way ; a lion is in the streets.

common. They were often united in such mental and spiritual elements as formed foundations for the religious negations of the one party and for the affirmations of the other.

The truth of this is fully compatible with the fact that a few thinkers, born at the beginning of the century, went much further than their fellows towards a complete repudiation of all beliefs, as far indeed as any one to-day.[1]

But for the most part the minds of liberals in early and middle Victorian times were rich in an optimism drawn from a capital of uncriticized assumptions. They were busy with emancipation from the entail of the past : their battle-cry was " Liberty." If pain was involved in the escape from old beliefs and institutions it was greatly mitigated for them by the conviction that the essentials of true religion and morality were unaffected by it. An energy in emancipation was given to them by—as it were—their " stance " upon a rock of belief, if not in God, at least in goodness as inherent in the natural order of things.

Such optimism lay behind their almost pathetic belief in education as the way of all salvation. It quickened their impatience with ecclesiastical dogmas and sanctions. It gave heart to men in their struggle with " Hebrew old clothes." It allowed that expansion of ethical fervour which, as in George Eliot, seemed but

---

[1] No doubt, to name one such conspicuous exception, there was John Stuart Mill in existence to separate himself scornfully from those " who reject revelation " and "take refuge in an optimistic Deism, a worship of the order of nature and the supposed course of providence, at least as full of contradictions and perverting to moral sentiments as any of the forms of Christianity " (J. S. Mill, *Autobiography*, p. 70) ; and to congratulate himself upon his wife's " complete emancipation from every form of superstition, including that which attributes a pretended perfection to the order of nature and the universe " (*ibid.* p. 108).

There was also Carlyle, to whom at one time as a young man "the Universe was all void of Life, of Purpose, of Volition, even of Hostility : it was one huge, dead, immeasurable Steam-engine, rolling on, in its dead indifference, to grind me limb from limb. O, the vast, gloomy, solitary Golgotha, and Mill of Death ! " (*Sartor Resartus*, chap. vii.).

Yet this was the revolt of a minority such as could be neighbours to a majority possessed of more positive convictions, just as in a parliament the views of an extreme radical section can coexist alongside of a mass of more moderate opinion. Moreover, for Carlyle, at any rate, such revolt was only temporary and a preliminary to his passage from " The Everlasting No " to " The Everlasting Yea."

to increase with the loosening of her grasp upon distinctively Christian doctrine. It reappeared in others in the assumption of the benevolence of nature to the individual. Here, indeed, for the heroes of political emancipation, the upholders of economic orthodoxy, and the believers in unrestrained competition and the doctrine of *laisser-faire*, was the very fulcrum to the lever of nineteenth-century liberty. Individual man, it was thought, needed only to be freed from artificial and traditional restraints, and to be set in a nature similarly liberated, for it to provide to each his meat in due season, and for him to fare as well as he deserved.

We can gauge the strength of this optimistic reliance upon nature if we observe its reaction upon Darwinism. Though the doctrine of the " struggle for existence " in itself cut at the roots of the belief in the benevolence of nature to the individual, many were quick to infer from the observation of a continuous upward development in the past added grounds for their general faith in progress for the future. "Progress," indeed, was the bottom layer of Victorian assumptions. It still survives among a superior minority that has disencumbered itself of any other convictions. It still appears in the " man in the street's " confidence in times of adversity that, thanks to the general order of things, " something is likely to turn up."

Nevertheless, Darwin was the sexton to these assumptions. Whether fairly or not, the change from Victorian to " modern " times is associated with his name. By his writings it was as though he made a channel through which waters, long dammed out, flooded in. Many are alive to-day to recall the swirl of the waters, whether of dogmatic and agnostic science, or of uncritical Bible criticism, as they rushed through the formerly impenetrable bulwarks of Victorian religion.[1]

---

[1] Compare, for the above, Henry Sidgwick's words in 1860 on *In Memoriam*: "Hence the most important influence of 'In Memoriam' on my thought . . . opened in a region . . . deeper than the difference between Theism and Christianity:

This generation is modern in the sense that it never knew the world " before the flood." While it has been growing up the assumptions of Mid-Victorian liberalism have been going bankrupt. Their capital has been running out. Even their last survivor, Progress, has been at grips with a doubt deeper than itself as to man's place in the universe. For the infection of a kind of cosmic nervousness has become widespread. Somehow the world is now felt to be less domestic than it was. The skies have darkened and men's minds have become more sombre. In some a sense of the mere scale and range of the world in size and time has prompted a philosophy of relativity wherein nothing is absolutely true or right at any passing moment. Others have been led by the observation of the effects of physical environment to ask whether matter is not dominant over mind and spirit. Others have been appalled to realize that nature (so far from being benevolent to the individual) aims only at the survival of the race, and cares nothing for its members except as contributing to the health of the species. In greater or less degree through all minds is spread the sense that they are in a world which is indifferent to their interests. And thereout springs a fear of being thrown upon its mercies : a consequent prudential reliance upon the weapons that

---

it lay in the unparalleled combination of intensity of feeling with comprehensiveness of view and balance of judgment, shown in presenting the *deepest* needs and perplexities of humanity. And this influence has increased rather than diminished as years have gone on and as the great issues between Agnostic Science and Faith have become continually more prominent. In the sixties I should say these deeper issues were somewhat obscured by the discussions on Christian dogma, and Inspiration of Scripture, etc. You may remember Browning's reference to this period—

> ' The Essays and Reviews debate
> Begins to tell on the public mind
> And Colenso's words have weight.'

During these years we were absorbed in struggling for freedom of thought in the trammels of a historical religion. . . . Well, the years pass, the struggle with what Carlyle used to call ' Hebrew old clothes ' is over, Freedom is won, and what does Freedom bring us to ? It brings us face to face with atheistic science : the faith in God and Immortality, which we have been struggling to clear from superstition, suddenly seems to be *in the air* : and in seeking for a firm basis for this faith we find ourselves in the midst of the ' fight with death ' which ' In Memoriam ' so powerfully presents " (quoted in *Tennyson: A Memoir*, vol. i. p. 301).

money can buy for the struggle for existence ; and a doubt whether morality is not the philosophy either of those who are paid to maintain it, or of those who can afford to be good.

Furthermore, the mind of society has become morbid with the sickness of an industrial order which has been built upon an economic philosophy of half-truths. The confident optimism of the era of the Great Exhibition and the Manchester School has withered away. The faith (which we are told appears again and again in the writings of Richard Cobden [1]) " that God is over all, and that Providence will right wrongs and check wickedness without our help," has faltered in the face of the results of individualistic competition, whose theological motto has run, " Every man for himself and God for us all, as the elephant said when he danced among the chickens."

Here indeed is a main reason for the waning of the ethical (let alone theistic) confidence which was found in men otherwise agnostic. The economic conditions of morality have been laid bare, and the relationship of all parts of society to one another has been recognized. The parts of the body politic which talk and write most have been found to be but margins upon a world of which the facts confute their theories. Yet the solidarity of the social whole ensures that none of its members can escape from the fortunes of the rest. Therefore the whole mind of our time is tainted by the moral powerlessness of men in modern competitive business— where the sway over human volition of uncontrolled and accidental forces is at its highest ; where the natural struggle for existence is made many times worse by the intricate devices of scientific ingenuity ; where men are as good as they dare be ; where it is most evident that the world left to run loose and not battled with is indifferent to the hopes and fears of individual human beings.

[1] John Maccunn : *Six Radical Thinkers*, Richard Cobden, p. 133.

Thus the firm footing of Victorian Liberalism whether in thought or practice has slipped. The revolt of a greater realism has proved its bed-rock of assumptions to be a false bottom. Discussion has gone further and invaded its sanctuaries. It seems as though its representatives sat in a circle in an increasingly hot room and took off their clothes one by one, upon the assumption that a point would be reached when they could sit both in comfort and decency. Their sons have passed any such minimum point. Some have tried to do with nothing on ; others are trying to get either out of their skins or out of the room.

For the heat in the room is thrown off by facts which are not good. It is a greater sensitiveness to cruel and evil facts in the world which puts the sons out of sympathy with the fathers. Somehow or other the rose colour has faded out of Victorian spectacles. The collision between the ideal and the actual, between belief and experience has grown more violent. It was a relatively tame world within whose empirical facts— as T. H. Green insisted—the ideal was to be recognized, " and not in an ideal world of guess and aspiration alongside of the empirical." [1] The world which Science presents to-day as that within which human ideals must find a home is wilder and more fearful. " That Man is the product of causes which had no prevision of the end they were achieving ; that his origin, his growth, his hopes and fears, his loves and his beliefs, are but the outcome of accidental collocations of atoms ; that no fire, no heroism, no intensity of thought and feeling, can preserve an individual life beyond the grave ; that all the labours of the ages, all the devotion, all the inspiration, all the noon-day brightness of human genius, are destined to extinction in the vast death of the solar system, and that the whole temple of Man's achieve-

---

[1] T. H. Green : *Works,* vol. i. p. 449. Cf. his allusion to the *outer world* as a "means through which the Deity, who works unseen behind it, pours the truth and love which transforms man's capabilities into actualities " (*Works,* vol. iii. p. 4).

ment must inevitably be buried beneath the débris of a universe in ruins—all these things, if not quite beyond dispute, are yet so nearly certain, that no philosophy which rejects them can hope to stand. Only within the scaffolding of these truths, only on the firm foundations of unyielding despair, can the soul's habitation henceforth be safely built." [1]

Such is the " modern " situation.

Doubtless, despite all that has been claimed for this generation, the mass of men in this country—certainly the majority of church-goers—have still to realize it. The many have still to pass through the transition which so powerfully staggered the few half a century ago. Roughly speaking, the average man has still to be assailed by the fear that his general view of the universe derived from Old Testament saturation is obsolete. He has still to follow in the steps of Mr. Wells and " be drawn out of the little world of short horizons and millennial expectations "—the world of the Father in Mr. Gosse's *Father and Son*—" into another world of endless vistas, of years whose blackness and vagueness are terrifying." He, too, in his measure, " will be smitten by the riddle : all this scheme of things, life, force, destiny, which began not six thousand years, mark you, but an infinity ago, that has developed out of such strange weird shapes and incredible first intentions, out of gaseous nebulae, carboniferous swamps, saurian giantry and arboreal apes, is by the same token to continue developing—into what ? " He has still to struggle with something of the obstinacy of Victorian religion against the destruc-

---

[1] Bertrand Russell : *Philosophical Essays*, The Free Man's Worship, p. 60 ; cf. p. 63 : "In this lies Man's true freedom : in determination to worship only the God created by our own love of the good, to respect only the heaven which inspires the insight of our best moments. In action, in desire, we must submit perpetually to a tyranny of outside forces ; but in thought, in aspiration, we are free, free from our fellow-men, free from the petty planet on which our bodies impotently crawl, free even while we live, from the tyranny of death. Let us learn, then, that energy of faith which enables us to live constantly in the vision of the good ; and let us descend in action into the world of fact, with that vision always before us."

tion of the cosmogony which was founded for him on the acceptance of the whole of " the Book " as true.

In truth, the biographies and the ecclesiastical history of the last half of the nineteenth century, and the state of mind of Anglican congregations to-day corroborate what we have already said. The engrained dominance of Scriptural ideas in British minds has given them an unnatural watertightness against currents which have been ready to flow into them ever since the time of Copernicus and the Renaissance. Hence the roar of waters as through a broken dam, when the Darwinian movement brought home the implication of the Copernican revolution. Hence the rapidity of the separation in mind between periods but little apart in time. Hence the ineradicable consciousness to-day of a modern point of view.

No doubt the average man, by virtue of freedom from the sophistications of culture, will be less moved by the force of currents that carried the more academic away. No doubt, too, the fact that others have endured the first shock of revolution will mitigate its effects upon himself. He will be spared the more callow phases of modernism. But he cannot wholly escape—he is not escaping—convulsion. He is ever reproducing the experience of a former generation, of being swept by violent tides out of old anchorages, both religious and moral.

II

If such be " the hurt of the daughter of My people," with what balm can it be healed? Who can be the physician?

Not the moral philosopher.

He, no doubt, will come forward to claim that morality is unaffected by these alarms, and that no general commotion can take from men an absolute sense of moral obligation. And yet the moral ideal to which a man's conscience is sensitive, and the conditions of his struggle towards its attainment, cannot be isolated from what he thinks—from his general view of things. The moral philosopher therefore may, if he likes, sit in his own room composing ethical treatises, but meanwhile the whole house is on fire. He may occupy himself, but he will not interest many others, with morality, while its presuppositions are to seek. The subject-matter of his exercises is man, and while man's place in the world is under challenge, he can moralize about man only to the degree that an artist can draw a model that will not sit still. There is a Victorian ring about the average British citizen's delusion, so familiar to the ears of parochial clergy, that "it does not matter what you think, so long as you do what is right." Here "thinking" means allegiance to distinctively Christian doctrine, whilst "doing" means the carrying out of duties implied in a belief in God, as yet undisputed, or in a morality, assumed to be self-evident.

But how if the undisputed comes under dispute? There are questions about which it *does* matter what men think if they are to act rightly. The spread of long-accepted tradition and custom has disguised this. There have been things which, in the words of John Stuart Mill,[1] men have "agreed in holding sacred ; which, wherever freedom of discussion was a recognized principle, it was of course lawful to contest in theory, but which no one could either hope or fear to see shaken in practice ; which" were "in the common estimation placed beyond discussion." A futility reminiscent of placards stating that "Trespassers will be prosecuted" hangs about these words. Discussion, theoretical and practical, has been more vagrant than Mill dreamt. Something impels his successors to abhor above all else an evasion of the worst questions. And as the questions are raised, so, little by little, the weight of once-accepted assumptions, sanctions, self-evidences,

---

[1] J. S. Mill, *Dissertations*, vol. i. p. 417.

and authorities is reduced, and the range of moral and
immoral possibility is widened.

Quo usque tandem? Are they right who say that
the passionate and appetitive elements in human nature,
ever impatient of anything but present satisfaction, will
quickly construe uncertainty about further issues into
reasons why a man should eat and drink ere to-
morrow he die? It is likely, indeed, that in the cool
retreats of segregated English culture the volcanic
capacities of human nature have been under-estimated.
But where revolt has been really radical and wholesale,
as among many in the student world abroad, there such
moral anarchy has followed as makes it plain that in
the future the side of the angels will be maintained,
not by an idle confidence in vague and common sentiment, but by those who have attained to conscious and
reasoned convictions about ultimate things.

The moral philosopher then, as such, will not be
found in possession of the balm in Gilead.

Nor will the Christian moralist. It is a further
sign of the changed times that men can no longer be
satisfied with viewing Jesus Christ merely as a gracious
moral teacher. That was possible last century for
some individuals aglow with the *Nachschein* of Evangelical pietism. It was possible when foundation truths
about God, the world, and man were thought to stand
fast independently of any Christian doctrine. Only the
slightness of their theological interest — in the strict
sense of the word—has allowed so many critics to treat
the Sermon on the Mount as a purely ethical discourse.

But latterly an anxiety over issues that lie deeper
than ethics has destroyed the blindness which overlooked the theology implied in Christ's ethical teaching.
It is being realized now that His maxims are inseparable from His ideas of God and man.

Hence a great discord. Just as the colours of a
picture toned and mellowed by age stand out in sharpness and brilliance when it is cleaned, so the ethical

maxims in the Gospels as they are re-read by the mind
of to-day acquire an intense sharpness of edge and
sting. The moral injunctions of Jesus stand out as
high-lights upon the picture of the world as He saw
it. And with the world-view implied the mind of to-
day finds itself in jangling discord.[1] Thought to-day
is this-worldly : the mind of Jesus seems to be im-
possibly other-worldly. He taught that the possession
of riches would make the kingdom of heaven hard of
entry. The difficulty has increased to-day with the
increase of riches whether of the mind or of the body.

And yet it is not enough simply to account for the discord by attributing it to an unworthy worldliness. For
concomitantly with the prevailing absorption in treasures
on earth, there exists a nobler impatience with treasures
in heaven, which is due to the sense in many good men
of the intolerable misery in this world of so many of
their fellows. There is a righteous demand for the
kingdom of heaven here and now, which revolts against
the seemingly illusory promise of a future bliss.

In many cases this demand is backed by the belief
that the kingdom of heaven could be brought in by
the successful adaptation of the wisdom of this world
to social ends. Gospels of " efficiency " and " agenda "
movements are the result. Elsewhere, as in a part
at least of the socialist movement, a franker materialism views social problems as made and therefore
remediable by money. Yet the confidence of those
who with whatever philosophy in mind are " hasten-
ing the kingdom " is increasingly abashed by the fact
that the chief centres of energy in the body politic
are indifferent to their aims. In a real sense the
whole world of reformers and philanthropy, as well
as that of culture and fashion, is parasitic upon
another world of industry and commerce. The latter

---

[1] A sense of this discord has led to the preoccupation of theologians with
eschatology. That is, the question has been forced to the front, whether the
other-worldliness with which Jesus looked at the kingdom of this world was not
due to His belief that it was speedily to pass away. But see Essay III. p. 107 ff.

world is inside and the former outside the actuality
of the social problem, in the sense that a crew is in
the race and its supporters or critics on the towing-
path are out of it. In an industrial and commercial
community change must originate from within industry
and business. Yet to-day it is precisely in these regions
that men seem most stricken by impotence to change,
and are most held in the clutch of necessity. Con-
trasting with the chatter of social reformers is the
sullen silence of business men, broken at times by
their cry in self-defence that " business is business."

Thus there has come into existence a mind which is at
violent discord with the ethics of Jesus Christ. There is
a hiatus between the philosophy of necessary and successful self-assertion and the promise to the meek that
they shall inherit the earth. It is no deeper than that
between the presuppositions of insurance companies and
the disparagement of anxiety for the morrow. Therefore the world turns from the advice of the Christian
moralist as from something which at best means only
the hallowing of failure. After all, was not the Preacher
of paradox on the Mount cut short in His prime by
death upon a cross ?

If it is so with the teacher of Christian ethics, how
is it with the preacher of the Christian Gospel?

It may be that the situation finds him well fortified within his traditional citadel, insensitive to the
cries outside, or only ready to chant the Athanasian
Creed at the heads of his enemies in the gate. If
not, then there is no other escape for him from the
pains of the Christian moralist. He has to share with
him the pain of the discord between this- and other-
worldliness. He, too, is on the bank of the stream
of industrialism in company with the other counsellors. Standing, often with an Anglican or academic
dignity, upon a margin of partial immunity, he is
acutely conscious of being less " in the world " and
its conflict than those to whom he preaches. Yet a

sense of solidarity shuts him off from recourse, in accordance with rich stores of precedents, to world-renunciation. He cannot save his own soul by escape from a naughty world, just because he cannot escape from the relationship which binds him to his brethren in the world. In an inmost monastic cell he still must eat, that is, he still will be in economic dependence upon his neighbours in the market. His saintliness and its conditions will be inseparable from the traffic outside in the souls of men — in a word, as a saint he will live off the sinner.

Driven, therefore, into the world of secular facts, what is the Christian preacher's message to it ? Is he, as some Roman modernists advise, to despair of it ? Is he, that is, to accept the belief that the world of fact is governed by the hard law of failure, and be content to surround a bloody reality with a halo spun out of his " religious " or mystical consciousness of a heaven beyond ?[1] Must he recognize the impotence of Christianity to take modern civilization within its grasp ? Must he resign himself to limping along with it as beside a soteriological ambulance in the rear of the world's war ?

He is, at any rate, drawn to the Cross. It is of a piece with the other facts: it matches the darkness of the world in whose panorama it appears. In it he sees the climax of a life of selflessness and sacrifice. Yet by itself it is empty of any Gospel of God. Indeed, approached as he approaches it, the Cross by itself only blackens the tragic in life, and suggests the question whether, after all, the Crucified was not wrong in His conception of God's relations to this present world, and died as a martyr to a great

[1] Compare with this in philosophy Bertrand Russell: *Philosophical Essays*, The Free Man's Worship, p. 65. ". . . Not by renunciation alone can we build a temple for the worship of our own ideals. Haunting foreshadowings of the temple appear in the realm of imagination, in music, in architecture, in the untroubled kingdom of reason, and in the golden sunset magic of lyrics, where beauty shines and glows, remote from the touch of sorrow, remote from the fear of change, remote from the failures and disenchantments of the world of fact."

mistake. No doubt this question will urge him past the Cross and on to the Resurrection. There, indeed, he can see a foundation on which the Christian redemption of this world—as contrasted with its renunciation —might rest. But then, on other grounds, he may be nervous about laying such stress upon the Resurrection. It brings to a head all the reluctance to commit himself entirely to belief in miracle, which he shares with his contemporaries ; and as a matter of " criticism " it is full of its own difficulties.

We can conclude that if the balm which we seek is in the Christian preacher's possession, too often he holds it in a trembling hand. For the insecurity of the situation reaches down to the foundations not only of Victorian assumptions but of the Christian religion. This, as we have seen, is not exactly new. What is new as compared with even the latter years of last century is that the crisis in the Christian faith implies a worse crisis in any other. The time is past when men could forsake their Christian allegiance on the assumption that they were left in untroubled possession of the essentials of religion and conduct. Unless it be in that wing of social democracy where a dogmatic materialism still is dominant, there is no other ark of security out of which men look with indifference at what they take to be the submergence of Christianity. It was only the unimpaired strength of assumptions, whether theistic or ethical, which used to put the Christian preacher into the position of a man making a great fuss about nothing. Given the immunity from criticism of those assumptions, Christianity was bound to look like a fire-brigade proffering its services where houses were not alight.

That at any rate is over. Revolt has gone deeper than merely rejecting the seeming irrelevancies of Christian dogma. It has undermined and shaken the ancient strongholds of belief in God and in man. It has rounded upon a civilization, the practical mani-

c

festation of whose supposed assent to the essentials of religion, is an industrial order which denies God and prostitutes man. At the hands of men who, in their best moments, desire above all things to look into the dark and face the worst, the surviving proprieties of the last two centuries, whether in religion or morals, are in course of disruption. Once more it is being realized, and for the first time for many generations in England, of what strange and terrible elements the world is made, and how dread a laboratory of good and evil is in the heart of man.

III

Therefore to-day is a day of new hope for the Christian religion: the pains of to-day are the travail-pangs of its new birth. After all it presupposed an emergency. It needed a bad day for it to be known as good news. It could never have brought salvation had there been no situation for men to be saved from. Not that it did not find much true religion or good philosophy or right conduct, much faith and heroism in the world to confirm and to fulfil. It could never have been recognized, nor been understood, nor have taken root but for their existence. But it did presuppose an uncertainty which went deeper than all else, a darkness prevailing over light, a root need. It was first preached to a civilization which for all its achievements was darkened in its understanding, "having no hope, and without God in the world."

This has been hard to recognize for many generations past. It is easier now. Voices of men who seem to be the chosen vessels of the *Zeitgeist*, proclaim the coming again of the days before the Gospel. Driven on to look at things as they are unblenchingly, they are giving expression to the pity and fear that life awakes in them. They are channels of utterance to the dumb and restless hearts of many of their fellows. Without illusions they are seeking and knocking for a central clue to the dark mystery of existence.

One day as they seek they will find. With a revulsion of delight in the truth of what seemed too good to be true, they will find Jesus Christ. For theirs is the temper and mind which disclose His potency. He came to seek and to save those who knew themselves to be lost. He has been impotent for centuries owing to the spiritual complacency of men. He has suffered every degree of patronage by intellectuals who have been interested in Him but have had no need of Him. He has been degraded by the transformation of His revolutionary disclosure into an established and conservative tradition at truce with the world and in bondage to propriety. But now His day returns, as human hearts are loosened to receive Him. A common need draws all the saints, both prodigals and elder sons, to reapprehend what is the breadth and length and height and depth, and to learn anew His love which passeth knowledge.

Nothing helps more to a fresh appreciation of this than a study of the hearts that did originally receive Him. It must suffice here rather to point to the importance of the study than attempt it. The study required is of Jewish psychology. Jewish hearts were the solitary medium whereby Christ and His Gospel were given to the world. Jesus appealed to the faith in God that He found in His fellow-countrymen. He found the hearts of many very humanly apathetic, occupied with the necessities of existence, deluded by the shows of life, drugged by familiarity and tradition. But amid such cinders of the Jewish religion He found an unextinguished flame still burning. He found the fire of prophetic faith still alive in those who looked for the consolation of Israel.

Modern research by its study of historical scenes, backgrounds, climates, and contemporary ideas allows us to stand beside those men, not as lay figures in the calendar, but as fellow human beings. By the same process, too, the Old Testament has been changed from a file of books into a line of men.[1] Hence in some measure we can stretch hands across the centuries and live with the great prophets whose inspired teaching, before ever its spirit was condensed into literalism by canon or tradition, led Israel from the lower levels of local and tribal religion to the heights of belief in One God of all the earth. Thus we are led into the very factory of the faith which Jesus Christ presupposed. Archaism and distance drop away from the words of psalmist, preacher, and prophet. We enter the company of men whose national experience had brought them to interpret the whole world in terms of God. But we also learn how the very strength of their acquired convictions gave birth to agony and distress. For it was faith in God, then as now, that rendered men sensitive to godlessness. It was the certainty of God in the men whose mind moulded the Jewish Scriptures that gave rise to their uncertainty. The more ardent their belief in God the more quick their sense of its contradiction by the way of the world. So the ancient words ring with the dismay and perplexity that were created by the collision of Israel's religion with reality.

When Jesus came He took the world as He found it. He did not explain away the things that challenged faith. He appealed to existing faith. He preached no new theology, but grafted His message of fulfilment into the stock of Jewish faith in God wheresoever it was alive.

He found that with the mass of His fellow-countrymen belief in God was often no more than an assumption that justified traditional observance and conduct. But for a few He was able to draw that belief out of the background of assumption and familiarity, and to quicken it into being the central impulse of their lives. He

[1] Cf. Essay II. *passim.*

filled it with an expectation that for the time drove out
of mind the thought of anything but glory and success.
He raised it to its highest power in the confession of a
follower that He, for all the smallness of the things of
His day, nevertheless was Messiah. All the more,
therefore, was that expectation overwhelmed by the
events which gathered into themselves everything
that any time had made the quick heart of the Jew
shrink. The darkness of all the hours in which present
fact had made Jewish trust in God falter was concentrated into an "hour of darkness." The hour of
Calvary, when at length it came, recapitulated all the
questions which men have asked about God and His
dealings with the world.

For Jesus had convinced a few Jews that all the
previous ages of hope and trust had been met at last by a
day of fulfilment. But that hope, in so far as it had been
more than a convention, had been ever under challenge,
ever eaten into by a sense of its own foolishness : never
able finally to drive out a doubt of itself—doubt whether
it were more than a projection of its own longings, or
a common assumption, or a tradition from the past,
doomed in the end to confutation by reality. And
therefore in the end, at the climax of the day of fulfilment, the Cross seemed to be the finally victorious
onset of a foe till then only kept at bay, and never
beaten under foot.

Hence the faith that sprang out of the Cross, or
rather, out of what followed it, was built on no lightly-
made assumption about God. Its essence was assumption
put to final proof on the hill where, as it were, the very
nerve of the world was laid bare. The faith in God
which Jesus found was uprooted by His cross to
be replanted in the revelation of His Resurrection and
coming in the Spirit. The foundations of trust in
God were convulsed to be relaid in Him who *nevertheless* was the Christ. We are sure of this as we read
the latter part of the New Testament. One thing

separates us from the men out of whose souls the written words flowed, namely, their certainty of God and of His relations to the world. The disclosure that had been made in and through Jesus Christ was the supreme disclosure—the one desire of all restless human hearts —namely, the truth of God Himself, found to be where it seemed that He could not be. " This is the message which we have heard from Him, and announce unto you, that God is light, and in Him is no darkness at all." [1] That is the infinitely wonderful outcome of that day of final decision, when God Himself—trusted to by Jesus, adjured by priest and ruler, despaired of by disciples—came into judgment.

This central truth, while it was still new, answered all other questions. It was the immediate and dominating fact that absorbed into itself everything else. As the truth of God it included the truth of man ; it contained within itself all the inferences and implications which the increasing energy of human thought in later days could draw out of it. Hence, for instance, the seeming simplicity of New Testament ethics. They can scarcely be disentangled from their plain secret, namely, the centripetal and mutual relationship of the soul to God in Jesus Christ. All maxims and philosophies were reduced to the simple task of walking in the light since the light had come.

But a change soon came. It could not be long before the one essential disclosure ceased through familiarity to hold the foremost place in human interest. The foundation of barest and most elementary faith in God once relaid came to be buried out of sight as men busied themselves with superstructures. Logical reasoning having accepted " the message " could not help but treat its chief purport as assumption and major premiss whence to draw out its necessary inferences. The minds of thinkers quickened to livelier consciousness were bound, as it were, to stand away from that which

[1] 1 John i. 5.

had come to them, in order to direct, analyse, explore, relate, and systematically to understand it.

The dangers of this are obvious, and Western thought has been busy since the Renaissance in pointing them out. No one can doubt that the proportion and perspective of the faith became altered by its intellectualization. It was made to wear the appearance of over-certainty about God. Because God was taken for granted, He was almost forgotten. He became the centre whence man's attention could stray to the circumference, to occupy itself with lesser objects of devotion. He was so far from being in doubt that undistracted energy could be devoted to precise controversies about His attributes, or to the dissection of the mystery of His sacramental presence, or to the association of His inspiration with every word of the Scriptures.

We can understand how static and immemorially founded Christianity came to appear, in days when Europe had become Christendom and Rome was still the centre of the world, when the East and South were far away, when the new world was yet unknown, and the dawn of the new knowledge had not broken.

We can understand, too, the relatively superficial character of the Reformation. Its convulsions never shook the foundations of the faith, but rather only laid them bare.

Finally, we can understand how, in regard to the primary elements of belief in God and man and nature, so many men came to look upon Christianity as relatively unimportant. The foundations once newly laid in Jesus were buried so deep that men came to look upon them as a part of the natural structure of existence. In a word, we can understand what we have called the Victorian attitude.

But the original conditions are coming round again to-day. The times of the impotence of Jesus Christ are passing. He was ever powerless with those who did not need Him. A knowledge of darkness is needed to urge indolent man upon the quest after the light. Once there was a bonfire lit in the world, of which the New Testament is a still flaming brand. Once men were darkness and once they became light in the Lord. Since then the light has been diffused into twilight, and in half-Christianized Europe generations have had no knowledge either of the light or of the darkness. But to-day all changes. The darkness of the far lands where the Gospel has never been, let alone grown old, lies close round Europe. The darkness of the veil of things seen and pleasurable hangs heavy over luxurious souls. The darkness of the universe in its incomprehensible age and vastness overcasts the vision of post-Darwinian science. The darkness of human hearts emancipated, and void of all allegiance but to themselves, creeps ever on.

Therefore to-day the light begins to shine anew, as men begin again to know the need of it.

Have not the times arrived the rumour of whose coming touched the prophetic heart of Robert Browning?

> . . . what whispers me of times to come?
> What if it be the mission of that age
> My death shall usher into life, to shake
> This torpor of assurance from our creed,
> Reintroduce the doubt discarded, bring
> That formidable danger back, we drove
> Long ago to the distance and the dark?
> No wild beast now prowls round the infant camp:
> We have built wall and sleep in city safe:
> But if some earthquake try the towers that laugh
> To think they once saw lions rule outside,
> And man stand out again, pale resolute,
> Prepared to die—which means alive at last?[1]

---

[1] *The Ring and the Book*, The Pope, line 1851.

II

THE BIBLE

BY

RICHARD BROOK

SYNOPSIS

PAGE

INTRODUCTION 27-32
In the past the Bible has been supreme as a creative and
sustaining power in the spiritual life 27
To determine whether it can continue to be this we must
ask what the Bible is and to what it owes its power . . 29
It is a living and vitalising record of religious experience :
its writers were "religious men" 30

I. THE CONTENT OF THE RELIGIOUS EXPERIENCE OF THE
BIBLICAL WRITERS 32-46
(a) The Old Testament Writers—
The primary and constituent elements of their religious
experience 32
The purpose and method of their writings . . 36
Theological and ethical development . . 38
(b) The New Testament Writers—
The new and characteristic element in Christian
experience 41
Its relation to that of the Old Testament writers . 42

II. THE ORIGIN OF THE RELIGIOUS EXPERIENCE OF THE
BIBLICAL WRITERS 46-57
The religious and the non-religious interpretation of life
contrasted 46
Three analogies which suggest the lines along which we
may formulate a theory of inspiration :
(1) The optimism of religion compared with the optimism
of science 49
(2) Genius for religion compared with genius for science, or
with genius for art or music 51
(3) Revelation in its more passive aspect compared with
a man's knowledge of his friend . . . 53
It is because they possess a special genius for religion that
the Biblical writers are able to apprehend God's self-revelation . 57

III. THE PERMANENT VALUE OF THE RELIGIOUS EXPERIENCE OF
THE BIBLICAL WRITERS 57-71
It has some evidential value even for those who do not share
it, but in the last resort the appeal must be to the experience
itself 57
Experience shows that the religious sense requires cultivation,
and can be cultivated in the same way as, e.g., the artistic or the
musical sense—by the study of the "great masters" . . 60
Threefold test of genius for art 63
Application of this test in the sphere of religion justifies the
view that the Bible is for religion what the "great masters" are
for art—"the classical and normative expression" of the
religious life 64
The Bible has a definite historical value, but
(1) It is for religion and not primarily for history or theology
that we go to the Bible 67
(2) All the writers were not equally inspired, nor is inspiration limited to them 69
The authority of the Bible is that of its own spiritual
supremacy and its proved spiritual power . . . 70

II

THE BIBLE

Sorrow is hard to bear, and doubt is slow to clear.
Each sufferer has his say, his scheme of the weal and woe.
But God has a few of us whom He whispers in the ear ;
The rest may reason and welcome.

These men see the works of the Lord : and His wonders in the deep.

To the plain man the Bible is no longer the Book of Books. On investigation we shall find that the plain man is wrong, but at first sight there is much to be said for his point of view. He is no critic and has no time for critical studies, but he has learnt that the Bible is not infallible in its statements of fact, in its ethical teaching or even in its theology. He knows what modern science has to say with regard to the creation narratives in Genesis, and he is vaguely aware that similar stories are to be found in Babylonian mythology. And in many other places, chiefly perhaps in the stories of the patriarchs and of the early monarchy, he suspects that there is a large element of folk-lore and tradition, and he has not the means of finding out what element of historicity the narratives contain. Consequently, he is invaded by a general sense of insecurity, and believing that many of its statements are untrue, he not unnaturally asks how the Bible can be regarded as in any real sense inspired, or, indeed, as having any particular value.

Moreover, he is not really interested in " the kings

of Israel and Judah." Why should he read these old
stories and legends, even supposing that they are true?
Still less is he interested in the ceremonial enactments of
Leviticus or in the symbolism of such books as Daniel
and Revelation, which he does not the least understand.
He has always been taught that the chief value of the
teaching of the prophets lay in their miraculous predictive powers, and now that he is told that the old
"argument from prophecy" is discredited, nothing
seems to remain. He perceives, too, that the ethical
standpoint of some of the Biblical writers is relatively
crude. He cannot but condemn, for example, the
treacherous act of Jael which is singled out for
special praise in the Song of Deborah. What, he asks,
is he to gain by reading such stories as these? And
he sees almost as little reason why he should read
the New Testament. He already knows, in broad
outline, the story of the life of Christ. Why should
he read it again? Is the Gospel narrative really trustworthy in all its details? And what is he to make of
the Pauline Epistles with their elaborate and obscure
arguments?

It is some such feeling as this, implicit if not explicit,
which accounts for the fact that nowadays men do not
read the Bible. This feeling is by no means confined
to those who have definitely broken with Christianity.
The ordinary Christian still clings to the belief that the
Bible is, somehow or other, different from other books,
but he finds it hard to provide himself with any clear
or sufficient reason for this belief, and as he has no
definite idea as to why or how or in what spirit he
ought to read the Bible, the natural result is that, in
many cases, he does not read it at all.

Yet it is an undoubted fact that up to our own
time the Bible has occupied a unique and a supreme
place as a creative, a moulding and a sustaining power
in the spiritual lives of Christian men. "In every
generation and wherever the light of revelation has

shone," says Coleridge in a fine passage, "men of all ranks, conditions, and states of mind, have found in this volume a correspondent for every movement towards the better felt in their own hearts, the needy soul has found supply, the feeble a help, the sorrowful a comfort. You in one place, I in another, all men somewhere and at some time meet with an assurance that the hopes and fears, the thoughts and yearnings which proceed from or tend to a right spirit in us, are no dreams or fleeting singularities, no voices heard in sleep, no spectres which the eye suffers but does not perceive."[1] Proof or illustration is really unnecessary, but the words of Heine may be quoted as typical. "Neither vision nor ecstasy, neither voice from heaven nor bodeful dream," he says, "has pointed the way of salvation to me. I owe my enlightenment quite simply to the reading of a book . . . The Book, the Bible. . . . He who has lost his God may find Him again in this volume, and he who has never known Him will there be met by the breath of the Divine word." But it is not necessary to go to the records of the past or to the lives of others. There is a court of appeal closer at hand. It would not be easy to find any one who habitually reads the Bible in a devotional spirit who could not add something from his own experience to give further confirmation to what is, after all, a fact of almost universal experience.

Accordingly the question we have to ask is whether this value of the Bible in the past was due to some inherent quality which the Bible itself possesses or to that conception of it as verbally inspired and infallible which has been held up to our own time and is now

---

[1] Quoted, Tyrrell, *Scylla and Charybdis*, pp. 66 *et seq.* Prothero, *The Psalms in Human Life*, provides an interesting commentary. Numerous instances covering the whole range of Christian History are given to show how men of all sorts and conditions have found in the Psalms the inspiration and support of their spiritual lives. "For every recorded incident there are millions of cases unknown beyond the secret chambers of the heart, in which the Psalms have restored the faith, lifted the despair, revived the hopes, steeled the courage, bound up the wounds of the struggling, suffering hosts of humanity."

seen to be untenable, whether, in fact, it was due to
what the Bible *is* or to what it has wrongly been supposed
to be. Surely it is more reasonable to think that
the former view is the true one ; that the Bible made
its appeal in the past not because but rather in spite of
those views of it which we have now abandoned, and
that, consequently, the more clearly we understand the
real nature of the Bible, the greater will be the power
of its appeal. What is needed, then, and what this essay
attempts to give, is a straightforward statement which,
taking accepted critical conclusions for granted, will
make it clear what the Bible really is. The plain man
knows well enough what it is not—he is tired of being
told that it is not infallible. But he does want to know
what it is and to what it owes its power : why, in the
past, men have read and loved it : why they have found
in it the support of their religious lives : why they have
believed it to be, in a unique sense, God's book : and
still more, whether and how it can continue to be for
us what it has been for our fathers.

The essence of the answer lies in the fact, which
modern scholarship has enabled us to recognise in its
full significance, that the Bible is God's book because it
is in a unique and universal sense Man's book. It is
the record of and the vehicle for transmitting a great
human experience—an experience of God, of human need,
and of God's response to that need. The authors, the
editors, the compilers of the various books and of their
literary sources are now seen to be men of flesh and
blood, linked to us by the possession of a common
humanity. They are not, as men had almost come to
think, like the dolls of a ventriloquist, or like children
repeating from memory a lesson they have learned but
not understood, quoting catch-words and phrases which
are not a part of themselves and find no answer within
their own experience, but they are living men, sharing
our joys and our sorrows, our hopes and our aspirations,
our needs and our fears, facing the problems and per-

plexities of life, " the old misgivings " and " the crooked
questions " which are the common heritage of humanity,
saying what they feel and know, and speaking with the
conviction which is born of personal experience.   It is
because we have a real kinship with them that we are
irresistibly drawn to them and that their power survives
" deep in the general heart of man."

But though we find in their lives an experience which
closely touches our own and makes them, through and
through, one with us, we also find—and it is this which
is the characteristic and distinguishing fact—that their
whole experience of life is changed and transformed by
a real and living religion.   They were religious men.
Their lives were inspired by an intense faith in God and
dominated by a sense of His presence, His holiness,
and His love.   They tell us of the faith that is in them
and of the struggle and the storm and the stress through
which they have come to the knowledge of God.   They
show us how their faith has brought them out of darkness into light, and how the God in whom they have
trusted has helped and saved them.

This is the real secret of the religious power of
the Bible.   To teach religion, as Carlyle said, the first
thing necessary is to find a man who has religion.   For
most men, their religion is vitalised and sustained by
their personal relations with religious men.   It is only
when we come into contact with men whose lives are
guided and controlled by the hand of God, and see the
power of the faith which makes them strong, that we
ourselves become sure of God and His love.   " Soul
is kindled only by soul."   This is the experience of all
who have ever known and loved a true servant of God.
And the Bible " teaches religion," leads men to God,
because its writers were men who " had religion."
The more we emphasise their real humanity, the
greater will be the power of their appeal.   As they
write they pour out the secrets of their hearts and admit
us to the innermost chambers of their lives, and as we

read" their story our hearts burn within us : we are fired
with their enthusiasm : their faith in God evokes a like
faith in us.

This is why men have always read and loved the
Bible—not because they regarded it as a text-book
of history or of science, or as a code of ethics, or as a
compendium of theological doctrines. It was once
believed to be this, and, as we now see, wrongly, but
its real value then, as now, lay not in this, but in the
irresistible appeal of the writers to the heart and
conscience, and in the power of their faith in God to
uplift men's thoughts and words and deeds, always and
everywhere. Men read the Bible because in it they
found God. The value of the various books for history,[1]
for ethics, and for theology must, and can only, be
determined by the application to them of those same
principles of criticism which we should apply to any
other book for the same purpose. Its religious value
depends upon the fact that it is a record, a living and
a vitalising record, of religious experience which must
be of worth while human nature lasts.

We may now proceed to examine in more detail the
content and the origin of the religious experience of the
Biblical writers and attempt to estimate its permanent
value.

I. THE CONTENT OF THE RELIGIOUS EXPERIENCE
OF THE BIBLICAL WRITERS

According to the Biblical writers, religion means one
thing and one thing only, communion with God.[2] It

---

[1] See below, p. 67.

[2] The Biblical writers assume the existence of God and are not concerned with
metaphysical speculation as to His nature and being. " It was as a living personal
force, not as a metaphysical entity, that Jehovah was adored by Israel, and so a
living faith was possible in spite of much vagueness and vacillation upon the very
points in the conception of the Godhead which, to our habit of mind, seem most
central" (Robertson Smith, *Prophets of Israel*, p. 63). As our present purpose is
merely to describe the religious experience of the Biblical writers, nothing is here
said of the grounds on which it is justifiable to assume the existence of God. For
a discussion of these, see Essay IX.

is essentially and intensely personal. Its primary and constituent element is the consciousness of God and of the self in relation to and dependence upon Him, that consciousness which Newman describes when he speaks of God and his own soul as the "two, and two only absolute and luminously self-evident beings." [1] It is not the mere assent of the intellect to the statement that God is, or even to the statement that God is good. Rather, it is the vivid realisation of God and His love, and the conscious and deliberate throwing back of ourselves upon Him and His power. It is the inner conviction of the heart that He loves us and cares for us, that our times are in His hands, that He is our refuge, and that underneath are the everlasting arms.

The deepening of this communion with God is the one thing for which the religious man cares, for he feels that this way only may he attain to fulness of life. "Like as the hart desireth the water-brooks : so longeth my soul after thee, O God. My soul is athirst for God, yea, even for the living God." This abiding and increasing sense of God's presence and love brings with it an inner security and an absolute repose. Not that the religious man feels himself protected in a sense in which others are not protected from physical danger, but rather that he is ready to face whatever may befall him, through good report and ill report, even rejoicing in tribulation, because nothing can happen to him without the will of God, who loves him. "Thou shalt not be afraid for any terror by night : nor for the arrow that flieth by day; for the pestilence that walketh in darkness: nor for the sickness that destroyeth in the noon-day."

"The Lord is my shepherd : therefore can I lack nothing."

"He shall feed me in a green pasture : and lead me forth beside the waters of comfort."

[1] *Apologia,* p. 4.

D

"Yea, though I walk through the valley of the
shadow of death, I will fear no evil : for Thou art
with me ; Thy rod and Thy staff comfort me."

To the writer of the Psalm, these words were real
and expressed the deepest conviction of his heart. His
sense of relationship to God, experienced not in some
wild ecstasy but continuously and throughout life, is the
supreme fact of his experience. It unifies, transforms
and animates the whole of his life and thought and action.

This consciousness of God and the desire for closer
union with Him permeates the minds of the Biblical
writers, but closely related to it, so inseparably connected
with it that it may even be described as an element of
their religious experience, is the consciousness of the
demand which God makes as the very condition of that
communion. The righteous Lord loveth righteousness.
"What doth the Lord require of thee, but to do
justly, to love mercy, and to walk humbly with thy
God." Religion, according to the Biblical writers,
cannot exist apart from, and must always manifest
itself in, morality. The sense of God and His goodness creates in those who possess it a passion for
righteousness.

"Lord, what love have I unto Thy law : all the
day long is my study in it."

"O that my ways were made so direct: that I
might keep Thy statutes ! "

"My delight shall be in Thy commandments ; which
I have loved."

Side by side with this passion for righteousness,
there is an overwhelming sense of the failure to
attain it. According to the Bible, the consciousness
of sin, not as a mere mistake, but as a deliberate
thwarting of the Divine will, is an essential element
of religious experience.[1] Isaiah's account of his call
is typical. The vision of the Lord of Hosts opens
his eyes so that he sees his own sin, and the sin of

[1] See Essay VI. pp. 272-3, 278.

his people. " Woe is me, for I am undone : because
I am a man of unclean lips, and I dwell in the midst
of a people of unclean lips." This, in fact, constitutes
his call. He is called to fulfil in his own life and in
the world around him that Divine will which is revealed
to him in his perception of God and His holiness.
But he feels he is not worthy of the mission which is
entrusted to him. Conscious of his sin, he dare
not go forth as the preacher of God's holiness, and
it is not until his iniquity is taken away and his sin
is purged that he can answer " Here am I ; send me."
It was the same with the writer of the 51st Psalm. It
was according to the multitude of God's mercies, and
His great goodness, that he perceived his own offences.
He prays for forgiveness, the comfort of God's help, in
order that his lips may be opened to show God's praise,
and that he may teach His ways unto the wicked.

Everywhere the sense of God carries with it a sense
of vocation. Life is viewed as a conflict between good
and evil, in which men are called to join. It is the
working out of great issues, and the powers of darkness
are arrayed against the powers of light. But the victory
is with God and with those who submit themselves to
Him, for they shall receive " power from on high."
Sure of God, they can throw themselves back on Him,
with the assurance of ultimate triumph.

It is, of course, really impossible to separate, even
in thought, these various elements in the religious
experience of the Biblical writers. They do not represent distinct and successive stages in the development
of the religious consciousness : from the first they are
united in a single progressive movement which is one
of growing intensity and not of differentiation. With
the different writers the different elements are differently
emphasised, but for all of them religion is a life
dominated and inspired by the knowledge of a Divine
Power working within, a Power which fashions according to its will those who submit themselves to it.

The religious man is the man who goes through life
sure in his heart of the living God and of His love
and care for men, with the determination to do God's
will because God loves him and he loves God, and
with the conviction that God will show him what that
will is and, despite his constant and repeated failures,
will enable him to perform it.

It will be necessary later on to consider the origin
of the religious experience of the Biblical writers and
its value to us. For the moment, however, we are
simply concerned with its existence as a fact, as *the* fact
of supreme importance in relation to the Bible. It is
the possession by the various writers of this religious
experience, the same in its essential character throughout, which gives to the miscellaneous collection of
books which form the canon a real unity, despite their
superficial diversity. Separated though they are from
one another by long intervals of time and by the
different environments, intellectual and ethical as well
as social, in which they find themselves, the writers are
united by their conviction of the goodness of God and
in their experience of His compelling and saving power.
They do not all attain to the same height of religious
insight. It would be absurd, for example, to place
Leviticus and Esther on the same level as some of the
Psalms or portions of Deutero-Isaiah.[1] The religious
experience of some of the writers is fuller and richer
than that of others, but though it may vary in its
intensity its character remains constant throughout, and
the difference, where it exists, is one of degree and not of
kind. It is one and the same faith which inspires all the
writers and shines through the pages of their record.

And the purpose with which they write is one and
the same. They write in order that they may communicate to others that knowledge of God, that living
faith, which they themselves possess, and that others
may share in that conviction of God's righteousness

[1] See below, p. 69.

which has transformed and given meaning and purpose to their own lives. "These things are written that ye may believe ; and that believing ye may have life." A necessity is laid upon them. The secret of God burns within their hearts, and they cannot rest till they have told it. "The lion hath roared, who will not fear ? the Lord God hath spoken, who can but prophesy ? " Their message, of course, is addressed to the men of their own age, and of necessity it takes different forms to meet the different needs of different times. The faith which is held "in divers portions" is expressed "in divers manners" and through divers forms. Sometimes the writers' aim is to embody and perpetuate their religion in legalistic and ritualistic enactments. Sometimes they use the past history of the race, the stories of its great teachers and leaders or of the origin of national institutions, as the vehicle of their message. It is not in the facts as mere events of past history that they are interested ; but rather in those facts as manifesting God's eternal purpose and revealing His will. Their method is selective, and they could not always distinguish between mere legend and reliable traditions, and they idealise and freely adapt their material to meet their needs ; and sometimes, as in Jonah and Job, they do not hesitate to employ a more conscious and direct form of parabolic teaching.

Nor is it only the past which they endeavour to interpret. In the light of their trust in God and His goodness they try to explain the present, the facts of present experience which seem to run counter to their faith—the fact of sin and suffering, the apparent lack of coincidence between virtue and reward : or they try to discover the religious significance of the great national crises through which they pass—the rise of Assyria, the fall of Samaria, the exile, the disillusionment which followed the return from Babylon. Sometimes their message is primarily a message of hope, and with eyes fixed on the future they picture in vivid and

highly symbolical language the glorious destiny of the
nation and the good things which God has prepared
for them that love Him. The predictive is no
accidental element in prophecy. Life is not what it
ought to be, and therefore, viewed from the religious
standpoint, not what it must and will be. The day
must come when God's will shall prevail, and "the
earth shall be filled with the knowledge of the glory of
the Lord, as the waters cover the sea"; when God
shall manifest His righteousness, and for His name's
sake, and His people's sake, shall establish His kingdom.
The Messianic expectation in all its varying forms, the
later apocalyptic ideas, the gradually growing belief in a
future life,—the calling in a new world to redress the
balance of the old—these are the product, and in some
sense the measure, of this faith.

Inevitably, of course, each writer expresses and
interprets his faith in the thought-forms of his age,
and, inevitably, as generation succeeds generation and
knowledge advances, these change and develop. A
living faith must express itself in a growing and developing theology. But theology is not religion, and it is
important to make the distinction clear. Theology is
the science of religion. It is the reflexion upon religious
experience, the attempt to interpret, to understand and
to systematise it. And as such it is necessarily subject
to development with every development of man's understanding and knowledge. The same religious experience
will be differently interpreted, not only at different
times, but even by different individuals at the same
time. The Professor and the Blacksmith, in so far as
they are religious, may have the same religious experience, but their "theological" views, their "thoughts"
about God, are and must be widely different. To
comprehend, to be able to understand and give adequate
intellectual expression to one's religious experience—if
and in so far as this is possible—is a higher state than
not to comprehend it; but the depth of the experience

is not determined by the capacity to understand it.   A full and rich religious life may express itself in terms of a crude theology, and the things which are hidden from the wise may be revealed to babes.   The best theologian is not necessarily the most religious man.[1]

This distinction between religion and theology will have to be borne in mind when we attempt to consider the religious value of the Bible for us to-day, and ask to what extent, if at all, later developments of thought, by showing the inadequacy of some of its theology, have lessened its value as the self-expression of a deep religious life.   It is, however, sufficient to notice here that the faith of the Biblical writers is not exempt from that theological development which always marks a living faith, and that modern criticism, by helping us to place the various books and their sources in their chronological sequence, makes it possible for us to trace this development through its many stages.[2]   The religious experience of the various writers is consistently the same in kind throughout, but it is more fully comprehended and more adequately expressed by the later than by the earlier writers.

At first the theology is crude and naïve ; primitive peoples, child races, like children, can only have a crude theology.   Just as the writers use the language of their time, so also they think its thoughts.   The neighbouring Semitic tribes, to take a single illustration, were monolatrous ; each had its national god and owed sole allegiance to him, but the gods of the other tribes were believed to be not less real.   In full accord with this

---

[1] Religion and theology are not, of course, completely independent, but they do not develop co-terminously.   They are independent in the same sense as art and the theory of aesthetics.   A good artist may be a bad critic.   This does not mean that art criticism is of no value to art, but it does mean that the capacity to see a vision of beauty and to communicate it to others is not the same thing as the capacity to reflect upon and interpret that vision.   The picture of the great painter provides data for the critic, as the record of the religious experience of the saint provides data for the theologian.

[2] Apart from the knowledge, for example, that Deuteronomy is not the work of Moses but belongs to a much later period, probably the time of Josiah, it is impossible to form any true conception of theological development in the Old Testament.

view we find in the earlier Biblical writers a conception
of Jahveh as a tribal deity, one among many gods. He
was the God of Israel as Chemosh was the god of
Moab, or Milcom the god of Ammon. Israel was
His chosen people. He fights their battles for them,
and leads their armies to victory and to the promised
land. It was not until the time of the eighth-century
prophets that this view was abandoned and a practical
monotheism taught. And it was still later before the
primitive anthropomorphic and materialistic conception
was superseded by the transcendent and spiritual view
of Deutero-Isaiah. Other illustrations might be given,
but our present concern is with the religious experience
of the writers, rather than with their various attempts,
often crude and inadequate, to interpret and systematize
it. The contention is that the Bible bears witness to
the existence of a common and constant faith in God
and His goodness, a faith which varies in its intensity
with the different writers, and is expressed in a gradually
developing theology.

And side by side with this theological development
we can also trace an ethical development, from a relatively low to a high stage ; but this does not affect the
fact with which we are at present concerned—that from
first to last the Biblical writers manifest an intense
passion for righteousness, and that this passion for
righteousness is an essential part of their religious
experience. Often enough their zeal for the Lord is a
zeal which, judged from a later and more developed
standpoint, is not, in St. Paul's words, "according to
knowledge." No one, least of all a Christian, would
maintain that what was said to them of old time was
ideally perfect : the "law of Moses," as our Lord Himself taught, was adapted to the hardness of the people's
hearts. Inspired and educated by the teaching of the
prophets, the moral sense, in course of time, became
better instructed and more wisely directed. What had
seemed good to one generation seemed to a later genera-

tion, at a more advanced stage of ethical development, to be wrong. Thus Jehu's massacre of the descendants of Ahab is narrated and approved by the author of 2 Kings[1] as manifesting his " zeal for the Lord," but, later on, it is denounced by the prophet Hosea[2] as a sin which the Lord will avenge by destroying the House of Israel. But this ethical development consists not so much in an intensifying of the passion for righteousness, which manifests itself in the earlier as well as in the later writers, but rather in the gradual recognition of the kind of act which God demands. Abraham was willing to sacrifice his only son, the child of his old age, in obedience to what he believed to be the will of God. His zeal was not, as the story itself plainly shows, " according to knowledge "—the story, in fact, is narrated primarily in order to show that Jahveh, unlike other Gods, does not demand human sacrifice—yet the crudity of Abraham's view as to what God demanded does not destroy the moral value of his willingness to do, at whatever the cost, what he believed God to command. If this were more clearly recognised it would obviously remove many of the difficulties which are ordinarily felt with regard to the Old Testament.

So far no mention has been made of the specifically Christian experience which is recorded in the New Testament. In the New Testament writers we find the same trust in God and His goodness, the same sense of His presence, and an even greater apprehension of His love and saving power.[3] But there is this

---

[1] 2 Kings x. 30.   [2] Hosea i. 4.

[3] " Penetrate a little beneath the diversity of circumstances, and it becomes evident that in Christians of different epochs it is always one and the same modification by which they are affected : there is veritably a single fundamental and identical spirit of piety and charity, common to those who have received grace ; an inner state which before all things is one of love and humility, of infinite confidence in God, and of severity for oneself, accompanied with tenderness for others. The fruits peculiar to this condition of the soul have the same savor in all, under different suns and in different surroundings, in Saint Teresa of Avila just as in any Moravian brother of Herrnhut " (Saint-Beuve, quoted James, *Varieties of Religious Experience*, p. 260).

difference, which is vital and fundamental. It was the life of the historical person, Jesus of Nazareth, which created Christianity. It was from Him that there came into being the new spiritual impulse, the new power, which manifested and still manifests itself in the Christian life. And therefore, for the New Testament writers, the person of Christ is absolutely central. He constitutes the beginning and the end of the religious experience of which they speak. For them, communion with God is mediated through and made possible by Him : it is through Him that they have access to the Father, and no man cometh to the Father but by Him. It is in and through Him, and primarily as members of the society of His followers, that God works in their lives and communicates to them His power. Where two or three of His disciples are gathered together in His name, He is present with them, all the days, even unto the end of the world, as Revealer, Redeemer, Sanctifier, giving them life and abundant life.

Thus a new element is added to the religious consciousness which produced the Old Testament—an intense conviction that the life of Christ, which is the source of the power of their inner lives, is God's own act for man. For every writer this is the starting-point of his religious life. In the life of Christ something has been done for him by God. In that life God Himself has spoken and acted. In time past He had spoken to the prophets in divers portions and in divers manners, but now He has spoken in a Son—in One who stands in such a relation to Him that He can say, " He that hath seen Me hath seen the Father," and " what things soever the Father doeth, these also doeth the Son likewise." [1] Therefore they feel that their attitude towards God is determined by their attitude towards Christ—" he that receiveth Me, receiveth Him

[1] The question as to the authenticity of these words does not affect the argument. The author of the Fourth Gospel expresses his conviction and voices the primitive Christian consciousness, that in Christ God, whom no man hath seen at any time, has revealed Himself, and that through Christ man may know God.

that sent Me " : that on the side of Christ they are on the side of God, and doing the will of Christ they are doing the will of God.

But not only has God revealed Himself. In the life of Christ He has also vindicated His faithfulness and manifested and achieved His purpose for mankind, the mystery which from all ages had been hid in God. Throughout the ages the prophets had looked for some manifestation of God's moral supremacy and for the fulfilment of His promises to the Fathers—" so that a man shall say, verily there is a reward for the righteous : doubtless there is a God that judgeth the earth." And through long ages they had looked in vain. But now, God *has* acted. He has wrought His mighty work and laid in Zion His foundation-stone. He who had brought the Fathers out of Egypt with a mighty hand and an outstretched arm has shown His power and His righteousness in that He has raised up Jesus from the dead. The prophets of old had looked for the day of the Lord, when God should pour His Spirit upon all flesh, and all men, from the least to the greatest, should know Him. And in Christ, and in the power of His risen life, that promise has been fulfilled. The salvation which prophet after prophet, in face of constant disappointment and disillusion, had ever proclaimed as near, has been achieved, and is now offered to all men —" to you is the promise, and to your children, and to all that are afar off."

" Blessed be the Lord God of Israel :
    For He hath visited and redeemed His people ;
    And hath raised up a mighty salvation for us :
    In the house of His servant David ;
    As He spake by the mouth of His holy Prophets :
    Which have been since the world began."

This triumphant certainty of and thankfulness for a salvation already won and freely offered, runs through the whole of the New Testament and strikes a new note. In place of the old sense of what God demands

from His people, there is the new sense of what He
has done for them. The new covenant is made. By
sin men are separated from God, but by God's act in
Christ they are reconciled to Him. "What the law
could not do, in that it was weak through the flesh,"
God, sending His Son in the likeness of sinful flesh,
has done and is doing. Like other men St. Paul feels
the need of a Saviour. He knows that in Christ, and
in the corporate life of the Christian community, he
has found one. Everywhere he sees men's lives ruined
by sin, and not least his own life. The good which he
would, he cannot do : the evil which he would not,
that he practises. "O, wretched man that I am," he
cries, "who shall deliver me from the body of this
death ? " And sure and certain is his answer, for it is
based upon a living experience—he knows the truth
of his own life : "I thank God, through Jesus Christ."
Through His acceptance of Christ he feels himself,
sinner though he is, at peace with God. In and
through Christ he knows himself able to overcome
the world. "I can do all things through Christ that
strengtheneth me." On the side of Christ he feels
himself driven along by a force that is higher than
himself and brought into the presence of God, and
this gives him, in every trial and every difficulty, the
assurance of ultimate victory. "I know in whom I
have trusted." "I live, yet no longer I, but Christ
liveth in me." And, be it remembered, this is not
mere meaningless jargon, the repetition of empty
phrases. It is the perfectly honest attempt of a man,
of like passions with ourselves, to describe the deepest
experience of his life. It cannot be doubted that it
was this experienced power of the life of Christ, as
a real force working in the world, drawing all men
to Himself and to God, which created in the Christian
community the consciousness that it was God who
was working in the life of Christ[1] and that He had,

[1] Cf. Essay V. p. 217.

in that life, fulfilled His promises to the Fathers. And it was this same experienced power which enabled the Church to survive the non-fulfilment of the expectation of the immediate return of the Messiah on the clouds of heaven and in great glory, and which still is the real basis of the conviction of Christian people that " the gates of hell shall not prevail."

Yet the hope which expressed itself in apocalyptic imagery, though it was gradually transformed, was never abandoned. Hope is an essential element of all religious faith, and the experienced power of the life of Christ intensified the Christian hope. God had spoken and acted,—that was the primary element in the Christian consciousness ; but there was still, as in the Old Testament, a looking forward, only now the hope was inspired by a new confidence. What God has done in Christ is the earnest of what He will do. It is because He *has* wrought redemption for His people, that " the earnest expectation of the creation waiteth for the revealing of the sons of God "—" even we ourselves, which have the firstfruits of the Spirit, groan within ourselves, waiting for our adoption." [1] " Now are we children of God, and it is not yet made manifest what we shall be. We know that, if He shall be manifested, we shall be like Him ; for we shall see Him even as He is." [2]

It is not necessary, for our present purpose, to consider the various attempts made by the New Testament writers to interpret and systematize their faith. There is considerable theological development both in the New Testament and throughout the whole course of Christian history. The experienced fact of

---

[1] Romans viii. 19, 23.

[2] 1 John iii. 2. " Christianity is—and will ever be—the religion of sure salvation, brought by Jesus and to be experienced by His believers already during their present life. This does not exclude Christian hope. On the contrary, the more present salvation is experienced in mankind, the stronger Christian hope will be. . . . The Christian is a new creature, but he looks for a new heaven and a new earth, and his prayer will be for ever as His Lord taught him—*Thy kingdom come* " (Von Dobschütz, *Eschatology of the Gospels*, pp. 205-7).

reconciliation to God through Christ (the fact of atonement) gave rise to the numerous doctrines of the Atonement; the experienced power of the life of Christ gave rise to all the subsequent Christological speculation.[1] With this theological development we are not here concerned; what is important for our present purpose is the religious experience itself—the same in its essential character as that described in the Old Testament, differing from it, however, in its degree and in its method—it is through Christ that men enter into that communion with God for which their souls thirst. But it is because they are religious men, because they are already conscious of communion with God and assured of His goodness and His love, that they see in Christ God's self-revelation to men.[2] No man can say Jesus is Lord, save in the Spirit : it is only the eye of faith which can see that Christ is Divine.

It is, as has been said, the existence among the Biblical writers of this faith in God which is the fact of supreme importance in relation to the Bible. Viewed simply as a fact it is, even to the non-religious man, to the man, that is, who does not share it, at the least an interesting phenomenon. In the nature of things the faith itself challenges attention and demands explanation. How are we to account for its origin ?

II. The Origin of the Religious Experience of the Biblical Writers

"The Lord, the Lord God, merciful and gracious, long-suffering and abundant in goodness." "Commit thy way unto the Lord, and put thy trust in Him." "The Lord upholdeth the way of the righteous; the way of the ungodly shall be broken."

---

[1] Cf. Essays IV., V. and VI.

[2] In this sense, at any rate, we see how the Old Testament is the preparation for the New Testament. It is, of course, also true that the New Testament is the climax of the Old Testament, and that the knowledge of God revealed in Christ must govern our whole attitude towards the Bible. Cf. Essay V. p. 219.

It is clear that this belief in God's goodness and over-ruling Providence is not a mere colligation of observed facts. To the non-religious man, the facts of life seem not only susceptible of, but insistently to demand, a widely different interpretation. Not so does creation reveal the Creator. Nature, "red in tooth and claw," hard, cruel and unsympathetic, careful of the type, careless of the individual life—

> The sin and sorrow in the world, the stream
> Of evil, gathering on from age to age,
> With all its rocks and all its wrecks of life ;
> And men's hearts hardened, and the tender lips
> Of women loud in laughter, and the sobs
> Of children helpless, and the sighs of slaves—

all shriek against this faith in the love and goodness of God. " In the measure that a man tries to live widely, deeply, and nobly, he is bound to become a pessimist. If optimism is usually associated with the youth and pessimism with the age of persons or peoples, it is because pessimism is the verdict of experience. Whether in himself, or in the world, if a man has ideals for both, he is bound to find not only failure, but an iron law of inevitable failure." [1] Doubtless this is an overstatement, but it is so far true that it makes it impossible to suppose that the faith of the Biblical writers in the goodness of God has been arrived at as an inference from the facts of the world.

Nor is it possible to explain the origin and persistence of their faith by supposing that they were blind to those facts which, to the non-religious man, seem inconsistent with it. Theirs was not the sheltered faith of

> . . . country folks who live beneath
> The shadow of the steeple,

and have no knowledge of what we call " the real facts of life." It is not merely a shallow criticism, but on the face of it wholly false, to speak of them as "arm-

[1] Tyrrell, *Christianity at the Cross Roads*, pp. 117-18.

chair optimists." They see all the difficulties and
state them boldly. They were as acutely conscious of
man's littleness in the vastness of the universe as any
modern. The God who measures the waters in the
hollow of His hands, and meteth out the heavens with
a span, who weighs the mountains in a scale and the
hills in a balance, before whom all nations are as
nothing—what can be the value to Him of a man's
life ?   "What is man that Thou art mindful of him, or
the son of man that Thou regardest him?"   Nor were
they blind to the evil, both moral and physical,
which there is in the world. They see it not less, but
more plainly than other men. The dominant note of
the Bible is not "All's right with the world," but
rather "Who will show us any good?"   Not the least
striking fact about the Bible is that those of its writers
who are most deeply convinced of the goodness of
God, are most keenly conscious of the existence of evil.

"There is none righteous, no, not one ;
There is none that understandeth,
There is none that seeketh after God ;
They have all turned aside, they are together be-
come unprofitable ;
There is none that doeth good, no, not so much
as one." [1]

Nor did the apparently conflicting facts, what we
call the problem of evil, present themselves to the
Biblical writers in any less acute forms than they do to
us to-day. Nowhere is the paradox of faith more
striking than in the life of Christ. No other teacher
so taught and so firmly held a belief in the love and
goodness of God, and in His universal Providence.
"The hairs of your head are all numbered."   "Be not
anxious for the morrow."   "Your Heavenly Father
knows what things ye have need of."   More than this,
He had a consciousness of a unique relationship to God

---

[1] Romans iii. 10-12. St. Paul repeats and endorses the Psalmist's sweeping
condemnation.

and of a unique vocation. No man ever claimed more for Himself, or so confidently asserted that His work enjoyed the favour of God. "All power in heaven and earth hath been committed unto Me." And in no other life have the facts so plainly seemed to contradict the faith which inspired it. His mission, judged by the ordinary standards, was not a success, and from the very first it was clear what the end would be. The shadow of the Cross darkens every page of the story. Rejected at Capernaum, refused a hearing at Nazareth, driven from Samaria, crucified at Jerusalem—it was all of a piece and all inevitable. He devoted His life absolutely to the service of God, and the result was the Cross. But though the life of Christ is the supreme illustration of the paradox of faith, it is not the only one. Calvary sums up in one dramatic moment the experience of all the prophets. Destitute, afflicted, evil entreated, they all died in faith, "not having received the promise." At the moment of his call, Isaiah knows that his preaching will be of no avail. The warning of Jeremiah falls, as he knows it will, on deaf ears.

And again the question presents itself to the non-religious man, Why is it that these men believe in God and devote their lives to His service, apparently failing, yet never despairing? What is the source of their unconquerable hope and undying faith? The heroism of it and the boldness fascinate and attract him. Clearly it is "of faith" and not "of knowledge." It goes beyond any induction from observed facts, and is incapable of complete verification in them.

This does not necessarily mean that it is either untrue or incredible. We sometimes forget that it is not only the religious man who must live by faith. The optimism of religion is, in fact, closely analogous to the optimism of science. The faith of the religious man in the goodness of God—or, in other words, his belief that every event has a moral purpose—finds a parallel in the faith of the man of science that the

E

Universe is a Cosmos, that every event has a cause, and is ultimately explicable in relation to the whole scheme of things.[1] In both cases the belief is incapable of complete verification. The religious man fully recognises that there are some events of which he does not yet see the moral purpose, and that, so far, his postulate is not completely verified. And so, too, with the man of science : the existence of research implies his recognition that there are some events of which he does not yet see the cause, and that, so far, his postulate is not completely verified. Yet neither will abandon the hope that the unexplained is not ultimately unexplainable. The difference is that the one is seeking an explanation in terms of moral purpose, and the other in terms of self-consistency.

And in each case, too, the hope or the faith is reasonable and persists only in so far as it finds adequate —though never complete—justification in experience. What the religious man calls "faith" is, up to a certain point, analogous to what the man of science calls "working hypothesis"; but, by the terms of the definition, the hypothesis must "work." The man of science admits that there is much that he has not explained in the light of his "faith," but, despite this, he maintains it because it seems to him to explain more of the facts than any alternative view, and he makes a venture of faith—from the known to the unknown. So, too, the religious man admits that there is much which he has not been able to harmonise with his faith ; but despite this, he maintains it because it seems to him to explain more of the facts of human nature and of life than the alternative theory of the non-religious man. He does not glory in a *credo quia impossibile.* He satisfies

---

[1] "Every synthesis of fact to fact, every attempt to know . . . is inspired by a secret faith in the unity of the world. Each of the sciences works within its own region, and colligates its details in the light of its own hypothesis ; and all the sciences taken together presuppose the presence in the world of a principle that binds it into an orderly totality."—Henry Jones, *Browning as a Philosophical and Religious Teacher*, p. 37.

himself, and he tries to satisfy others, by appealing to those facts which are explained by and do justify his faith, to the manifestations in history and in life of the power not ourselves, which makes for righteousness.

Thus the Biblical writers try to show how behind the maze of history with its apparent contradictions and its apparent arbitrary occurrences, there is the hand of God guiding and controlling it all, and that in it all and through it all there is a Divine purpose slowly fulfilling itself in the ordered sequence of events. Where they cannot do this, they, too, make a venture of faith, from the known to the unknown, and trust that somehow good will be the final goal of ill. Because He believes in the goodness of God, Jesus Christ is sure that His death cannot mean either the end of His life or the ruin of His work. His faith leads Him to see in the apparent failure of His ministry the vindication of the teaching of Deutero-Isaiah as to the redemptive value of suffering, and therefore He sees in the Cross the salvation of mankind, and beyond the Cross the triumph of His risen life.[1] Doubtless this was a venture of faith, but essentially it was a venture which faith was bound to make.

But though both with the man of science and the prophet the faith only persists because those who hold it find it progressively justified in experience, it still remains true that in neither case is it arrived at as an inference from the facts of the world. The faith interprets the facts, and without the facts it would not have arisen, but by themselves the facts do not explain or create the faith.

> Truth is within ourselves : it takes no rise
> From outward things, whate'er you may believe.

We may carry the comparison a stage further. Alike in the sphere of science and of religion there are the great discoverers and revealers of truth,

[1] Cf. Essay III. pp. 124 *et seq.*

men with special faculties of insight, which enable
them to see deeper and with greater clearness of
vision than other men. The great scientific discoverer
in an intuitive flash sees cosmos where others see
only chaos, and the great religious teacher sees an
eternal purpose of righteousness and love slowly
fulfilling itself, where others see only blind force
directed to no moral end. The same, of course,
applies in every region of mental activity or spiritual
life. There are great poets and musicians and painters,
just as there are great men of science, each possessing,
in their respective spheres, faculties of insight which
enable them to perceive aspects of truth or beauty
which others, less gifted, cannot see. Such genius is
mysterious in its origin, and, so far as we can see,
subject to no general laws. We cannot account for the
appearance of a great man of science or of a great poet.
We cannot explain why one man has an ear for music
and another has not, or why the great painter sees
beauty to which others are blind. And it is the same
in the religious sphere. The great painter is differentiated from other men in that he has, in a special
degree, an eye for colour, or a feeling for line ; and a
great prophet is differentiated in that he possesses
special faculties of insight in the region in which man
holds communion with God. In the case of the
prophet these perceptive powers may be called "a
religious sense," and the existence of religion is the
evidence of the existence of this religious sense, just as
the existence of poetry or music is the evidence of the
existence of a poetic or musical sense. There are some
men who seem to have little or no religious sense.[1] To
them the language in which the Biblical writers describe
their religious experience sounds as meaningless as a
sonata of Beethoven does to those who have no musical

---

[1] But see below, p. 61. It need not follow that Christianity has no message
for those who seem to have no religious sense. For them, the support of their
religion will depend, in the first instance, upon those philosophical, moral and
historical considerations which are discussed in the later essays in this volume.

sense. But there are others in whom this religious sense exists in a highly developed form, who have a special genius for religion, as others have for art or music. Whether and to what extent others beside the Biblical writers possess this genius for religion need not, for the moment, be considered ; that the Biblical writers do possess it is a fact which will not be denied.

We may go further than this. The Biblical writers have their own theory as to the origin of their faith—a theory which is, in fact, an essential part of their faith. For them, religion, as has been said, is not the mere assent of the intellect to a certain view of God's existence and nature. It is not the mere belief that God is good and that every event has a moral purpose—like the belief of the man of science that every event has a cause. Still less, of course, is it a mere hypothesis which is held tentatively and laboriously verified. " What constitutes religion," says von Hügel, " is not simply to hold a view and to try to live a life with respect to the Unseen and the Deity, as possibly or even certainly beautiful or true or good ; but precisely that which is over and above this—the holding of this view and this life to proceed somehow from God Himself, so as to bind my innermost mind and conscience to unhesitating assent." [1]

One and all the Biblical writers assert that their faith is due to the direct action of God upon their lives. This is the ground of their confidence and certainty—" Thus saith the Lord," " God said," " The Word of the Lord came unto me, saying." Their language was probably more than mere symbolism,[2] but at the least it represents their conviction that their knowledge of God was due to direct relationship with Him.

Thus the analogy which has been drawn between the faith of the prophet and that of the man of science, and between the religious and the aesthetic sense is

---

[1] *The Mystical Element of Religion*, vol. i. p. 46.
[2] Cf. Essay III. p. 95.

inadequate, because there is a fundamental difference between the two experiences which are being compared. The experience of the religious man in his perception of God differs from the experience of the painter in his perception of beauty in the fact that in the former case the object perceived (viz. God) is regarded as personal and as personally active in the perceptive process. The knowledge of God which the Biblical writers claim is conceived of in terms of personal relationship, and consequently an analogy which includes such relationship may be more adequate. The knowledge of God which they claim may, in fact, be compared with the knowledge of a man which his friend possesses, a special knowledge peculiar to him in virtue of his friendship. I know that my greatest friend is a good man. He is accused of theft, and all the facts seem against him. Other men think him guilty, but I know that he is innocent. I cannot prove this either to myself or to any one else. My belief in his innocence is " of faith " and not " of knowledge "—it may not be susceptible of complete verification—but this does not weaken the strength of the conviction with which I hold it.

This faith of mine in my friend is closely akin to that faith in God which is found in the Biblical writers. " Though He slay me," says Job, " yet will I trust Him." Here, too, the faith goes beyond a colligation of observed facts. To some extent a man's words and acts reveal his character, and by examination of and reflection on these all men, without personal intercourse, may have some knowledge of him. But such knowledge is inadequate. His acts and words are capable of widely different interpretations, and only those who know *him* can understand them. So far from judging him solely by his acts and words, the friend judges and estimates these in the light of that personal knowledge which is the result of his friendship. And that this friendship may exist, that there may be this communion of soul with soul, two things are necessary. There

must be, on the part of my friend, a willingness to
reveal himself to me. " I can only know that person
who chooses to reveal himself to me. I may be in his
presence several hours during each day, and for six days
in each week, and yet at the end of ten years know him
no better than the servant who brushes his clothes. . . .
Unless there is self-revelation, we are almost as far off
from knowing the person as though we had never seen
him." [1]   And, also, there must be on my side some
response, a sympathetic insight which will enable me to
understand and apprehend his self-revelation.   Where
there is no community of spirit, no essential kinship,
there can be no friendship or personal knowledge.

> You must love him, ere to you
> He will seem worthy of your love.

And experience shows us that as there are men who
have a genius for science and for art, so also there are
men who have a genius for friendship, a special capacity
for understanding their fellow-men and entering into
the closest relationship with them.

The various analogies which have been given are only
analogies, and the last one is crudely anthropomorphic,
but they suggest the lines along which we may find an
answer to the question we are considering in this section
—What is the origin of the faith of the Biblical writers ?
In other words, they may help us to formulate a theory
of inspiration and revelation.

Assuming, as we have done throughout, that the
communion with God which the Biblical writers claim
is real and not illusory,[2] we may draw three conclusions.
First, that their knowledge of God is and must be
revealed knowledge.   It is, of course, obvious that man
can have no knowledge of God which God does not
will him to have.   I can only know my friend if and
in so far as he wills to reveal himself to me ; still less

---

[1] Walpole, *Vital Religion*, p. 12.
[2] The justification of this assumption is discussed in Essay IX.

can I have any knowledge of God apart from His self-revelation. And, secondly, that this knowledge of God is due to the fact that they possess a special faculty for apprehending His self-revelation. If God speaks, He can only speak to those who have the capacity for hearing, and in proportion to that capacity. And, thirdly, that as the condition of this speaking and hearing, of this communion between God and man, there is and must be an essential kinship between the Divine and human nature ; in other words, if man is to "know" God, he must, in Biblical language, be made in the image of God. I can only understand the picture of an artist if to some extent I share his mind ; I can only know my friend if there is some real community of spirit between us. "The spirit of man whereby he knows God," says Hegel, "is the spirit of God Himself." And this is the view of the Biblical writers. "The Spirit Himself beareth witness with our spirit, that we are children of God."[1] "We have received the spirit which is of God, that we might know the things that are freely given to us of God."[2]

This capacity for entering into communion with God, this special insight which enables men to apprehend His self-revelation, is termed by the Biblical writers "the gift of the Spirit." It has been spoken of above as "the religious sense," and for the present we may adhere to this designation of it. This religious sense, the indwelling Spirit of God, the spirit of truth which leads men to the truth, is the condition and the medium of Divine revelation. We shall therefore no longer think of revelation as the communication to man from without of certain pieces of information about God, but rather as an act of God within. It is not so much that God speaks to one man and not to another, as that the one man has the capacity to hear and the other has not. What we call inspiration is the quickening and intensifying of

---

[1] Romans viii. 16.   [2] 1 Corinthians ii. 12.

this religious sense, an increase of the gift of the Spirit, which produces the religious genius, as, for example, the quickening and intensifying of the poetic faculty produces the great poet.[1]

It is because the Biblical writers possess, in a highly developed form, this religious sense, because they have a special genius for religion, that we speak of them as in a special sense inspired.[2] "They were holy, spiritual men," says Luther, "therefore God spoke with them in their consciences, which the prophets held as sure and certain revelations." What was given to them was a special insight so that they could apprehend God. Their eyes were opened so that they could see Him, and their ears so that they could hear His voice. Their sense of God and His goodness is the act of God within their lives and constitutes His self-revelation to them. Beyond this we cannot go. "The wind bloweth where it listeth, and thou hearest the sound thereof, but canst not tell whence it cometh, and whither it goeth : so is every one that is born of the Spirit."

III. The Permanent Value of the Religious Experience of the Biblical Writers

It remains to consider the value for us of the religious experience of the Biblical writers. It may, however, first be noted that for them, and for all who share it, the experience is its own evidence. In this sense, at any rate, William Law was right in saying, "The spiritual life is as much its own proof as the natural life, and needs no outward or foreign thing to bear witness to it." The Biblical writers are sure and

---

[1] "The revelation to the prophets is seen to have been a quickening of their ethical insight, of their spiritual apprehension, of their sense of close filial unity with God in this life. . . . Revelation is education, not instruction."—"The Idea of Revelation," in *Cambridge Theological Essays*, pp. 236-7. I am much indebted to this essay.

[2] Every religious man is, to the extent to which he is religious, inspired. How far the Biblical writers may be regarded as inspired in a unique degree is considered in the following section.

certain that God is what they say He is. Their faith in Him represents the deepest conviction of their inner lives. They neither argue nor reason about it : they simply state it as true.

Whoso hath felt the Spirit of the Highest
Cannot confound nor doubt him nor deny :
Yea with one voice, O world, tho' thou deniest,
Stand thou on that side, for on this am I.

On the other hand, to those who do not possess it— and except to the extent to which they do possess it— it has, in one sense, no value.[1] It is their experience, their faith, not mine, and I cannot, at any rate permanently, substitute for my own convictions an intellectual assent to the convictions of other people. Faith, to have any value for us, must be our own faith.

But there is a sense in which the religious experience of the Biblical writers has some evidential value even for those who do not themselves share it. There can be no doubt that the experience itself is real : the only doubt is as to what it is an experience of, or, in other words, whether its cause is, as they maintain it is, God Himself. The experience must have some cause, but it does not follow that that cause must be God. " The primary evidence of the existence of any perceived object must be our perception of it ; and if it is to be shown notwithstanding that what we suppose ourselves to perceive, does not really exist, this cannot mean that we perceive nothing. It can only mean that what we perceive is not what we think it to be : in other words, the question is not so much *whether it exists* as *what it is.*"[2] The existence of religion, that is, does not prove the existence of God. On the other hand if, apart from the fact of religious experience, we have other and

---

1 " Mystical states, when well developed, usually are, and have the right to be, absolutely authoritative over the individuals to whom they come. No authority emanates from them which should make it a duty for those who stand outside of them to accept their revelations uncritically " (James, *Varieties of Religious Experience,* p. 422).
2 Webb, *Problems in the Relations of God and Man,* p. 6.

adequate grounds for believing in the existence of God, the intuitions of the religious consciousness are facts of which account must be taken when we speculate as to the nature and being of God.[1] Granted even the probability of the existence of God, there is nothing intrinsically unreasonable in the supposition that He may have revealed Himself. Rather, the burden of proof lies with those who deny and not with those who assert.

Yet it still remains true that the ultimate appeal for each is to his own experience. This must necessarily be the case. It may be possible to justify a belief in God by processes of abstract reasoning, but there is a world of difference between the purely philosophical and the religious conception of God. It does not follow that the two are ultimately incompatible, nor does it follow that, even though it was arrived at not by processes of pure philosophy but rather intuitively and through direct spiritual apprehension,[2] the religious conception cannot be rationally justified. Yet the fact remains that truth which is spiritually perceived cannot be fully apprehended by any purely logical process. I cannot " prove," for example, that a picture is beautiful. I may point out its merits, but in the last resort my argument will only carry conviction to those who possess——and to the extent to which they do possess— a capacity to appreciate beauty when it is presented to them. And so, too, it must be with regard to that conception of God which is found in the Biblical writers. It may not be impossible to justify it on rational grounds, but it is impossible to " prove " it by any purely logical process to those, if there are any, who do not possess a religious sense. " Profane men," says Luther, " desire and insist to have it proved by reason that Moses and the prophets were divinely inspired. But I answer that the testimony of the Spirit is superior to reason. For, as God alone can properly bear witness

---

[1] Cf. Essay IX. pp. 501 *et seq.*   [2] Cf. Introduction, p. ix.

to His own words, so these words will not obtain full
credit in the hearts of men until they are sealed by the
inward testimony of the Spirit. The same Spirit,
therefore, who spoke by the mouth of the prophets
must penetrate our hearts, in order to convince us that
they faithfully delivered the message with which they
were divinely entrusted." The same truth is stated
with equal force in the Westminster Confession : " Our
full persuasion and assurance of the infallible truth and
divine authority (of Holy Scripture) is from the inward
work of the Holy Spirit bearing witness by and with
the word in our own hearts." Translating this into
the language which we have hitherto been using, we
may say that as it is only the man with a sense of beauty
who can perceive beauty and express it in a picture, and
also only the man with a sense of beauty who can judge
and appreciate the beauty of the picture when it is
painted, so it is only the man with a religious sense
who can truly know God and reveal Him, and also
only the man with a religious sense who can fully
apprehend the truth of the message about God which
the prophet proclaims. That same Spirit which enables
the religious genius to know God enables us—so far as
we share it—to know the truth of what he says about
God. Only those who possess the gift of the Spirit—
or, as we have called it, the religious sense—are able
fully to apprehend the products of it.

Experience, however, shows that those other senses
with which we have compared the religious sense are
capable of development and cultivation, and, more than
this, actually require it. In a well-known passage in
his autobiography, Darwin tells us how in later life he
lost his taste for pictures and music : he even found
Shakespeare "intolerably dull." This was almost
inevitable. If we never look at beautiful things, we
shall soon cease to love them. " If I had to begin my
life again," Darwin concludes, " I would make a rule
to read some poetry or to hear some music at least once

a week." Accordingly it is legitimate to suppose—
and experience justifies the supposition — that the
religious sense is capable of and requires cultivation not
less than these other senses.   It is hardly likely that
men will be able to know God without at least that
amount of trouble which is required for the appreciation
of literature or music.   Reference has already been
made to the fact that there are some men who seem to
have little or no religious sense.   It would, perhaps,
be truer to say that in such cases—which are more
numerous than we sometimes think—the religious sense
is either undeveloped or atrophied through disuse, than
that it is non-existent.   It may well be that the " light
which lighteth every man " has, for them, become
darkness, because they have failed to " stir up the gift "
which is in them.

But if God is what the prophet declares Him to be,
it follows that this ¯ilure to develop the religious sense
by which man en.ers into communion with God and
knows Him, results in an impoverishment of the whole
life in a sense, because to a degree, quite different from
that in which the failure to develop, for example, the
musical or the artistic sense impoverishes life.   There
are men who seem to have so little capacity for ap-
preciating music that, while recognising their lack of
musical sense as a defect, we should feel that they
might more profitably devote themselves to the development of other faculties which they do possess and in a
higher degree.   But if that conception of God which
the prophets proclaim is true, the case with regard to
religion is wholly different.

> Religion's all or nothing ; it's no mere smile
> O' contentment, sigh of aspiration, sir—
> No quality o' the finelier tempered clay
> Like its whiteness or its lightness ; rather, stuff
> O' the very stuff ; life of life, and self of self.

If God is what the prophet declares Him to be, the
life of the man who does not know Him is not merely

incomplete, but defeated and half unfulfilled. The revelation of God which the prophet gives is life and abundant life.[1]

Further, it is reasonable to suppose that the method by which the religious sense may be cultivated and developed will be the same as that by which those other senses with which it has been compared are developed. What this method is may be illustrated from the artistic sense. Most of us begin by liking bad art, and even continue to do so though we are conscious that it is bad. " I know which pictures I like, but I don't know which are good," adequately represents the position of the ordinary man. And if ever we are to be able to appreciate or recognise the great masters, we must deliberately attempt to train and cultivate our taste. For this purpose we go to the expert, to one whom we recognise as qualified by his experience and knowledge to tell us which are the great masters and why, and then we study these pictures ourselves. And the result of this study of the great masters is that in course of time our taste is educated and stimulated, and we become able to appreciate the greatness of their pictures and to pass judgment upon them. We become, in fact, experts ourselves.

This, of course, involves an appeal to authority, an appeal which is capable of misuse, and, in the religious sphere, at any rate, has been misused. But *abusus non tollit usum.* Under certain conditions it is both legitimate and inevitable. As applied in the case we have considered, there is no authoritative imposition of beliefs on grounds which are irrational, and there is nothing which conflicts with the claims of reason. The appeal to authority is, in fact, based upon reason : it is simply the recognition of the fact that the opinion of one man is not necessarily as true as that of another, but that on his own subject the judgment of the expert is of more value than that of the ordinary man. *Cuique*

[1] Cf. Essay IX. p. 479.

in sua arte credendum. On his own subject, on the subject, that is, for which he has unique capacities and gifts, the specialist has a unique knowledge, and so can speak with a unique authority, and the ordinary man must be ready to learn from him, to take advantage of his wider experience, and train his own perceptions by his help. He must make, in fact, the venture of faith, and accept, provisionally, the judgment of the expert. But he does this with the expectation that, since the judgment of the expert is probably right, as his own experience widens and deepens, his judgment will become the same as that of the expert. What he accepts on authority he will afterwards verify in his own experience, but the acceptance of the authoritative judgment is the essential starting-point.[1] Faith, it has been well said, is an experiment which ends in an experience : it is not believing instead of knowing, but rather believing in order to know. Applying this method in the religious sphere, we may say that as in the case of music or art we train our perceptions and cultivate our taste by the help of the great musicians and artists, so also we must train our religious perceptions and cultivate our spiritual sense by the help of those who have a special genius for religion.

But how are we to find the religious genius? How are we to distinguish the true prophet from the false, and where is the "expert" who will show us which are the "great masters" of religion ? Here, too, the analogy we have drawn between religion and art will help us again. How do we recognise or test genius in art ? There is, perhaps, a threefold test. First, the genius is the man who possesses special faculties of insight which enable him to catch some glimpse of truth or beauty which the ordinary man cannot see. " He is the greatest artist," says Ruskin, " who has embodied, in the sum of his works, the greatest number of the greatest ideas." And, secondly, he is one who is able

---

[1] Cf. Essay VIII. pp. 366-7.

through the medium of his work to create, in those who study it, emotions akin to those which in him inspired that work. Not only does he see a vision himself, but he opens our eyes so that we can see it too.

> For, don't you mark, we're made so that we love
> First when we see them painted, things we have passed
> Perhaps a hundred times nor cared to see ;
>   . . . Art was given for that—
> God uses us to help each other so,
> Lending our minds out.

By means of his picture, the great painter conveys to us "thoughts that do often lie too deep for tears," and as we look at his picture the vision which inspired him inspires us, and we catch a glimpse of the beauty he saw. And, thirdly, the work of the genius must stand the test of time. It must possess "Catholicity." The power of the great picture is not limited to any particular age or time : the appeal is to men at all times and in all places—not to all men (popularity is not the test of greatness), but to those whose artistic sense is cultivated and who have the right to judge.

If we apply this threefold test in our search for the religious genius—for those by whose help we can train our religious sense—it is, first and most, to the Bible that the facts of history and of experience point us. The Bible is for religion what the great masters are for art. It is, as has been well said, like "a picture gallery of the old masters."

As we turn back the pages of history we see how particular nations and peoples seem to have possessed special gifts. Rome had a genius for law and organisation, as Greece had for art and letters. So, too, the Hebrew people had a special genius for religion. In an especial and unique sense religion was their life : it moulded the national constitution, it directed the national policy, it created the national literature. The Hebrews, as only the historian adequately recognises, have been the great religious teachers of the world ;

we, who have learnt from them, are apt to forget how
wholly unique their religion was when it first made
its appearance in the world—they saw God and knew
Him as no other nation—and how largely indebted to
them for its religions the rest of the human race is.
The religions of Greece and Rome, of Babylon and
of Egypt have perished, and of the great religions
which, in addition to the Jewish, still live, two,
Christianity and Mohammedanism, have their roots in
Judaism. To those who see a Divine power working
out the purpose of its will in the whole course of
history, and who believe that each people has its own
contribution to make to the building up of the perfect
people of God, the Hebrews stand out pre-eminently as
selected in order to give religion to the world.

And it is in the Bible that the religion of the
Hebrews finds its highest and its noblest expression.
Through the medium of their words, the Biblical
writers enable us to see God as they saw Him, and to
share that communion with Him which inspired their
writings. This is simply a statement of fact. As we
read, our hearts burn within us : we feel ourselves
brought into the presence of God, and are assured of
His love and power and goodness. We share in the
experience of the writers. In the presence of Christ
the disciples felt themselves in the presence of God.
In the Gospels they so tell us the story of that life,
that He still lives in their record, and, as we read, our
experience becomes the same as theirs. It is told of
Bishop Creighton that to one who was dying without
faith and asked for help he said : " The only thing I
can recommend is the Gospel according to St. John.
Read it, and weigh it, and consider the view of life
which it contains." As we read, we become sure in
our hearts of God's love ; we feel that the God who
rules the world is on the side of, in and with the life
of Jesus, and that as we surrender ourselves to Him we
shall be enabled to realise all the potentialities of our

F

own lives. Like the first disciples we feel the call of Jesus, and are irresistibly drawn to Him ; their faith in Him is communicated to us. It was the Spirit of God working within their hearts which enabled them to see God in Christ, and it is the same Spirit working within our hearts which enables us to see God in the portrait of Christ which they have drawn.

And the appeal of the Bible is catholic. Religious men always and everywhere have found in it the inspiration and support of their lives. It has made them " wise unto salvation," strong in the Lord. This fact was the starting-point of our inquiry, and need not be further emphasised now.[1] It need only be said that it is this proved power of the Bible in the past which really constitutes its authority for us to-day. The place which the Bible has occupied in the religious history of mankind, and in particular in the Christian Church, marks it as "the classical and normative expression of the religious life." And it must be accepted as such for the same reason that the works of Shakespeare or of Fra Angelico are accepted as " classics," that is, on the authority of the expert.

For the Christian, this authority is that of the Church. In religion, it is the saint who is the expert, and the authority of the Church, the *consensus sanctorum*, represents the living and abiding voice of a corporate experience, wider than that of any individual or of any age, which testifies to the supreme value of the Bible as a creative and sustaining power in the spiritual life. We go to the Bible in order to deepen and correct our religious lives by the aid of the Biblical writers : we read the Bible in order that we may find God in the way in which religious men at all times have found Him. " As well imagine a man with a sense for sculpture," it has been said, " not cultivating it by the help of the remains of Greek art, or a man with a sense of poetry not cultivating it with the help of Homer or Shakespeare,

[1] See above, pp. 28-9.

as a man with a sense of conduct" (or, we may add,
with a sense of religion) " not cultivating it by the help
of the Bible."

No attempt has been made in this essay to estimate
the historical value of the various books of the Bible.
It has been contended that the primary purpose of the
writers is religious and not strictly historical, and that, in
many cases, they idealise and freely adapt their material
in accordance with this purpose.[1] This must not, however, be taken to imply that their writings have little or
no value for the historian.   As regards the Old Testament, some of the books, viewed simply as historical
documents, are of very considerable value.   In the case
of others, the historical value is only slight, or rather,
is mainly indirect.[2]   In the light of modern criticism it
has become necessary for us to modify, in many important respects, the traditional view of Jewish history ;
still it is mainly in the Old Testament itself that the
historian finds the material by means of which he can,
with some certainty, reconstruct this history.   But
the general result of criticism has been to shift the
centre of interest for religious purposes from the historical books to the Psalms, the writings of the Prophets
and the Wisdom Literature.
   As regards the New Testament, the case is somewhat different, as we are here dealing with documents
which are contemporary, or nearly contemporary, with
the events narrated.   The Gospels provide us with the
materials for an account of the life and teaching of the
Historic Christ,[3] and the other New Testament books
enable us to trace the history of the primitive Christian
community in Palestine and the rise of the Gentile

---

[1] See above, p. 37.

[2] Sometimes the writers provide the historian with valuable information as to
the historical situation at the time at which they write, rather than with regard to
the events of the past which they purport to narrate.   And it is no paradox to say
that the writings of the Prophets are, in many cases, of greater value to the historian
than the so-called " historical books."

[3] Cf. Essay III. pp. 80 et seq.

church in the critical period prior to the fall of Jerusalem. It is, however, important to remember that no
ancient historians are, in the strict and modern sense of
the word, scientific. The movement in that direction
made by Thucydides and Polybius was not sustained.[1]
Later writers were more concerned to paint a portrait or
draw a moral than to test authorities or to secure accuracy
in minor details ; and even a writer like St. Luke, who
more than the other evangelists possesses something of
the historian's outlook and purpose, is unfairly treated
if he is judged by the standard of a Mommsen instead
of by that of a Plutarch. But though the historical
value of the New Testament is undoubtedly superior to
that of the Old Testament, it is not on this account,
but rather on account of its far greater religious value,
that we assert its fuller inspiration.

Two further points must be mentioned to prevent
misconception. In the first place, it must be stated that
it is for religion, and not necessarily for theology, that
we go to the Bible. The distinction between religion
and theology has already been pointed out, and, this
recognised, it will be clear that the religious value of
the Bible is not determined by the adequacy or
inadequacy of its theology. We can learn more
religion from the humblest saint than from the greatest
theologian. The same holds true in the case of art.
Andrea del Sarto, " the faultless painter," knew how to
draw and mix his colours, but he is not as great a
painter as Fra Angelico. He is not equally inspired,
and he has less to reveal to us. And in the Bible the
religious genius of the writers manifests itself despite the
limitations of their theology. In some ways our theology
may be more adequate than that of St. Paul,[2] but for
that religion, of which our theology is the intellectual
interpretation, we may, or rather we must, go to St.

[1] Cf. Bury, *The Ancient Greek Historians*, esp. lectures v. and viii.
[2] The Nicene Creed may be only the making explicit of what is implicit in the
earlier theology, but just in so far as it is this, it marks an advance in theology.

Paul, and we shall find in his religious experience our inspiration and the data for our own theology.

And, secondly, it must be explicitly stated—though the point of view adopted throughout should already have made it plain—that it is not suggested that all the Biblical writers were equally inspired, or that inspiration is limited to them. Precisely the opposite is meant. The view that all the canonical books have the same religious value—though it seems to underlie the Anglican Lectionary—is as untenable as the old mechanical theory of verbal inspiration, and no one really holds it. "How is it," a modern writer asks, "that the Bible of the simplest saint will be well worn and thumbed, perhaps actually torn, at the Psalms and in the Gospels, and the page quite clean in Leviticus and Esther? . . . They might not acknowledge in words that there are degrees of inspiration in the Bible : but their markings in the Bible make it perfectly plain that in effect they do." [1]

And, further, on the principle we have maintained, it is equally clear that some books not included in the Canon, such, for example, as the Book of Wisdom or the *Imitatio Christi*, show a higher degree of inspiration than some of the canonical books. To some extent this is partially recognised by the Church of England, which directs the public reading of parts of the Apocrypha. But it is of the essence of the position we have adopted that we should believe that God is ever revealing Himself, and that all knowledge of Him is from Him.

> God sends His teachers unto every age,
> To every clime, and every race of men,
> With revelations fitted to their growth
> And shape of mind.

It is because we believe this that we pray that God will inspire continually His Holy Church and bestow

[1] Munro Gibson, quoted *Absente Reo*, p. 54.

upon us the gift of the Spirit, which will enable us to
have a right judgment in all things and lead us into
all truth.

Yet it remains true that all men have not the same
capacity for apprehending God's self-revelation or for
communicating it to others. There are men of religious
genius, men, like Moses, who speak with God "face
to face." These men become the founders of great
religious movements and are the religious teachers
of mankind. We know them by their fruits and
we speak of them as inspired in a unique degree.
That we, too, may speak with God "face to face,"
that we may have that knowledge of Him which
they possessed, we seek the help of those to whom
He spoke in the past. If first and most we go
to the Bible, it is because, as has been shown, the
facts of history and of our own experience lead us
to it. The authority which the Bible possesses is that
of its own spiritual supremacy and its unique spiritual
power. "On the great deep of Holy Scriptures we
float away from our prejudices and preconceptions,
and afar from the creeping mists and rocky barriers
of the narrowing coast, and alone with God, can see
in open vision the vastness of all His loving purposes.
They who haunt these mighty tides 'see the works of
the Lord and His wonders in the deep.' . . . Our
own souls must be continually bathed in those living
streams if we would keep them apt and ready for
heavenly visitations." [1]

What is claimed for the Bible is just that which
the facts demand. If less is claimed our religious
life will be infinitely poorer and weaker than that of
our fathers and we shall be disloyal not only to the
past but also to the future. For in disinheriting
ourselves we shall be disinheriting the generations
that are to come. What the Bible has done for
others it can do for us. "As if on some dark night

---

[1] Wilberforce : Ordination Addresses, IX.

a pilgrim suddenly beholding a bright star moving
before him should stop in fear and perplexity. But
lo ! traveller after traveller passes by him, and each,
being questioned whither he is going, makes answer,
' I am following yon guiding star ! ' The pilgrim
quickens his steps and presses onward in confidence.
More confident will he be if, by the wayside, he should
find here and there ancient monuments, each with its
votive lamp, and on each the name of some former
pilgrim and a record that there he had first seen,
or begun to follow, the benignant star." [1]

And so I go to the Bible, as others have gone before
me, to learn from those who have heard God speak,
seeking by their help to see the vision they saw, and
finding in their words inspiration and power. As I
read, the spark of faith is kindled in me, and, in part,
I see God as they see Him. But if I cannot see the
visions they see and hear the voices they hear, I do
not conclude that they were deceived and that there
were no visions and no voices, but that the fault lies
with me, because I have not the eyes with which to
see or the ears with which to hear. And so I go back
to the Bible with the conviction that as my own
experience widens and deepens it will become the same
as theirs, that I shall know God as they know Him,
because they know Him as He is. The day will come
when I shall believe

> the words that one by one
> The touch of Life has turned to truth,

not " because of their saying," but because I have seen
for myself and know.

[1] Coleridge, quot. Tyrrell, *Scylla and Charybdis*, p. 66.

III

THE HISTORIC CHRIST

BY

BURNETT HILLMAN STREETER

SYNOPSIS

	PAGE
The point of view of Modern Scholarship	75
The origin and historical value of the Gospels . . .	80
Apocalyptic Eschatology and the Messianic hope . . .	87
John the Baptist	92
The Call of our Lord and the psychology of the Prophetic mind .	94
Apocalyptic or Warrior Christ ?	99
The Teaching of our Lord : its theme and character . .	103
The Ethical Teaching : its relation to the Law, to Eschatology, and to the Divine Forgiveness	105
The Kingdom of God	111
The Son of Man	116
The value of the Apocalyptic idea	119
The Death of the Messiah and its significance . . .	121
The Resurrection	127
The Vindication—*Vicisti Galilaee*	141

III

THE HISTORIC CHRIST

THE POINT OF VIEW OF MODERN SCHOLARSHIP

TWENTY years ago Orthodox Theology was awakened
with a start by the present Bishop of Oxford to a
clear recognition of the fact that the human knowledge
of our Lord was limited within the scientific and
historical horizon of the mind of His own age. And
I imagine that at the present time there are few
theologians by whom this position is not accepted,
not merely as being plain on the very face of the
Gospel narrative, but from the further reflection that
we cannot logically deny it without making His
humanity unreal. To do that would be to capitulate at
the last to that recurrent tendency, against which, under
the names of Docetism, Apollinarianism, or Monophysitism, the Church fought hard and long in earlier
ages. Those who would forbid us to consider the
mind of Christ as that of an historical individual
largely moulded by the special environment and the
special culture of His own country and His own
time, virtually forbid us to allow Him a truly human
mind at all. What, then, is left of the "humanity
of Christ"—a humanity without a truly human mind?
   In the last few years the turn has come for
"Liberal Theology" to experience the shock of a
not dissimilar awakening at the hands of Johannes

Weiss, Schweitzer, and other writers of the "Eschatological School," of whom the best known in this
country are the late Father Tyrrell and Professor
Burkitt of Cambridge. Liberal Theology had always
recognised that on the intellectual side the mind of
our Lord belonged to His own age and not to ours,
but it had quite unconsciously made the tacit assumption that His moral and religious ideals were only a
glorified forecast of those of cultured respectability
in the nineteenth century, "tuning His denial of the
world to our acceptance of it." The name of Christ
in Christendom is so closely bound up with every
conception of what is highest in morals and religion
that all unsuspectingly each man reads back into the
mind of our Lord the ideals of his own class and
culture, his own age and country, or it may be of
his own fragmentary branch of the Church Universal,
and takes for granted that the principles most valued
by himself were central to the Master also.

The Eschatological School protests that this is an
anachronism, and that the key to the understanding
of His life and teaching is to be found in those
religious hopes and ideas which recent researches in
the field of what is known as Apocalyptic Eschatology
have shown to have dominated the minds of so many
of His contemporaries. "As of old," says Schweitzer,
"Jacob wrestled with the angel, so German theology
wrestles with Jesus of Nazareth and will not let Him
go until He bless it—that is, until He will consent
to serve it and will suffer Himself to be drawn by
the Germanic spirit into the midst of our time and
our civilisation. But when day breaks the wrestler
must let Him go ; He will not cross the ford with
us. Jesus of Nazareth will not suffer Himself to be
modernised. . . . But He does bless those who have
wrestled with Him, so that though they cannot take
Him with them, yet, like men who have seen God
face to face and received strength in their souls, they

go on their way with renewed courage, ready to do battle with the world and its powers." [1]

Modern lives of Christ, whether written from a radical or from a conservative standpoint, have been too modern. The pseudo-Romantic Christ of Renan, and the "bourgeois Christ" of Rationalistic liberalism are quite as far removed from the actual historical figure as the personified abstraction of scholastic logic or the sentimental effeminacy dear to Christian Art. But if we agree with Schweitzer here, yet it is not without a feeling that he himself cannot quite escape the charge of modernising, and that his own boldly-outlined portrait is a little like the Superman of Nietzsche dressed in Galilean robes.

From the point of view of a purely historical interpretation the advance made by the Eschatological School is threefold. Firstly, it approaches the subject not from the standpoint of the twentieth century, but from one which recent discovery has shown to have been normal in the Judaea of our Lord's own time. Secondly, it can accept at their full face value all the sayings of our Lord reported in the Synoptic Gospels. Many of these had to be explained away and interpreted in an unnatural sense by the older Orthodoxy. The older Liberalism either did the same thing or took the shorter cut of affirming that they were not authentic. The new school accepts them as they stand. Thirdly, the "great gulf" supposed by all who had felt the influence of the Tübingen School of Liberal Theology to have been fixed between the Christology of St. Paul, even in its earliest development, and that of the Twelve simply disappears, and with it the paradox that historical Christianity was created by St. Paul and not by Christ. [2]

From the point of view of religion the gain seems to be no less. Ever since the "Illumination" of the eighteenth century orthodox theology has been on

---

[1] Schweitzer, *Quest of the Historical Jesus*, p. 310.   [2] Cf. Essay IV. p. 157.

the defensive—obliged to concede this, but still holding to that ; surrendering *x* but clinging desperately
to *y*. A more hopeless position can hardly be imagined
for a religion of which the very life and essence consists
in its being an attack and a challenge to the world. A
Christ whom apologists have first to "save" is little
likely to save mankind. Liberal Theology, on the
other hand, seeking, or rather assuming, in Christ
the rationalist's ideal could at best only discover one
less "rational" than the seeker. The student, then,
had to face the uninspiring choice between a Liberalism
that could almost patronise its Christ and an Orthodoxy that must needs "defend" Him,—and neither
conception to be found in the Gospels without some
violence to the text. But the Christ whom this newer
school reveals is a solitary arresting figure, intensely
human, yet convinced of His call to an office and a
mission absolutely superhuman—a conviction which
one will attribute to fanaticism, another to inspiration,
—calling men to follow Him along a path which to
some will appear the way of folly, to others the way
of life. He came not to bring peace but division,
and to "separate them one from another as a shepherd
divideth the sheep from the goats."

Fresh light is always blinding, especially to those
who see it first, and new views rarely secure attention
except when pushed to extremes. That this is the case
with the Eschatological School, and especially with
Schweitzer, its literary genius, few will deny. Nor is
the work of the great scholars of the older generation,
the great conservatives of this country, and the great
liberals of Germany, superseded. One who in his
enthusiasm for the things which to-day has found
forgets the discoveries of all the years of yesterdays
will never see but a broken fragment of truth.

Out of the crucible of criticism, kept at white-heat
by all the schools combined, the metal has been poured,
and as the moulding sand is brushed away we catch a

first glimpse of the finished statue—a portrait of the
Master alive and life-transmitting, one which His
followers will not need, or rather will not presume, to
"defend." They will only point to it, and "many
will be offended," but some will "see God." "Two
women shall be grinding at the mill ; the one shall be
taken and the other left."

And this portrait is no other than that which the
ordinary reader, once given the clue, can find for
himself in the Gospels. That is the strange thing with
Science, Art, Religion, and indeed all human activities.
Clear, simple, and seemingly obvious results are only
achieved as the reward of the long and arduous toil of
many minds, after many an experiment and many a
failure, continued often through many generations.
"Prophets and kings have desired to see those things
which ye see, and have not seen them."

But, some one will ask, what bearing has all this on
that belief in the Divinity of Christ which has been from
the beginning the mainspring of Christian inspiration ?
The subject is treated in detail in a later essay in this
volume ; in this place a single paragraph will suffice.

To the Christian, Christ is the "portrait of the
invisible God" (Col. i. 15), "the impress of His
essence" (Heb. i. 3).[1] This *should* mean that a study of
the Historic Christ is a principal source on which to
model our conception of the inner nature of the Divine.
It is a natural instinct to approach the subject from the
other end, and to read into our conception of the
Historic Christ the *a priori*, and possibly misleading,
ideas which we happen to have formed of the Divine.
The instinct is a natural one, but in the past it has
often led men to construct a portrait of the Master
which is certainly not human, and can only be called
Divine if we think that in our own minds there is
present a more adequate conception of the Divine *before*

---

[1] In this Essay I have quoted A.V. or R.V., or given my own rendering, at
discretion.

we have studied the person and work of the Historic Christ, than there will be afterwards. Christ we know, but "no man hath seen God at any time, the only-begotten Son, . . . he hath declared Him."

The discussion of the critical and historical problems raised by the Gospel records, and the endeavour to reconstruct the social and intellectual background of Judaea in the first century of our era, have for the last hundred years occupied minds learned and acute in many countries. Few, certainly not the present writer, can claim to have mastered the immense literature of the subject, fewer still to adjudicate upon its final results. What follows makes no attempt at completeness or finality ; it is an individual impression, confessedly and inevitably one-sided and inadequate, of a few of the more important aspects of that portrait of the historic Jesus which modern scholarship is restoring to us. Considerations of space and time preclude a discussion of doubtful points of evidence or interpretation. The tacit assumption as fact of what appears to me to be the more probable conclusion in many a debatable point is not to be taken to imply a dogmatic disregard of other views.

The Origin and Historical Value of the Gospels

The oldest of our Gospels is that according to St. Mark. This is not only the oldest, but, according to the practically unanimous judgment of modern scholars, it was the principal source of information used by the authors of the first and third Gospels. I see no sufficient reason to reject the very early tradition that it was written by St. Mark, the companion of St. Peter and St. Paul. It is a probable conjecture that the Gospel according to St. Matthew owes its name to the fact that it incorporates, in addition to the story of Mark, a document drawn up by the Apostle whose name it bears. It will, however, be convenient to refer by the name " Matthew " to the compiler of our present Gospel. As for the third Gospel, there are to my mind adequate reasons for assigning it to St. Luke the physician, the companion of St. Paul.

About two-thirds of Matthew and about half of Luke appear to have been practically transcribed from Mark, with trifling alterations, so that in so far as their story is parallel to Mark's it has no independent value,[1] save as a witness that the existing text of Mark has not very seriously been tampered with, and as an evidence of the high degree of authority attributed to that Gospel in the first century. St. Mark gives no account of the birth and infancy of our Lord, and, as is well known, the evidence of MSS. and Fathers, combined with considerations of internal evidence, is conclusive against the authenticity of the last twelve verses of the Textus Receptus, which describe the appearances after the Resurrection. The genuine text, after giving the message of the angel at the empty tomb, breaks off short, in what appears to be the middle of a sentence, with the words ἐφοβοῦντο γάρ—the original conclusion having obviously disappeared.

The stories of the birth and infancy of our Lord, and of His appearances after the Resurrection, seem to be derived by Matthew and Luke respectively from independent and indeed widely-divergent documents or traditions, the historical value of which is hotly debated. With this most important exception Matthew and Luke have very little in the way of *incident* to add to Mark, and in some cases these additions seem to be of doubtful historicity.[2]

The outstanding value of the Gospels of St. Matthew and St. Luke consists in the fact that they are our main authority for the *teaching* of our Lord. For His

---

[1] Indeed there are not a few cases where an important little point in St. Mark's version is lost or obscured by some slight omission or verbal alteration by Matthew or Luke ; cf. p. 98 *note*, p. 117 *text and note*.

[2] *E.g.* Matt. xxvii. 52-53.

G

deeds we look in the first place to St. Mark, for His words to Matthew and Luke. A great deal of this teaching is found to occur in *both* Matthew and Luke, and this fact seems best accounted for by the supposition that they had another written source to draw upon beside Mark—a source consisting mainly of sayings of our Lord. This hypothetical document is usually referred to as "Q." It is generally believed that Q is older than Mark. I myself incline to the view of those who think that it was probably the work of the Apostle Matthew, whence his name got attached to one of the two later Gospels which, by incorporating, superseded his original work. It is more than likely that, besides the passages which Matthew and Luke agree in reproducing, a number of passages which occur in Matthew only or in Luke only, especially the former, were also derived from Q.

Besides Q both Matthew and Luke, but more especially St. Luke, must each have had access to a rich mine of information inaccessible to the other. Hence come three-fourths of the parables, including nearly all the longer ones, and some other material. So far as St. Luke is concerned, we know of a two-years' residence in Caesarea which would have given him access to good traditions. But the great majority of the parables and sayings peculiar to Matthew and Luke need no external guarantee ; they authenticate themselves by showing both in style and spiritual grasp the clear impress of the same master-mind which speaks through the other sources.

The Gospel according to St. John has been the great battlefield of criticism, and only those who have merely trifled with the problems it suggests are likely to speak dogmatically on the subject.[1] There are cases where in matters of circumstance and date it seems to correct or supplement the Synoptic account as if with high authority ; there are sayings which seem to rise too

---

[1] The subject is further discussed in Essay IV. p. 202 ff.

profoundly from the very heart of the Master to be other than authentic ; in particular, in this Gospel is more deeply felt that element of mysticism so conspicuous in all great religious teachers, and therefore antecedently to be expected in our Lord, of which, however, only glimpses are seen in the Synoptic tradition. Yet on the whole I myself feel that the mystical and theological interest of its author dominates if it does not swallow up the biographical. In his mind, after years and years of pondering and teaching, the facts and their interpretation have become inextricably blended, and his Gospel should primarily be regarded not so much as an historical authority as an *inspired meditation* on the life of Christ. But in so characterising it I would underline the word " inspired " as well as the word "meditation." A theological and philosophical interpretation of the meaning for mankind of the person and work of Christ need not be a false or illegitimate interpretation. "The Spirit shall guide you into all truth." A literary analogy at once suggests itself in the representation of Socrates in the *earlier* dialogues of Plato, in which it is impossible to distinguish between the thought of the master and its interpretation by his great disciple. For the purpose of a complete life of Christ it would be necessary to attempt to appraise and incorporate the purely historical contribution of the Fourth Gospel ; for a sketch like the present it will be sufficient to use the materials provided by the three Synoptic Gospels alone.

The question of the historical value of the Synoptic Gospels in general next demands consideration. The special question, however, of the Resurrection it will be convenient to reserve for a fuller treatment at a later point (cf. p. 127 ff).

A strong presumption in favour of the substantial reliability of the general impression given by them of the life and teaching of our Lord seems to arise from the following considerations. The main tradition appears to be derived from sources which we can identify as likely to be well informed ; much of it was stereotyped and committed to writing at a comparatively early date ; it reflects throughout a vivid and accurate local colour ; lastly, each of the separate streams into which the tradition can be analysed presents what is substantially the same portrait of the same Figure—a sufficient indication that they are all, generally speaking, faithful renderings of the one original.

When we come, however, to consider points of detail a distinction must be drawn between the tradition of the words and that of the deeds. The Oriental mind is trained to commit to memory and accurately reproduce the words of the religious teacher. It was so in the schools of the Rabbis, it is so to-day in Cairo or Constantinople. And though the Disciples cannot be regarded as a " school " in this sense (indeed, even the Rabbinic schools had not as yet achieved the formal method and organisation of later times), it is probable that the sayings of our Lord were remembered with far greater accuracy than would have been possible to modern minds accustomed to have recourse at once to writing. Nor must we forget that He was a master of expression, and the memory more easily retains the exact wording of a striking phrase than the minor details of a striking scene. Moreover, the unconscious reaching after the effective, which inevitably influences a twice-told tale, has less scope where what is repeated is already expressed in an arresting way.

On the other hand, as regards His deeds, it must be recognised that the case is otherwise. The Gospels were written mainly for practical and devotional purposes ; their authors had not the same interests as a modern scientific historian. Hence many facts which would have been of the greatest interest to us, though known to these writers, are left unrecorded. Moreover, they are largely indifferent to that correct chronological sequence of events which is deemed essential by us moderns. All who study at all closely the combination of parallelisms and divergences in the first three Gospels, which constitute the Synoptic Problem so-called, are struck at once by the numerous omissions and re-arrangements made by Matthew and Luke in reproducing Mark's stories ; and we cannot suppose that Mark in his turn would have dealt otherwise than they did with *his* sources of information, whether these were written or oral.[1]

Moreover, the faculty of accurately observing facts and of clearly distinguishing between what is actually observed and what is merely inferred therefrom, an essential characteristic of the modern scientific habit of mind, comes only from a kind of training which found no place in ancient education. Every one is familiar with the fact that even to-day, and that not only among the uneducated, a good story, as we say, loses nothing in the telling. The narrator has his mind fixed only on the main point and how he may present that in the most effective and telling way. Thus quite unconsciously he emphasises one detail and overlooks another, and is quite unaware that he has altered the balance of the facts, until he is confronted in the witness-box with the cross-examining counsel or questioned in the study by a scientific observer.

A minute comparison of the text of Mark with those passages in Matthew and Luke which are derived from him, in several instances shows this tendency actually at work. And if the tendency could operate even after the tradition had been reduced to writing, it is obvious that its operation must be allowed for in our estimate of St. Mark, our earliest and principal authority for the Life, especially since the author was admittedly not an eye-witness, and was writing perhaps

[1] Cf. my essay on the "Literary Evolution of the Gospels," in the *Oxford Studies in the Synoptic Problem* (edited by Dr. Sanday), for a fuller account of the influences which determined the composition of the Gospels.

some thirty-five or forty years after the events he records. It is also obvious that the tendency would operate more especially in stories which have already in them a strong element of dramatic interest, such as the miracles. For instance, had the events underlying the famous story of the Gadarene swine been reported by a trained scientific observer, we may readily believe that some facts would have been added and others differently presented, the vital significance of which was unrealised by one who explained what he noticed on the theory of possession by demons and their migration.

Nevertheless the realism and naturalness of St. Mark's representation, and in particular the candour and simplicity with which he records incidents implying something of human limitation in the Master, or of human infirmity in the Twelve—incidents which even in the other Synoptics are toned down, ignored, or explained away,[1]—and lastly, a convergence of smaller indications which cannot be here enumerated, make it evident that the tendencies noted have only operated to a limited extent, and that the element of deliberate or conscious misrepresentation is entirely absent.

One final *caveat* must be entered. Christ is reflected to us only through what His disciples remembered and recorded of Him, and what we can infer from that. But what great man have his followers completely understood? Christ is greater than His disciples, greater therefore than the earliest records of Him. The later records show a tendency to magnify and idealise. The historian must note and allow for this, but he should beware lest in allowing for that which has exalted he overlook that which has impaired the picture. In all transcending genius there is an element which eludes analysis and soars beyond the analogies of our experience of lesser men. And if, as has been said, in the last resort every great man is a

[1] Cf. *op. cit.* p. 223 ; also Hawkins, *Horae Synopticae*, 2nd ed., p. 117 ff.

Great Unknown, how much more must this be true of
Him who is the subject of this essay ?

> Others abide our question—Thou art free !
> We ask and ask—Thou smilest and art still,
> Out-topping knowledge !   For the loftiest hill
> That to the stars uncrowns his majesty,
> Planting his steadfast footsteps in the sea,
> Making the heaven of heavens his dwelling-place,
> Spares but the cloudy border of his base
> To the foil'd searching of mortality.

APOCALYPTIC ESCHATOLOGY AND THE MESSIANIC HOPE

Prophets of Israel confident alike in the righteousness
and might of their God, and in the consequent necessity
that He would ultimately vindicate His people (or rather
the godly " remnant " of them), in the darkest hours
of danger from without and misgovernment within
had confidently proclaimed a greater, better, happier age
to come.   Plato's ideal State, and modern pictures of
Utopia and the Millennium, normally picture the ideal
state of society as a highly organised system based
on a more or less republican constitution.   But the
prophets of early Israel were familiar only with the
simplest political, industrial, and military organisation,
and were entirely without experience, either in their
own case or their neighbours', of any form of state
other than monarchical.   Dreamers in such a stage of
civilisation would most naturally picture their Utopia,
their ideal state, as an ideal monarchy ; for patriarchal
monarchy was the only form of state they knew.   For
an ideal monarchy the principal requisite is an ideal
king.   Hence the hopes of many of the prophets centre
on the figure of such a king—" a shoot from the
stock of Jesse," a uniquely gifted " Son of David," who
would restore the traditional glories of David's reign—to
whom the name Messiah or Christ came later on to be
applied.   But the house of David failed to produce

this king ; and the nation went into exile, it returned
again, it waited century after century still subject to
the foreign yoke, still with its promised destiny
unfulfilled.

In the time of Isaiah it had not seemed beyond the
bounds of possibility that a greater David, with some
assistance of a not unprecedented kind from the God of
battles, should repel Assyrian aggression and then
proceed to reform abuses at home. But the Babylonian
had taken the place of the Assyrian, the Persian of the
Babylonian, and the Macedonian of the Persian, soon
the Roman replaced the Macedonian. Each power
was succeeded by one of greater military strength than
its predecessor. What son of David could cope with
this ? And Antiochus Epiphanes, a monarch of the
Syrian Macedonian house, did what the others never
did: he tried to stamp out the religion of the nation.
This at last it was felt must stir up the vengeance of
the Lord of Hosts, and seeing that the armies of Israel
were no more, " with His own right hand will He
get Him the victory." Thus the prophetic hope takes
on a new shape. Israel is to be restored, not by the
valour of a uniquely endowed sovereign of David's
line, but by the direct catastrophic interference of God
Himself.[1]

Not only is the nature of the Messianic hope
changed, the form of its literary expression changes
also, and from the persecution of Antiochus dates the
rise and prevalence of *Apocalyptic* with its characteristic
Eschatology.[2] The vivid directness of the ancient
prophet is replaced by a complicated symbolism, to our
modern taste fantastic and bizarre, influenced somewhat, it is thought, by Babylonian and Persian models.

---

[1] Direct Divine action of a kind is no doubt contemplated in some of the earlier
prophets, but it is conceived on a smaller scale and in far less catastrophic terms.

[2] Strictly speaking Apocalyptic (= Revelation) is the name given to this type of
literature on account of its *form*, *i.e.* revelation through visions expressed in a particular
kind of symbolism. Eschatology is a name which more properly attaches to its *matter*,
the description of the " Last Things," the end of the present world-order. The
words, however, are often used as if they were synonymous.

Unheard of tribulations, angelic and demonic conflicts, lead up to catastrophes shaking earth and heaven. The dead shall rise to judgment, and the righteous people of God, both those newly arisen and those who had not experienced death, in bodies glorified and transformed shall enter into a life of blessedness in a New Jerusalem on a renovated earth.[1] Moreover, instead of delivering his message in his own person like the old prophets the seer now commits it to writing under the aegis of the name of some great one of the past, of an Enoch, Moses, Baruch, Daniel.

Apocalyptic in its more elementary stages occurs as early as some passages of Ezekiel, but hardly till Daniel [2] (written about 167 B.C., just before the Maccabean revolt) has it attained its characteristic form. Daniel was followed by a long series of similar works, the recovery and historical interpretation of which has been one of the greatest achievements of modern Biblical scholarship. The Christian Church continued the tradition, and produced a number of Apocalypses, one of them being the book which appears in our Canon as the Revelation of St. John—both in luxuriance of poetic imagery and in spiritual power the greatest of them all.

Logically the Apocalyptic hope of the restoration of Israel by direct and catastrophic Divine intervention did not need the ideal King—warrior, upright judge, and pure administrator—dreamed of by the earlier prophets. The kingdom of God thus established needs no king but God Himself, and many of the Apocalyptic writers make no mention of the Messiah. But the fact that inspired prophets had foretold such a personal deliverer could not be ignored. In the "Similitudes" of the Book of Enoch—a book quoted as inspired

---

[1] The belief in a *real* immortality for the *individual* is the great contribution of Apocalyptic to Hebrew religion. In later writers the earthly Messianic Kingdom lasts 400 to 1000 years, and not till then is there a *general* resurrection and judgment; after which the righteous are sublimated into heaven. A last great conflict precedes, in which the powers of evil are sometimes led by a kind of Anti-Christ, variously named.

[2] But the short post-exilic apocalypse Isaiah xxiv.-xxvii. is probably earlier.

in the New Testament[1] and some early Fathers, and still so regarded in the Ethiopic Church—the two conceptions are combined. In the Book of Daniel (vii. 13) there had been recorded a vision of "one like unto a Son of Man coming with the clouds of heaven," which the author himself appears to interpret as symbolising collectively "the saints of the Most High." But in Enoch this "Son of Man" is interpreted as a supernatural being, who with His angels shall confound the kings of the earth, sit on the throne of God, judge the world, and in general be God's agent in introducing the new era of the Apocalyptic hope.

"And there I saw One who had a head of days, and His head was white like wool, and with Him was another being whose countenance had the appearance of a man, and his face was full of graciousness, like one of the holy angels. And I asked the angel who went with me and showed me all the hidden things, concerning that Son of Man, who he was, and whence he was, and why he went with the Head of Days? And he answered and said unto me, ' This is the Son of Man who hath righteousness, with whom dwelleth righteousness, and who reveals all the treasures of that which is hidden, because the Lord of Spirits hath chosen him, and his lot before the Lord of Spirits hath surpassed everything in uprightness for ever. And this Son of Man whom thou hast seen will arouse the kings and the mighty ones from their couches, and the strong from their thrones, and will loosen the reins of the strong and grind to powder the teeth of the sinners. And he will put down the kings from their thrones and kingdoms because they do not extol and praise him, nor thankfully acknowledge whence the kingdom was bestowed upon them' " (Enoch xlvi. 1-5, Dr. Charles' translation).

"And at that hour that Son of Man was named in the presence of the Lord of Spirits and his name before

---

[1] Cf. esp. Jude 14, " Enoch, also the seventh from Adam, prophesied of these." The section known as the " Similitudes " appears to have been written before 64 B.C.

the Head of Days. And before the sun and the signs were created, before the stars of the heaven were made, his name was named before the Lord of Spirits. He will be a staff to the righteous on which they will support themselves and not fall, and he will be the light of the Gentiles and the hope of those who are troubled of heart. All who dwell on earth will fall down and bow the knee before him, and will bless and laud and celebrate with song the Lord of Spirits. And for this reason has he been chosen and hidden before Him, before the creation of the world, and for evermore " (Enoch xlviii. 2-6).

This conception of the Messiah as Son of Man, that is, as a pre-existent supernatural being, destined to be manifested at the close of history to usher in the new era, is by far the most important if we are to understand the general outlook of the original disciples and of the writers of the New Testament. But it did not displace either the name or the conception of the ideal Son of David. In the Psalms of Solomon, for instance—a collection of Pharisaic hymns of the first century b.c.— we find the expectation of a new era to be introduced, not by the sword of man but by the direct act of God Himself, and accompanied by a resurrection of the righteous, as in the Apocalyptists. The Messiah in himself, however, is not described in supernatural terms, though phrases like " He shall destroy the ungodly nations with the word of his mouth," [1] taken in connection with the statement that he will not depend upon the ordinary means of warfare, may imply greater than human powers.

Moreover, it is probably quite incorrect to suppose that the conception of the warrior Messiah was entirely eliminated from the popular expectation by this purely supernatural Apocalyptic conception. The exploits of Judas Maccabaeus and his line, let alone the belief in

[1] Cf. 2 Thess. ii. 8, " Whom the Lord Jesus shall slay with the breath of His mouth," and Rev. i. 16, " Out of His mouth went a two-edged sword."

"blood and iron" which is innate in human nature, forbade the extinction of the hope that some day there would rise One who should draw the sword, and summon the tribes, like Deborah of old, "to the help of the Lord against the mighty." Theudas (cf. Acts v. 36) seems to have been such an one, and the immense response which at a later date Bar-Cochba, who *did* claim to be a Messiah of this kind, was able to evoke, shows that the older conception, though slumbering, was still alive. But these various conceptions of Messiah, though logically irreconcilable, were doubtless combined in the mind of the average Jew. In popular theology two and two need not necessarily make four, and dreams of future happiness find the picturesque language of poetry more congenial than prosaic logic.

In some circles there seems to have been a curious amalgam of two phases of the Messianic hope. Dating from Maccabaean times there had always been two sections among the Jews, those who frowned down political unrest and preached that deliverance by the arm of the Lord alone must be awaited,[1] and those, like the followers of Judas of Galilee—the Zealots as they were called—who were always ready to draw the sword the moment a leader or an opportunity appeared. Judas and such as he were not regarded as Messiahs. It was believed rather that if Israel had faith to draw the sword in their support, at the crisis of the war which must ensue, just at the moment when a crushing defeat seemed inevitable, the supernatural Christ would appear.

JOHN THE BAPTIST

Such in brief were the somewhat diverse hopes passionately entertained by the people, when suddenly there appeared in the desert the wild ascetic figure of

[1] Of such would be the circle of quiet devout souls, "looking for the consolation of Israel" (Luke ii. 25), pictured in Luke i. and ii. Prof. Lake (*Earlier Epistles of S. Paul*, p. 393) tentatively suggests that the existence of a Zealot propaganda gives an additional point to maxims like "Resist not evil."

John the Baptist, preaching "the kingdom of God is at hand."[1] The Day of Judgment and the New Era, so long foretold by Prophet and Apocalyptist, are at last in sight.

All great movements, political and religious, have in them something of the element of reaction, all go back to an age behind the present and revive a principle or ideal of the past which the present has forgotten or obscured. John Hampden made his appeal to the ancient liberties of England, the French Revolution looked back to the Republicanism of Brutus and Cassius, Luther and Calvin to the writings of the Apostles, Newman and Pusey to the Caroline Divines and the Fathers of the undivided Church.

But no revival can really bring back the past: unconsciously its message combines with the conceptions of that past to which it recurs, much of that present against which it appears to protest. The later centuries of Judaism had produced a great religious literature—"Wisdom," Psalm, and Apocalyptic—but all or almost all was anonymous or pseudonymous. There had been lacking the personal appeal of the ancient prophet speaking, because he *must* speak, with an authority none could question, "Thus saith the Lord." The preaching of John is a revival of the prophetic method of the past: anonymity is thrown off, he speaks in his own person in the spirit and the power of an Elijah. But what has intervened is not forgotten. Apocalyptist and Prophet, the new and the old, are in him combined. In the little that is preserved of his teaching we feel the grand simplicity, the ethical directness, which is the note of the prophets of the eighth century B.C. The vision is the apocalyptic vision of the Kingdom, akin to Enoch's, but it is preached in the spirit of Amos. Before John, Apocalyptic was largely a literary tradition tied up in ingenious symbolism. Now it becomes a direct prophetic message from God to the masses of the people.

---

[1] Matt. iii. 2, probably from the Q version of John's preaching.

The interesting question as to a possible connection between John the Baptist and the sect of the Essenes does not here concern us. It is, however, essential to recognise that he set in motion a " revival " or wave of religious movement of great importance. This is attested not only by the considerable emphasis laid on him and his relations with our Lord in all our Gospels, and by the hesitation of the authorities even to seem to speak against one whom " all held to be a prophet" (Mark xi. 32), but also by the fact that his influence had reached as far as Ephesus (cf. Acts xix. 3) ahead of Christianity ; while Josephus, if the passage is authentic, speaks of him and of our Lord as if they were popular prophets of equal importance. That our Lord felt much in sympathy with the Baptist's message,—direct, intelligible to all, at once prophetic and apocalyptic,—is shown by His coming Himself to be baptized by him, as well as by His emphatic reference to him as one than whom none greater has been born of woman.

The Call of our Lord and the Psychology of the Prophetic Mind

Like John our Lord appeared to His contemporaries pre-eminently as a Prophet [1] (Mark viii. 28)—that He claimed to be Christ was not suspected at first even by the Twelve. And if our speculations as to His inner mind are to avoid the anachronism of being merely modern ideas read back into the past, we may only penetrate the mind of the last and greatest of the Hebrew prophets by studying the psychology of the other prophets of His race.

The most striking difference between the Hebrew prophet and the religious and social reformer of modern times is the sense of complete possession by the Spirit of

---

[1] Cf. also Mark vi. 4, Luke vii. 16, 39, xxiv. 19, etc.

God, the feeling of being a mere instrument, a mere voice, by means of which the Divine message is to be given. The modern reformer speaks of his own convictions, he backs them up by proof and argument. The Hebrew prophet says simply, " Thus saith the Lord." The modern speaks of his enthusiasm for the cause, of his duty to advocate it. Contrast the words of Amos, " The lion hath roared, who will not fear ? the Lord God hath spoken, who can but prophesy ? " Differences of national temperament and the tendency to depend on argument rather than on intuition— largely the result of centuries of education, first in the analytic rationalistic categories of Greek philosophy, subsequently in those of modern science—have made it impossible nowadays for any but a half-mad impostor to speak like this. But the great Hebrew prophets were the antithesis of that.

Such a conviction of possession and message seems normally to date from some great moment in the prophet's life—his Call. "The Lord took me from following the flock," says Amos. "I saw the Lord sitting upon a throne," begins the famous vision of Isaiah. Similar experiences are recorded by Jeremiah and Ezekiel. The visions and the voices they speak of are no mere pieces of conscious symbolism or imaginative fine writing, any more than was the rapture into the third heaven which St. Paul records in 2 Corinthians.

To certain types of mind, especially at certain stages of culture, the voice of conscience or the conviction of vocation at the supreme crises of a life become translated into what the subject can only regard as visible or audible experiences. In old days anything that came by way of a vision came with an added authority. Nowadays the prejudice is the other way. A vision is commonly regarded as evidence for an unsound mind, and as even discrediting the thing "revealed" in it. A sounder psychology would seem to indicate that both prejudices are equally irrelevant. The value of an idea, or the inspiration of its propounder, is to be judged by intrinsic quality, not by the manner of realisation. Men do not gather figs of thistles, or creative thought from lunatics. *Kubla Khan*, one of its author's finest poems, came to him in a vision—part of which he could never recall. The difference between such an experience and that sudden flash of insight which more usually accompanies all special moral, artistic, or intellectual apprehension in modern times, is very largely due to differences in temperament, education, and environment. All great ideas, all new solutions, whether in science,[1] ethics, art or practical life arise, apparently unbidden, to the mind.

Considerable light is thrown on the nature of the Prophetic Call if it be studied in connection with the wider phenomenon known as Conversion—conversion, that is, of the sudden and immediate type—a phenomenon to which psychologists have of late given special attention. It would appear that such a conversion differs from the more gradual awakening of the conscience to the claims of a higher life, which is in modern times the more familiar experience, at any rate in Anglican circles, chiefly in the fact that influences which have been all along actually at work, have, in the case of a gradual awakening, been more or less consciously recognised and even welcomed, whereas, in the case of a sudden conversion, their operation has been unknown to the subject or, if known, has been consciously and strongly resisted.[2]

The difference between the Hebrew prophet, to whom his message comes in a sudden unexpected intuition so strong as to be externally visualised or made audible, and the modern reformer, to whom his convictions have come by a more gradual awakening of interest and a consciously inductive study of facts and conditions, seems to present a close psychological analogy

---

[1] Cf. esp. the description of his own experience in Poincaré, *Science et Méthode*, ch. iii.
[2] Cf. James, *Varieties of Religious Experiences*, lectures VIII.-X.

to that between the suddenly converted and the gradually illuminated type of Christian experience.

This does not mean that before his Call the prophet was in the moral state of the "unconverted sinner." A call is not the same thing as a conversion. The one is a summons to a new work, the other to a new ideal ; the one is merely a change of activity, the other a change of heart. Doubtless the two often go together, as for instance in the case of St. Francis of Assisi, but they are separable both in thought and experience. They are, however, alike in that they both involve an added stimulus, a changed "focus of interest," to use Professor James' phrase, a concentration, and as it were a crystallisation, of tendencies hitherto more or less latent. Such a change of focus, such a reconstruction and rearrangement of the balance of interest, is very commonly (though by no means exclusively) brought about under the influence of the psychological ferment caused by a religious revival, and even in modern times is sometimes accompanied by voice or vision.

"Conversion," as James points out, is only for the "twice-born," that is, for those who before the crisis through which they attain inward peace and conviction have passed through a period more or less clearly realised of struggle, stress, and doubt. Similarly we may suppose that a call, even in the cases where it is not the accompaniment of a conversion, presupposes a period of intense but baffled interest in some spiritual or moral problem leading up to the moment of illumination which provides the prophet with his message.[1] Thus the difference between ancient prophet and modern reformer is more psychological than material. Yet the man to whom at the last all comes in a flash, seems to apprehend with a clearness, and to be fired with a passion unknown to him whose eyes have been gradually opened. And when a call comes in a voice or vision

[1] So Poincaré, *loc. cit.*, emphasises concentrated interest as pre-requisite to the flash of scientific discovery.

H

which he who sees or hears cannot but regard as the act of God external to himself, it produces a tempest of conviction not otherwise attained.

It was a celestial vision on the road to Damascus that made of Saul the persecutor, the Apostle who "laboured more abundantly than they all." It was a celestial vision—the vault of heaven rent asunder, the Spirit descending as a dove, a voice, "Thou art My beloved Son"—that certified a greater than St. Paul of His supreme vocation.[1]

In a psychological crisis like this dim premonitions and unseen potentialities are brought to a climax ; the personality, so to speak, comes into its inheritance and at a bound attains maturity. But the meaning of the crisis is determined by the quality of the personality itself, and by the sum of all the influences which it has assimilated to itself from its environment during a long course of years. The external stimulus which precipitates the crisis may be the least important factor in the final result. In the present instance the external stimulus is not far to seek. The wave of religious expectancy stirred up by the preaching of the Baptist would naturally induce a special susceptibility to a religious call. The moment of Baptism, the rite of mystic initiation into the Kingdom proclaimed so near at hand, would not unnaturally be to our Lord the moment of illumination as to His own position in that kingdom.[2]

But though this may explain the moment and manner of the Call it throws no light on the growth of a Personality which could be responsive

[1] In St. Mark's version (Mark i. 10) the Call is clearly a vision personal to our Lord. "He saw the heavens rent asunder, and the Spirit as a dove descending upon Him." In St. Luke's version (Luke iii. 22) it is said that "The heaven was opened, and the Holy Spirit descended in a bodily form, as a dove"—a materialised interpretation, though probably unconsciously so, of the original tradition. It is probable that the stories of the Baptism and Temptation are ultimately derived from an account given to the disciples by our Lord Himself.

[2] It will be remembered that later on our Lord expressly (Matt. xvii. 12-13) identifies John with the Elijah who, as Malachi had foretold (Mal. iv. 5), was to appear immediately before "the great and terrible day of the Lord." For the original significance of the rite of Baptism cf. Essay IV. p. 162.

to such a call, and which could respond to it in the
particular way in which He did. Nor is it likely that
we should be much the wiser on this point if we knew
far more than we do of the environment of His earlier
years—of the family and education, of the synagogue
and social life of a Galilean village. We do not
explain a Shakespeare in terms of the Parish Church
and Grammar School of Stratford. Historical research
may reveal the forces which condition but not those
which produce the epoch-making individual.

One reflection, however, is suggested by the facts we
know. " Blessed are the pure in heart, for they shall
see God." To see God means—among other things—
to estimate the world according to a scale of values
other than the common. It is to see the littleness of
much that man calls great, the greatness of much that
man calls little. It is to consider the lilies of the field,
and to see that Solomon in all his glory was not arrayed
like one of these. It is to see the worth of man as
man, undazzled by the external differences that go with
wealth and place. It is to see that whoso would be
truly great must be the servant of his kind. To One
who looked at life like this it might not seem so great
a paradox that the Christ of God should be chosen
from the ranks of those whose lot it is to labour and
to serve. Nevertheless, in all great minds, and notably
in all religious minds, there is an element of deep
humility, and without some such an experience of voice
or vision as that attested by the earliest tradition it would
be difficult to understand His absolute conviction that
He was indeed Lord of lords and King of kings.

Apocalyptic or Warrior Christ ?

The detailed story of the Temptation, found in
St. Matthew and St. Luke (as well apparently as the
Baptism), seems to have stood in Q, the oldest source
which criticism has detected. It may perhaps be

interpreted as a kind of parable of the events of those days—our Lord was fain to speak in parables. Or it may be a reminiscence of something He told the disciples, insensibly cast by them in the re-telling into more pictorial form. It is even possible that the effects of a long hunger combined with the nervous reaction of the stirring experience of His Call actually caused His inner conflict to become visualised in the form related. In any case its psychological appropriateness to the situation is undeniable. A moment of intense spiritual exaltation is inevitably followed by a period of depression. Always after vision comes struggle, after a call the temptation most pertinent to it.

The revelation that He was the Christ, attested as it was by an audible voice divine, did not admit of doubt. But being the Christ, how He was called upon to act must have been a problem of no small perplexity. Once that was decided, the powers, miraculous or otherwise, necessary for the part might be presumed. One by one arise before His mind current ideas of what the Christ should do or be, one by one they are rejected as entailing faithlessness to the highest ideal.

"Bid these stones become bread." The value He set on the outward trappings of royalty may appear from the satirical allusion to those " that wear soft raiment " to be found " in kings' houses." Its more material advantages, the command of all the means of gratifying physical and other wants, might for an instant attract one brought up to know the pinch of poverty, and feeling at the moment the actual pangs of hunger. But to use for such a purpose the gift of miracle (a gift, be it remembered, which was postulated by His Messiahship according to contemporary ideas [1]) was inconsistent with the scheme of ethical values of one who could say, " How hardly shall they that have riches enter into the kingdom of God."

---

[1] The Anti-Christ even was expected to have this power ; cf. 2 Thess. ii. 9, Mark xiii. 22.

"All the kingdoms of the earth and the glory of them." The rejection of this temptation is the final rejection of the office of a "Warrior Christ" who would "wade through slaughter to a throne "; a Caesar on the throne of David, albeit ruling, when He got there, in the spirit of righteousness.

"If thou be the Son of God cast thyself down from hence." This is usually interpreted as the temptation to secure a general recognition of Himself as Messiah without effort and without appeal to any moral interest in His message, but simply by a dramatic miracle, in fact, to convert an evil and adulterous generation by a sign. I would, however, hazard another suggestion, based on the fact that St. Luke, preserving, as I believe, the original order of Q,[1] places this *after* the Temptation to act as a Warrior Christ. If the kingdom is not to be established by the sword, it can only be by an act of God such as the Apocalyptists picture. But if so, is the Christ to wait and work, or should He by some startling act precipitate the consummation ? The Son of Man was expected to appear in the sky with attendant angels. Should He then fling Himself from the highest pinnacle of the Temple in sight of all Jerusalem, trusting that God, to save His Christ from destruction, would send a flight of angels to His support ? Such an attempt to "force the hand" of God, inconsistent with the trust in the Heavenly Father taught elsewhere, is decisively rejected : "Thou shalt not tempt the Lord thy God."

The conception of Warrior Christ being rejected absolutely and *in toto*, there remained only the conception of the Christ to be Apocalyptically manifested. From this fact, and from the fact that our Lord so often speaks of Himself as Son of Man, it would appear that it was *along the lines of that conception* that He interpreted His office. But "along the lines of that conception" is all we are entitled to say. His independent inter-

---

[1] Cf. *Studies in the Synoptic Problem*, p. 152 (*c*).

pretation of the Old Testament and His trenchant criticism of the traditions of the Scribes, forbid us to impute to Him a slavish literalism in the acceptance of contemporary apocalyptic symbolism. But of this more will be said hereafter (cf. p. 116 ff.).

The definite rejection of any political conception of Messiahship and the acceptance of the apocalyptic symbol of the Son of Man, even though interpreted in an original and independent way, brought with it the determination of His immediate course of action. The manifestation of the Son of Man was part, and, in the vision of Daniel at any rate, not even the first part, of the Great Restoration to be brought about by immediate Divine intervention. It was obvious, therefore, that His Messiahship was only, as it were, that of a Messiah presumptive. Not till the time came for the Kingdom to be established would He appear as King.[1] His obvious duty, then, for the present lay in the continuance of the work of John the Baptist, *i.e.* in urging men to prepare themselves for the Kingdom that was soon to be : " Repent ye, for the Kingdom is at hand."

The fact that the Christ has come, but the time for His Kingdom has not yet come, *ipso facto* turns the Christ-designate into a Prophet—a rôle not originally included in the conception of the Christ. Thus as in the case of John the Baptist, in the first stage of the great religious movement we are studying, so in the second stage with our Lord Himself, we have a reaction to and a revival of the methods and ideas of the great ones of the past. The ordinary religious teacher of the time was the Rabbi—professedly only a commentator. Original inspiration when it existed took an anonymous or pseudonymous form, mainly Apocalyptic. Like John, our Lord came forth " speaking with authority " like one of the ancient prophets.

---

[1] A partial qualification of this statement will be found on p. 119.

THE TEACHING OF OUR LORD : ITS THEME AND
CHARACTER

For a while, then, the Christ-to-be becomes, as it
were, His own forerunner, and thus the last of the long
succession of the Prophets. On the interpretation
and application to life of the teaching thus, almost
incidentally, given, treatises have been written and
sermons preached for nineteen hundred years. But
for our present purpose it is not so much with its
practical application as with its relation to the background of the thought of the time that we are concerned.

In the doctrine of the Fatherhood of God distinguished modern scholars have seen the essence of
His teaching. It would be more correct to point to
this, rather as being the presupposition and background
of His teaching, than as the conspicuous feature in its
actual content. Nothing, indeed, can be more obvious
than that God was ever present to our Lord's mind as
the one great reality, more real and actual than the
external world. In His mind, too, that "fear of the
Lord," which looms so large in Hebrew literature, has
been swallowed up in the "perfect love which casteth
out fear." Hence He speaks of God naturally and
normally as "My Father," as "your heavenly Father." [1]
But this is not done as though it were some new
conception of God which it is His special and primary
duty to proclaim. Indeed, it was not in itself new,
being found in earlier Jewish thought, [2] though, of

---

[1] It is noticeable that He is never reported as saying "Our Father." This may
be accidental, but it may imply that the difference between His own special relationship to God and that of other men was never overlooked. The opening words of
the Lord's Prayer are no exception, for it is not given as a prayer for His own use.
In the Synoptics the title "Son of God" is commonly a synonym for Messiah, but is
only twice clearly used by our Lord, in the form "the Son" (Mk. xiii. 32, Mt. xi.
27 = Lk. x. 22) ; though it is implied by "Son" in Mk. xii. 6, Mt. xxii. 2.   In Mt.
xi. 27 it appears to have a mystical sense as well ; cf. p. 119.

[2] In the O.T. the actual word "Father" is never clearly used of the relation of
God to the individual, but the idea of a Providence tender towards the individual
seems to be the inspiring thought in Psalms like "The Lord is my Shepherd"

course, it was new to make it normative and central in
the conception of God's attributes.

The Gospel representation leaves no room for
doubt that the *specific* message which at that crisis our
Lord felt primarily called to preach, and the message
which He bade the Twelve to preach, was not this. It
was the message of John the Baptist, " Repent ye, for
the Kingdom of God is at hand " (Mk. i. 15 ; Mt. x. 7).

The message has two aspects, the ethical, " repent,"
and the eschatological, " the Kingdom is at hand." In
the detailed working out of either aspect we see that
same feature of continuity with the present combined
with reaction to older ideals, which has been already
noticed in the mission of John the Baptist. We call
to mind His saying about the " Scribe instructed unto
the kingdom of heaven, . . . which bringeth forth out
of his treasure things new and old " (Matt. xiii. 52).

Controversy has raged round the question how far
the teaching of our Lord can be called " original."
Much of it has been beside the mark. Great minds
do not seek after originality but after truth ; incidentally, along with the old, they light on new truth. A
more specific characteristic of greatness is the power of
seizing upon the essential and eliminating the irrelevant.
It is this which in Science distinguishes the discoverer
of fresh light from the plodding student, which in Art
differentiates the master from the copyist. It is the
secret of what in letters we name " style." In that form
of " originality " which is always straining after
novelties, it is conspicuously absent. In practical life
it appears as that rare gift paradoxically known as
common sense. In character—the instinctive capacity
for right thought and action—it is seen as simplicity,
directness, and an unerring sense of value.

To understand the main features of our Lord's

(Ps. xxiii.), or " Whoso dwelleth under the defence of the Most High " (Ps. xci.).
Cf. " Like as a father pitieth his own children " (Ps. ciii. 13). But the title " Father "
is applied to God in early portions of the Talmud.

message we need only to trace the operation of this one principle in His attitude to the chief elements in contemporary religion—the Law and the Eschatological hope. But this simplicity and directness of perception is not confined to these departments, nor is it the result of laborious analysis or conscious theory. It flows naturally from the simplicity and directness of His whole outlook on life. "If thine eye be single, thy whole body will be full of light." "What shall it profit a man, if he gain the whole world, and lose his own soul?" It is seen again in the famous word about the lilies—the one aesthetic judgment of His which has come down to us—"that Solomon, in all his glory, was not arrayed like one of these." It lies behind the "one thing needful" which chides the "fussiness" of Martha, and it is perhaps the inner meaning of the baffling saying, "Except ye become as little children ye shall not enter into the kingdom of heaven."

A biting simplicity and directness is no less characteristic of the *form* of His teaching—more often given in spontaneous *obiter dicta* of penetrating brevity than in set discourse, illuminated with vivid illustration from the household or the farm, abounding in paradox, irony, and humour. Too often, however, we miss their point. Familiarity has dulled the freshness of His words, nor are we schooled to look for qualities like these in books canonical; but did St. Francis altogether miss the mark when he styled his followers *joculatores domini*, "the Master's Merrymen"?[1]

THE ETHICAL TEACHING

(a) in relation to the Law

"Repent."—To the Jew the moral law was the law of Moses, there was no other. Hard things said about the

---

[1] Cf. *Speculum Perfectionis*, ix. 100. For a discussion of the form of our Lord's teaching I would refer to a fascinating study in Mr. Glover's *Conflict of Religions in the Roman Empire*, p. 117 ff. The occasional humour in the Gospels is also noticed in *Memoirs of Archbishop Temple*, vol. ii. p. 681.

Law by St. Paul in the heat of controversy have tended to make some moderns—children of the Reformation, exulting in the "glorious liberty of the children of God"—forget that these sayings give only a one-sided account even of St. Paul's views. Whatever its short-comings, a law which could call forth in its praise Psalm cxix. was a real source of moral and religious inspiration to a nation ever ready to bleed in its defence. The casuistry and pedantry of its interpreters are scathingly denounced by our Lord, but nowhere is a word said by Him against the Law itself. Yet towards it His attitude is one of entire independence and discrimination. He changes fundamentally the whole method of approaching it, making the essential thing to consist, not in what the letter of the Law actually prescribed, but in those moral and religious ends which the Law, in so far as it was God's Law, was intended to help men to attain. Like all great educationalists He aimed at leading men to understand and to originate, not merely to accept and to obey.

He goes back behind the Law to the ancient Prophets, and in the spirit of him who said, "I will have mercy and not sacrifice," He lays down principles in which are implicit a complete revolution in the methods and content of the Law. "The Sabbath was made for man, not man for the Sabbath"; "because of the hardness of your hearts, Moses *permitted* divorce"; "not that which goeth into a man defileth a man, but that which cometh out"; "whosoever looketh on a woman to lust after her hath committed adultery"; "love God, love man, on these two commandments hang all the Law and the Prophets." Here are great ethical and religious principles which sift out in a word the wheat from the chaff and supply at the same time a new stimulus, a new outlook, and a new approach to the moral ideal.

I have argued elsewhere [1] that the actual form of our Lord's own teaching may have been to some

---

[1] *Studies in the Synoptic Problem*, p. 221 f.

extent determined by His clear apprehension of the innate human tendency to conceive of right conduct as a system of rules, of which Pharisaism is only an extreme instance. It is at any rate remarkable that He nowhere lays down rules. A rule as such necessarily invites a casuistic interpretation ; we cannot help asking whether such and such a thing is or is not "within the meaning of the Act." But, by means of Parable or Paradox, principles can be laid down without this danger. Even the most ingenious could not extract a cut and dried rule as to the comparative claims of the family and religion from the saying " He that hateth not his father and his mother . . . cannot be my disciple." Yet in the mouth of One who taught a gospel of love its meaning cannot be misunderstood.

The principle that morality is a disposition of the soul, not a code of rules, has a further and specially characteristic application. If it is the change of heart, the direction in which a man is moving, that matters most, it follows that the stage of actual achievement which he has already reached at a particular moment is *relatively* unimportant.[1] Hence the Publican, who clearly sees the great gap between himself and his ideal, is ethically in a more hopeful state than the Pharisee, naïvely unconscious that there is a gap at all. Progress is most possible where it is most desired, and the messenger of God has more in common with admitted sinners than with the grave and solemn personages ironically described as " needing no physician."

(*b*) *in relation to the eschatological background*

Such principles commend themselves at once as self-evident and of universal application. But there is another element in our Lord's teaching of which this

---

[1] Similarly St. Paul speaks of a man being "justified" once and for all at his conversion, in spite of his frequent experience that the process of "sanctification," the building up of a stable character, was in many cases painfully slow.

cannot be said. I mean those "world-denying" injunctions which have always provided such plentiful food for discussion. The discovery of the eschatological background of the Gospels has turned the discussion into a new channel, and the question has been raised of late, whether it may not be the case that He Himself regarded much of His teaching as a merely temporary ethic, valid only for the few short years or even months of strain and stress, which were expected to intervene before the Kingdom of God should appear.

As we shall see later the Gospels imply, and the early Church certainly believed, that He taught that the Kingdom of God, and with it the end of the present world-order, was very near. Supposing Him to have held this, had this expected catastrophe no influence on His view of the appropriate conduct for mortals in the brief interval remaining? If "the hammer of the world's clock had risen to strike the last hour," *ought* not in fact His teaching to have been an *interimsethik* [1]— the morality for a short period of transition?

It may help towards attaining the right point of view for a solution of this lately formulated problem if we note that the same question might be asked with regard to St. Paul's ethics, for he, too, held the same view of the "shortness of the time." Yet, save in one passage concerning marriage,[2] there is little obvious reaction of his eschatological views upon his ethics.

There is something timeless about the great ideals of Righteousness or Beauty, and it would seem that the specific genius of Prophet, Poet, or Artist cannot but seize and body forth the things it sees in forms of eternal meaning. The fine frenzy of intuition soars above the logic of the world-view of its possessor. A close examination seems to show clearly that the rule holds good in the present instance. Doubtless had the

---

[1] It is worth remarking that for the believer in immortality even in the twentieth century, this life of threescore years and ten might make some use even of an *interimsethik*.

[2] Cf. 1 Cor. vii. 26-31.

Master explicitly contemplated the centuries of slow development still awaiting humanity, the actual form and phrasing of many a precept would have been different. Doubtless, too, He would have let fall a word or two on the creative moral value of institutions like the Family and the State. But the heart of the question is not here, but in those great anti-worldly paradoxes which have ever constituted the " offence " of Christian ethic.

" One thing thou lackest ; sell all that thou hast, and come, follow Me." " Be not anxious for the morrow." "If a man smite thee on one cheek, turn to him the other." " Lay not up for yourself treasures upon earth," and the like. Do precepts like these represent the Master's estimate of real and fundamental values ? Or did He only mean that wealth, forethought, self-assertion were good enough things in times past, and that preoccupation with them is foolish now *only* in view of the approaching catastrophe ?

Two main reasons seem to preclude this interpretation. Firstly, the approaching end of the world is not as a matter of fact adduced as a motive in the case of many of the most startling of these precepts. Men are urged not to be anxious for the morrow, not for the eschatological reason that to-morrow they may awake in another world, but because God's providence is daily shown in His feeding the fowls of the air and clothing the lilies of the field. Whether the end be far or near, moth and rust will still corrupt, and thieves break through and steal, and wealth is disparaged primarily because the love of it distracts the soul in conflicting ways : "No man can serve two masters" ; "Where your treasure is, there will your heart be also." " Love your enemies " is commanded, not because the time is too short for petty squabbles, but " that ye may be sons of your Father which is in heaven, for he maketh his sun to rise on the evil and on the good, and sendeth rain on the just and on the unjust."

But a further consideration arising even more from

the very heart of the matter is this. Every word and act of our Lord makes it clear that the love of God and man which was for Him the fundamental principle of life was not a mere emotional sentiment, neither was it a mere academic criterion for discriminating between the essential and non-essential elements in traditional morality. It was a consuming passion for service, that passion which dedicates whosoever is inflamed therewith to a life of renunciation, conflict, and reproach, and which demands the absolute sacrifice and surrender of all that would hinder devotion to the cause.

" Whoso hateth not his father and his mother—yea and his own life also—cannot be My disciple." Sayings such as these are no doubt intentionally paradoxical in their expression, but they spring not from the eschatological expectations of His age but from His own inward passion for God and man, and he who would neglect, explain away, or tone them down has missed the secret of the Master's power. Herein lies the heroic element in Christianity, which alone has made it, and alone can make it, a religion fit for heroes.

> Give all thou canst : high heaven rejects the lore
> Of nicely calculated less or more.

(c) in relation to the Divine Forgiveness

Yet to lay emphasis only on this stern summons to absolute singleness of purpose and absolute surrender to the ideal at whatever cost would give a one-sided impression of His message in its totality. Equally conspicuous is the tenderness and sympathy for those who have fallen short, even of a far less exacting moral ideal than that which He Himself both taught and lived, for the publican, the sinner, or the man whose sickness was due to his own sin (cf. Mark ii. 5). The ideal is infinite ; infinite, too, is the compassion for those who miss it.

After the pattern of the ideals of a man's own mind

are the predominant characteristics of that image of the Divine nature which he is capable of realising. To the old prophets God was pre-eminently a God of justice, stern and terrible, a God " that loveth righteousness and hateth iniquity." Another note, indeed, is struck from time to time in the Old Testament, and we hear of " the loving-kindness of the Lord " (cf. Psalm lxxxix. 1). In our Lord's mind it is this aspect which lies uppermost, though the sterner side is not forgotten. In His teaching, the stress on the Divine forgiveness at times almost drowns the warning note of judgment. Parables like the Prodigal Son ; sayings like " your heavenly Father knoweth that ye have need of these things before ye ask " ; " not one sparrow falleth to the ground without your Father " ; must be set side by side with " strait is the gate " and " let him take up his cross," if we would realise the full meaning of His call to repent.

Just as the duty of man is no longer taught as the negative " thou shalt not harm," but the positive " thou shalt do good," so the Divine compassion is no longer conceived merely as that negative mercy which remits the just penalty for offences done, but as the overflowing tenderness which goes forth " to seek and to save that which is lost." It is under the figure of the Good Shepherd that the mind of Europe has loved best to think of Him who thus taught, and perhaps this aspect of His teaching is that which His Church has least conspicuously failed to keep alive.

The Kingdom of God

" The Kingdom is at hand." His attitude towards contemporary eschatological conceptions seems, as we should expect, to be characterised by that same blend of acceptance and independent interpretation that is shown in His attitude towards the Law.

Jewish Apocalyptic was based on a geocentric

picture, now long outgrown, of Heaven, Earth, Hell, tier above tier, populated by angels and demons, highest of all, God in supra-regal splendour seated on an almost material throne. Its conceptions of the method of the Divine working in history are fantastic, bizarre, often even repellent, to the modern mind. But the spirit which to the men of that age and that culture found a natural embodiment in these forms was a passionate faith in the Divine justice and the Divine providence, which, in a downtrodden section of a small nation crushed for centuries by corrupt and powerful empires, is not one of the least heroic manifestations of the religious spirit of man.[1]

Just as in His ethical teaching our Lord disentangles and develops the weightier matters of the Law, so in His language about the eschatological Kingdom attention is concentrated on the essential points, Judgment and Eternal Life. Contemporary Apocalyptic does not lack conspicuous ethical and prophetic elements, but its main efforts are expended in elaborating fanciful and detailed pictures of the precise nature of the tribulations, the demonic conflicts, the cataclysms celestial and terrestrial, which are to precede the great deliverance ; in giving mysterious signs to calculate its date ; or in vivid descriptions of the various stages of blessedness and torment in the intermediate state and in the world to come.

Of all this there is nothing or next to nothing in the teaching of our Lord.[2] Again we are reminded of the great prophets of the eighth century in whom the detail and the stress is all devoted to the ethical and

---

[1] Cf. the remarks in Essay IV. p. 200 f. on the Apocalypse of St. John.

[2] The only real example is the section Mark xiii. 6-27, where the detailed emphasis on various signs is in the manner of ordinary Apocalyptic. There are, however, good reasons for believing that this chapter contains a large admixture of unauthentic sayings ; cf. my remarks in *Studies in the Synoptic Problem*, p. 179 ff. In the Appendix to the same volume I pointed out that if we compare the eschatological sayings in Q, Mark and Matthew, there is a distinct movement in the direction of making our Lord's sayings conform more closely to the conventional apocalyptic pattern. The fact is an important one, though the conclusions I was then inclined to draw from it were, I now think, somewhat too sweeping.

religious exhortation, while the "Day of the Lord" looms out dimly in the future, awful, certain, but undefined. What the Day of the Lord is to the old prophets, that the coming of the Kingdom is to our Lord—an essential part of His message, but not its main content.

Another trait of independence in our Lord's preaching of the Kingdom must be touched upon. Two different types of teaching about the Kingdom occur in the Gospels. On the one hand words are frequent which imply or expressly state that He taught that that present "generation should not pass away till all things were accomplished," that the disciples would not have time even to "go through the cities of Israel before the Son of Man be come," and that the final consummation of the Kingdom would come "like a thief in the night," in sudden and catastrophic form.

Such sayings are so numerous, and in many cases are so intimately bound up with the context and with other sayings, that they cannot be explained away without grave risk of explaining away along with them the historical character of the Gospels altogether. Moreover, even if such language could be eliminated from the Gospels, the universal belief of the primitive Church—testified to in practically every one of the Epistles—could hardly be accounted for, except as based on something in our Lord's teaching.

On the other hand I must needs think, in spite of the opposition of some distinguished scholars, that it is equally unscientific to explain away the collective force of certain passages of a different tenor.[1] Such are the Parables of the Mustard Seed and Leaven, the Seed growing secretly, the Hidden Treasure, and the Pearl of great price, also certain shorter sayings like, "If I by the finger of God cast out devils then is the Kingdom of

---

[1] Both sides of the question are presented in some detail in a series of articles in *The Interpreter*, Jan. to Oct. 1911, which contain a friendly controversy between Professor Burkitt, Archdeacon Allen and myself on the subject.

God come upon you," "the Kingdom of God is within you,"[1] or again the mention of the fact that "the blind see, the lame walk . . . the poor have the Gospel preached unto them," as a token to John the Baptist that our Lord was the Expected One. And there are other less striking utterances, all of which seem to imply that there is a sense in which the Kingdom is already present. Many of them, indeed, also imply, and all are consistent with, the view that in another sense it is still future, and that only in the light of the richness of that future will the real importance of the present be seen. The future, indeed, is the harvest, but the present is the seed.

The conviction that the salvation of God is in one sense here and now, yet in another and larger sense still awaiting consummation, that in the present life man can enjoy a foretaste or "earnest" of that which shall be, is fundamental as much in the religious experience of the world's great mystics as in that of the ordinary man. It is perhaps especially characteristic of that age-long strain in Hebrew religion represented in the Psalms. Hence the attempt to eliminate this double element from the central theme of our Lord's teaching by explaining away the sayings last enumerated is not merely a *tour de force* of exegesis but runs counter to the analogies of the religious consciousness.

But there is not really even a verbal inconsistency between the two classes of sayings. "Kingdom of God" is on the whole a misleading translation of the original. "Reign or rule of God" would usually be the better rendering ; cf. especially the paraphrase in the Lord's Prayer "Thy kingdom come," that is, "Thy will be done on earth as it is in heaven." Wherever the forces of the evil one are put to flight, whenever the sick are healed, whenever men hearken to the

---

[1] I must needs think that "within you," and not "among you," is the natural rendering of ἐντὸς ὑμῶν. This, of course, does not rule out speculation as to whether the Greek correctly represents the Aramaic phrase used by our Lord, but the burden of proof lies with those who maintain that it is a mistranslation.

call to repent, these things are no mere sign that the Kingdom is near ; they are, so far as they go, an actual instalment of the realised reign of God on earth. They are not the flash-light from a distant coast, the mouth of the harbour is already reached.

Here again our Lord reverts back to an earlier conception. The latest stage of Apocalyptic, as Dr. Charles points out, differs from the earlier Apocalyptic, and still more from the old prophetic view, in despairing of the regeneration of this world by any means however supernatural, and in hoping only for a *new* Jerusalem coming straight down from heaven on to a *new* earth. But the Kingdom of God as preached by our Lord entailed also a regeneration of this earth, of which it had been written, " The earth is the Lord's, and the fulness thereof." Thus His conception, combining the earlier Prophetic with the later Apocalyptic, includes two ideas which modern thought must needs hold apart — the idea of a corporate national regeneration on this earth, and the idea of individual immortality in a supersensuous sphere.

We see here that same reinterpretation of contemporary religious beliefs in the light of their underlying principles, which we have already seen in His treatment of the Law. The essential idea of the Kingdom is the realisation of the rule of God ; wherever then evil is being rebuffed and good is triumphing, the Kingdom is, just so far, in the act of being realised. In St. Paul we find that " the Kingdom of God is not eating and drinking, but righteousness and peace and joy in the Holy Ghost " (Rom. xiv. 17), and that the present indwelling of the Spirit is " an instalment of our inheritance " (Eph. i. 14).[1] In this, as well as in his more definitely eschatological hopes, his teaching is essentially implicit in his Master's.

---

[1] Cf. also 2 Cor. i. 22, v. 5.

THE SON OF MAN

So much for the Kingdom—what of the King? The importance of His deliberate choice of the title, Son of Man, has been already indicated (p. 102), but it is not easy to be sure of the exact meaning He attached to it.

A word must be said as to the actual phrase itself. In the Old Testament, Son of Man is a poetical equivalent for man. "Lord, what is man that Thou art mindful of him, or the son of man that Thou regardest him?"[1] The equivalent phrase in later Aramaic simply means "man"; whether this was already so in the dialect used in Galilee in our Lord's time is a disputed point among Aramaic scholars. In any case the title may be fairly represented in English as "the Man."

We have seen, however, that the Book of Enoch shows that, at any rate in some circles, it had acquired also a technical sense as a Messianic title. A confusion between the ordinary and the technical use of the words was thus possible, both in the minds of the original hearers of our Lord and in the tradition of His sayings. For instance, the saying, "The Sabbath was made for man, not man for the Sabbath, therefore the Son of Man is Lord also of the Sabbath," seems more pointed if the latter half means, not that the Messiah, but that man *as such* is master of the Sabbath. Again, the difficulty that the saying (Mark ii. 10), "The Son of Man hath power to forgive sins," does not seem to have been interpreted as an open claim to Messiahship, would be met if the Pharisees had understood, possibly misunderstood, Him to mean by the words no more than "man."

As a rule, however, in the Synoptics the phrase is

---

[1] It is notable that it is usually found in passages where the contrast of man's lowliness with God's power is implied. Thus Ezekiel is always addressed by God as "son of man." In Gen. vi. 2 the parallel phrase "daughters of men"＝women is also found in contrast to "sons of God."

clearly used as the title of the Apocalyptic Christ. It is used in two sets of passages, in the one with the emphasis on His glorious coming in judgment ; in the other, almost in irony, to illustrate the Christian paradox, " Whoso would be greatest let him be servant of all." For instance, " The Son of Man hath not where to lay His head " ; " the Son of Man shall suffer and be put to death " ; " the Son of Man came not to be ministered unto but to minister, and to give His life " ;—passages of which half the point is lost if we forget that Son of Man was the title of a King of kings, the Vicegerent of God Himself.

Some difficulty is created by the fact, abundantly clear from St. Mark's Gospel, that His claim to be the Messiah at all was a secret, unknown even to the disciples till at Caesarea Philippi it was divined by St. Peter in a moment of inspired intuition. I believe that Schweitzer and others are correct in inferring from the form in which the cries of the multitude are given in St. Mark, the oldest version of the story, that even at the Triumphal Entry they still regarded Him, not as being Himself the supernatural Messiah of the apocalyptic hope, but as a Prophet, the forerunner of the Messiah—in fact, a second John the Baptist, as Herod had once satirically named Him (Mark vi. 16). Even if they had heard some of those sayings about the Son of Man, to us so clearly personal in their reference, they would naturally have supposed He could only mean them of some glorious being yet to come.[1]

Hence from the first there was an element of mystery about His use of the title. However, His

---

[1] Cf. Burkitt, *American Journal of Theology* for April 1911, pp. 180-190. Schweitzer argues that John's question, " Art thou he that should come? " (Matt. xi. 3) means, not " Art thou the Christ? " but " Art thou the Elijah who is to precede the Christ? " (Mal. iv. 5 ; cf. Mark viii. 28, ix. 11), the " baptizer with fire " whom he himself had foretold. This may be correct. The view that John recognised our Lord as Messiah at the Baptism is implied no doubt in the Fourth Gospel, and in Matt. iii. 14-15, " I have need to be baptized of Thee," etc.—an addition to the Marcan version, which on other grounds has been regarded as inauthentic— but may be a mistaken inference of later Christian tradition.

reply to the solemn adjuration of the High Priest makes it clear that the passage in Daniel (vii. 13-14) in connection with its personal application in the Book of Enoch must be taken as normative, though not exhaustive, for any sound interpretation.

"I saw in the night visions, and, behold, there came with the clouds of heaven one like unto a son of man, and he came even to the Ancient of days, and they brought him near before him. And there was given him dominion, and glory, and a kingdom, that all the peoples, nations, and languages should serve him : his dominion is an everlasting dominion, which shall not pass away, and his kingdom that which shall not be destroyed" (Dan. vii. 13-14).

To this day the Oriental mind expresses itself with a luxuriance of imagery unfamiliar to the West. Especially characteristic is this of the Hebrew Prophets. Their language is the language of poetry, not of sober Saxon prose. And even beyond the norm of these the language of our Lord is rich in parable, metaphor, and paradox. If in the agony in the garden it was natural for Him to speak in conscious metaphor of the cup that He must drink, we may not press too literally a direct quotation of an ancient Scripture whose whole style was avowedly symbolic. Again, His answer to the challenge of the Sadducees with regard to the Resurrection of the Dead—another of the central ideas of contemporary eschatology—shows a clear perception of the inadequacy of the more materialistic imagery of Apocalyptic (cf. p. 137).

But while all due allowance must be made for these considerations, we may not read into ancient Galilee our own modern rationalising interpretation. Such language would be to His mind neither purely meta-phorical nor absolutely literal—the word "quasi-symbolic" may be coined to represent the case.

A further consideration of no small importance is this. We have seen that the Kingdom was in the main

still future and yet in part and in germ already present.
It would seem to follow that His Kingship is already
realised in just such a partial and germinal way. "All
things have been delivered unto me . . . neither doth
any know the Father, save the Son, . . ." (Mt. xi. 27,
cf. p. 103 *n.*) implies at least a Messianic Sonship
already mystically realised in the present. Moreover, if
to His mind, the essence of Kingship is service (Mark
x. 42-45), in so much as He was already serving He
was already King ; in so much as He had not yet
performed the supreme service He was as yet uncrowned.
That supreme service, that coronation act, as our next
section will make clear, was to begin when He should
"give His life a ransom for many."[1]

The Value of the Apocalyptic Idea

The eschatological teaching of our Lord is a simpler,
wider, and greater thing than ordinary Jewish Apocalyptic,
but for myself I am coming more and more to feel
that to water down and explain away the apocalyptic
element is to miss something which is essential. Much
of the unique moral grasp of the New Testament is in
one way directly a result of the eschatological background of the period.

The summits of certain mountains are seen only at
rare moments when, their cloud-cap rolled away, they
stand out stark and clear. So in ordinary life ultimate
values and eternal issues are normally obscured by
minor duties, petty cares, and small ambitions ; at
the bedside of a dying man the cloud is often lifted.
In virtue of the eschatological hope our Lord and His
first disciples found themselves standing, as it were,
at the bedside of a dying world. Thus for a whole
generation the cloud of lesser interests was rolled away,
and ultimate values and eternal issues stood out before

[1] Cf. the interpretation of the words "from henceforth ye shall see," given in
Essay V. p. 262 *text and note* 4.

them stark and clear, as never before or since in the history of our race. The majority of men in all ages best serve their kind by a life of quiet duty, in the family, in their daily work, and in the support of certain definite and limited public and philanthropic causes. Such is the normal way of progress. But it has been well for humanity that during one great epoch the belief that the end of all was near turned the thoughts of the highest minds away from practical and local interests, even of the first importance, like the condition of slaves in Capernaum or the sanitation of Tarsus.

" Men feared," says Schweitzer, " that to admit the claims of eschatology would abolish the significance of His words for our time ; and hence there was a feverish eagerness to discover in them any elements that might be considered not eschatologically conditioned. When any sayings were found of which the wording did not absolutely imply an eschatological connection there was great jubilation—these at least had been saved uninjured from the coming *débâcle*. But in reality that which is eternal in the words of Jesus is due to the very fact that they are based on an eschatological world-view, and contain the expression of a mind for which the contemporary world with its historical and social circumstances no longer had any existence. They are appropriate, therefore, to any world, for in every world they raise the man who dares to meet their challenge, and does not turn and twist them into meaninglessness, above his world and his time, making him inwardly free, so that he is fitted to be, in his own world and in his own time, a simple channel of the power of Jesus." [1]

But we have something more to learn from Apocalyptic. The conception of evolution has proved so illuminating in every department of thought that it has inevitably distracted men's attention from the fact that, in human history at any rate,[2] the greatest advances

[1] Schweitzer, *Quest of the Historical Jesus*, p. 400.
[2] But see remarks on "the unprecedented in Nature," p. 137 *fin.* 138.

are frequently *per saltum*. They occur in epochs or moments of crisis, as in the Apocalyptic parable of "the Day of the Lord."[1] The Reformation, the French Revolution, or the rebirth of the Far East in our own time, are conspicuous examples, but in a measure this is no less true of nearly all considerable movements. Such crises, no doubt, are the result of causes which can to some extent be traced, and have been prepared for by a slow and gradual development. But in their realisation they are catastrophic, and take even the wisest by surprise. "As in the days of Noah they were eating and drinking and knew not until the flood came," so it has ever been at "the coming of the Son of Man." In each such epoch we may see a partial Advent of the Christ, but is the Apocalyptic word amiss that Anti-Christ is also then abroad ? Such times are times of tribulation, devastation, and demoralisation as well as of deliverance and advance.

And what is true in the history of the great world holds good no less commonly in the inner history of the microcosm of the individual soul—"in an hour when he knoweth not his Lord cometh."

The Death of the Messiah and its Significance

For the moment our Lord was called to play the part of prophet ; one day He would be manifested as the expected Son of Man. We cannot but ask the question whether from the first He had a clear conception how the transition from the one to the other was to be effected, or whether He was content to wait for this to be shown in God's good time, letting "the morrow be anxious for the things of itself." The answer to this question depends on the answer given to a further question, Did He from the first clearly anticipate that His earthly career would end in death ? The evidence at our disposal does not allow of a certain

---

[1] Cf. Lake, *op. cit.* p. 438 ff.

answer being given, but it would seem probable that His realisation of this was progressive, changing gradually from a dim premonition to an absolute certainty, as though the Cross towards which He journeyed cast a shadow, faint at first but darkening at every step.

At any rate, some time before the end, if not from the first, hard facts, the opposition and plots of Scribes and Pharisees, not to mention the lessons of history, must have made it evident. Written broad across the face of history—and not least conspicuously of the history of Israel—is the fact that humanity persecutes its prophets. Written broad across the Gospels is our Lord's clear recognition of this. "So persecuted they the prophets which were before you"; "Ye build the tombs of the prophets and hereby bear witness that ye are the true sons of the men who slew them"; "O Jerusalem, Jerusalem, thou that killest the prophets and stonest them which are sent unto thee." [1]

The idealist temper hopes all things, and the story of Gethsemane shows that even to the last He thought it was just possible He might not have to drink the cup; just as the soldier who volunteers for a forlorn hope does so, not expecting, yet just hoping, to return alive.

According to St. Mark, He several times distinctly and clearly foretold His death. [2] Critics have suggested that the exact correspondence of some of these prophecies with the details of their fulfilment casts suspicion on their authenticity; perhaps this may be admitted as regards some of them, even perhaps as regards the exact wording of all of them. But a parallel tradition in St. Luke, perhaps derived from Q, guarantees the main fact that He foreboded the end. "I have a baptism to be baptized with, and how am I straitened till it be accomplished" (Lk. xii. 50). "Go and say to that fox, Behold I cast out demons and

---

[1] Cf. also Luke xi. 50, "the blood of all the prophets," and Mark vi. 4, "a prophet is not without honour, save," etc.

[2] Cf. Mk. viii. 31, ix. 12, ix. 31, x. 33-34, xiv. 27-28; in nearly all of these passages the Resurrection is also foretold.

perform cures to-day and to-morrow, and on the third day I am perfected. Howbeit I must go on my way to-day and to-morrow and the day following, for it cannot be that a prophet perish out of Jerusalem" (Lk. xiii. 32). Such a foreboding, too, is clearly implied in the reply to James and John, "Can ye drink of the cup that I drink of?" (Mk. x. 38); in the Parable of the Wicked Husbandmen (Mk. xii. 1 ff.); and again in the saying "She hath anointed my body beforehand for the burying" (Mk. xiv. 8).

In this connection scholars have asked why was it that our Lord went up to Jerusalem; was it to preach or was it to die? To those who have studied the psychology of great religious leaders the question is irrelevant—as well ask, Why did St. Paul go up to Jerusalem when the Spirit in every city testified that bonds and imprisonments awaited him? The modern reformer may study tactics and opportunities, but the great prophets of old on great occasions follow without questioning the admonition of an inner voice.[1]

Designated as that Christ whom Prophet, Psalmist, and Apocalyptist had foretold, on whom were concentrated the hopes of Israel; guaranteed by the Divine voice to be that Son of Man at whose manifestation Abraham, Isaac, and Jacob, and all the righteous dead were to arise and sit at meat in a new Jerusalem, the centre of a renovated world; He went up to that city of immemorial sanctity with more than a foreboding, with an expectation, that there He was to die. Here is a situation challenging the most searching thought. Can we suppose that as the time drew near He, who felt so irresistibly called to face it by Divine compulsion, had given no thought to find the reason of that death, if haply such should be required of Him. May we speculate as to the line His thought would take?

---

[1] Cf. Acts xvi. 6-9, the admonitions which determined the plan of St. Paul's second missionary journey. The experience known in some religious circles as "leading" is not essentially different though usually fainter in degree.

He was face to face with a mystery—the mystery of mysteries and the problem of problems. Man's instinct for justice demands that the bad should suffer and the righteous should escape. The course of this world is ordered otherwise. "He maketh his sun to rise on the evil and on the good," and it would sometimes seem as if the vials of His wrath were poured out alike upon the just and on the unjust. In some of the Psalms, and more especially in the Book of Job, the problem is raised but hardly answered. But there is one place in the Old Testament where it is faced, and a profounder answer is suggested—the 53rd chapter of Isaiah. Our Lord's answers to Satan at the Temptation, His reply to John's question "Art Thou He that should come?" His answer to the High Priest, and the cry on the Cross show that at all great crises in His life His mind instinctively found a natural expression in Scriptural phrase. Especially familiar to Him was the Book of Isaiah. At times He quotes it directly, more often His own language is coloured by its phrasing. Can we believe that His thoughts did not recur to it in such a crisis?[1]

"He was wounded for our transgressions, He was bruised for our iniquities : the chastisement of our peace was upon Him ; and with His stripes we are healed. All we like sheep have gone astray ; we have turned every one to his own way ; and the Lord hath laid on Him the iniquity of us all. . . . When His life shall make an offering for sin, He shall see His seed, He shall prolong His days, and the pleasure of the Lord shall prosper in His hand. He shall see of the travail of His soul, and shall be satisfied : by His knowledge shall My righteous Servant make many righteous : and He shall bear their iniquities. Therefore will I divide Him a portion with the great, and He shall divide the spoil with the strong : because He poured out His soul unto

---

[1] He expressly quotes Is. liii. 12 (Lk. xxii. 37), and λύτρον ἀντὶ πολλῶν (Mk. x. 45) is probably reminiscent of πολλούς . . . ἀνθ᾽ ὧν παρεδόθη in the same verse.

death, and was numbered with the transgressors : yet
He bare the sin of many, and made intercession for the
transgressors " (Is. liii. 5-6, 10-12).

There is no sufficient evidence that this passage had
ever hitherto been interpreted of the Messiah. The
thoughts of the Prophet himself would appear to have
been directed mainly to the problem of the purpose
of the suffering and oppression of Israel, or of the
righteous element in Israel, symbolically spoken of as
"the Servant of the Lord." But the words of genius,
or, shall we say, of inspiration, have always an eternal
application far wider than the actual occasion of their
original utterance. The Prophet's solution is profoundly
true over a far wider field. Prosperity and suffering in
this world are not proportionate to desert, yet it is by the
labours and the suffering, not only of the great idealists,
martyrs, and reformers whose names are known to
fame, but equally of the great multitude of humble,
quiet, honest toilers ; it is by constant sacrifice to the call
of duty, or to the love of family and friend, and by
these alone—that the effects of human ignorance and
guilt are mitigated, and the very existence as well as the
progress of the race made possible.

"His life shall make an offering for sin " (R.V.
marg.), " He shall bear their iniquities." The words are
suggested by the ritual of the Temple sacrifice. The
unique distinction of the long line of Hebrew prophets
is their protest against the crude external ideas of
sacrifice universal in early religions. "Behold to obey
is better than sacrifice," "I delight not in the blood of
bullocks or of lambs," "The sacrifices of God are a
broken spirit, a broken and a contrite heart, O God,
thou wilt not despise." Yet it was a deep and sound
instinct that still kept alive the reformed sacrificial
system of the second Temple, burdensome, trivial, and
superstitious though so much of it seems to us.
Penitence and obedience, indeed, are the only sacrifice
that has value in the sight of God, but how little of

this can each one offer, even for the sins he clearly recognises? And what of the sins to which his hardened conscience is insensitive, what of the sin of the community—that atmosphere of false ideals and evil customs which enters insensibly into our inmost being? Something more than individual penitence for the sins which the individual knows as such is wanted, something that shall avail to "take away the sins of the people," something that shall set a different standard, start a fresh tradition, create a new power.[1]

It has been seen already how in regard both to the law of conduct, and to the eschatological hope, our Lord went back behind contemporary ideas to the prophets of old in such a way as to unite the quintessential elements of both. The last act of His life was to do the same for the third of the chief features of the old religion—the Atoning Sacrifice.

The Prophet had written that the ideal Servant of the Lord was to suffer and to die, to "bear the sin of many." And who, we may conceive the Master asking, should act as the ideal Servant of the Lord if not the Christ the Son of God? Already He had rejected the Satanic offer of all the kingdoms of the earth, for the part of a hungry, homeless teacher. The foxes have holes and the birds have nests, but the Son of Man, designate the Monarch of Futurity, has not where to lay His head. He had taught "Blessed are ye poor," "Blessed are ye when men persecute you." One act, one lesson more was left.

"And Jesus called them to Him, and saith unto them, Ye know that they which are accounted to rule over the Gentiles lord it over them ; and their great ones exercise authority over them. But it is not so among you : but whosoever would become great among you, shall be your minister : and whosoever would be first among you, shall be servant of all. For verily the Son of Man came not to be ministered unto, but to

[1] Cf. Essay VI. p. 294, p. 285.

minister, and to give His life a ransom for many"
(Mark x. 42 ff.).   Not enough was it to have proclaimed the new ideal in penetrating phrase, not enough
to have lived a life of service and self-denial.   Of him
who was to be the supreme agent in the regeneration
of mankind, the supreme sacrifice of all is asked.   From
such an act there goes forth power.   One thing more
is lacking ere humanity is redeemed from the miseries
of this present life.   Before the Kingdom of God can
appear, a price must be paid—and the price is the life
of the King.

The future is now clear.   The Servant of the Lord
whom Isaiah told of, was by his suffering and death to
bring about redemption, and to him a triumph beyond
the grave, glorious and complete, is promised.   To the
Son of Man is predicted a coming with the clouds of
heaven.   Both prophecies are to be realised through
one act.   That He may return in glory He must first
depart in suffering and shame.   Standing, therefore,
before the High Priest, mocked, deserted, helpless,
marked down for death, He can confidently answer the
question " Art Thou the Christ the Son of the Blessed ? "
with a triumphant reference to Daniel's prophecy, " I
am, and ye shall see the Son of Man sitting at the right
hand of power, and coming with the clouds of heaven "
(Mark xiv. 62).

A few hours later hanging on the Cross He uttered
the cry " My God, my God, why hast thou forsaken
me ? "   And after nineteen centuries the end that He
proclaimed so near has not yet come.

There is matter for reflection here.

THE RESURRECTION

Years before the belief in a life beyond the grave,
at least for the righteous, had been taught by Jewish
Psalmist and Apocalyptist, by Greek philosophers, by
many of the Sages and Prophets of the East.   If we

may suppose that there is anything of justice or benevolence in the Power which upholds the Universe, the startling contrast between merit and reward so often seen in this world seems almost to compel the belief that our present life is but the porch to a wider and more glorious edifice. To a similar conclusion we are led by the reflection that even the noblest lives on earth, lives seemingly on the road to a perfection which would be a worthy end and crown to the toil and moil of all their efforts, and (if we may say so) of all God's efforts, break off, so far as this world is concerned, before that end is reached. Those again who, like the psalmists and the saints, have felt themselves to be, at any rate in supreme moments, in spiritual communion with the Divine, have always felt the confidence that to this communion death could not be an interruption—rather would it remove a barrier. Lastly, all who believe that there is a dignity and worth in any individual life, which constitutes it a thing of permanent and intrinsic value, must see that its extinction would be an irreparable loss to the totality of existence. "Ye are of more value than many sparrows," and the loss of a single soul is the detriment of God. It was a thought like this on which the Master Himself based His argument for a resurrection, " the God of Abraham, of Isaac, and of Jacob "—a God in whose sight the individual is of worth—"is not the God of the dead but of the living." No one who really believes in a Divine Providence at all, least of all one who believes in a Heavenly Father such as our Lord spoke of, can believe that the life of Jesus ended upon the Cross.

Much in this Universe in which we live seems to reveal a great creative mind ; much in the history of mankind, much in the experience of each individual points to " a divinity which shapes our ends, rough-hew them how we will." But there are things that seem to point the other way. And in moments when our

faith is low, when it seems that Heaven is blind to
human suffering, dumb to human cries, a great doubt
arises. If that Man who alone in the history of our
race solely and single-heartedly lived and worked and
gave all for the love of God and man, died as a
criminal, mocked by His enemies, deserted by His
friends, forsaken, as it seemed to Him, by God Himself,
the question which rises instinctively to our minds is
a very fundamental question. The spectacle of the
ideally good man brought to the ideally bad end
raises a question which concerns, not the immortality
of man, or the Divinity of Christ, but the very
existence of a God at all. Surely, if ever in history,
this was the moment for God, if there be a God, to
lift the veil which hides His working and within the
sphere of visible and palpable experience vindicate His
governance of this visible and palpable world ; we
desiderate some *proof*, like the men of old we ask
" a sign."

Herein lies the force of the persistent demand of
man for miracle. It is not so much to prove that
Jesus lives, nor yet that *we* shall rise again—both these
would follow if we could be sure that God rules all.
Rather it is because in this, the test case as it were in
human history, we in the weakness of our faith demand
a sign that God *does* rule.

" An evil and adulterous generation seeketh after a
sign and there shall no sign be given to it." " If they
hear not Moses and the prophets neither will they be
persuaded though one rose from the dead." Doubtless
in proportion as our hearts are set against the ethical
ideal He taught, and dumb to the united witness of
the prophets of our race, we must expect to find no convincing proof forthcoming. But is there no sign given
to those who would wish to follow Him, but whose faith
is dim and halting, as there was given to them of old,
" not to all the people," still to a faithful few, " witnesses
that were chosen afore of God " (Acts x. 41) ?

K

"For I delivered unto you first of all that which also I received, how that Christ died for our sins according to the Scriptures ; and that he was buried ; and that he hath been raised on the third day according to the Scriptures ; and that he appeared to Cephas ; then to the twelve ; then he appeared to above five hundred brethren at once, of whom the greater part remain until now, but some are fallen asleep ; then he appeared to James ; then to all the apostles ; and last of all as unto one born out of due time, he appeared to me also " (1 Cor. xv. 3-8).

This is the earliest and best authenticated record of the sign which was given to them, a sign which was *to them* all-sufficient and convincing. But if that same sign is to be a sign equally convincing to us, we must needs ask what exactly was the nature of those appearances whereby they were convinced. We must ask for details as to the time, the place, the manner of them.

Our most reliable authority would, of course, have been the original conclusion of our earliest written Gospel, St. Mark. But that has gone, and we have only secondary authorities to fall back upon. And the accounts derived from these and from St. Paul cannot be fitted into a consistent story without rearrangements and cross identifications largely hypothetical.

We are bound also to consider the evidence in relation to the background of contemporary thought. The resurrection of the dead was one of the most conspicuous features in apocalyptic eschatology. It is often mentioned in the New Testament as one of the points which divided the Pharisees, who represented the main body of religious orthodoxy, from the Sadducees, the party of an unenthusiastic but highly placed minority. It was believed that with the advent of the Messianic Kingdom the dead would be raised with the bodies in which they had been buried, unchanged, it might be even wounded and mutilated, as they had been at the moment of death, and that these bodies would then be to some extent transformed and "glorified." The degree of transformation thought to be necessary to fit the body for eternal life naturally varied very considerably with individual writers. It has always been the case that some minds interpret religious phraseology in the most literal and material-istic sense, others with greater refinement of spiritual perception. There were those who thought that eating and drinking and marrying would still go on, others believed that the righteous "shall be made like unto the angels and equal to the stars" (Apoc. Baruch 52).[1]

Now the various accounts in the Gospels of the appearances of the Lord to His disciples after the resurrection imply a conception of the resurrection body as being physically identical with the body placed in the tomb, yet as having undergone some measure of transmutation and, so to speak, dematerialisation in general accordance with these popular eschatological ideas. Hence we cannot refuse to consider the possibility that many of the details in the stories as we have them may have been insensibly read into the facts actually observed from the popular presupposi-tions in the light of which they were interpreted. Few even nowadays always distinguish between a fact observed and a seemingly obvious inference made from it at the time ; and the operation of such a tendency must be allowed for the more since there is reason to believe that the stories as we have them are not accounts at first-hand by eye-witnesses.

But leaving on one side the question of evidence, the theory that the actual physical body laid in the tomb was raised up seems to involve (as indeed Article IV. baldly states) that it was subsequently taken up,

---

[1] Cf. H. St. J. Thackeray, *The Relation of St. Paul to Contemporary Jewish Thought*, pp. 111-119.

" flesh and bones," into heaven—a very difficult conception if we no longer regard the earth as flat and the centre of the solar system, and heaven as a definite region locally fixed above the solid bowl of the skies. In the mediaeval universities the question was seriously debated whether the body of our Lord was taken up into heaven clothed or naked. To us the very idea of such a debate seems irreverent and absurd, and I know of no living theologian who would maintain a physical *Ascension* in this crude form, yet so long as emphasis is laid on the physical character of the *Resurrection* it is not obvious how any refinement of the conception of " physical " really removes the difficulty.

A further difficulty of a purely religious nature arises from the following consideration. All recognise the fact that the material particles which enter into the constitution of our fleshly bodies are constantly changing, and that the actual material particles which form part of our bodies when laid in the grave may and do, through the indirect medium of vegetation, enter into the composition of other human bodies. For this and other reasons the belief is gradually being abandoned that the mode of being—or " body," if that be the term with which to describe it—in which we ourselves hope to enter into immortality will be materially identical with the physical body we have had on earth. The essence of what we mean by the hope of the resurrection of the body is surely contained in its emphasis on the survival of a full and distinct personality, and in the idea which finds expression in the lines of Tennyson—

> Eternal form shall still divide
> The eternal soul from all beside ;
> And I shall know him when we meet.

But if this be the case, then for us, with our changed philosophical and scientific outlook, to apply literally to the resurrection of our Lord the naïve eschatological conception of the resurrection of the body natural to the men of that day, is to differentiate, in a way which the writers of the New Testament would have vehemently repudiated, between the nature and the manner of His resurrection and of ours. " Christ the first-fruits, afterwards they that are Christ's," loses much of its essential meaning if the resurrection of our Lord was in one wise and our own is to be in another wise.

Nevertheless, however much we may recognise the difficulties involved in the traditional conception, the fact remains that the disciples were convinced that the Master had risen and had "shown Himself alive by many infallible proofs," and that this conviction was the cause and the inspiration of the Church they founded. If the traditional explanation be rejected, the historian is bound to seek an alternative.

An alternative which commends itself to a large number of scholars and thinkers of the present day, more especially on the Continent, is that which is commonly known as the "Subjective Vision" theory.[1] It is suggested that what the disciples saw was a series of visions caused by some acute psychological reaction— the hopes which He had raised in their hearts, the impression of His personality upon them, refusing to submit to the hard fact of His death. Might not such appearances retold from mouth to mouth in the lapse of years be insensibly materialised into the stories in our Gospels ? I do not think that conservative theologians always do full justice to the considerations which may be urged in favour of this hypothesis. On the other hand the holders of the theory do not seem to me to give due weight to the considerations which can be advanced against it. In the main these amount to pointing out that none of the psychological analogies adduced exactly cover this particular instance ; and

---

[1] This should be carefully distinguished from the "Objective Vision" theory— *i.e.* the view that, though the form of the vision was determined to some extent by the subjectivity of the disciples, it was directly caused by the Spirit of the risen and living Christ. Such a view should be classed among the possibilities mentioned on p. 136.

further that although, and indeed even because, the men of that age were in the habit of taking visions very seriously as Divine messages, it is difficult to resist the impression that they did very clearly distinguish between the appearances of the risen Lord and the ordinary visions which are so frequently mentioned in the New Testament and elsewhere; and considering the vital importance to them of the question, one ought at least to weigh gravely the probability that they had reasonable grounds for making the distinction. And lastly, any purely subjective theory seems inadequately to account for that conviction of spiritual communion with the Risen Christ which has been a determining factor throughout the history of the Church.

The discovery of the empty tomb, assuming the story to rest on adequate historical evidence, which personally I believe to be the case, is often supposed to determine the decision in favour of the traditional theory. This, however, is not really so, for with a little ingenuity it is not difficult to imagine more than one set of circumstances which might account on purely natural grounds for the tomb being found empty. Various suggestions have been put forward, as for instance that the Romans, fearing a possible disturbance, took advantage of the Sabbath quiet to remove the body out of the reach of the disciples. Of course neither this nor any other one definite suggestion has any claim to be regarded as *in itself* particularly probable,[1] but where a natural explanation of an event is at all possible, there must be very special reasons for falling back upon an explanation of a supernatural character.

The possibility of a naturalistic explanation of some kind or other would doubtless be assumed as a matter of course were the story told of any ordinary person. But it may be urged that the case in question is not

---

[1] It need hardly be said that the least probable of all is that which is also the oldest, "His disciples came by night and stole him away while we slept" (Matt. xxviii. 13).

that of an ordinary person.   If, on other grounds, we
are in general impressed with the claims of Christianity,
are we not entitled, or rather are we not bound, to
approach the evidence for this particular event in the
light of these other and wider considerations?   Such
are—the uniqueness of our Lord's person, the place
occupied by the resurrection in Christian experience,
its relation to the whole view of the world implied by
belief in a God who might be supposed to be ready and
willing to manifest His moral governance in the sphere
of physical existence.   Moreover, if it be allowed that
the discovery of the empty tomb was to some extent a
factor in confirming the Apostles in their belief in the
resurrection, the admission of a naturalistic explanation
carries with it the admission that to just that same
extent the founding of Christianity was assisted by,
even if it did not rest upon, a mistaken inference.   It
may be argued that these and similar considerations
render it fitting and natural to suppose that the body
of our Lord would not have been "suffered to see
corruption," and that historical evidence which would
be inadequate to prove an occurrence in itself intrinsically improbable may well be accepted as sufficient when
the contrary is the case.

Such a view is entertained by many whose opinions
I am bound to regard with respect, including several
of the contributors to this volume ; but for myself I am
not content to regard the Traditional and the "Subjective Vision" theories as alternatives which exhaust
the possibilities of explanation.   Behind most dilemmas
lurks a fallacy.   The fact here to be explained is in
the first place one which was a turning-point in the
spiritual history of mankind ; and in addition our interpretation of it is in a sense normative of our apprehension of so spiritual a concept as the nature and mode
of human immortality.   It is a fact in a twofold way
both spiritual and unique, and to shut up the range of
possible explanation within the limits of our experience

of things material is virtually to deny the existence of the spiritual altogether.

Both the alternatives suggested above seem to me to be materialistic, only in different ways. Apocalyptic, on the one hand, is more closely allied to poetry than prose ; it is " picture-thinking," and naturally expresses the belief in immortality in materialistic symbols. On the other hand, much of modern thought is materialistic in another way ; it thinks in terms of the lifeless categories of matter and energy mechanically conceived. But I decline to consider myself bound to explain an event of such spiritual significance in the terms of one of two materialisms, whether it be the imaginative materialism of Jewish eschatology or the philosophic materialism of modern naturalism.

Only if the possibility of personal immortality be dogmatically denied can there be any real difficulty in supposing that the Master would have been able to convince His disciples of His victory over death by some adequate manifestation ;—possibly by showing Himself to them in some form such as might be covered by St. Paul's phrase, " a spiritual body " ; possibly through some psychological channel similar to that which explains the mysterious means of communication between persons commonly known as telepathy ; or possibly in some way of which at present we have no conception. On such a view, the appearances to the disciples can only be styled " visions," if we mean by vision something directly caused by the Lord Himself veritably alive and personally in communion with them.

> No visual shade of some one lost,
> But he, the Spirit himself, may come
> Where all the nerve of sense is numb ;
> Spirit to Spirit, Ghost to Ghost.

If it be objected from a conservative standpoint that there is something strange and novel about this way of regarding the subject, I would reply that this is not the case. The argument used above is neither a new one nor my own ; it is only another way of stating the self-same argument used by our Lord Himself on the only occasion in which He is recorded to have directly dealt with the question of the nature and manner of the resurrection of the dead.

When the Sadducees (Mk. xii. 18 ff.) endeavoured to pose Him by the story of the woman who was seven times married, and the question : " In the resurrection whose wife shall she be of the seven ? " the whole point of their argument lay in the tacit assumption of the dilemma that *either* the resurrection must be conceived of in the materialistic terms of the cruder popular eschatology, *or*, as they themselves held, that there could be no resurrection at all. To them our Lord replies: " Do ye not therefore err, because ye know not the Scriptures nor the power of God, for when they shall rise from the dead they neither marry nor are given in marriage, but are as the angels in heaven." " Ye know not the Scriptures," that is, ye interpret the words of prophets and apocalyptists in a crude materialistic sense ; " nor the power of God," that is, ye limit the possibilities of Divine action within those conditions which are familiar to your own experience ; " they are as the angels in heaven," that is, the nature of the resurrection life must be conceived of in spiritual terms. Accordingly the suggestion made above, that there is a *via media* between the cruder conceptions which traditional theology has inherited from Jewish eschatology, and the pure rationalism of many moderns, is merely a re-affirmation—hardly even in form of statement modernised—of our Lord's own explicit teaching on the matter.

Nor is it a valid objection to such a view to say, as is sometimes done, that it postulates an occurrence of an unprecedented kind, and is therefore as difficult on the score of " miracle " as the traditional theory.

In Nature the unprecedented is always occurring.

Upon that fact rests the possibility of evolution. The whole modern theory of the origin of species depends on the assumption that the parent of each new species is a variation or mutation of the type, which in relation either to the type, to the environment, or to both, is unprecedented, and recent biologists are emphasising the view that such mutations have been frequently of a striking and outstanding nature. The continuity of nature does not mean that the unprecedented does not occur, but that, when it does so, it appears as something organically related to what has preceded and not as a catastrophic intrusion. It is to the occurrence of an unprecedented event of this description that the probabilities and the evidence taken together appear to me to point.

Whether the Resurrection so conceived can properly be called a miracle is entirely a question of definition. In popular usage the word Miracle includes two conceptions, in themselves quite distinct and of very different value. First, a miracle is regarded as an act or event which, to adopt a current phrase, shows "God making manifest His moral governance in the physical world"; that is to say, it is an occurrence which, though from the point of view of God it may possibly be predetermined and in that sense can be regarded as in accordance with Law, is from the point of view of man, and as it stands related to the rest of our experience, a special and *ad hoc* manifestation or "intervention" of the Divine, for a definite end ethically determined.

The second element is the assumption that such Divine action occasionally, if not normally, takes the form of an interruption of the ordinary course of physical nature and that of a catastrophic kind. The scientific, metaphysical, and historical difficulties which arise if this element in the conception of miracle is insisted upon are too well known to be worth repeating.

Only the first of these elements—the belief in Divine

guidance and "intervention"—is really essential and
valuable in the popular conception of miracle, and this, I
would affirm, is essential to Religion. It may be
admitted that the evidence for it falls short of mathe-
matical demonstration, yet the view that the Universe is
not the result of, and governed by, blind forces acting in
accordance with rigid mechanical law, but rather of a
process guided by an overruling Providence, does rest
upon a reasonable basis of extended and verifiable experience and legitimate inference. I would mention only
the fact, no less stupendous because usually taken for
granted, that in the past the evolution of apparently blind
forces has led to Progress ; the reflections suggested
by the crises great and small in the history of nations ;
the evidence for "guidance" in the lives of individuals;
cases of answers to prayer ; and the less tangible
phenomena to which the term Religious Experience
is applied.

Miracles in this sense are occurring every day, but it
needs no pointing out that in these the Divine is seen
to manifest itself by using, if we may so speak, and not
by superseding, the ordinary working of nature. It may
be, as some philosophers maintain, that such manifestations, seen *sub specie aeternitatis*, are determined. Or
it may be, as I would myself hold, that they are to
some extent contingent, and act as a corrective to the
havoc wrought by the vagaries of the human will. In
which case it would seem as though the Divine " Personality " has in this respect an analogy to human personality in that its " freedom " operates by combining,
arranging, and directing, rather than in adding to or
subtracting from, the system of forces which make up
the normal working of nature ;—though of course the
analogy must not be pressed to the extent of conceiving
the Divine activity as being in a Deistic sense external
to nature.[1]

The Resurrection Appearances of our Lord, if con-

[1] Cf. also the remarks on Miracle in Essay IV. p. 167.

ceived in some such way as I have endeavoured to suggest, should then be regarded as a Divine intervention of this kind. There are some, I know, to whom such an interpretation of them seems lacking in reality and substance, but for myself I feel I am on firmer ground than if I were to rest all on a view of miracle which the lapse of time and the growth of knowledge seems ever to be making less secure, and which in the last resort appears to mean that God did things in Palestine nineteen hundred years ago which He will not or cannot do for us to-day, and that Christ was raised from the dead in a way that we shall not be.

Here, however, we are brought back to the point we started from. We set out to seek a sign. But the brief sketch given above makes it quite clear that the nature of the historical evidence is such that the empty tomb and the series of appearances—the sign which satisfied the Apostles—can, from the nature of the case, be no convincing sign to us. It *may* be that the old interpretation of the facts is right, and no one, I imagine, would abandon it without a pang, hallowed as it is by old associations and venerable tradition. But it can only be sustained, if at all, after a complex analysis of philosophical presuppositions, and after difficult and delicate discussions, critical and historical, which the plain man cannot follow, and where the experts are not agreed ; and to call a conclusion so reached " a sign " is only to mock that cry for patent proof we fain would gratify. Christian theology will never be more than an ineffective, purely defensive "apologetic," until it has squarely and candidly faced this fact.

But facts fairly faced soon lose their bitterness, *si crucem portas portabit te.* The sign which was given to them is and can be no convincing sign to us. But it does not follow that we are left without a sign at all, that is, without *anything* in the sphere of the visible

and material world which we can point to as a vindication of God's rule and of His Christ. To us another
sign is given, and that one which was not and could
not be given to the disciples nineteen hundred years
ago. Every century that passes makes the sign which
convinced them, to us more remote and less convincing;
every century that passes adds conviction to that other
sign which is given to us—I mean the vindication in
history of the claims He made.

The Jewish people, it was believed, had always stood
in a quite special relationship to God and had enjoyed
a unique revelation of His character and will, and the
long history of God's dealings with them, and incidentally through them with mankind in general, was
to reach its climax in the appearance of the Messiah.
Thus the Christ was, so to speak, the "last word" in
the dealings of God with man. Our Lord believed He
was the Christ—a remarkable belief for one obviously
sincere, disinterested, and sane to hold. He believed,
moreover, that His own death was the means appointed
for the accomplishment of His mission, and that after
this He would be vindicated in some complete and
startling way. This was an even more remarkable
belief, but it had one obvious merit. It admitted of
being put to the test of experiment. He put it to the
test—and the experiment did not fail.

THE VINDICATION—"VICISTI GALILAEE"

We have seen that though the force of isolated texts
may be impugned, though the influence of the beliefs
of His followers on the tradition of His sayings may
be fully allowed for, yet withal it is impossible for
candid criticism to doubt that He expected the consummation of the present course of this world to come
at least within the lifetime of those who heard Him.
No doubt, unlike some of the old prophets or apocalyptists, He gave no date. "Ye know not the day nor

the hour." "Of that day or that hour knoweth no man, no, not the angels which are in heaven, neither the Son, but the Father." Still, nineteen hundred years have passed and the end is not yet ; nor will be, so far as science can foresee, for uncounted years to come.

Then was the message, "the Kingdom is at hand," that message at once of judgment and of hope, an empty dream ? He rebuked those around Him who could prognosticate the weather but could not read the signs of the times. The hollowness and formalism of the established religion, the corruption and oppression of the ruling powers cried aloud, "And shall not God avenge His elect, who call day and night to Him, and He forbeareth ? I say unto you, right soon shall He avenge" (Luke xviii. 7). That judgment *did* fall. Forty years after these words were spoken His prophecy about the Temple was fulfilled that "not one stone should be left upon another," after a siege of which the horrors have no parallel in history. The special glory of Israel, the task of being a "light to lighten the Gentiles," was left to the little remnant that acknowledged Jesus. Not three and a half more centuries and the stupendous fabric of the Roman Empire, the "world" as it was called (Luke ii. 1), undermined by slow internal decay, came crashing down—and of all that magnificent civilisation only that survived which could shelter itself under the protection of the Christian name.[1] The judgment did fall.

He taught that the leaven which He brought was to leaven the whole lump. The process has been slow indeed, the lump is far larger than could have been contemplated in that age, yet it cannot be denied that the movement which He initiated, at a time when the highest civilisation the world had yet seen was consciously[2] decadent and despairing, has been the great

---

[1] This is really as true of the surviving Eastern Empire as of the West, since its inner coherence and stability were due almost entirely to the Church.

[2] The optimism reflected in the literature of the Augustan Age disappears with Tiberius.

ethical turning-point in the history of the race. And
that leaven is working still. Theologies and churches
may seem to totter, but never before in history has the
real spirit of Christianity had more influence on national
and social life. His Kingdom has not yet come, but
salvation is surely nearer now than when men first
believed.

But His claim went far beyond the prophecy of an
impending judgment and the preaching of a new
ethical message. " Ye shall see the Son of Man sitting
at the right hand of the Almighty,[1] and coming in the
clouds of Heaven." Granted that the words were
"quasi-symbolic," at least they are a confident assertion that the God and Father in whom He trusted
would signally vindicate Him and His cause—vindicate
Him not only in the eyes of a select and spiritually-
minded few, but also before the eyes of worldlings and
decriers—vindicate Him not only as a good man, or
a true prophet, but as that One to whose appearance
Prophet and Psalmist had looked forward, in whom
was to be consummated, as in its finest blossom, all the
previous history of Israel, as the spiritual if not also
the temporal Lord and Judge of humanity. The
claim was a tremendous one. Was this an empty
dream?

Shortly after the appearances which convinced His
disciples that He was still alive, there came upon them
an immense influx of spiritual power. They had been
men, they now were giants, and the secret of the
change in them was not merely that they believed the
Master *had* risen, but that He was *still and now* their
constant though unseen Companion. The lapse of
time, instead of weakening, increased the intensity of
this conviction, and all through the ages since a similar
conviction, or rather experience, has been the central

---

[1] τῆς δυνάμεως. It was common in Jewish, as indeed often in modern English
usage, to use synonyms for the name of God, *e.g.* "Heaven" (Mark xi. 30 and
Luke xv. 18), "The Blessed One" (Mark xiv. 61).

element in the lives of innumerable of His followers—
"to me to live is Christ." And, broadly speaking,
those who have felt this most strongly have in their
lives brought forth fruits consonant with the view that
the experience was no illusion. An intense mystical
consciousness of the presence of Christ is not universal
among Christians, or even among good Christians, and
from the nature of the case can only carry full conviction
to those who have themselves shared it strongly. Yet the
phenomenon is sufficiently widespread both in respect of
time and place and race to give it a reasonable claim to
the serious attention of the dispassionate observer.

But there remains a "sign" palpable and visible to
all, a sign unconvincing, indeed, to the "evil and
adulterous generation" whom no sign will convince,
but sufficient for the only class to whom when on earth
the Master cared to give a sign, those who are drawn
to His teaching but whose faith is weak.

To found an institution which shall outlive the
centuries, to create an influence which shall dominate
the future, to mould the mind and outlook of mankind,
to leave a name which posterity shall venerate with
wonder and admiration,—this has from the beginning
been the ambition of emperors, statesmen, and warriors
with nations and armies at their back to achieve their
aim ; it has been the ambition of thinkers and poets
with all the wisdom and culture of the ages at their
command. In the roll-call of fame are names like
Alexander, Caesar, Charlemagne, Napoleon. There
are names like Plato and Kant, Newton and Darwin,
Dante and Goethe, and on the history and the mind
of our race each of these has left a great and enduring
mark. They have left their mark ; their name and
their influence is still a power. But which of them
has done a work, has left an influence or a name like
the village Carpenter, unlettered and unarmed, who
dreamed that God would redeem the world through
Him, and died to make the dream come true ?

" All kings shall fall down before Him : all nations shall do Him service."

" For He shall deliver the poor when he crieth : the needy also, and him that hath no helper."

" He shall live, and unto Him shall be given of the gold of Arabia : prayer shall be made ever unto Him, and daily shall He be praised."

" His Name shall endure for ever ; His Name shall remain under the sun among the posterities : which shall be blessed through Him ; and all the heathen shall praise Him."

In ecstasy and hymn like this, Prophet and Poet had hailed the glorious Christ that was to come.

There stood a prisoner before the High Priest's throne, mocked, buffeted, His cause discredited, friends disillusioned and dispersed, Himself awaiting death in ignominy and torture.

" Art *thou* the Christ? " " I am," replied the Prisoner. " Blasphemy," pronounced the Priest. And History has judged between them.

IV

THE INTERPRETATION OF THE
CHRIST IN THE NEW TESTAMENT

BY

A. E. J. RAWLINSON

AND

R. G. PARSONS

NOTE.—For the final form of this essay Mr. Rawlinson is throughout responsible : but it is so largely indebted to notes and suggestions supplied by Mr. Parsons, especially in the first six sections, that it seemed best to describe it as a joint production.

SYNOPSIS

I. THE PRIMITIVE COMMUNITY.

I

The Church at Jerusalem : its theology the articulation of its experience. The earliest Christology to be sought in "Q" and in the opening chapters of Acts. Belief in the Resurrection and its significance for the first disciples. Messiahship of Jesus interpreted eschatologically. The note of their religious life is expectancy 151

II

The Spirit (i.) a pledge of the nearness of the Kingdom : but also (ii.) a *present* power in their lives. Inadequacy of what was in form a "theology of the future" to express the richness of Christian experience here and now 158

III

Relation of the primitive Church to Judaism. Baptism and the Eucharist as eschatological sacraments of the New Israel. Here also a "theology of the future" inadequate as the expression of present experience. Necessity for growth and expansion of thought : this only possible as the result of growth and expansion of the Church 161

II. THE WORK OF ST. STEPHEN.

St. Stephen, a Hellenist Jew, takes up the Hellenist attitude towards Law and Temple. In this he was essentially at one with our Lord, and like Him he is put to death for blasphemy. St. Stephen as the precursor of St. Paul . . . 164

III. THE CONVERSION OF ST. PAUL.

To St. Paul his conversion always a miracle. Modern theory of conversion suggests psychological explanation. The "religious" conception of miracle not destroyed by "scientific" explanation of the "miraculous" occurrence. Effects of the form of St. Paul's conversion on his Christology . . 166

IV. St. Paul's Early Preaching.   PAGE

St. Paul's early Gospel eschatological in form and substantially identical with that of the Twelve. His difference from
them was on the question not of the Messiah but of the Law.
His "Liberal" attitude towards the Law was determined by his
experience of the "free gift of God" in his conversion. St.
Paul as a thinker : he is not an exact or a consistent theologian,
and his mind is Jewish and not Greek   168

V. The Development of Paulinism.

The Cross the centre of St. Paul's preaching : he transforms
it from a stumbling-block to a Gospel : his efforts to explain
its significance :—
(a) The Servant of the Lord and the idea of Vicarious
Suffering   172
(b) The "Son of Man" conception, connoting pre-existence
in glory : the Cross to be explained as an act of voluntary self-
abasement determined by love, a love which was at once Christ's
and God's   173
(c) New life in Christ explained by doctrine of New Creation.
Christ as Second Adam. Hebraic conception of racial solidarity   176
Difficulties of St. Paul's theology of atonement arising from
static form of its expression, but he is not strictly consistent
here   177
Doctrines of faith, of life in the Spirit, and of mystical union   178
St. Paul as *doctor gentium* : his experience of missionary work
influences the form of his doctrine. Parallel between the
theology of St. Paul and that of the Mysteries. The Gentiles
accept Christianity as a superior kind of Mystery Religion.
One result of this an *ex opere operato* interpretation of the
Sacraments, which St. Paul corrects in 1 Corinthians. Inci-
dentally we are enabled to trace in his exposition of Eucharistic
doctrine a development of thought parallel to that which had
taken place with regard to Christology   .   .   .   180
Ethical character of St. Paul's doctrine as further exemplified
in his transvaluation of "spiritual gifts." The supremacy of
Love   186
Growing exaltation of the significance of the Christ in St.
Paul's thought. Knowledge "after the flesh" and "after the
Spirit".   187

VI. The Latest Stage of Paulinism.

The paradoxes of a static conception of redemption resolved
by the idea of development. Doctrine of the Purpose of God
for mankind through the Church : the *gradual* realisation or
fulfilment in human life of the "Christ that is to be".   .   189

VII. The Epistle to the Hebrews.

The author a Hellenist Jew of the school of Philo. His
conception of faith : and of Christ as (a) Pattern of faith,

(*b*) Author of Salvation, (*c*) Image of God. Practical purpose of
the Epistle. Contrast of the Two Covenants. Interpretation
of Christ in terms of priesthood and sacrifice derived from
Jewish Law. Necessity of a sympathetic understanding of
ancient idea of sacrifice. Hellenist criticism of animal sacrifices.
Interpretation of priesthood and sacrifice of Christ as their
fulfilment "within the veil." This conception underlies
Catholic eucharistic liturgies. The author interprets sacrifice
ethically   191

VIII. The Apocalypse.

The Apocalypse the work of a Christian prophet. Differs
from majority of Jewish apocalypses in not being pseudonymous.
Must be understood nevertheless in the light of the Jewish
Apocalyptic tradition.
The Christ conceived (*a*) as exalted to the throne of the Universe
and yet (*b*) as sharing in the trials and sufferings of His Church.
Visions of the World Struggle and of the End of the Age.
The symbolism of the book, which to-day appears fantastic,
was not so to contemporaries   198

IX. The Fourth Gospel and the First Johannine Epistle.

The Fourth Gospel anonymous but *prima facie* suggesting
authorship of John the son of Zebedee. The critical issue
still *sub judice*.
The book to be understood as a "spiritual Gospel," a
meditation on the life of Christ by a "man of the Spirit"   .   202
Yet the author does not regard his book as an allegory, but
claims that his Gospel is a Gospel of fact : he speaks from
experience the things which he has seen and known   .   .   203
Uncertain whether he had been an eye-witness of the
Ministry and Passion, or whether his narrative, historical in
intention, has the value of history in its details. The picture
is a picture of the Christ of history as interpreted by the
"Christ that speaketh in him" as he writes : in many cases it
is suggestive to translate sayings put into the mouth of Jesus
from the first person to the third. The revelation of Christ
through the Spirit in the Church a fuller revelation than was
possible in the days of His flesh   205
The Gospel is substantially Jewish and not Greek : but its
Hebraism is transmuted and coloured by a Greek environment   207
The author's doctrine of the glory of suffering. The
earthly life of Jesus becomes in the light of this doctrine itself
a revelation of the divine Glory, and men ought to have
recognized it   208
The essence of the revelation of God in Christ is Love.
The Evangelist here at one with St. Paul.
Concluding remarks on New Testament Christology   .   209

IV

THE INTERPRETATION OF THE CHRIST
IN THE NEW TESTAMENT

Τὰ πάντα καὶ ἐν πᾶσι Χριστός.
COL. iii. 11.

I. THE PRIMITIVE COMMUNITY

I

THE conclusion of the story of Jesus in the Gospels is the introduction to the history of the Christian Church. We may otherwise express the same truth by saying that the immediate result of the Crucifixion and Resurrection was the formation of a new Jewish sect. Jesus had been put to death by the authorities ; but His followers within a day or two affirmed that He was alive. His tomb, they asserted, had been found empty ; but more than that, they had seen Him. They waited in Jerusalem for what further might happen.

The picture set before us in the opening chapters of the Book of the Acts is the picture of a little group of men and a few women, waiting for a promised baptism with a " Holy Spirit."[1] Within a little while, as the outcome of events represented for us by the story of Pentecost, the promise is fulfilled. The

---

[1] It was a received doctrine of the later Judaism that the coming of the Messianic Age would be heralded by an outpouring of the Spirit.

"Spirit" which had wrought in Jesus came upon the disciples and wrought in them. An overmastering inward Power laid hold of them and transformed them. Those who in the hour of Calvary had been a rout of terror-stricken fugitives now stand forth as the pillar-Apostles of the infant Church. They are found witnessing boldly in the name of Jesus.

It is not the purpose of the present essay to follow out in detail the external history of the early Christian community. Our task is rather to ask what were their distinguishing beliefs, to trace the process by which they came to develop their thoughts about their Master, and to show how thoughts and beliefs alike sprang out of their experience. It is of the last importance to recognize that the development which is traceable in early Christian ideas about Christ was not the product of abstract speculation in the study. It was something beaten out by the stress of immediate controversial and apologetic necessities : even more, it was something determined by the disciples' own inherent need of giving progressively less inadequate expression to the dominating fact of Christ and the transforming experience of His Spirit in their lives.

If we ask what was the Christology of the earliest Christian community we must find it in the document called "Q," and in the speeches in the earlier part of Acts. "Jesus of Nazareth, a man approved of God unto you by mighty works and wonders and signs, which God did by Him in the midst of you, even as ye yourselves know : Him being delivered up by the determinate counsel and foreknowledge of God, ye by the hand of men without the Law did crucify and slay : whom God raised up, having loosed the pangs of death. . . . Let all the house of Israel, therefore, know assuredly, that God hath made Him both Lord and Christ, this Jesus whom ye crucified." Every one in the Jerusalem of that day was familiar with the career of Jesus—His preaching, His mighty works, His astounding claims. And every one knew, too, that He had been crucified. It was of Him—this well-known, ill-starred Prophet and Healer—that these men declared that He and none other was God's Anointed, the Christ who should come. How (we are constrained to ask) did they come by so amazing, and, as it seemed to contemporaries, so blasphemous a conviction? The documents themselves have only one answer to give, namely, the Resurrection and the coming of the Spirit. It was by these and by these alone that the disciples were finally convinced that Jesus was verily and indeed the Christ.

The Lord Himself, it will be remembered, had interpreted His mission in terms of the Jewish doctrine of Messiahship or Christhood. The disciples in the course of their association with Him had been led to recognize Him in that capacity, or rather, they had recognized in Him One who, in the counsels of God, was destined to be manifested as Messiah hereafter. But all this for them was shattered by the Cross; and the numbing effects of that disaster nothing short of the Resurrection could have availed to undo. It is true, indeed, that the appeal of our Lord's personality and the impression of His life and teaching upon the disciples' minds had been such, that whatever happened they could never be as though they had not known Him. It is true, again, and most important, that " if there had been in the disciples the least trace of a doubt as to the purity of Jesus—if they had marked in Him but a breath of ambition, of self-seeking, of irreligion— the Easter experiences would not have had the power to overcome this impression, and to keep the disciples true to Jesus through persecution and death. The purity and truth of Jesus had become for them so self-evident that nowhere in the New Testament writings is the smallest attempt made to vindicate or to prove His guiltlessness. This was the source of their power to overcome the scandal of the Cross. However important the appearances were for the first settlement of their faith, the firm anchorage of—as we say—an 'ethical' conviction was rendered possible only by the fact that the pure and sublime Image of Jesus exercised a lasting power over the disciples' souls and banished every doubt."[1] The disciples were, indeed, convinced that the Lord's life on earth had manifested from first to last a flawless perfection of moral beauty, truth, and goodness, which the negative term "sinlessness" fails utterly to express.[2] Nevertheless by itself such a conviction could but have served to deepen the gloom of Calvary and to render more heartbreaking and poignant the shattering of all their hopes. To-day it is possible that men may be found who are content to see in the Cross simply the sublimest climax of all tragedy, and who have no wish to look beyond. The first disciples of Jesus were simple peasant folk who were incapable of so essentially literary a detachment : to them the Cross even as viewed in the light of Easter remained something of a scandal—until by the Pauline paradox it was transformed from a gibbet into a throne.

The problem of the Resurrection, considered as an event in history, is discussed in the preceding essay.[3] We are here concerned rather with the disciples' faith in it. That faith for them certainly involved not merely the sight of the Risen Lord, but also the knowledge of the empty tomb. No doubt to the minds of men to-day this emptiness of the tomb is attended by serious difficulties either way : orthodox explanations of it suggest metaphysical difficulties and unorthodox explanations historical ones. But in the case of the disciples it was certainly a providential circumstance which turned their thoughts away from a dead body and a grave and centred them upon a living Person exalted at God's right hand. Had they known

---

[1] Johannes Weiss, *Christus.*   [2] Cf. p. 305 (*note*).   [3] Cf. pp. 127 *sqq.*

or believed that the dead body of the Lord was lying
somewhere in Jerusalem " seeing corruption," the
Pentecostal proclamation would have had a completely
different ring. Explanations would have been demanded
and devised for the existence of the mortal remains.
In all probability we should have heard either of the
veneration or of the desecration of the sacred relics.
But that very emptiness of the tomb, which has
rendered it perhaps unduly prominent in recent
apologetic, caused it in the earliest days to pass quite
into the background. The Apostles had something
far more positive and overwhelming to which to bear
witness in the actuality of the Living Lord and the
present power of the Spirit.

If we ask what precisely for the Apostles was the
significance of the Resurrection, we discover that this
was not for them at first what it subsequently became
for a St. Paul or a St. John—the overcoming of death
by life. They did not as yet speak of Jesus as the
firstborn from the dead who has opened unto us the gate
of everlasting life. Rather to them the Resurrection
was the *vindication* of their Master and the justification
of His claims. God by raising Jesus from the dead
had openly declared Him to be His Chosen, had
exalted Him to His own right hand in heaven, thereby
making Him " both Lord and Christ." The Resurrection was emphatically not regarded as a " return into
this life " ; it was rather a necessary means to the
Ascension and Glorification of Jesus and to His Advent
as Messiah.

According to this earliest thought, the Lord in the
days of His earthly ministry had not as yet become
in the full sense " Messiah." The document which
New Testament critics have agreed to call " Q "—the
source containing " sayings of Jesus " which underlies
portions of our first and third Gospels—regards Him,
indeed, as having been *designated* Messiah and as having
received the " anointing " of the Spirit at His baptism ;

and of course the significance of His sayings as of His life, which made it worth while to compile either a collection of the former or a narrative of the latter, lay in the fact that they were the life and sayings of Him who was the Messiah, and who was shortly to be revealed in that capacity. It remains true, however, that the Messiahship during the earthly ministry was looked upon as something veiled or concealed : it was a secret about the future. St. Peter in speaking of his Master's earthly ministry and crucifixion uses such titles as " the Holy and Righteous One," " the Prophet like unto Moses," the " Servant," that is, the " Servant of the Lord " ; [1] it is now, as the result of His Resurrection and Exaltation, that He enters upon His full Messianic dignity : and although for the present " until the times of restoration of all things " the heaven must receive Him, He is expected shortly to be manifested as " the Judge of quick and dead " to inaugurate the Messianic Age.

The dominant note, therefore, in the religious life of this earliest band of Christian disciples was that of expectancy. They were looking for the visible return of their Lord in triumph on the clouds of heaven, and the great event was daily and hourly awaited. What was necessary in the meanwhile was that men should repent and be baptized and believe the Good News that the Messiah was at hand, and that He was none other than Jesus.

No doubt in considering the *form* of this eschatological hope which so manifestly held the central place in the thoughts and beliefs of the earliest disciples, we ought to allow something for a certain crudeness of mind in them and a defect of spiritual perception which persistently interpreted the sayings of the Lord in a sense more crass and materialistic than that which they had originally been intended to bear. It is possible that a tendency of this kind has influenced the form

[1] Acts iii. 13, 26. Παῖς is the Septuagint rendering of " Servant " in Isaiah liii.

of those sayings as they have been reported in the Gospels.[1] So, again, the apologetic need of explaining away the scandal of the Cross in controversy with Jewish opponents might easily operate in the same direction. To the difficulty " Why was the Messiah crucified ? " the disciples made answer that in the first place it was necessary that He should fulfil the prophecy of the Suffering Servant in Isaiah liii., but that, secondly, the time was at hand when every eye should see Him and they also which pierced Him should then acknowledge Him.

Nevertheless, whatever weight may rightly attach to either or both these considerations, they are quite insufficient in themselves to account for an emphasis and a mode of thought which was surely no invention of disciples, but in essentials goes back—as is now beginning to be generally recognized by scholars—to the teaching of the Lord Himself. It has been pointed out in the preceding essay[2] that it is one of the great gains of recent criticism that we are now enabled to see the Christology of the Twelve as organically continuous with that of our Lord and the Christology of St. Paul as organically continuous with that of the Twelve. Christianity from first to last—in its origin quite as much as in its developments—appears as a doctrine about the Messiah, never as an ethical or religious code to which the Person of the Founder is irrelevant.[3] And yet when this has been said we must go on to add that the Christology—the Messianic doctrine—was not in itself new, any more than was the eschatological hope of the Kingdom. What was new was the identification of the Messiah with Jesus, and the proclamation of the Kingdom as immediately at hand. The assertion of the disciples was not so much that " Jesus is the

[1] See *Oxford Studies in the Synoptic Problem*, Appendix, pp. 425-436.
[2] Cf. p. 77.
[3] Had the theories of certain modern theologians been well-grounded, should we not have expected the early disciples to be known at Antioch not as *Christians* but rather as *Jesuits* ?

Messiah," but rather, "The Messiah is this Jesus, and *therefore* the Kingdom cannot be long delayed."[1]

II

Of this nearness and immediacy of the Kingdom they found yet a further pledge in their consciousness of possession by the Spirit. The events of the Day of Pentecost are interpreted by St. Peter in terms of the prophecy of Joel (whose book has been justly described as "an important and much-neglected apocalyptic work"), according to which a notable outpouring of the Holy Spirit was destined to herald the near approach of the "great and terrible Day of the Lord," that is to say, the Day of Messianic Judgment with which the Kingdom would begin. The Spirit accordingly is consistently spoken of in the New Testament as the pledge or instalment (ἀρραβών), which guarantees the fulness of the future Kingdom as shortly to appear.

Nevertheless, although the Spirit thus possessed for the *thought* of the disciples a specifically eschatological significance, it was in their actual *experience* far more than a mere earnest of the future. It was a present Reality which dominated and possessed them, a transforming Presence by which they were moulded and inspired. Outwardly it was manifested in ecstatic utterances, in the enthusiasm of prophesyings, in healings and works of power. Inwardly it wrought in them as a fountain of love and joy and peace, a certainty of salvation so glad and strong and free that it could face rulers and kings, suffering and persecution and death, and "count all things but loss for the excellency of the knowledge of Christ Jesus" their Lord.

Herein, surely, lay the secret of their attraction and of their power. It was not the *thought* of the disciples, not their Messianic doctrine as such, which

---

[1] It has been pointed out by Professor Lake that in Acts xviii. 5, 28, the words εἶναι τὸν Χριστὸν Ἰησοῦν ought to be translated "that the Messiah was Jesus," and not (as in A.V. and R.V.) "that Jesus was the Christ."

won over those to whom they preached and caused souls to be added to the Church. It was this magnificent, irresistible certainty in them, this triumphant consciousness—hardly as yet articulated into a doctrine —that in Jesus, God, according to His promise, *had* visited and redeemed His people : [1] it was the reappearance in their lives of the lineaments of the self-same spirit of love and sacrifice which had wrought in Christ, whereby men were constrained to " take knowledge of them that they had been with Jesus."

The Spirit at work in them was the Spirit of Jesus—recognizably and manifestly such, even to the eyes of those without. St. Paul, when, years afterwards, he had come to know the Christian Spirit both from intercourse with others and from experience of its working in himself, set himself in one of the epistles which have come down to us to sketch the type of character in which the Spirit should bear fruit. " Love, joy, peace, long-suffering, gentleness, goodness, faith, meekness, temperance "—we recognize the well-known lines of the picture in the Gospels. In like manner the familiar thirteenth chapter of 1 Corinthians—the Apostle's lyrical ode to Charity— is virtually an inspired portrait of that Master whom in the flesh it is probable that St. Paul had never seen.

And if the Spirit was the Spirit of Jesus, the Spirit of Jesus was the Spirit of God. This new life of the Spirit which possessed them was something veritably and indeed Divine. It was God made manifest in the flesh. It was the disclosure of God's nature as an eternal passion and energy of love. In the love of God shed abroad and made known through the grace of the Lord Jesus Christ, and realized in human hearts and lives through participation in the Spirit bestowed upon believers,[2] we find ourselves already

---

[1] Cf. Essay II. p. 42.

[2] Cf. 2 Cor. xiii. 14, " The grace of the Lord Jesus Christ and the love of God and the communion of the Holy Ghost."

in the presence of all the elements of that Divine self-disclosure which later Trinitarian theology was elaborated to express.

As the intellectual expression of a religious experience so rich and vivid and actual in its contents as this, the Christology of the earliest preaching, already outlined, was utterly inadequate. The Person of Jesus was too great to be fully expressed in terms of Messiahship and coming Kingdom, and soon burst through the categories of that early faith. It has been recently pointed out with truth as a fact full of significance that every one of the terms in which men have tried to set forth the Person and work of Jesus—Messiah, Son of Man, Son of God, Sacrifice, Passover, Lamb of God, Logos [1]—so far from making Jesus more intelligible to us than He is without them, needs interpretation to-day. "These are the accounts that men have given of Jesus Christ, and He has been more than they. He has transcended, He has gone through one picture of Him and another, one description and another : He has been more, far more, than any of these conceptions, taken by themselves or taken together, have been able to represent. They are inadequate, and there is He, the great fact." [2]

In the movement of expansion which resulted in the formation of a larger Christology the first impulse was given by St. Stephen, and by the great disciple of St. Stephen—Saul of Tarsus. In order, however, to make clear the precise significance of the work of these men, it is necessary to revert to the subject of the original Christian Community, and to consider the relation in which they conceived themselves to stand towards the Judaism of their upbringing and environment.

---

[1] "No one sings 'How sweet the name of Logos sounds'" (Rendel Harris, quoted by Glover in *The Death of Christ*).

[2] T. R. Glover, *The Death of Christ*, an address delivered at a Conference of the Student Christian Movement, Liverpool, 1912, and printed in *Christ and Human Need.*

III

To the original group of disciples it did not occur —indeed, it is hardly too much to say that to no body of devout Jews could it ever possibly have occurred— to regard themselves as adherents of a new religion, or as constituting a new Church other than that of the ancient Commonwealth of Israel. Our Lord, it is true, is reported to have spoken on one occasion of "His Church," [1] as something destined to be founded on the rock of St. Peter : but it is clearly in His capacity as Messiah—whether present or future —that He utters the words. The Church of the Messiah—the Messianic Congregation—was not a *new* Church to be distinguished from the old : it was *the* Church, the inheritance of all faithful Israelites, the same Church which (in St. Stephen's phrase) had been "in the wilderness," which had lived through all the experiences and vicissitudes of Israel's history, and which was now most truly represented by those who, recognizing in Jesus the true Messiah, awaited in patience and hope the coming of His Kingdom.

Nevertheless, the Messiah when He came would not find the true Israel co-extensive with Israel after the flesh : the Kingdom would be inaugurated by a Judgment. There would be a separation of wheat from chaff, a "thorough purging" (as John the Baptizer had put it) of the floor. This had ever been the message of prophecy—"*Woe* unto you that desire the Day of the Lord." It is in view of this expected visitation in judgment—the "wrath to come"—that we are to understand the urgency of the Apostolic preaching of Repentance and of Baptism. It was not enough, after all, simply to be a Jew : membership

---

[1] "St. Matthew" alone attests this saying, but it may well be authentic. The confident assumption of many critical writers that our Lord "could not" have used the phrase "My Church," appears to be determined mainly by anti-ecclesiastical prejudice.

of the chosen people would not necessarily of itself ensure salvation. What was all-important was membership in the "remnant" who would be able to stand in the day of Messiah's Judgment, and to whom would be given an inheritance in Messiah's Kingdom.

It is from this point of view in all probability that we must understand the original significance of sacraments, and the stress which from the first appears to have been laid upon them. Baptism—the rite of admission into the immediate circle of the adherents of the Messiah—was at once a token of repentance and a pledge of the remission of sins. It "sealed" those who received it as the destined inheritors of the Messianic salvation. The laying on of hands, which formed the complement of baptism, was the reception of the baptized into the fellowship of believers, with prayer that they might receive "the earnest of the Spirit." The Eucharist in like manner was probably regarded as an "earnest" of the Messianic Banquet,— that "eating and drinking in the Kingdom of Heaven" which was an element in the traditional apocalyptic hope.[1]

But just as in the case of the doctrine of our Lord's Person, so also with the theory of the Sacraments, the original thought-forms by which they were interpreted, with their predominating emphasis upon the future, proved inadequate to express the fulness and richness of spiritual experience in the present. In actual experience Baptism, with the laying on of hands which normally accompanied it, was discovered to involve a break with the past and a transforming access of spiritual life and power which made of it a veritable "new birth." In actual experience the Eucharist was

[1] If we may trust in this particular the record in the Gospels, this thought seems to have been in our Lord's own mind at the Last Supper, in association, however, with ideas derived from the institution of sacrifice, and a mystical identification of Himself with the Victim whose offered life should inaugurate a "New Covenant" (cf. Jeremiah xxxi. 31) in His "Blood," which eventually suggested, as we shall see, an interpretation of the Eucharist in sacrificial terms.

discovered to involve a present consciousness of realized communion with the Lord, a present gladness, a gift of spiritual strength and refreshment ever renewed, which broke through and transcended the purely eschatological aspect of it as an earnest of the future Feast. In the Breaking of the Bread the Presence of the Risen Lord was made known to the disciples as a fact of the spiritual order here and now : and the actuality and vividness of Eucharistic experience demanded a more adequate Eucharistic theology.

In the development of New Testament thought the two processes of reinterpretation at which we have hinted went on side by side and reacted upon each other : the fuller sacramental doctrine at once suggested, and was suggested by, the larger Christology. Neither process can profitably be studied in isolation, but neither could really begin so long as Christianity continued to exist merely as a movement within the closed circle of orthodox Judaism. The larger theology required for its development the freer atmosphere of Liberal Judaism as it existed outside Palestine in the synagogues of the Dispersion, and Liberal Judaism in its turn opened the door to the still wider world of Graeco-Roman civilization and its Hellenistic culture.

Upon the existence and the nature of Liberal Judaism in the period immediately antecedent to the coming of our Lord the researches of modern scholars have thrown considerable light. We learn by implication from a passage of Philo[1] that in the cities of the Dispersion in his day you might meet with Jews who not only—with Philo himself—saw a symbolical hidden meaning in the institutions and ceremonial of the Law, but who even maintained that the hidden meaning was the only valid meaning, and abandoned the literal

---

[1] *De Migratione Abrahami*, quoted by Lake, *Earlier Epistles of St. Paul*, p. 24. Philo was an Alexandrian Jew of high family, born probably about 20–10 B.C. His extensive writings are the classical expression of the Liberal Jewish school of thought which allegorized the Old Testament and cherished as its ideal the fusion of Judaism with what was best in Greek philosophy.

observance of Judaism, in so far as it was a ritual and ceremonial system, as unnecessary and burdensome. Extremists of this type were doubtless comparatively few, but there were many who, while maintaining the literal observances as binding upon Jews by birth, readily waived their necessity in the case of Gentiles, and encouraged the growth of a class of "God-fearers" or Gentile adherents of the synagogue who, though not actually circumcized, accepted monotheism and endeavoured to fulfil the "weightier matters" of the moral as distinct from the ceremonial law. It was in fact inevitable that in the case of Jews domiciled outside Palestine the ritual law and the ideal of the Temple worship and sacrifices, however important in theory, should in practice fall more or less into the background. By sheer force of circumstances the perspective was wholly different with regard to these things according as one lived in Jerusalem under the actual shadow of the Temple, or remote from Palestine in one of the Greek-speaking cities of the Empire.

II. The Work of St. Stephen

Bearing these points in mind we can understand the significance of the work of St. Stephen. Himself a Hellenist Jew, as his name suggests, he came to combine the Hellenist attitude towards the Temple and the ceremonial law with the Messianic hopes and ideals of the early Christian disciples, with the result that the whole balance of emphasis in the Christian preaching was profoundly modified. Our Lord Himself, it will be remembered, had been accused of undermining the Law, and had foretold the destruction of the Temple. It was by outspoken utterances about Law and Temple that the hostility against Him which culminated in the Crucifixion had been primarily aroused. It was not, indeed, that our Lord was fundamentally opposed to these things : He claimed not to destroy the Law but to fulfil it, and that He venerated the true ideal of the Temple is made evident by His cleansing of it. He had, however, set the spirit of the Law above its letter, and opposed the traditions of men : and He had looked for the dawning of the new supernatural order which would render the Temple unnecessary. His original followers proved incapable of entering into His deepest mind upon these subjects. As devout Jews waiting for the Kingdom they clung to the ideals of Pharisaic righteousness and were zealous in the observance of the Law.

To the Hellenist Stephen, on the other hand, Temple and Law were not merely transitory but unessential : too much reverence for them was indeed almost wrong, so soon were they to be swept away at the glorious appearing of the Messiah.[1] As the great deeds of God in old time in His dealings with the Patriarchs and Moses had been done independently of the Temple and its worship, so would it be now in the New Age that was on the point of dawning. We can understand how it came about that such teaching aroused opposition, and that the result was the same in St. Stephen's case as in his Master's : another death for blasphemy ensued. Nevertheless a great step forward had been taken. The religion of Jesus, thanks to Stephen, began to emerge clearly as a system opposed to institutional Judaism : and moreover Saul of Tarsus, as he kept the clothes of them that stoned Stephen, had marked how one in whom the Spirit of Jesus wrought could die. Our next task, accordingly, is to follow out the results for Christian thought of the conversion of St. Paul.

[1] Cf. the charge brought against Stephen—"This man ceaseth not to speak words against this holy place, and the law " (Acts vi. 13).

III. The Conversion of St. Paul

St. Paul regarded his conversion as miraculous. To his consciousness it presented itself from first to last as an event which burst in upon him in spite of himself : it was against his own will that he had been taken captive, at a time when he was kicking against the pricks. By a free gift God had been pleased to reveal His Son in him ; that was enough.

No doubt it is possible for us to-day to see predetermining psychological causes at work in him by which the way was in all probability subconsciously prepared. A Pharisee of Pharisees by education and conviction, a man of intense piety and zeal for " the customs which Moses delivered," a patriot ardently longing for " the hope of the promise of God made to the fathers," he had been unspeakably shocked by the contention of the Nazarenes that the Messiah was to be identified with the crucified Jesus. He embarked with enthusiasm upon the task of persecution and repression, yet found himself, as we must needs think, increasingly abashed and perturbed by the bearing of the Christians in their hour of trial. The witness of Stephen and others could not have been without its effect, and the contrast between the glad confidence of Christians in the possession of the Spirit, and his own restless conscience and sense of spiritual dissatisfaction (as he describes it in the seventh chapter of Romans) could not but have suggested, were it only subconsciously, a lurking doubt whether it might not be that these people were right after all. Obviously we have here all the conditions which—given favourable circumstances—might be expected to lead to one of those " sudden " conversions of which religious history affords numerous examples. The vision of the Christ on the Damascus road, for all its apparent " objectivity," might quite well turn out to be more or less explicable along psychological lines, as a product

of auto-suggestion induced by the inner conflict of
Saul's spirit. Such a view of the matter has a
plausibility in his case which does not attach to
similar explanations of the appearances of the Risen
Master to the original Apostles. The fact remains
none the less that to St. Paul's own mind his conversion
was an act direct from God—a miracle; and this fact
is of fundamental importance if we are to understand
the origin and growth of his Christology.

It may be remarked in passing, that it is high time
that a protest was made against the prevalent notion
that we are not to see the work of God in the processes
of the human mind, such as go to bring about a great
spiritual crisis. God is not a God of disorder—the
words are St. Paul's own—and the laws which govern
human thought and affection and work themselves out
in character are just as much God's laws as are the
laws by which the flowers grow or the stars move in
their courses. The recognition of predetermining
psychological causes as operative in St. Paul's conversion
does not make that conversion, when it came, any the
less real or remarkable, or (for the matter of that) any
the less miraculous. A miracle, in any sense in which
the term is defensible, does not mean, as we are too
often apt to suppose that it means, a sudden and
unexpected jerk, as it were, of the Almighty hand that
controls the machinery of the universe. The best
definition of a miracle is that it is something which
when we are confronted by it compels us to say, " This
is the Lord's doing, and it is marvellous in our eyes " :
it is no less marvellous if after our first sense of wonder
has calmed down we are enabled to see a little further
into the divinely-ordered process by which the event
was brought about. St. Paul's conversion was the
Lord's doing : and it is marvellous in our eyes, as it
was in his.[1]

In any case, whatever the account which we may

[1] See further on the subject of miracles, Essay III. pp. 138 sqq. and Essay V. p. 259.

give of the vision which came to St. Paul, to St. Paul's own consciousness it presented itself as something wholly objective. He had *seen* the risen Christ—seen Him as truly and objectively as any of the original Apostles—revealed in the blinding radiance of heaven. "He appeared to Cephas ; then to the Twelve ; then . . . to above five hundred brethren at once . . . last of all . . . He appeared to me also." True, the essence of the revelation was inward : the light that shone round about him above the light of the sun and that blinded his natural eyes would not have converted him, were it not for the light that broke inwardly upon his soul, the overwhelming realisation which forced itself upon him that the voice of Jesus was one with the voice of conscience and the words of Jesus were the words of the Spirit of God. But the fact that he believed himself to have actually *seen* the risen Lord as a glorified heavenly Man was not without its influence on the form of his Christological thinking. In common with Peter and James and the others who were Apostles before him, St. Paul believed our Lord to be the Messiah, not because of the excellency of His teaching and the sublimity of His character while He lived as man upon the earth, but because he had seen Him manifested alive after His Passion, and manifested in glory. It was the Saviour, risen and glorified, whom Paul worshipped and Paul preached, the Son of Man who had apprehended him on the Damascus road, who had laid hold of him and made him henceforward His slave.

IV. St. Paul's Early Preaching

If we ask what was the Gospel which Paul preached we shall find that it did not differ essentially either in substance or in form from that proclaimed by the original disciples. It was the Gospel of the coming Kingdom, the hope of the glorious appearing of the Son of Man from heaven. How thoroughly "eschatological" was the earlier Paulinism is plain from the Thessalonian Epistles : the suggestion that "the Day of the Lord has set in," or "that we are already living in the Day of the Lord," is emphatically repudiated,[1] and the thought of the Apostle moves within the received lines of Jewish Apocalyptic, from which the doctrine of the "signs of the end" and the anticipated manifestation of the Antichrist or "man of Sin" is borrowed. The account in the second chapter of Galatians of St. Paul's colloquy "after fourteen years" with "them who were of repute" is a further proof of the substantial identity of his preaching with that of the original Twelve. There was, however, a difference. St. Paul in the days before his conversion had as an orthodox Jew lived "after the straitest sect" : he had taken his stand upon the exclusive Covenant, the promise made to Abraham, and had sought to attain to salvation "by works of the Law." One result of his conversion was a violent reaction from all this. He passed over at a bound to the extreme Liberal camp of Judaism, which minimized the significance of law and temple and literal observance, regarded Gentiles as admissible to the covenant of Israel "after the Spirit," and preached a doctrine of salvation by faith.[2]

In this respect he appears as the follower of St. Stephen rather than of the Twelve ; but his changed attitude towards the Law was not simply a doctrine taken over upon Stephen's authority. "For I make known to you, brethren, as touching the gospel which was preached by me, that it is not after man. For neither did I receive it from man, nor was I taught

---

[1] 2 Thess. ii. 2. Apparently "sayings" or "letters" claiming St. Paul's authority had been circulated to this effect (ὡς ἐνέστηκεν ἡ ἡμέρα τοῦ Κυρίου). The word ἐνέστηκεν does not mean either "is past" or "is imminent" but "is present." (See Lake, *op. cit.* p. 94.)

[2] It is an interesting fact that the question whether Abraham was justified by faith or by works was not new, but had already been debated in Judaism prior to the rise of Christianity. Gen. xv. 6, and Hab. ii. 4, were already in all probability recognized "proof-texts" upon the Liberal side before they were quoted by St. Paul.

it, but by revelation of Jesus Christ." In other words St. Paul's teaching in this as in other matters flowed from, and was determined by, his own immediate personal experience. He had tried and found wanting the method of salvation by meticulous legal observance : it had brought him only a growing consciousness of sin, of failure to fulfil the ideal. As the result of his new-found relation to the Crucified all was changed. Instead of the burden of the outraged law and its terrors, there was a new joy and deliverance. The " free gift of God " which he had experienced in Christ Jesus had brought with it peace in the present and strength and hope for the future, a veritable resurrection of his soul from spiritual death.

When all is said, it is in his witness to this experience that the kernel of St. Paul's message is to be found. It is here that we discover most profoundly his significance for the spiritual life of humanity. The eschatological gospel, the hope of the near approach of the Kingdom, which is prominent in his early preaching, is never indeed discarded ; allusions to it are to be found even in his latest epistles, and we need not remind ourselves that, *in a transmuted form*, that which we know as the " Advent Hope " is an integral element of permanent value in the Christian consciousness of to-day. But the present experience in himself and others of redemption from the power of sin was from the first a central and dominating element in St. Paul's witness ; and the doctrines by which he endeavoured to give intelligible expression to it are his most distinctive contribution to Christian thought about Christ.

St. Paul was one of the world's great thinkers, but he was in no sense what we should now call an exact theologian. His thought was continually living and growing : and it was expressed, moreover, not in the precise and formal categories of abstract philosophy, but in the pictorial imagery and concrete symbolism of Hebrew Scripture and Rabbinic tradition. Some acquaintance with the leading philosophical conceptions of Stoicism and such other Greek systems as were most in vogue in the pagan world of his day it is possible that he may have possessed ; but his mind never moved easily in Greek channels, and he remains "an Hebrew of Hebrews" to the end. These considerations must be borne in mind in approaching the study of his doctrine. We must not expect to be able to fit together everything which we find in him into a single coherent and logical system. For one thing, he has nowhere left us a formal exposition of his teaching—we have to infer its main outlines as best we may from casual allusions in his letters and from discussions of particular points which happened to have been misunderstood or controverted. But even apart from this it is probable that his doctrine did not exist in the form of a completed or rigid system in the Apostle's own mind. We may nevertheless discern with sufficient clearness the main lines along which his thought developed.

V. The Development of Paulinism

We have already seen that to St. Paul the compelling fact of spiritual experience for which expression and explanation must be found was the consciousness of salvation through Christ and deliverance from the yoke of the law. In the effort to give an account of it his thoughts concentrated themselves instinctively on that which to him had been the greatest paradox and stumbling-block—the Crucifixion. For the first disciples the death of their Master had been almost forgotten in the wonder of its reversal.[1] St. Peter, for instance, according to the account given in Acts of his discourse on the Day of Pentecost, was content simply

---

[1] This statement is based upon the evidence of the early chapters of Acts. The occurrence however, of the words "how that Christ died *for our sins* according to the Scriptures," in St. Paul's account of the primitive tradition (1 Cor. xv. 1 *sqq.*) may possibly be held to justify the view that the antithesis between his doctrine and that of the Twelve on this point was less sharp than we have represented it as being.

to refer to it in passing as a crime of the Jews which
God had foreseen, and would forgive if they now
repented. St. Stephen in like manner regards it merely
as yet another instance of the Jews' wilful rejection of
God's messengers. But Saul, the Pharisee, had been
among those who had approved of the death of Stephen,
and *a fortiori*, therefore, of the death of Stephen's
Master. For him the Crucifixion stood out with awful
vividness as the great and central mystery in the life
and character of Him whom he had been so strangely
brought to acknowledge as the Christ. He could not
be satisfied with the view that it had merely been permitted by God in order to give Him an opportunity to
show His power and vindicate His Christ. Somehow,
he felt, in the death of the Lord there must be discoverable a vast positive significance ; bound up in some
manner with the Cross of Jesus was the secret of His
saving power. He looked for light to break upon its
mystery ; and when the light for him had broken, we
find him preaching the "word of the Cross" with ever
increasing emphasis. Here, in fact, was the very core
and centre of his message. "God forbid," he cries,
"that I should glory, save in the Cross" ; and again,
"We proclaim a Messiah on a Cross, to Jews a scandal,
and to Gentiles an absurdity, but to those who are
called, both Jews and Greeks, a Messiah who is God's
power and God's wisdom."

What were the conceptions which enabled St. Paul
thus to interpret the Cross no longer as a stumbling-
block but as a Gospel? The first Christians had already,
in all probability, quoted the 53rd chapter of Isaiah
as a Scriptural justification of the idea of a suffering
Messiah. The same idea, moreover, based upon the
same passage of Scripture, seems to have formed part of
our Lord's own conception of His mission.[1] "Thus it
behoved the Messiah to suffer, and to enter into His
glory." We cannot doubt that St. Paul had deeply

[1] Cf. Essay III. p. 124.

pondered the line of thought thus suggested. "He hath borne our griefs," the prophet had written, "and carried our sorrows . . . The Lord hath laid on Him the iniquity of us all." St. Paul has the same thought —"Him Who knew no sin " God " made to be sin on our behalf." Christ " became a curse on our account," and thereby " redeemed us from the curse of the law " ; God " delivered him up " (*i.e.* to death) " for us all." It is not perhaps, strictly speaking, true that St. Paul here preaches a doctrine of vicarious punishment, but undoubtedly he preaches—what is indeed clearly implied not only in his own phrases but in the Isaianic passage which underlies them—a doctrine of vicarious suffering. To say, however, that our Lord suffered on our behalf, and died that we might live is, after all, rather to state the fact of an atonement than to render it intelligible ; and St. Paul's doctrine did not stop short with a bare assertion of vicarious suffering, but included other elements of the highest interest and importance. In order to understand what these were we must go back to the conception of the Son of Man.

Except in the words attributed to the dying Stephen, the actual phrase " the Son of Man " does not occur in the New Testament outside the Gospels ; but the *conception* implied in the phrase underlies St. Paul's doctrine of our Lord as the " last Adam " or " Man from heaven." [1] It will be remembered that it was as a human figure revealed in bright light that St. Paul had seen our Lord in vision on the Damascus road ; and that the primitive Christian Gospel had proclaimed Him as the Messiah who should come upon the clouds of heaven in the glory of the holy angels. We have seen, moreover, that this latter conception goes back ultimately to the vision of Daniel as interpreted and amplified by the Book of Enoch.[2]

---

[1] ὁ δεύτερος ἄνθρωπος ἐξ οὐρανοῦ (1 Cor. xv. 47). The words ὁ Κύριος which underlie the A. V., "The second Man is *the Lord* from heaven," are probably a gloss. They are omitted from the text of the Revised Version.

[2] Cf. Essay III. pp. 90 sqq.

Now, in the Book of Enoch the "Son of Man" is not regarded as coming into existence for the first time at the moment of His manifestation upon earth, but as pre-existent from all eternity, dwelling in righteousness with the Ancient of Days "before the sun and the signs were created, before the stars of heaven were made." Jesus, therefore, acknowledged to be the "Son of Man" of apocalyptic expectation, must be conceived to have pre-existed in heavenly splendour before His life on earth : from the beginning He had dwelt with God, " chosen and hidden before Him before the creation of the world." His appearance upon earth at all, then—at least under conditions so remote from the surroundings of supernatural glory which were expected to herald the coming of the Son of Man— could only be explained as an act of sheer grace and loving-kindness. He who was to come in glory had stooped to come in lowliness—not having where to lay His head. " Ye know the grace of the Lord Jesus Christ, that though He was rich yet for our sakes He became poor, that ye through His poverty might become rich." " Let this mind be in you which was also in Christ Jesus, Who, being in the form of God, thought not equality with God a prize to be grasped, but nullified [1] Himself, taking the form of a servant, and was made in the likeness of men : and being found in fashion as a man, He humbled Himself, and became obedient even unto death, yea, the death of the Cross."

Theologies have been built upon these passages, but St. Paul's words are not exact theology, and it is absurd to treat them as precise metaphysical statements : in the contexts [2] in which they occur in his letters they are not even introduced for their own sakes, but merely as the ground of an appeal, in the one case for generous alms-giving, in the other for the avoidance of self-seeking, by

---

[1] It is clear from other passages in which the word is used (*e.g.* Rom. iv. 14, 1 Cor. i. 17, ix. 15) that κενοῦν in late Greek had come to bear the meaning "to make void," "to nullify," rather than "to make empty."

[2] 2 Cor. viii. 7 sqq. ; Philipp. ii. 3 sqq.

reference to the Lord's example. It is all the more significant of the lines on which the Apostle's thought had developed that he is able thus allusively to take for granted as common ground between himself and his correspondents a conception so striking and suggestive. From the throne of glory to the death of the Cross! Here, indeed, was a theme for wonder and thanksgiving. If the Cross meant *that*, then it was something more than a mere unexplained mystery of suffering : it was something voluntarily sought out and endured, an act of love surpassing anything that it had ever entered into the heart of man to conceive.

And, moreover, the love shown forth in the Cross was not simply the love of Christ : it was the love of God. Any separation between God and Christ was here unthinkable. God had " sent forth " His Christ—the " Son of His love "—to be a " propitiation " for our sins. We must not press too insistently the force of the word " propitiation " : St. Paul adopts the term in passing from the sacrificial system of Judaism, but he does not stop to enquire too closely who or what is being " propitiated." He seems, indeed, to regard the death of Christ as intrinsically necessary to display the severity and justice of God—human sin could not be passed over lightly, and it was only at this tremendous cost that man could be "ransomed " from its power ; but his main thought is of the *love* of God as manifested in the Saviour's self-forgetting sacrifice—a love which had prevailed in spite of men's sins and of the " wrath " which in themselves they must have aroused. " God was in Christ reconciling the world unto Himself" and " God commendeth His own love towards us, in that, *while we were yet sinners*, Christ died for us." [1]

Clearly (St. Paul felt) it was with a great act of the Divine Love operative for man's redemption that in the death of Christ he had to do. But this was not all. The recognition of the Cross as a revelation at

[1] Cf. Essay VI. pp. 314-315.

once of God's love and severity was still not adequate
as an explanation of his experience. The Law, as St.
Paul understood it, had pronounced upon sin the
condemnation of death, and St. Paul himself, under the
Law, had been "dead," that is, morally and spiritually
powerless, the slave of sin. By his union with Christ
he now knew himself to be "alive." What had
happened ? Had God repented of the condemnation
pronounced ? That surely were impossible. Does
God, then, receive the wicked as if they were righteous ?
To do so would be to combine injustice with falsehood ;
moreover, the proof that the "enmity" between
St. Paul and God was at an end lay precisely in the fact
that the power of sin in him was broken, that in Christ
Jesus he was "a new creature."

Who, then, was Christ Jesus, and what was this
"new creation" ? St. Paul recalled the story of the
original creation in Genesis, and was led to express,
and to endeavour to explain, the contrast between the
old creation and the new—between the life of sin and
the new life in Christ,—by the help of the conceptions
of the first and the second Adam. "Adam" is simply
the Hebrew word for "man," and Adam in the ancient
legend was the ancestor of mankind. Now, an ancestor,
according to the Hebrew way of thinking, already implies and, as it were, includes the whole of his descendants. Thus, for example, the writer of the Epistle
to the Hebrews speaks of Levi as paying tithes to
Melchizedek, because "he was yet in the loins of his
father"—Abraham—"when Melchizedek met him"
(Heb. vii. 10). Accordingly "Adam" for St. Paul is
not merely the ancestor of mankind : he represents,
and in fact he *is* mankind ; the sin and death of Adam
is the sin and death of all men. But Jesus Christ is a
second Adam. He, too, stands for, and as it were
includes, all mankind ; and as in the first Adam all
died, so in the second Adam all shall be made alive.
The first Adam—formed, according to the story in

Genesis, of the dust of the ground—was "of the earth, earthy"; but the second Adam, the glorious, pre-existent Son of Man, was from heaven. From the first Adam was derived man's natural life—"the first man Adam became a living soul"; from the Christ, the second Adam, man's new-found spiritual life was de-rived—"the last Adam became a life-giving Spirit." As Adam reproduced himself in his descendants by physical begetting, so in Christ men were spiritually begotten anew, and He in them was reproduced.[1]

Clearly if this way of stating the "work of Christ" can be maintained, whatever is morally objectionable in the idea of the Redeemer's sufferings as vicarious is thereby eliminated. The point after all is not so much that Christ died for us as that we died in Him. In Him we died, and in His resurrection we rose. His death is identically our death and His resurrection our resurrection, and all who come to share the manhood of the second Adam are dead and risen—dead to sin and alive unto God. Moreover, since Adam stands for mankind, so Christ is or represents all mankind. The thought is all through intensely corporate and social. Man is corporately sinful, and corporately redeemed. The ancient mind, it is often said, was defective in its failure adequately to recognize the principle of in-dividuality; and this, no doubt, is true. But the abstract individualism of much modern thinking loses sight of the deeper truth of human solidarity, and it is just here that ancient thought is strong.[2]

There are, however, difficulties in St. Paul's con-ception. There is, for example, in his use of the terms "life" and "death" a recurring ambiguity. They denote, of course, in the first instance life and death in the ordinary physical sense of the words; but they are used also to denote spiritual life and death—the new-found capacities of spiritual achievement in souls that are "risen with Christ," the moral impotence and

[1] Cf. Essay V. p. 246 and pp. 253 sqq.   [2] Cf. Essay VI. pp. 297-298.

spiritual entombment of souls "sold under sin"; and
in St. Paul's thinking the two senses run into one
another and cannot be clearly distinguished. Thus the
physical death and resurrection of Christ are regarded
as carrying with them the "death to sin" and rising
again to *spiritual* life of all men; but further, the
physical death which is the common lot of all men is
regarded as the "wages" of sin; inasmuch, however,
as all men died in Christ's physical death, the "wages"
have already been paid and received—"he that hath
died is justified from sin"; consequently all shall rise
in Christ's resurrection : He is "the first-fruits of them
that slept."

Again, since the first Adam involved the whole race
in sin, the second Adam ought in strict logic to have
imparted the new life to all ; and, moreover, inasmuch
as in Him *they* died and rose again—died to sin and
rose again to righteousness—sin in strict logic ought to
be henceforward impossible.

All such criticism, however, is really beside the mark.
St. Paul, as has been already insisted, was not a
strictly logical thinker, still less a theologian con-
structing a system. He was a supreme religious
genius struggling to express and make intelligible new
facts of religious experience. He does not as a fact
conceive redemption in the static fashion which his
argument, considered logically, would require. On the
contrary the Christian salvation, theoretically and
potentially effectual for all men, requires to be
individually appropriated by "faith," and "faith" for
St. Paul, whatever else it may be, is certainly not mere
"belief"; it is not a "hearty assent" to anything,
neither is it independent of "works"; it is "active
through love" (Gal. v. 6).[1] How far St. Paul's
doctrine of the Atonement is from being narrowly
logical is clear from the fact that there is still something

---

[1] Faith for St. Paul has its beginning in personal loyalty to Christ and its
consummation in mystical union with Him.

left for man to do. We have to walk worthily of our new life ; to bring forth fruits worthy of our changed mind ; to eject sin from our members and "yield them as instruments of righteousness." St. Paul is not afraid of a paradox. "If ye then *be risen* with Christ, *seek* those things which are above." The Atonement is complete, and yet it remains for us to complete it.

On the other hand, St. Paul is clear that the power of faith in us, "active through love," is a Power not of ourselves. It is Christ operative within us. It is the Spirit of Christ indwelling and possessing us—"Christ in you," as he expresses it, "the hope of glory." "To me to live is Christ," he cries, "to die is gain." "I live, yet not I, but Christ liveth in me, and the life which I now live in the flesh, I live by the faith of the Son of God, who loved me, and gave Himself for me." In this intensely mystical consciousness of the indwelling Christ, ever with him as the guiding and inspiring principle of his life, St. Paul is typical of all the great Christian saints ; and, indeed, the experience is shared in greater or less degree by sincere Christians in all ages.

Christ and the Spirit of Christ : St. Paul does not sharply differentiate the two conceptions in the way that later theology came to do ; his is the spontaneous and unstudied language of experience, and the Power which wrought in him and in others to the subduing of passion and the conquest of sin, the Power which gave life meaning and purpose, a new vision and a new joy, which inspired to suffer and to serve and if necessary to die, was as plainly the power of Christ as Christ Himself was the power of God. That a man should have the Spirit of Christ in him was the same thing as that he should have Christ in him or that he should have the Spirit of God in him. "Ye are in the Spirit if so be that the Spirit of God dwelleth in you. But if any man have not the Spirit of Christ, he is none of His. And if the Spirit of Christ is in you, the body is dead because of sin ; but the Spirit is life because of

righteousness." "Now the Lord is the Spirit; and
where the spirit of the Lord is, there is liberty."
"Stand fast, therefore, in the liberty wherewith Christ
hath made us free."

Righteousness, life, freedom—it is because St. Paul
(and the Christian Church following his lead) was thus
able to grasp the inner significance of the Personality
of Jesus the Messiah, and to express it as a life-giving
Spirit, that Jesus has been for humanity what He has
been. It was this which made St. Paul pre-eminently
doctor gentium—the Apostle of the Gentiles. So long as
the Christian preaching was merely the proclamation of
a Jews' Messiah it could have had to the pagan world
no more than a passing interest, comparable to the
interest which we ourselves feel when we read in the
papers of the appearance of another Mullah, mad or
sane, in Somaliland or elsewhere. If there had come
into the world one who was to be a Saviour for
Greeks and Romans, Barbarians and Scythians, learned
and ignorant, bond and free, he must be one of whom
more could be asserted than that he was the Messiah
of the Jews.

St. Paul in fact came, as we have seen, to assert far
more about our Lord than the bare fact of His Messiahship : and although we have seemed to find in the
Apostle's personal history a clue to that modified
emphasis in his preaching whereby the present grace
of salvation came to assume an even greater importance
than the future hope of the Kingdom, we need to
remember also that his experience was not simply the
experience of a Christian but of a Christian missionary.
It was not merely that the first Apostles had known
Christ first in the days of His humiliation, and had
only afterwards come to understand His glory, whereas
in St. Paul's case the experience had been reversed,
and for him the Christ seen in glory on the Damascus
road was less a man who had been exalted than a
heavenly Being who had condescended to become

human. It was not merely that for St. Paul the central thing was his deliverance in Christ from the power of sin and the curse of the law. The Gospel with which he had gone out into the Gentile world, so far as we can gather it from the Thessalonian Epistles, was (as has been already observed) the Judaic, eschatological Gospel, unaltered even in form : and if St. Paul came to modify or supplement it, to find modes of expression which did fuller justice to his own central experience, we may be sure that, like every teacher, he learnt much from those he taught.

It was not, indeed, that for his own part he at any time ceased to be essentially a Jew, or that his thought moved upon other than Jewish lines. But he discovered by experience that some ways of putting his message were intelligible to Gentile minds, as others were not. In particular, the conception of a Divine Being—a God—who had died and come to life again, and whose dying and rising, mystically shared by the initiated, were the pledge of their salvation in this life and the next, was one which—as it is now coming to be generally recognized—was already familiar in the Graeco-Roman world of the day.

Throughout Asia Minor, in the great cosmopolitan Greek towns, and in Rome itself, what are known as "Mystery Religions," derived from Egypt and the East, were widely popular. They seem to have had their roots, far back in the dim past, in primitive nature-worships. In the Phrygian system Cybele, in the Egyptian system Isis, representing the Earth Mother, bewailed the death in autumn of the vegetation-spirit, Attis or Osiris,[1] and celebrated joyfully his resurrection in the spring. This original crude basis, however, was allegorized and practically dropped

---

[1] The worship of Mithras, the best known of these mystery religions, did not, as it would appear, become widely disseminated in the Roman Empire before the end of the first century of our era. It presents, externally at least, many close parallels to Christianity, and during the period of its greatest vogue it was for some time a serious rival to the Church.

out of sight in the later developments of these cults, and in the forms in which they spread over the civilized world of Greece and Rome the mythical figures of Osiris and Attis appear rather as redeemer-gods who represent the principle of life out of death and guarantee a blessed immortality to their votaries. Men were initiated by means of solemn washings and purifications, and in sacred meals and mystic sacraments participated in the divine drama, constantly renewed and re-enacted, of the life, death, and joyful resurrection of their god. In spite of ritual survivals which were in some cases of a savage and even revolting kind, it must be recognized that much of what was highest and most spiritual in the religious aspirations of the age sought, and in some measure found, both outward expression and inward satisfaction in these mystic cults ;[1] and although their direct influence upon Christianity may easily be exaggerated, it will readily be seen that familiarity with the language and ideas of the mysteries would provide a point of contact in the Gentile mind which rendered intelligible St. Paul's Gospel of the death and resurrection of the Christ. In this sense Christianity may be said to have fulfilled the unconscious " Messianic prophecies " of the Mystery Religions.

But if the Gentile mind thus tended to accept Christianity as a " mystery religion," it was certainly a mystery religion of a new and superior kind. For one thing, its Christ was no mere mythical figure of the past, but an actual Person whose life and death and resurrection were attested by men who claimed to have seen and known Him, and whose living Spirit, operative in their lives, bore fruit in a type of character which the mystery religions could not boast. For

---

[1] For a valuable account of the Mystery Religions see Cumont, *Les Religions orientales dans le Paganisme romain* : a discussion of their bearing on the Gospel as preached by St. Paul will be found in Lake (*op. cit.* pp. 40 *sqq.*). There is nothing in the evidence to suggest that any of the fundamental conceptions of St. Paul's Gospel *originated* in the Mystery Religions : the utmost that ought to be asserted is that they may have come to have some influence upon the forms of its presentation.

another, the appearance upon earth as Man of this
wonderful Person whose sufferings and death were
effectual for man's redemption was proclaimed as a
voluntary act springing from sheer love, and that the
love of God. And in point of fact, although the
theology of the mysteries helped to make Christ intelligible to the Gentiles, as the theology of Messiahship
had made Him intelligible to the Jews, it remains as
true in the former case as in the latter that the secret
of the Gospel's power, and the explanation of its
victories, is not to be found in the doctrinal forms of
its expression. In Greece and Asia Minor, as truly as
in Jerusalem, the really effective Christian apologetic
was the Christian life. " It is the Spirit that quickeneth :
the flesh profiteth nothing."

It is probable, indeed, that the influence of the
theology of the mysteries did not always operate
wholly for good. It suggested in some cases an
unethical and even a magical interpretation of the
Gospel—as though a man, having once been purified
in baptism, and having duly received, through participation in the Eucharist, the risen life of the Redeemer,
was henceforth " safe " and might with impunity ignore
the obligations of morality, as one who was in any case
secure of ultimate salvation. The Christian sacraments, that is to say, were in danger of being interpreted
as magical charms justifying antinomian practice. It is
this problem which St. Paul has before him in his
discussion of the significance of the Eucharist in the
first Epistle to the Corinthians ; and the manner in
which he deals with it makes clear incidentally the kind
of development which Christian thought had sustained
in relation to sacramental doctrine, and specifically in
relation to the Eucharist.

Attention has already been called to the close mutual
connexion and interaction of Eucharistic and Christological thinking : we are prepared for the discovery that a
less exclusively eschatological interpretation of the Christ

had brought with it also a less exclusively eschatological doctrine of the Eucharist. The primitive thought of the Kingdom is still, indeed, a part of its significance—" ye do proclaim [1] the Lord's death *till He come* " : but combined with it we now find other conceptions expressive of what the Eucharist was discovered to be in the actual experience of the faithful. It is, for example, a " memorial " of Christ : that is to say, not merely a reminder of His *death* as an event in the past, and not merely a foreshadowing of His *Kingdom* as a hope for the future, but rather something which brings home to the hearts and minds of the worshippers the whole of what Christ is, the Redeemer, Crucified and Risen, as a present fact of the spiritual world. So, too, the thought of sacrifice [2] has been introduced ; the " table of the Lord " can be both compared and contrasted with those sacrificial meals of Paganism which St. Paul calls the " table of devils." In the Eucharist the Christian enjoyed a true and actual communion with his Lord, as the pagan worshipper conceived himself to hold communion " with the idol." The blessing of the Cup and the breaking of the Bread involved a partaking of or sharing in the Body and Blood of Christ, analogous to sharing in or partaking of the flesh of a sacrifice. The Eucharist, in other words, was the spiritual meat and drink of Christians ; and as it united them to the Christ on Whom they fed, so it united them in Him to one another ; by virtue of participation in the " one Bread " which was Christ, they who were many were " one Bread, one Body."

The description of Christians as the " Body of

---

[1] What is the meaning of καταγγέλλετε? Or rather *to whom* is the " proclamation " made ? One is inclined to say not to man, for there would be none but believers present at the Eucharist, and Christian believers did not need to proclaim *to one another* the fact that Christ had died : on the other hand καταγγέλλετε is hardly the natural word to use for " proclaiming " or " pleading " before God. St. Paul seems rather to regard that death of shame which had become the Church's glory as proclaimed in triumph before the unseen presences of the spiritual world. Cf. Eph. iii. 10.

[2] It is important to distinguish the ancient idea of sacrifice from that which became current in mediaeval times. See below, pp. 194 sqq.

Christ," already established in 1 Corinthians and developed at length in Ephesians, has to-day become so
familiar as a synonym of the Church that men forget to
notice its extraordinary character or to ask themselves
how St. Paul originally arrived at it. Here, as elsewhere, it is probable that it was the Eucharist which
gave the clue. If the Church was called the Body of
Christ, it was because her members partook of that
Eucharistic Bread which was also so described. " The
Bread which we break, is it not a communion of the Body
of Christ ? seeing that we, who are many, are one Bread,
one Body : for we all partake of the one Bread." [1]

A double process was in fact at work : the doctrine
of Christ influenced that of the Eucharist ; the fuller
doctrine of the Eucharist suggested in its turn yet
further developments of the doctrine of Christ. This
will become clearer as we proceed. Here we would
only notice that the motive of what St. Paul has to say
about the Eucharist is not so much to set forth a
positive exposition of his doctrine with regard to it, as
to correct the unworthy views of the Corinthians, who
were interpreting it *ex opere operato*, to the detriment of
Christian morals.

The Corinthians had in fact failed to grasp the true
nature of that Divine Spirit whereof they had been
made to drink. The same people who regarded the
sacraments as mechanical guarantees of salvation are
found preferring the more external and superficially
striking manifestations of the Spirit, in "speaking
with tongues [2]" or healings, to that inner transformation

---

[1] The doctrine of Baptism in like manner now appears as closely related to the
same conception. Cf. 1 Cor. xii. 13 " In one Spirit were we all baptized into one
Body." Baptism is no longer merely a pledge of forgiveness and " seal " of the
future Kingdom : it is regarded as the outward vehicle of a spiritual incorporation
into the " Body " of Christ, here and now.

[2] The phrase " speaking with tongues " (γλώσσῃ λαλεῖν) in 1 Cor. xii.-xiv.
appears to denote the ecstatic utterance of unintelligible sounds under the stress of
religious emotion. The phenomenon is not unparalleled in the history of religion.
Cf. Schmiedel in the *Encyclopedia Biblica* (*s.v.* Spiritual Gifts) ; Weinel, *Die Wirkungen des Geistes und der Geister*, pp. 71 sqq. ; and for modern psychological theories
see Lake, *op. cit.* pp. 241 sqq.

of character and motive which to St. Paul was all in all.

St. Paul's view, as contrasted with theirs, is ethical through and through. The mere fact of participation in the Eucharist (considered simply as an external rite) no more guarantees the Christian's salvation, independently of his moral state, than the fact of having received the Manna and the water from the Rock guaranteed the safety of the Israelites of old. Of those who desired not to "eat and drink judgment unto themselves," it was required that they first "examine themselves," that they "discern the Body," that they "eat not the Bread nor drink the Cup of the Lord unworthily."

So in like manner with regard to "spiritual gifts." "Speaking with tongues," healings and the rest, remarkable though they might be, were not of any intrinsic value in themselves. At most they were the transitory forms of the Spirit's manifestation, and the Spirit was more than they. In its inmost character and essence the Spirit was the Spirit of Charity, the Spirit of Love : and "though I speak with the tongues of men and of angels, and have not charity . . . it profiteth me nothing"— I might as well be beating a piece of brass, or clanging a cymbal in the orgies of Dionysus.

The praise of Charity is St. Paul's supreme delineation of the Christian Spirit, and there is implicit in it an entire transformation of the crude popular view of spiritual workings which was current in the primitive Christian communities. "The community," writes Professor Gunkel, "regards as pneumatic or spiritual the extraordinary in the life of the Christian, Paul the ordinary ; they that which was peculiar to individuals, Paul that which was common to all : they that which occurs abruptly, Paul that which is constant : they the special in the Christian life, Paul the Christian life itself. Hence the value which the primitive Church attaches to miracles, Paul attaches to the Christian state.

No more is that which is individual and sporadic held to be the divine in man: the Christian man is the spiritual man."[1] But if we thus express the difference by saying that St. Paul regards the Spirit as manifested in what is normal or ordinary in the Christian life, this must not be taken to imply that the Christian life itself, as St. Paul conceived of it, is something ordinary. If it is odd that a respectable citizen should suddenly begin to speak with tongues, it is at least equally odd that he should love his neighbour as himself.

The Eucharist as spiritual food and drink, the Spirit as the Spirit of Love—what was the reaction of these conceptions upon the Apostle's Christology? We have already noticed that St. Paul discovered an analogy to the Eucharist in the Manna and the water from the Rock which had sustained " the Church in the Wilderness." To his mind this was more than a fanciful comparison, it was an actual fact. The story as given in the Book of Exodus is for him literally true—he even accepts and mystically interprets a Rabbinical legend to the effect that the " Rock " with its miraculous stream of life-giving water followed the Israelites from halting-place to halting-place in their wilderness wanderings : and he boldly identifies the Rock with Christ. From this identification it at once followed that the Christ, pre-existent in glory, had also been effectively operative in human history from the beginning. Not merely had He been hidden with God before times eternal : in some degree and in some sense He had been already manifested in the entire age-long process of revelation and grace. Calvary was but the climax and consummation of a vast Divine Purpose of redemption and love in Christ Jesus which was the supreme law of the universe according to the eternal world-plan of God. The Christ, in whom Christians were created anew, was the same Christ through whom

---

[1] Gunkel, *Die Wirkungen des heiligen Geistes,* quoted by G. B. Stevens, *Theology of the New Testament,* p. 440.

in the original Creation, "all things were made." He
assumes in the thought of the Apostle a significance not
for human history alone, but for the Cosmos : redeemer
of men and goal of corporate humanity, He is also
" before all things, and in Him all things consist."

Such was the tremendous and ever-growing significance
which the Christ who had taken him captive, and made
and moulded and transformed his life, came to bear in the
thought of the Apostle : so to know Him was to know
Him, as St. Paul expressed it, " not after the flesh but
after the Spirit." This is not to say that for St. Paul
the Christ had ceased to be a living Person and become
a mere abstract idea or principle. On the contrary, his
doctrine from first to last is rooted and grounded in
concrete facts of experience, and that an experience of
One whom the Apostle affirmed unhesitatingly to be
none other than Jesus of Nazareth. Few critical judgments are more perverse than that which persists in
taking the knowledge of Christ " after the flesh," which
St. Paul informs us he had abandoned, to mean an
acquaintance with the facts of our Lord's human life
and death. The Apostle's entire Gospel implies the
precise opposite of such an idea. For him the spiritual
Christ and the human Jesus are one and the same Person :
it is not a " *Christ* after the flesh " but a " *knowledge* "
of Christ " after the flesh " that is devoid of spiritual
value. To know Christ after the flesh is to know Him
as St. Paul had known Him before his conversion : it is
to know merely the bare external facts of His career
and to see in them only a stumbling-block and a blasphemy. To know Christ after the Spirit is to know Him
as St. Paul now knew Him : to see in those very facts, as
well as in the power of the present Spirit, the gospel of
God's grace and the ground of Christian glorying.[1]

----

[1] It would follow from this that the effect of " Paulinism " was not to destroy
men's interest in the earthly life and Passion of the Lord, but rather to stimulate
it ; to this fact it may be that we owe the existence of St. Mark's Gospel. It is
curious to observe that the critical school which has insisted most strongly upon the
alleged indifference of St. Paul to the " Jesus of history " has also been the most
quick to discover in St. Mark the operation of a " Pauline tendency."

VI. THE LATEST STAGE OF PAULINISM

Thus far our exposition of Pauline thought has been based almost exclusively upon the Epistles of St. Paul's early and middle periods, though already in touching upon the Apostle's doctrine of the cosmic significance of the Christ we have drawn one of our quotations from Colossians.[1] In the group of writings which may be held to represent the maturest expression of his thought—the Ephesian and Colossian Epistles—we have presented to us a conception of the Christ and an interpretation of His significance which is in some ways even more profound and far-reaching than any we have yet considered.

We have seen that St. Paul had originally shared the standpoint of those who looked for an immediate coming of the Lord, and that although he never abandoned either in word or in fact the hope of the Kingdom as the first disciples had conceived of it, yet as time went on it came to occupy no longer the central place in his teaching. We have seen, again, that the doctrine of the second Adam, in the form in which St. Paul had stated it, involved certain difficulties or paradoxes which appeared to run counter to facts of experience. If we died in Christ's death and now live with His life, sin henceforth should be impossible to us. Already, however, in the circumstances which led to the writing of Galatians the Apostle had found himself confronted by what must have been a constantly recurring problem—the problem of converts who for a time " were running well," but

---

[1] The Pauline letters may be thus classified :

Early Paulinism : I and II Thessalonians.

Middle Paulinism : Galatians, I and II Corinthians, Romans.

Late Paulinism : Philippians, Ephesians, Colossians, Philemon.

The Pastoral Epistles (I and II Timothy and Titus) are doubtfully Pauline, the Epistle to the Hebrews definitely non-Pauline. Many critics still dispute the Pauline authorship of Colossians, and an even larger number refuse to regard Ephesians as the work of St. Paul, though in our judgment without any very sufficient reason : in any case the Epistles in question represent a legitimate development of Pauline ideas.

who afterwards showed signs of falling away. Experience showed that the "old Adam" died hard; that evangelisation was not necessarily conversion. More and more it was borne in upon the Apostle's consciousness that the process by which Christ was formed in the human soul was the work not of a moment but of a lifetime. He came to realise that the work which must be done before the Christ at His coming should find a people prepared for Himself, fit to be citizens of His Kingdom, was vaster than he had ever imagined when first he set out upon his task. He no longer expects to see with his own eyes the consummation; he is ready to depart, and to be with Christ,[1] leaving it to others to continue what by God's grace he had been enabled to begin.

As his life of missionary labour drew to its close he sends forth from his Roman prison "one supreme exposition, non - controversial, positive, fundamental, of the great doctrine of his life—that doctrine into which he had been advancing year by year under the discipline of his unique circumstances—the doctrine of the unity of mankind in Christ, and of the purpose of God for the world through the Church."[2] He sees in the Christ, whose he is and whom he serves, the secret of that increasing Purpose which runs throughout the ages, the supreme end and goal to which the whole creation moves. The world as we know it is not the world as it shall become. Humanity as we now know it is not the humanity that shall one day be. Imperfect, partial, divided, unbalanced, and untempered as it now is, mankind is yet in process of being completed and perfected into One; and the Christ, who all in all is being fulfilled, though He stands already in His own divine-human nature, perfect and complete in Jesus of Nazareth, waits, as it were, at the consummation of history, until all men

---

[1] Philipp. i. 23.
[2] Armitage Robinson, *The Epistle to the Ephesians*, p. 10. Cf. also Essay VII.

have grown up into His ideal and come into realized
oneness with His Person, " until we all attain unto
the unity of the faith and of the knowledge of the
Son of God, unto a full-grown Man, unto the measure
of the stature of the completion of the Christ." The
Christ that is to be, the unity of the New Man full-
grown—that is to be the goal of Christian striving,
and the promise of it standeth fast like the strong
mountains. The Apostle, who for his own part
" counts not himself to have apprehended," strives
still towards the mark, for the prize of that high
calling, and with Christians then and since " yearns for
the sign " of Christ's fulfilling, and " faints for the
flaming of His advent feet."

St. Paul has travelled far indeed from the form of
the original Gospel preaching : but has he departed
from its spirit ? Is his doctrine, in all the magnificent
range and reach of its development, anything more
than the drawing out in more adequate terms of
implications which were already contained in the
revelation of the Son of Man in the Gospel ? The
answer is written broad across the face of Christian
history, in which multitudes who have found in St.
Paul's experience the echo of their own have been
content to express its significance in words and phrases
no other than his.

VII. The Epistle to the Hebrews

Influenced by St. Paul, and yet approaching the problem of the interpretation of the Christ from a standpoint and with antecedents which were wholly unlike
St. Paul's, the next great Christian writer whom it falls
to us to consider is the anonymous author of the
Epistle to the Hebrews. St. Paul had been an orthodox Jew, brought up after the straitest sect at the feet
of Gamaliel. The Judaism of the author of Hebrews
may, in a certain sense, be said to be orthodox, but it

is no longer the Judaism of Palestine or of the Jerusalem rabbis. It is the liberal, Hellenized Judaism of the Alexandrine school of Philo : a Judaism which saw in the earthly Law and Temple only the shadows and patterns of things eternal—fleeting symbols in time and space of the abiding realities of heaven.

Thus, for example, " faith," as understood by this writer, is the faculty in us whereby we are enabled to grasp, behind the outward show of the world as it presents itself to our senses, the inward substance of " things not seen." To have faith is to " endure as seeing Him who is invisible " ; and Jesus is regarded as faith's Pattern and Example—" He who trod the path of faith before us, and trod it perfectly to the end." [1] We find, accordingly, great emphasis laid upon the human experience of the Saviour, the inner struggle in Him against the temptations which in all points beset Him even as they do ourselves, the perfecting of His life through suffering, the " strong crying and tears " by which He learned obedience and was enabled to offer up His life unto the Father, thereby becoming " the author of eternal salvation unto all them that obey Him."

Yet Christ is more than the pattern of the life of faith—more even than the author of salvation. For the writer of Hebrews as for St. Paul, He is the crown and consummation of the whole long process of God's self-revelation to man. " God who of old times spake unto the fathers by divers portions and in divers manners, hath at the end, in these days, spoken unto us by His Son, whom He appointed heir of all things, through whom also he made the worlds ; who being the effulgence of His glory and the express image of His substance, and upholding all things by the word of His power, when he had made purification of sins, sat down at the right hand of the Majesty on high." The terms and phrases of Philo lie behind this descrip-

---

[1] Τὸν τῆς πίστεως ἀρχηγὸν καὶ τελειωτὴν Ἰησοῦν (Heb. xii. 2).

tion : "image" of God,[1] "effulgence" of the Divine
Glory. These were expressions which Philo, combining
Judaism with the philosophy of Plato, had applied to
the "Word" — the Divine Utterance or Creative
Reason—by whom, as a "second God" side by side
with the Supreme, all things (according to Philo's way
of thinking) came into existence and were maintained
in being. In his use of them the unknown writer
approximates very closely to the thought which was
destined in the Fourth Gospel to become explicit—the
thought, namely, that in the life of the historical Jesus
the "Word" became flesh, that in Him the Mind,
Reason, or Character of God was once for all embodied
and revealed. The Christian idea of Christ, without in
any way losing its grip upon the concrete facts of history
and experience, is yet in process of becoming more reflective, more philosophical, less Jewish and more Greek.

Yet the Epistle has a practical purpose : it is written
to warn Christian converts against apostasy, and more
especially against the danger, which is evidently
regarded as a serious one, of a relapse into mere
Judaism. The contrast between the New "Covenant"
and the Old, with which the major portion of the
Epistle is occupied, is intended to enforce a very
definite moral—that of the greater responsibility which
goes along with greater privilege. It is in the drawing
out of the details of this comparison that the author
introduces what is in some ways his most distinctive
contribution to Christian thought, viz.—the interpretation of Christ in terms of priesthood and sacrifice
derived from the Jewish Law.

St. Paul had applied sacrificial analogies to the
Eucharist, and a background of sacrificial ideas is
suggested in the terms of its institution. A Christo-
centric sacrificial rite implied *ipso facto* a sacrificial

---

[1] It should be noticed, however, that the phrase "image of the invisible God"
($\epsilon i\kappa\grave{\omega}\nu$ $\tau o\hat{v}$ $\Theta\epsilon o\hat{v}$ $\tau o\hat{v}$ $\dot{a}o\rho\acute{a}\tau o v$) already occurs in Colossians i. 15, and "image of God"
($\epsilon i\kappa\grave{\omega}\nu$ $\tau o\grave{v}$ $\Theta\epsilon o\hat{v}$) in 2 Cor. iv. 4.

interpretation of the Christ, and we find accordingly that already in St. Paul Christ is spoken of as " our Passover, sacrificed for us," as " making peace by His blood," as being in some sense a "propitiation." What for St. Paul is an occasional illustration or a momentary point of comparison,[1] is for the author of Hebrews a substantive idea, which is worked out with great fulness and elaboration of detail in an argument which extends through several chapters.

Ideas of sacrifice and priesthood are apt to appear remote and uncongenial to modern minds, and the evil associations of controversy cling round the ancient phrases in a manner which renders it difficult for us to do justice to the thought contained in them. If we are to arrive at any understanding of the argument of Hebrews, it is before all things necessary that we should rid our minds of mediaeval and modern conceptions of sacrifice, and think ourselves back into a world in which animal sacrifice was an actual and familiar religious usage. The word "sacrifice" to-day bears primarily a metaphorical sense : to the men of New Testament times it signified primarily a concrete rite, a religious action : something done, not something thought or believed. No doubt the external rite of sacrifice represented and embodied certain ideas : sacrifices were offered for definite reasons, with specific ends in view, and were understood to have a more or less definite meaning. Nevertheless, it remains true that the ritual of the sacrifice was

---

[1] Apart from the three phrases quoted in the text, and the statement in Ephesians v. 2—" Even as Christ also loved you, and gave Himself up for us, an offering and a sacrifice to God for an odour of a sweet smell "—where the self-oblation of Christ is compared not to a sin-offering but to a burnt-offering, there do not appear to be any passages in St. Paul which interpret the work of Christ in sacrificial terms. The statement in Galatians iii. 13 that Christ " became a curse for us " has nothing to do with sacrifice, but is an inference from the manner of Christ's death in the light of Deut. xxi. 23—" He that is hanged is accursed of God." Sacrificial victims were never regarded as " accursed " but, on the contrary, as " most holy." So also the idea of vicarious suffering, frequent in St. Paul, has nothing to do with sacrifice. The only animal in the Levitical system which is ever conceived as a " sin-bearer " is the " scape-goat " of Lev. xvi. But the scape-goat is not sacrificed, but escapes : and, moreover, it is not a " goat for the Lord," but for Azazel (Lev. xvi. 8 [R.V.]) : its function is to bear away the forgiven sins of the people to Azazel, the demon of the wilderness.

determined with greater precision than its significance, that the deed was regarded as of greater importance than the doctrine. In a general way sacrifices of a certain kind were understood to take away sins ; so long, however, as this was admitted, the question how or why they had this effect was left conveniently vague.

Certainly the theory of mediaeval times—that in order to meet the requirements of justice the death penalty was by a legal fiction inflicted on the sacrificial victim in the sinner's stead—does not correspond to the ancient thought of sacrifice. The nearest approach to a theory of sacrifice contained in the Levitical Law is to be found in the words, " The life of the flesh is in the blood : and I have given it to you upon the altar to make atonement for your souls : for it is the blood that maketh atonement by reason of the life " (Lev. xvii. 11). In other words the efficacy of sacrifice, in so far as any orthodox rationale of it existed at all, was understood to lie in the fact that it was not primarily an infliction of death, but an offering of life. The death of the victim was merely incidental and pre-liminary to the sacrifice proper, viz.—the offering of the blood (representing the life) upon the altar. The offering of the blood was the work of the priest : the slaughter of the victim was performed by a Levite or, in the case of private sacrifices, by a layman.[1]

The attitude of the Liberal Judaism of Alexandria towards the sacrificial system of Jerusalem was a some-what equivocal one : it was necessary on the one hand to justify the provisions of the Law, but on the other hand it was impossible seriously to regard sacrifice, in so far as it was an external rite, as having any positive or intrinsic efficacy. The argument of Hebrews on its negative side is a rationalistic criticism of animal sacrifice from this point of view. " It is impossible that the blood of bulls and goats should take away sins." But the Law, with its " sanctuary of this world "

[1] Cf. Essay VI. p. 306, footnote 1.

and its system of sacrificial worship, was nevertheless God's ordinance : in the unreal and transitory sphere of things visible it was ordained to be the symbol and shadow of the true sanctuary, the "pattern" laid up in heaven, which was "shown" to Moses on the mount.

In the historical Jesus shadow and substance had become one. It was the assured testimony of Christian experience that what the blood of bulls and goats had been powerless to effect Christ had finally accomplished. It followed that His sacrifice was the reality which Jewish sacrifices had all along foreshadowed. Christ had died once for all upon Calvary ; but the significance of His sacrifice was eternal ; nay, the sacrifice itself was an event not of the temporal but of the eternal order. "If He were on earth, He would not be a priest at all."

The symbolism of the ritual law is in fact maintained strictly. Calvary, which corresponds to the slaying of the victim, is but the preliminary to the sacrifice proper : that sacrifice consists in the offering of the life which is the blood. It is conceived mystically, as a reality eternal in the heavens. Christ, according to the thought of the author, "abideth a priest for ever" : He "ever liveth to make intercession" for His people : He offers eternally in the heavenly sphere the sacrifice of His "blood." [1] Thus for Christians the true altar is not the altar of Judaism but the altar in heaven : it is not the type but the reality. Of that true altar they which serve the sanctuary upon earth "have no right to eat," [2] though Christians receive its virtue in the Eucharist: Judaism and Christianity, in other words, are incompatible, and the "Old Covenant" is in principle abolished by the coming of the "New." "He taketh away the first, that He may establish the second."

The theology of the Epistle to the Hebrews underlies all the Catholic eucharistic liturgies, and it is only

---

[1] Cf. Essay VI. p. 322.
[2] "We have an altar, whereof they have no right to eat which serve the tabernacle" (Heb. xiii. 10).

in the light of it that they can be understood.[1] To the
modern mind the entire conception is apt to seem
merely fantastic ; propounded as a theology of atonement and a rationale of Christian worship it appears
frankly unintelligible. Granted that the author's
Platonic philosophy enabled him to regard the earthly
worship as the symbol of a heavenly worship which alone
was real, to us who do not share his Platonic premisses
these relations are reversed. The *heavenly* altar
becomes a symbolical conception, modelled upon the
earthly altar of Judaism and less concretely real than
its prototype : and moreover the imagery of tabernacle,
altar, and sacrificing priest, which to the ancient world
suggested much, to us suggests little.

Yet as the vehicle of worship a symbolism of some
kind is after all inevitable in practice: and for Christianity
the symbolism of the New Testament must as inevitably
bear something of a classical character. It is the part
of wisdom not to discard tradition but to understand
it ; and we may still give a real meaning to the ancient
language of sacrifice, provided we are at the pains to
recognize the symbolism for what it is, and to penetrate
to the essential meaning of the ideas for which sacrifice
and priesthood stand. To such an understanding of
sacrifice the author of Hebrews himself gives us the
clue : for him as for ourselves the essence of sacrifice is
after all discovered to reside not in any merely external
ritual, whether on earth or in heaven, but in the
voluntary oblation and dedication of life for others'
sake, in uttermost obedience, even unto death.

Wherefore, when He cometh into the world, He saith,
Sacrifice and offering Thou wouldest not,
But a body didst Thou prepare for Me :
In whole burnt offerings and sacrifices for sin Thou hadst no
  pleasure ;
Then said I, Lo, I am come
(In the roll of the book it is written of Me)
To do Thy will, O God.

[1] Cf. Essay VII. pp. 343-346 ; Essay VIII. p. 392.

The oblation of the eternal Priest " after the order of Melchizedek," and the obedience of the Servant of the Lord whose life is given "a ransom for many," are, in effect, not two things but one; and the Sacrifice which is the ground of the Christian's confidence "to enter into the Holy Place . . . . by a new and living way " is itself offered through that same "eternal Spirit "[1] of love and service whereof the Christian too partakes, and in whose power he is enabled also to offer himself a living sacrifice to God.

The theology of sacrifice in the Epistle to the Hebrews is assuredly no unworthy thing ; and the work of its unknown author fitly takes its place in the New Testament canon side by side with the writings of a St. Paul or a St. John.

VIII. THE APOCALYPSE

We have used the name of St. John : as a matter of fact it is quite uncertain by whom—whether by the son of Zebedee or another—the books which in the New Testament canon are ascribed to St. John were actually written : it is still more doubtful whether the Apocalypse and the Gospel can be the work of the same individual. For our purposes the question is largely irrelevant ; the Apocalypse, Fourth Gospel, and Johannine Epistles are in any case closely related, and represent a type of Christian thought which was current at Ephesus towards the end of the first century of our era ; and the Apocalypse, upon any showing, stands somewhat apart from the Gospel and First Epistle of St. John, and is probably of rather earlier date.

The author of the Apocalypse is a Christian prophet. His writing is in line, indeed, with the general apocalyptic tradition of late Jewish and early Christian times,

---

Heb. ix. 14 — " Christ who through the eternal Spirit offered Himself without blemish unto God "—is the profoundest statement in the New Testament at once of the significance of sacrifice and of the sacrificial view of Christ.

and can only be properly understood and appreciated by those who have made themselves familiar with the apocalyptic literature as a whole. Nevertheless, in one most important particular it differs from almost every other writing of its class. Instead of throwing what he desires to say into the form of a vision supposed to have been seen by one of the worthies of old time, the author writes in his own name,[1] and openly sets forth his message as a "revelation of Jesus Christ, which . . . He sent and signified by His angel unto His servant John." In common with the New Testament writings as a whole his book is the record at first hand of an immediate personal experience: it is instinct from first to last with the consciousness of that "spirit of prophecy" which is the "testimony of Jesus."

Dwelling in Asia Minor at a time when persecution had already befallen the Church, and a further persecution was plainly imminent, "John" writes with the primary purpose of cheering and encouraging the Christians in their hour of trial. He has "in the Spirit" found himself "in the Day of the Lord": "things to come" have been revealed to him, and he is charged with a message "to the seven Churches which are in Asia." He shows them the Christ as He has revealed Himself to him, risen and reigning in glory. He who was dead is alive, and has the keys of hell and of death. The "Lamb that was slain" is the object of the adoration and the praises of the heavenly hosts. The despised Man of Nazareth is exalted to the throne of the Universe.

Nevertheless the exalted Christ still shares in the warfare, the trials and the suffering of His Church on earth. He knows very accurately and minutely what

---

[1] The author's name was almost certainly John, though it does not follow that he was John the son of Zebedee. Dr. Charles has pointed out that the literary expedient of pseudonymity was adopted by the apocalyptic writers of Judaism in deference to the late Jewish doctrine that the age of prophecy had ceased and the prophetic canon was finally closed. In the Christian Church prophecy had been revived and was recognized and held in honour. It was no longer necessary, therefore, for the writer's identity to be concealed.

is going on in the communities of those who profess His name. He sends to the several "Churches" by His servant John messages of comfort, of warning, and of counsel, according to the needs of each, together with the assurance of ultimate victory to those who remain faithful in the "great tribulation."

There follows a vision of the future in the approved apocalyptic manner. Symbols and pictures, to modern taste often bizarre and fantastic, follow one another across the stage in quick succession like the phases of a kaleidoscope, and the Church's conflict with her persecutors is set in the context of a vast titanic world-struggle between Good and Evil, between Christ and Anti-Christ, between God and Satan. Rome appears as the Mystic Babylon and the Great Harlot, the woman drunken with the blood of the Saints, and Nero as the Beast [1] whose death and reported resurrection is a diabolical parody of that of the Christ. The "tribulation" reaches its climax in a series of plagues, which lead up to the "war of the great Day of God the Almighty," the last great battle in "the place which is called in Hebrew Har-Magedon," the final triumph of the Christ, and the "marriage supper of the Lamb." The book concludes with a description of the heavenly Jerusalem and the ultimate blessedness of the saints. "I saw a new heaven and a new earth : for the first heaven and the first earth were passed away . . . and I John saw the holy city, new Jerusalem, coming down from God out of heaven, prepared as a bride adorned for her husband."

It is difficult, perhaps impossible, to arrange the successive visions of the Apocalypse in any coherence of logical scheme or order, and some of the scenes appear practically in duplicate. A few scholars hold that the book is composite, while others, who agree that as a whole it proceeds from a single author, consider

---

[1] The "number of the Beast"—666—is to be explained as a Hebrew anagram upon the name "Nero Cæsar."

that "John" has incorporated fragments of earlier Apocalypses with his own. In one or two instances this may be the case : and even where the visions are plainly original they are described in the terms and phrases of earlier writings, echoes being especially frequent of the language of Ezekiel, Zechariah, and Daniel. Yet the resultant impression is certainly very far from being that of a mere literary patchwork. The author's inspiration is living and immediate, and we are to explain the literary characteristics of his writing rather after the analogy of the modern preacher, who, in moments of high exaltation, is moved to speak of spiritual things not in words of his own, but in the familiar phrases and cadences of Holy Scripture, borrowing the language and imagery of the Bible as the best instrument at his command to express his meaning.

The symbolism which, whether we will or no, sometimes weighs upon our spirits to-day with a certain sense of incongruity, was in the age when the book was written luminous and manifoldly suggestive. Apocalyptic was then a living tradition, and the forms of its expression congenial and familiar. Its imagery had not as yet been translated mercilessly into colour and shape by a too realistic religious art, and the prosaic literalness of the Western mind was wholly lacking in the ancient East. To-day we stare so hard at the technique as to miss too often the point of the picture ; but for those who have eyes to see, the visions of John are still pregnant with spiritual meaning, and the spirit which inspires and breathes through them is still—if we except one or two passages in which under the stress of persecution, the fiercer spirit of Judaism breaks out in cries for vengeance upon the oppressor— the Spirit of that Jesus whom John owned as Master and Lord, and whose voice he had heard speaking to him in the solitudes of Patmos.

IX. The Fourth Gospel and the First Johannine Epistle

The Fourth Gospel, unlike the Apocalypse, is anonymous, though its contents almost inevitably suggest, and the twenty-first chapter—added as an appendix, perhaps by the author, perhaps by a later hand—definitely states, that the author is that " beloved disciple " who appears frequently in the narrative and is most naturally identified, at any rate upon a *prima facie* view, with St. John the Apostle who was of the number of the Twelve.

Controversy has raged, and rages, as to the character of this Gospel, whether it be history or symbolism or both : in the present state of opinion with regard to it no individual estimate of its significance is likely to command general acceptance. A full discussion could not in any case be attempted here : and what follows is accordingly put forward—to adopt words used by St. Augustine in connexion with a profounder theme— *non ut illud diceretur, sed ne taceretur.*[1]

When all is said, the religious value of the Fourth Gospel is in a very great degree independent of the question of its authorship or even of its value as history. Critical complexities and historical scepticisms are alike powerless to destroy (even for those who share them) the simplicity and depth of its spiritual appeal : the words and phrases of the Evangelist strike home with irresistible force and directness to the hearts of learned and simple alike.

[1] We have tried to draw attention to a few of the points in which the Fourth Evangelist's interpretation of the Christ is most distinctive : but in the main we have confined ourselves to the suggestion of a mode of approach to his Gospel : and what we have written should be read as an introduction to it rather than as an interpretation of its teaching. In particular we have designedly omitted to consider afresh in this connexion doctrines or ways of thinking about our Lord's Person which are common to the Fourth Evangelist and to St. Paul ; though the Gospel, in so far as it reaffirms Paulinism, does so with the added weight of twenty-five years' experience. Its very lateness in this sense adds to its value ; for it is a paradox to maintain that the longer men thought about our Lord the less they understood Him.

And the secret of the strange power of this "precious and only Gospel, far to be preferred above the others," lies in the fact that the writer has lived it. His work, even if it be regarded as history, is surely history as seen through a medium of Christian experience and reflexion: a "spiritual Gospel," as Clement of Alexandria called it long ago, the work of one of those "men of the spirit" in whom the early Christian communities recognized a peculiar faculty of insight and illumination.

Like the author of the Apocalypse, the writer lived at a time when men still had revelations to give to the Church, revelations confessedly new and wonderful, which were accepted for that very reason as proceeding from a spiritual source identified with the Holy Spirit, because displaying the operation of the same spirit which the community already possessed. Professor Weinel has suggested that the very form of the sentences and discourses in the Gospel is due to this : that the evangelist's dark, mysteriously suggestive manner of expression, with its short, simple, co-ordinated sentences and almost mesmeric rhythm, betrays the "man of the Spirit" as author ; and that he instinctively represents the Lord as speaking thus because He was, above all other, the ideal "Man of the Spirit" to whom the Father had given the Spirit "without measure." "He shall take of Mine and shew it unto you"—words which the Johannine Christ is represented as saying to the disciples with reference to the Spirit—express a truth of which the Gospel is itself the most conspicuous example ; and as it conceives our Lord as the Way, the Truth, and the Life and Light of the World, so in its doctrine of the Spirit it presents us above all with the conception of the Holy Ghost the Illuminator who is to guide the Church into all truth.

Yet the Gospel is no vague allegory ; so far from sublimating the life of Jesus into dreamy speculation, it is a protest against an idealising tendency which the Alexandrine doctrine of the Word or Logos was bringing

into the Church.[1] The point of the Gospel is not so
much the doctrine of the Word as the insistence that
the Word became flesh. It is not " truth embodied in
a tale " by literary genius : it is the drawing out of
that revelation of Divine truth which had been embodied
not by man but by God, and not in allegory but in
fact. The writer insists on the reality of the Gospel
facts, the manifestation of the Word made flesh in the
historical life of Jesus, in order to claim a like reality
for the spiritual manifestation of the Christ which had
followed it.

In a word, the author of the Fourth Gospel shares
the common characteristic of the New Testament
writers : he is less a theologian than a witness. He
is speaking in the Spirit the things which he has seen
and known. If we may assume, as we surely may,
that he is the same person who wrote also the first of
the Johannine Epistles, the tremendous declaration
with which his Epistle opens forms his own commentary upon his Gospel. " That which was from
the beginning, that which we have heard, that
which we have seen with our eyes, that which
we beheld, and our hands handled, concerning the
Word of life (and the life was manifested, and we
have seen, and bear witness, and declare unto you
the life, the eternal life, which was with the Father,
and was manifested unto us) ; that which we have seen
and heard declare we unto you also." Behind these
words lies half a century of Christian experience, and
the writer gives his message to the world in the form
of a Gospel, a written narrative of the life and Passion
and Resurrection of the Saviour, precisely because he
is absolutely persuaded that for those who had insight
to perceive it, the whole of that which the Christ had
come to be in the experience of the Church, all that
wealth of meaning which Christians had discovered in

---

[1] The tendency reached its culminating point in the later Gnostic systems. For
the permanent value of the Logos doctrine see also Essay V. pp. 214 *sqq.*

His Person and in His work, was actually implicit from the beginning in the historical facts of His life and mission.

Of those historical facts he may or may not have been himself wholly or in part an eye-witness;[1] nor is it in either case probable that he describes them exactly as they would have been described at the time by those who saw them. It is an "after-Gospel," reflective, interpretative, in a certain sense mystical. Incidents are selected for their symbolic value, and the meditations of fifty years have coloured the words and deeds. Nevertheless it is emphatically not the case that the writer is consciously idealising: he does not deliberately substitute parable for history, neither is he indifferent to historical truth. His emphasis throughout is on the living and the concrete; and the eternal truth which he discovers in the facts is not, he feels, a reading into them of what was not originally there, but a reading out of them of what was implicit from the first.

So, too, with the words which he puts into the Saviour's mouth: they may not be always the literal words of Jesus in the days of His flesh: but the evangelist feels that they are the words of "the Christ that speaketh in him"[2] even as he writes. If the Gospel had been written in our own time by a modern evangelist the third person and not the first would in most cases have been used; ancient literary canons differed from ours,[3] and in this Gospel the Church's controversy with the Jews and her beliefs about her Lord are put into the mouth of Him who is the Truth because the evangelist is assured that they are true. The discourses,

---

[1] Upon this point the authors of this volume are not unanimous.

[2] Cf. 2 Cor. xiii. 3, τοῦ ἐν ἐμοὶ λαλοῦντος Χριστοῦ.

[3] It is worthy of remark that in Greek and Latin literature (with the possible exceptions of the *Memorabilia* of Xenophon and the discourses of Epictetus) there appears to be nowhere any instance of an attempt to reproduce the *ipsissima verba* of connected speeches or discourses attributed to any of the characters introduced. The practice of Rabbinical writers was, of course, very different, and the *Synoptic* Gospels clearly conform in this respect to the Jewish and not to the Greek tradition.

if they are to come home to us with their proper force, require in many cases to be turned for modern purposes from the first person to the third.

Thus, for example, it is really the Church who in the person of Christ is saying to the Jews, "Ye search the Scriptures, because ye think that in them ye have eternal life, and these are they which bear witness of *Him*, and ye will not come to Him that ye may have life." Or again, "Even though He bare witness of Himself, His witness was true, for He knew whence He came and whither He went; but ye know not whence He came or whither He went." . . . "It is Another that beareth witness of Him, and *we* know that the witness which He witnesseth of Him is true." It is the Spirit in the Church who is witnessing to the truth of Christ, and men are rejecting His witness. The evangelist writes his Gospel for a testimony against all such, and he claims that the interpretation which he gives of the significance of the rejected Messiah is itself the fruit of an inward experience of Him, as real and concrete as the outward and palpable knowledge of Jesus in the flesh.

Nay, it represents a fuller knowledge and a further revelation. At the time the disciples had not understood : the Fourth Gospel is at one with the Synoptists here. "As yet they knew not the Scripture." We even read that " there was as yet no Spirit "—a startling phrase indeed, yet one which bore no such meaning to the Evangelist as it would have done to a Greek thinker of the fourth century. For the Spirit, the sphere in which Faith and Knowledge, Light, Life, Liberty, and Truth have their being, is to him a power rather than a substance. The conception of revelation which pervades this Gospel is essentially dynamic. It colours all the characteristic words of St. John. Instead of "faith" we have the verb "to believe," instead of "knowledge" the verb "to know." Both are processes incomplete, nay only inchoate in our experience, but

stretching out before us into the infinite. " The Light "
in this Gospel is not the white radiance of eternity
but a light that *comes* into the world and burns and
shines more and more unto the perfect day. It is "the
light of life." The " Truth " is not a collected body of
facts, a *summa theologiae*: it is the power that makes
us free. " The Life " is not the deferred reward of
goodness, but an inexhaustible spring of divine energy
—a divine energy which transforms and makes eternal
even the life that now is. And so in the days of His
flesh "there was as yet no Spirit, because Jesus was not yet
glorified " ; and therefore " it is expedient for you that
I go away : for if I go not away, the Paraclete will not
come unto you ; but if I go, I will send Him unto you." [1]

It is often said that in the Fourth Gospel what is
Jewish is replaced by what is Greek : that in particular
the doctrine of eternal life is *substituted* for that of the
resurrection and the future Kingdom, and the contrast
of the temporal and the eternal for the antithesis
between the present age and that which is to come.
This is an overstatement. Eschatology is not discarded
in this Gospel any more than in the later Epistles of
St. Paul, and so far from being wholly Greek the
language and ideas of the Gospel are at bottom Hebraic
through and through. The prologue alone brings us
face to face in the Logos doctrine with a definitely
Greek conception [2] ; and this it is probable that the
writer did not himself introduce for the first time into
Christian thought, but rather took over from the language of those around him. It is, however, true that the
Jewish ideas of the Gospel are transmuted and coloured
by the mental atmosphere of a Greek environment, and

[1] The substance of the above paragraph is drawn (for the most part *verbatim*) from
a "praelection" delivered by Dr. Inge at Cambridge in 1907.
[2] Many scholars, however, hold that the affinities even of the Logos doctrine are
rather with the quasi-personified " Memra " or " Word " of God in late Jewish
Wisdom Literature than with the Platonic or Philonic Logos. Certainly the idea
of the pre-existence of the Christ (*e.g.* " Before Abraham was, I am "), which is often
thought to be a distinctively Greek conception derived from the Logos-theology, is
already implicit in our Lord's use of the title, " the Son of Man " (cf. *supra*, p. 174,
and Essay III. p. 91).

that the process by which eschatology became less central in the Christian outlook here reaches its culminating point within the New Testament.

The reason is not far to seek : there is all the difference between a young man's hope of the future and an old man's reminiscences ; and in this Gospel the wonder of the Christian life, as the writer has lived it in the power of the Spirit and seen it lived by those around him, swallows up the future and illuminates the past, so that he sees revealed in the Saviour's earthly life of lowliness and suffering the glory of the Son of Man. " The Word became flesh, and we beheld His glory." The suffering of the Messiah had been to the first disciples a stumbling-block ; and if St. Paul had found in it a ground for glorying, it was because in His sufferings the Son of Man had emptied Himself of His glory for our sakes. The " beloved disciple," taught by the Spirit, has penetrated more deeply the mind of the Master. He has grasped the great unifying thought that to serve, to suffer, and to save is itself supremely the essence of the Divine Glory, in such sort that the human life of Jesus is the veritable incarnation of the Word, the revelation of that God and Father of mankind whose nature and whose name is Love.[1] Therefore at once in all that Jesus did a new significance is discovered. The words were the words of eternal life ; the deeds were " signs " manifesting His glory. Even in the first miracle at Cana of Galilee His Messiahship was declared : it could not be but that *even then* " His disciples believed on Him." There was no room for a *gradual* dawning, as in the Synoptic story, of the truth of His Messiahship. His glory was manifest : surely everybody must have seen it ! The Jews, too, ought to have seen it. How blind people had been ! The Evangelist is angry with those who had rejected Him, and his indignation breaks through in what is often felt to be the slightly rasping

---

[1] Cf. Essay V. p. 219.

tone of the polemic against the Jews which is put into our Lord's mouth in this Gospel.

Christ is the revelation of the Father, and the revelation is a revelation of love. The Fourth Evangelist is here at one with St. Paul. To know Christ is to know the love of God which passeth knowledge. " Herein is love, not that we loved God, but that He loved us, and sent His Son to be the propitiation for our sins." " Beloved, let us love one another : for love is of God ; and every one that loveth is born of God, and knoweth God. He that loveth not knoweth not God ; for God is love." In these sentences from the Epistle the Evangelist sums up the substance of the Gospel : for him as for St. Paul the kernel of the whole matter is love, and we may match with St. Paul's great praise of Charity the hymn of mystic love in the Johannine First Epistle.

" God is love, and he that dwelleth in love, dwelleth in God, and God in him."

" God is light, and in Him is no darkness at all."

" This is the true God, and eternal life."

St. John's writings close the Canon ; the development of Christology in the New Testament has run its course.[1] It has been the aim of this essay to exhibit it in the rich variety of its manifestations as the product of a single process, determined throughout by a living experience which amid all diversities remains essentially the same. " All these worketh the one and the self-same Spirit, dividing to each one severally even as He will." Certainly it has not been the verdict of Christian experience that the writings which are latest in date are furthest removed from the Spirit of the Master. We have recognized frankly a development,

[1] The Epistles of St. James and St. Jude and the First Epistle of St. Peter have been omitted from our survey, not because they are not important, but because they add little that is new to Christological development. They are all, probably, earlier in date than the Fourth Gospel. The Second Epistle ascribed to St. Peter may be later.

a shifting of emphasis, a modification of values. We have seen the clear-cut, realistic expectation of the Lord's immediate Coming, which marks the earliest Christian writings, pass half a century later into the quiet mysticism of St. John—"Beloved, now are we sons of God, and it is not yet made manifest what we shall be. We know that, if He shall be manifested, we shall be like Him ; for we shall see Him even as He is." It is probable that the language of St. Paul in Thessalonians is closer to the letter of our Lord's own words : shall we say that it is closer to their spirit, or represents more truly that which essentially He meant ?

V

THE DIVINITY OF CHRIST

BY

WILLIAM TEMPLE

SYNOPSIS

PAGE

I. THE FACT AND THE PROBLEM . . . 213-223

    The doctrine of the Incarnation primarily a doctrine about
God 213
    Men's experience of Christ has forced them to regard Him
as the revelation of God ; but this can only be justified if it
is rationally defensible and even rationally necessary ; *i.e.* if
it makes sense 215
    Certain implications of the doctrine made clear . . 218
    Relation of the doctrine to the fact of evil . . . 219
    If Christ reveals the actual Life of God, He thereby also
reveals the ideal Life for Man ; here is the Problem . . 222

II. THE CLASSICAL ATTEMPTS TO SOLVE THE PROBLEM 223-242

    The intellectual apparatus at the disposal of the Greek
Fathers 223
    The significance of the controversies down to 451 A.D. . 226
    The significance of the formula finally adopted . . 230
    The gain and loss of the Western method of treatment . 233
    Augustine and Anselm 235
    Merits and defects of Abelard's treatment . . . 240

III. AN ATTEMPT TO RESTATE THE FACT . . 242-263

    St. John our natural starting-point 242
    Christ's Divinity only credible if His Humanity is in some
way representative and inclusive 245
    He is not *a* God but God ; how ? 246
    He is not only *a* Man, but Man ; how ? . . . 253
    Our statement aims at gathering together the merits of
previous attempts 255
    Yet it is inadequate, as from the nature of the case all such
statements must be ; we must make successive attempts to
formulate, expecting progress but not finality . . . 258
    " He that hath seen Me hath seen the Father " . . 260

V

THE DIVINITY OF CHRIST

"Lord, shew us the Father, and it sufficeth us."

I. The Fact and the Problem

THE central doctrine of Christianity has been made unduly difficult by the way in which believers inevitably tend to state it. It is really a doctrine about God; but it is made to appear as if it were primarily a doctrine about a historic Person, who lived at the beginning of our era. We are presented with the story of a historic life, and we are asked whether or not we regard the Man who lived it as divine. It is thus assumed that we know already what is meant by the word "*Divine*"; and to some extent no doubt we do; the religious experience of mankind and the labours of philosophy have to some extent determined its meaning. But two difficulties arise at once. The "logical attributes" of God do not seem applicable to the historic Christ; and the "moral attributes," which are conspicuous in Christ, are not obviously characteristic of the Ruler of the Universe. Thus, for example, the word "*Divine*" suggests Omniscience; then where is the evidence that Jesus of Nazareth was omniscient? He suffered surprise and disappointment and openly stated that He did not know the hour of the Judgment. The word suggests Omnipresence; what can be meant

by saying that Jesus of Nazareth was omnipresent?
It suggests Omnipotence; where is the evidence that
He was omnipotent? He "could do no mighty work"
in face of unbelief.

When we pass to the moral attributes the difficulty
is of another kind. Does the word " *Divine* " mean just?
In a world where the wicked flourish, what is the
evidence that the Ruler of the Universe is just? Does
it mean loving? Look at the only part of the Universe
we know.

The fact is that most of us are not able to attribute
any such meaning to the word "*Divine*" as will enable us
to use that word of Christ, unless we have first seen
God in Christ Himself. To ask whether Christ is
Divine is to suggest that Christ is an enigma while
Deity is a simple and familiar conception. But the
truth is the exact opposite to this. We know, if we
will open our eyes and look, the life and character of
Christ; but of God we have no clear vision. "No man
hath seen God at any time."

It is this which makes St. John the most modern of
theologians. He can meet the agnostic on his own
ground. There is, admittedly, some governing force
which (if anything is) must be Divine. In the language
of that day, the name of this supreme power is the
Logos—the Word.[1] To begin with the doctrine of
the Logos is as if a writer of to-day should begin with
the doctrine of Natural Law; only philosophers could

---

[1] The history of the term Logos begins with Heraclitus of Ephesus. He was
profoundly impressed by the uniformities of nature, and to the principle of Natural
Law suggested by them he gave the name Logos, whose authority he attributed to
God : " The sun will not transgress his measures; were he to do so, the Erinyes,
aiders of Justice, would overtake him. He who speaks with understanding must
take his foothold on what is common to all, even more firmly than the city stands
on the foothold of law; for all human laws are nourished by the divine law.
Though this Logos—this fundamental law—existeth from all time, yet mankind
are unaware of it, both ere they hear it and in the moment that they hear it "
(Gomperz, *Greek Thinkers*, i. p. 74). With the last clause cf. John i. 5, 10, 11.
With the Stoics the term Logos had come to stand for the principle not only of
order but of life; cf. John i. 4. Philo had combined it with the Word of the Lord
in the Old Testament, and had made it the mediating term between the Infinite
Eternal God and the finite transitory world.

give a full account of it, but every one would know in
general terms what was intended, and every one would
accept the starting-point.

Whenever the human mind has been active for a
considerable period, it is brought back to the belief
that the world is a rational system governed by a
rational principle. Science will trust reason against all
appearances, and believes that the conclusions to which
it leads are indubitable facts. It believes, because
Reason leads to it, that the earth goes round the sun,
and that the chairs on which we sit are composed of
whirling electrons. It assumes that reality is rational,
that the principle of Reason governs it. But still it is
possible to ask, what is the *character* of this principle of
Reason ?

The belief in the unity of the world, which the
advance of science has made a dominant idea in the
minds of our contemporaries, gives an altogether new
prominence to certain problems and particularly to the
problem of evil. The Supreme Being is not now
conceived as acting only here and there or now and
then ; He (or it) acts everywhere and always. "Apart
from Him hath not one thing happened," as St. John
declares ; and he goes on to declare that the character
of this Unknown Almighty Power is revealed in a
historic Figure—Jesus of Nazareth. And in what
follows we shall, accordingly, not start with theological
presuppositions which have to be fitted on somehow or
anyhow to that historic Person ; we shall begin with
the historic Person Himself and see what the experience
of those who know Him compels us to say concerning
Him. God we hardly know ; but Christ we know,
and one who knew Him best declared that in Him
"the Word became flesh . . . and we beheld His
glory."

But why are we to take Jesus as the embodiment of
the Supreme Principle, and to believe that its nature is
the character of Jesus? Historically, men came to do

so because of the effect which He produced upon them. Men found that as they associated with Him, power came into their lives ; evil habits that had been irresistible disappeared ; the sense of alienation from God vanished ; even after His Death, they were conscious of His living Presence among them—whether visibly or invisibly. And as they looked back, with their knowledge of what had happened to them, at the time they had spent in His company, the Figure seemed perpetually vaster and more august ; the words were the same, but their significance grew—

> What first were guessed as points I now knew stars :

the actions were the same, but they were charged with new meaning ; the Death was the same, but it detached itself from its place in history and became something eternal—something enacted from the foundation of the world. The whole meaning of infinity was packed into that one event—

> Ye would withdraw your sense
> From out eternity, strain it upon Time :
> Then stand before that Fact, that Life and Death,
> Stay there and gaze, till it dispart, dispread,
> As though a star should open out all sides,
> Grow the world on you, as it is my world.[1]

And this impression is not limited to those who lived with Him in Galilee or in Jerusalem. Through all the centuries from then till now there have been men who have been conscious of the presence of one who seems to them no other than the historic Jesus, and whom they are irresistibly impelled to worship as the Ruler and Sustainer of the world.

> That one Face, far from vanish, rather grows,
> Or decomposes but to recompose,
> Become my universe that feels and knows.

Just as He Himself must needs state His Mission in terms of the Messiahship, because no less exalted con-

---

[1] Browning : *A Death in the Desert* (the best commentary on St. John's Gospel).

ception was adequate to the work that He had to do,
so His disciples, and all who in prayer or work or
suffering have sought and found communion with Him,
are impelled to exalt Him above other men, and to
render to Him worship which can only be given to
God. Historically, it is men's actual experience of
Christ that has led them to believe that in Him the
Supreme Power is made known.[1]

But this is not a final justification of any such belief;
this belief, like any other, can only be justified by the
fact that it makes sense. And this must mean that it
justifies experience alike to the moral and to the
theoretical reason. It is not enough that we should at
the end of our philosophy have merely vindicated the
postulate of all science and philosophy,—the conviction
that the universe is a logically coherent whole; we
must have found satisfaction for the moral side of our
nature also.[2] Now the only tenable explanation of the
world is the doctrine that it proceeds from and expresses
the Reason and Will of an Absolute Being.[3] A complete theology would also be a complete metaphysic, and
would give us not only the solution of all problems in
the moral and spiritual life, but also the explanation of
the motions of the planets and all other physical facts.
But it has never been supposed that the revelation of
God in Christ is directly relevant to such questions,
though, of course, truth in one department cannot
be isolated from the whole body of truth, or indeed be
fully grasped without an understanding of the whole.
If, however, the Christian doctrine is true, it must
contain the solution of all spiritual problems of actual
human life; for it claims that God is revealed in Christ
so far as that revelation can be made in the mode of a
human life, and such a revelation must give the answer
to human problems.

Chief among these is the question, What is the

---

[1] Cf. Essay II. pp. 41-46.   [2] Cf. Essay IX. pp. 471-477.
[3] Ibid. pp. 446-460.

Purpose of God for Mankind? Till that is known, nothing is of any consequence. It is only lack of imagination that enables men to say that duty and ideals can retain their full hold of us even though it be true that the whole Universe is indifferent to us and all will be at last as though we had never lived or striven. But if God has a purpose for us, what is the meaning of all the evil in life, and how, if at all, is it being justified or even remedied? What is the nature of the Life Divine or of the ideal life for man, and how, if at all, are we to enter into that life?

Let us trust for a moment to the guidance of the impulse which led men to take Christ as the embodiment of the Divine, and see what light it brings. Does this belief make sense?

(1) It is important to understand what we are doing. We are to make trial of the belief that God is absolutely and completely revealed in Christ so far as the Divine can be expressed in human terms at all. Some would say, "No doubt, Christ is Divine; but so is Buddha, and Socrates, and many another." In that sense everything is the self-expression of God, and to Christ and Buddha and Socrates we must add Nero and Cesare Borgia and Mont Blanc, and moreover all dull and commonplace things imaginable. God is the Maker of the Universe; knowledge of anything in it is knowledge of His work; and if we see any part in its context we shall therein see something of the purpose of God. But the position of which we are now making trial, is not merely that Divinity is to be found in Christ, but that the Character of God is the Character of Christ; and if so, it cannot also be the character of Socrates or of Buddha, for these are not the same.

(2) But also we need to remember that if the Character of God is the Character of Christ, it is not also the character of Jehovah as set forth in certain parts of the Old Testament (*e.g.* Isaiah lxiii. where Jehovah is represented as red with the blood of Edom).

We are to take Christ Himself as the climax, and
therefore the standard, of the revelation ; whatever in
Old Testament or other revelation is in conflict with
His, must be pronounced as due to the imperfection of
the prophet or other medium through whom the
revelation is given.

(3) Moreover, the belief is that in the historic Life
of Christ the Life Divine is manifest. St. Paul sometimes speaks of His life as a period of humiliation
between two eternities of glory. No doubt we must
appreciate the truth in this view. The Almighty Lord
of Life need not concern Himself about us ; and if He
reveals Himself as loving us constantly and boundlessly,
even as suffering on account of us, this is a self-
emptying of joy and peace which He has foregone
for love of us. But this view is not the deepest ; it
suggests that the heavenly glory is something quite
different from the earthly Life of Christ—a splendour
which He left and to which He returned. But if we
are to believe that in Christ we see the Father, we must go
further and say with St. John that the self-humbling
and self-emptying and the self-forgetting sacrifice are
themselves part of the eternal glory of God. There was
no leaving of Heaven when He came on earth. " The
Word was made flesh . . . and we beheld His glory."

This impulse to worship Christ is in harmony with
the ineradicable instinct of mankind to conceive of the
Supreme Power as good. But both are apparently
contradicted by the evil in the world which God has
made. And the evil of the world can only be justified
before Reason or Religion if it is being destroyed ; it is,
moreover, so deeply rooted in the nature of things that
only God can destroy it. And in a world so full of
sin and misery, the Creator can only be worthy of our
worship if He is bearing the burden of it.[1]

If we may say—as for myself I should wish to say [2]

---

[1] Cf. Essays VI. pp. 315, 321-322, and IX. p. 511.
[2] Cf. Bosanquet, *Individuality and Value*, vi. : specially pp. 254-255.

—that a world redeemed is better than a world that had never known evil ; if the great moments in human history or in our own lives are not the moments of undisturbed enjoyment, but the moments of victorious struggle, even at great cost, against some form of evil—then we shall say that if there were no evil, much of what is best in our experience would be impossible.

But this would only show that some evil may be justified ; it does not justify the world we know, where innocent suffering is common, where evil seems often to be triumphant, where, in the animal creation, speaking broadly, enmity and fear are supreme, and lives are wasted wholesale. Pain and Sin, as we know them, cannot be dismissed by general considerations about the excellence of sympathy or moral victory ; we must find real sympathy for all real suffering, real conquest of all real evil.

Let us first consider the lesser problem of Pain. If God is revealed in Christ the sympathy and the conquest are sure. God suffers and God conquers. When we suffer, we share the experience of God. In all our afflictions He is afflicted ; and all the pain is permitted for the joy that comes out of it, the joy of hearts united for ever in the bond that common suffering makes ; and because our fellow-sufferer is God, we can believe that for all innocent pain there is the sympathy that redeems it. This is not proved, of course, but it is credible ; it makes sense, and nothing else makes sense, of Pain.

It may be doubted whether suffering is altogether evil. It is apparently not only a condition of the realization of some forms of good, but also an essential part of much that is best in life—heroism and self-sacrifice. But sin is unquestionably altogether evil. Sin is selfishness ; it is the assertion of a part against the whole—of part of a man's self against his whole self, or of a man against the society of which he is a part.

This selfishness is the law of animal life; though already in their devotion to their young and, in some species, in their corporate existence the animals have the germ of a life that is human and even divine. But selfishness, as we know it, must always yield to love, if only the love is really understood. How does Christ, assumed for the time to be the revelation of God, meet the selfishness of man as it thwarts His purpose and conspires to kill Him? "When He was reviled, He reviled not again; when He suffered He threatened not." "Father forgive them, they know not what they do." His bearing throughout the Passion is the exact counterpart of His own teaching about God. We are to love our enemies and thereby become like to God. "Love your enemies and pray for them that persecute you, that ye may be sons of your Father which is in heaven; for He maketh His sun to rise on the evil and the good, and sendeth rain on the just and the unjust . . . ye therefore shall be perfect in the way that your heavenly Father is perfect."

If we would realize what our sin means to God, we see it in the Cross. If we would know how He regards us as we wound Him, we see it in Christ during the Passion. No man can go on for ever wounding one who bears the blow like that; no man is insensitive to love if once he realizes that he is loved. We may wantonly persist even in the injury of love, but not for ever. Love, if understood, always prevails at last; and it does so by making itself known; and it makes itself known by sacrifice. The sacrifice of the Love of God is the means by which sin is conquered; it is God's sacrifice of Himself, and therefore may reach and conquer all at last. And in conquering the sin, it justifies it; for the love thereby developed and won back is richer and deeper than is possible without the struggle.[1] The Principle of Reason which governs the world is the eternal victory of Love over selfishness

---

[1] Cf. Luke vii. 47; xv. 3-10.

at the cost of sacrifice. This is not proved, of course, but it is credible; it makes sense, and nothing else makes sense, of Sin.

But this same Sacrifice is the very Essence and Glory of the Godhead. Heaven is not the selfish reward for unselfish conduct; it is self-forgetfulness in the fulness of love. Some day the love will be returned, and Heaven will be "pleasure for evermore"; but that pleasure is one that a selfish man is by his selfishness incapable of enjoying. The life Divine is the Christ-life, the life of utter self-forgetfulness; and in this period that means real suffering and sacrifice—until all love is returned. It is not a man only of a certain time or place, but it is God who says : "If any man will come after me, let him ignore himself and take up his cross," and who answers our desire to share His glory with the words "Can ye drink of the cup that I drink of?" It is God who pleads with us when we are slack or weary in discipleship, "Could ye not watch with me one hour?" The age-long agony of Redemption is the glory of God; can we think of any greater glory? Other glories no doubt there are,

> For God has other Words for other worlds,
> But for this world the Word of God is Christ.[1]

God is Love; that is His Name and Nature; and all that is meant by that is true of Him.

Thus we find, not only a clue to the mystery of evil, but the revelation of the Life Divine which is the ideal life for Man. Not only of the vision of truth but also of the life of love we may use the great words which Aristotle borrowed from Plato—" Such a life would be more than human; for it is not by his human powers that a man will live thus, but in virtue of a divine element within him. . . . We ought not to listen to those who bid us, being mortal men, to content ourselves with what is human and mortal, but

[1] Mrs. Hamilton King : *The Disciples*.

we should to the uttermost live the life immortal." [1]
What, then, are we to say is the Divine element within
us ? It is the love which love calls forth, and we enter
the life immortal as we yield to the irresistible appeal
of the Love of God made manifest in the Life and
Death of Christ.

The instinct that has led men to worship Christ as
God is not illusory ; this faith makes sense, and it
alone makes sense, of our experience.

God has revealed Himself in Jesus Christ : that is
the central truth. But if so, we are driven to ask who
or what is Jesus Christ. Is He a man like any other
man ? or is He a Divine Being breaking in upon our
world, a God in a human body ? Neither suggestion
can explain what He has done. Somehow or other He
must be "Perfect God and Perfect Man."

II. The Classical Attempts to Solve the Problem

(a) The Theology of the Eastern Church

Before attempting to suggest the lines along which
our own thought may profitably move in its effort to
solve, or at least to restate, the problem, it is desirable
that we should trace the attempts to express it in the
thought of previous ages, which led to the formulation
familiar to us through the Creeds, and to the phrases
of traditional piety in hymns and elsewhere.

It is important to remember the main intellectual
differences between our own day and that of the early
theologians ; for only so shall we rightly understand
their meaning or find how to express it (supposing we
wish to do so) in our own language.

(1) We have first to ask what was the intellectual
apparatus with which the early theologians had to work.
It was a philosophy derived from Plato and Aristotle,

---

[1] *Eth. Nic.* x.

but cruder and coarser than it had been in the hands of those great masters. It attempted to explain the fact, that many individual objects may be called by the same name in virtue of a common quality, by regarding this quality as an independent substance which was somehow present in each of the objects. Thus if two objects were green, it was because greenness was present in both ; if two objects were beautiful, it was because beauty was present in both ; if two actions were just, it was because justice was present in both. The greenness or beauty or justice, in virtue of which things become green or beautiful or just, were regarded as independently existing objects. Whether, or in what sense, this was really the view of Plato and Aristotle does not now concern us. It was with this belief in independent real qualities—the belief called Logical Realism—that the early theologians had to work ; and students of Logic will remember that Realism was long insisted on by the Church, Roscellinus being condemned at the instance of St. Anselm for teaching that a Universal—*e.g.* green, beauty, justice —is only a name that may be applied to different objects, the latter alone having real existence.[1]

This led to the view that "Humanity" is a substance or substantial entity independent of all individual men, but possessed by them ; and "Divinity" was another such. Now the realm of objects, according to the philosophy of the period, had two great divisions— the transitory or perishable, and the eternal or immortal. Humanity belonged to the former and Divinity to the latter. As there was in Greek philosophy no real doctrine of progress, it was impossible to represent Humanity as capable of developing, under the right influences, into something Divine ; and if we attempt

---

[1] At Soissons, 1092 : but the Church afterwards came to terms with Nominalism. Indeed it was not Nominalism merely as a logical doctrine that was objected to, but the tritheistic statement of the doctrine of the Trinity to which it led.

It must not of course be inferred from my rejection of Realism that I accept Nominalism ; both of these doctrines rest on that belief in "abstract universals," the repudiation of which is one of the great achievements of modern Logic.

to bridge the gulf between the imperfect human and the perfect divine by any other theory than that of a development of the former into the latter,[1] we shall find that we are degrading the conception of God by assimilating Him to what is imperfect and evil. The early theologians therefore had to express themselves in terms of Humanity and Divinity conceived as substances absolutely distinct from one another.

(2) These writers had very little grasp of personal individuality ; they did not see clearly that because I am I, I cannot be any one else ; thus we find that they did not at first perceive any difficulty in regarding the same Person as both God and Christ, though certainly in Old Testament and Apocalyptic thought God and the Messiah are different Persons. And this lack of any vivid sense of individuality is bound up with their lack of any psychology of the will ; the importance of this defect will become plain as we proceed. These two defects explain the ease with which they came to speak of Christ's Humanity as impersonal, maintaining that in Him there was united to the Godhead Humanity as a whole—that whole "substance," by sharing in which any individual man is human. The Incarnation could thus be represented as the deification—potentially at least—of all men.

(3) The intellectual machinery at their disposal and the defects in it which we have just noticed made it inevitable that the change of spirit, which, as a fact of undoubted experience, followed acceptance of the Lordship of Christ, should be expressed as a commingling of substances. Humanity is one of the perishing substances, and we therefore shall perish unless there be infused into our substance another which is imperishable. This Christ has done, for by His Incarnation, especially as continued in and mediated through the Sacraments, He has united our human

---

[1] The difficulty of this is shown by the crudeness of the attempt known as Dynamic Monarchianism.

substance with the Divine. For the Greek Fathers Redemption is rather a change of substance than a change of will, and that from which we are delivered is rather death than sin. I am speaking, of course, of theories, and we may well remind ourselves at the outset that a man may be a great saint though his theology is defective ; and it is an undoubted fact that complete personal devotion and a vast wealth of religious experience shines through the theology of the Fathers. We shall endeavour to see what were the chief elements in this experience at the close of our investigation. At present we need only remind ourselves that they were endeavouring to formulate the real facts of their experience, and not to elaborate mere fancies.

Logical Realism, then, as described above, was the tool which the early theologians had to their hands, and all theology has been influenced by the fact. Psychology was not yet ready to be used in such an enterprise, and is only now beginning to be of service. In 1857 Archbishop Temple wrote to his old Oxford tutor, Robert Scott : "Our theology has been cast in a scholastic mould, *i.e.* all based on Logic. We are in need of and we are being gradually forced into a theology based on psychology. The transition, I fear, will not be without much pain ; but nothing can prevent it." [1]

We shall endeavour in the last part of this essay to suggest lines on which this transition may be carried out. But we must not forget that there was a very early attempt to accomplish it ; such an attempt was made by Paul of Samosata, who was condemned in 268 A.D. He saw serious difficulty in the formulation of the Church's belief concerning Christ so long as this was expressed in terms of substance, and tried to express it in terms of will.[2] Owing to his defective psychology,

---

[1] *Memoirs*, vol. ii. p. 517.
[2] Cf. Harnack, *History of Dogma*, vol. iii. pp. 40-42, and the passages there quoted —especially τὰ κρατούμενα τῷ λόγῳ τῆς φύσεως οὐκ ἔχει ἔπαινον, τὰ δὲ σχέσει φιλίας κρατούμενα ὑπεραινεῖται. Throughout this historical section I am indebted to Harnack's great work.

however, he made will appear less real than substance, and
therefore made the unity of God and Man in Christ less
real than it was represented by the orthodox formulae.
The Church, rightly insisting that, whatever else this
unity may be, it is undoubtedly real, condemned Paul's
view as heresy. The mere fact that Paul sharply distinguished between "will" and "substance" or "nature"
shows that his own conception of will was rudimentary
and far from being sufficient to support a theological
superstructure.

Paul's failure, or rather the general intellectual context which conditioned it, necessitated the formulation
of Christian experience in terms of substance ; and
so the Church was inevitably involved in the Arian
controversy. The Johannine identification of Christ
with the Logos had originally meant, in the writings
of the Evangelist, " You believe in a single world-
principle, but you do not know its character ; we do ;
it was made flesh in the person of Jesus of Nazareth."
But the philosophers who had given currency to the
term Logos had been occupied with a different problem ;
their aim was to bridge the gulf between the eternal
changeless God and His imperfect transitory creation ;
the Logos therefore had been practically a second God
—δεύτερος θεός : and unless this secondary character was
emphasized, the term was useless as an explanation of
the created world. Hence Arius was logically right,
from his own point of view, in pressing his logical point
that a son cannot be co-eternal with his father. If
Christ is " of one substance with the Father," He could
not be the Mediator of *Creation* in the terms of contemporary thought, because He could not act as the
link between the eternal God and the perishable world ;
to fulfil this function, He must in His own Nature be
something between the two.

But on the other hand, in the terms of that same
thought, He cannot be the Mediator of *Redemption* unless
He is of one substance with the Father. For, as we

have already seen, if we are to think and speak in terms
of substance, and without the help of any doctrine
of development, we must either regard the division
between God and Man as absolute or else trifle with
the problem of evil. Mediation by an Intermediary
is impossible, because the Intermediary Himself must
either be perfect (and therefore, in the terms of that day,
of one substance with the Father, and not intermediary
at all) or imperfect (and therefore incapable of imparting perfection).[1] Hence if we attend to the problem
of creation we are logically required to be Arians ; if
to that of redemption, to follow Athanasius. And
quite clearly Athanasius was right, though his position
is defective in its failure to account for the origin
of finite existence and evil ; he was right because
Redemption is a matter of primary religious importance,
whereas the explanation of the world's origin is at least
secondary. Here the world is, sure enough, however
it may have come here, and our explanation will not
alter the fact ; but the means of its redemption is
something to which we cannot be indifferent. The
real significance of Athanasius is this : at a time when
there was great danger that the Church would become
a philosophical society upholding a particular modification of Neo-Platonic Cosmology, he insisted on its
religious and practical function, and by the triumph of
his cause perpetuated the formula by which, at that
time, this function was represented. The distinction
between " like substance " and " same substance " seems
to us abstract enough and quite remote from most
men's living interest ; at that time it represented the
whole difference between philosophy in its narrower
sense and a full, living religion.[2]

---

[1] Athanasius commonly stated this distinction in the terms "Corruptible" and
"Incorruptible."

[2] The spiritual value of Semi-Arianism, with its Christ who is not God but is like
God, has been epigrammatically expressed in the following fable :—

Child. I want Mother.

Nurse. I don't know where your Mother is, but here's Auntie.

The religious value of the Athanasian doctrine lies in the union of the two natures or substances ; God united Himself to Humanity (the Incarnation) in order that in and through that act Humanity should be united to Him (the Atonement). "He became human that we might be made divine." [1] The effort of orthodoxy in the next epoch was to retain this fusion of natures without detriment to either of the natures so united.

But Athanasius had not explained his theory— probably he was not interested in explanations. His analogy of the King, who by living in only one house in a city does honour to the whole city,[2] does not explain how Christ by uniting His Divine Nature to Human Nature in one instance can glorify or deify the humanity of every one else. Later on this achievement was made logically plausible by the use of complete logical Realism ; the Human Nature which Christ assumed was that of all men, not only in the sense of qualities discoverable in Him and in others, but in the sense of an indivisible essence which inheres in us all. The complete formulation of this doctrine was the work of the Cappadocians and of John of Damascus.

The triumph of Athanasius raised the question how this union of Natures was to be related to the historic Jesus. Thus the Church was involved in the Christo-logical controversies. The starting-point of all parties was the complete division between God and Man. Apollinarianism saw that, in that case, to be both God and Man in the full sense is not merely inex-plicable but impossible ; Christ is then a Divine Spirit in a Human Body, not a Divine Man. This doctrine, however, destroys that unity of human nature with the Divine on which the Atonement depends ; it also abolishes the disappointed, suffering, historic Christ of the believer's affectionate trust. On the former ground

---

[1] Αὐτὸς γὰρ ἐνηνθρώπησεν ἵνα ἡμεῖς θεοποιηθῶμεν. Athanasius, De Inc. LIV.
[2] De Inc. IX.

it was condemned,[1] and on both grounds it prepared
for the reaction of Nestorius which virtually attributed
to the historic Christ two personalities, one human and
one divine. Nestorius saved the historic, human Christ,
but again broke up the indispensable unity of God
and Man in His Person. His condemnation [2] led to
a revival of the main position of Apollinaris, with
modifications, by Eutyches, in whose doctrine the
Humanity of Christ was merged in His Divinity.
The condemnation of this view [3] led ultimately to the
secession of the Monophysites, who would not accept
the formula of Two Natures in One Person which was
declared as orthodox by the Fourth Ecumenical Council.

This formula is peculiarly interesting. Cyril of
Alexandria had accepted "Two Natures" in 433 ; [4] but
the authority of the phrase came from the West. Leo's
celebrated letter became, by a chapter of accidents, the
basis of subsequent orthodoxy. This was due partly
to the fact that both Leo and the new Emperor Marcian
wished to lower the pride and power of Dioscurus, who
had succeeded Cyril as Patriarch of Alexandria, but
much more to the fact that Leo was provided with a
way of speaking which was legal in origin, and which
to the Greek world meant nothing in particular, and
therefore nothing plainly disastrous.

The formula of Chalcedon is, in fact, a confession
of the bankruptcy of Greek Patristic Theology.[5] The
Fathers had done the best that could be done with the
intellectual apparatus at their disposal. Their formula
had the right devotional value ; it excluded what was
known to be fatal to the faith ; but it explained nothing.
To the Latin mind there was little or nothing to be
explained ; the same man may be both consul and
augur, the same Christ may be both God and Man.

---

[1] At Constantinople, 381. It seems doubtful whether the views actually condemned as Apollinarian really represent the deepest thought of Apollinaris himself.

[2] At Ephesus, 431. The remark above applies also to Nestorius.

[3] At Chalcedon, 451.   [4] Cf. Harnack, *op. cit.* vol. iv. pp. 188 ff.

[5] But it preserved belief in our Lord's real Humanity !

This is true if one is thinking of functions, but is irrelevant if one is thinking of substances. The formula merely stated the fact which constituted the problem ; it did not attempt solution. It was therefore unscientific ; and as theology is the science of religion, it represented the breakdown of theology.[1]

That breakdown was inevitable, because the spiritual cannot be expressed in terms of substance at all. The whole of Greek Theology, noble as it is, suffers from a latent materialism ; its doctrine of substance is in essence materialistic. For the root difference between matter and spirit is not that matter is extended and ponderable and impenetrable while spirit is none of these ; it is that matter is dead while spirit is living, matter is only an object while spirit is subject as well, matter can only move in space or enter into new combinations while spirit thinks and feels and wills, and exists in these activities. The "substance" of the Greek Fathers, whether divine or human, has the material, not the spiritual, characteristics ; it is, in fact, an intangible matter.[2] God consists of one sort ; man of another. The Incarnation (which is also the Atonement) is found precisely in the communication of the divine substance to man through the union of the two natures. No doubt this was most fully expressed in Cyril's own original formula μία φύσις τοῦ θεοῦ λόγου σεσαρκωμένη,[3] and it is hard to see how Cyril could accept the "Two Natures" of the Creed of Union in

---

[1] To Western Theology the Incarnation was always a fact, whereas to the Greeks it was also a philosophy. When Western Theology developed a complete scheme of its own (in Anselm), the Incarnation appeared as merely the necessary preliminary to the Death of the Incarnate God which was the pivot of the new system. With the Greeks the vital point was the Incarnation of God ; with the Latins it was the Death of God Incarnate.

[2] It is no accident that Gregory of Nyssa should be at once the chief exponent of the conception of a single and undivided human nature which Christ took as a *thing* which He has and which, identically, we also have, and also the leader in the theory which makes the Eucharistic Sacrament a continuation of the Incarnation, by which the receiver takes into his own substance the divine substance. On this cf. Essay VII. pp. 343-347.

[3] "One nature incarnate of the divine Word." The following words—"not as though the difference of natures were abolished on account of the union "—save the orthodoxy of the formula at the cost of its intelligibility.

433. But Cyril's phrase was not clear as to the real humanity of Christ, which was and is of vital importance for devotion ; and consequently the philosophically valueless formula of Chalcedon was preferred.

The chief result of Greek theology so far was to show (not indeed to contemporaries) the impossibility of a theology in terms of substance. But in addition to this it has one great defect and one great merit. The defect is its relative neglect of the moral problem. Redemption for it is primarily not from sin but from death. The distinction between God and Man is represented, not so much as a distinction between the Holy One and sinners, but rather as between the Eternal One and the transient generations. This is part of the inevitable failure of a "substance"-Theology. In emphasizing difference of substance and a change of substance as the method of redemption, it inevitably ignores the will and with it the moral problem. The Greek Fathers are not to be blamed for this ; they had to use the current intellectual coin, and they did with it the best that can be done. It is true that in the two great masters of Greek thought a more perfect appreciation of spiritual facts can be found—in Plato's doctrine of the soul as the self-mover and the controller of creation [1] and in Aristotle's doctrine of Energy or Activity, especially as combined with Plato's " self-mover " ; [2] but their successors had not been able to carry on the argument at that high level. The more spiritual view appears, indeed, in the most philosophical of the Fathers, when Origen insists that Christ must have a human soul because only with the soul could the Logos be united. But this does not take us very far. Thought was still largely under the dominion of imagination—not issuing in it and controlling it, but starting from it and controlled by it —and the imagination is in its very nature static and

---

[1] Cf. *Phaedrus* 245 c-246 D.
[2] Cf. *Eth. Nic.* vii. 1154 b 26 ; x. 1176 a 30-1178 a 8 ; *Met.* Λ, 1071 b 3-1076 a 5.

materialistic, except when some great artist forces his images to suggest what they manifestly are not. Hence comes the particular form of the great controversies, and hence, too, the failure of the Greeks to construct a fully satisfactory theology.

In its substance-doctrine we find the key to the chief defect of that theology—its comparative neglect of the moral problem. But this same doctrine—and that, too, in its worst form—enabled it to express with unsurpassed force the unity of the Christian with his Master and the spiritual elevation of the race accomplished by the Incarnation. If a man can really believe in a Human Nature existing as a separate and indivisible thing apart from all human beings, so that the adoption of this by the Divine Word deifies all who have that nature, by all means let him use this conception to express the central fact of Christian experience—the fact which a man of God in our own time expressed in the words, " If I did not believe that Christ had by His Incarnation raised my whole life to an entirely higher level—to a level with His own—I hardly know how I should live at all." [1] This central point—the unique value of the appearance of the Divine in human form in the person of Jesus of Nazareth—has never been more powerfully emphasized than by the Greek Fathers ; and therein lies their great service to the Church.

(b) The Theology of the Western Church

Western Theology represents a very real advance on the Eastern, because it is always consciously concerned with the moral problem, and uses relatively spiritual terms ; for the juristic method of handling the matter at least recognizes that the problem concerns " persons," the subjects of rights and duties, not " substances."

---

[1] *Memoirs of Archbishop Temple*, vol. ii. p. 709. Cf. St. Paul's "To me to live is Christ " ; " Christ liveth in me" (Phil. i. 21, Gal. ii. 20).

But it purchased this advance at a great cost ; for the juristic method necessarily insists on the complete separateness of the individuals concerned, and consequently sacrifices to a great extent (and entirely when it is quite logical) the conception of a corporate life in Christ which the Eastern Church so nobly emphasized ; worse still, it concentrates attention on deliverance from the penalty of sin rather than on deliverance from sin itself, and thus remains incompletely spiritual with a tendency to a self-centred pietism.

Western Theology commences its independent career with the Pelagian controversy ; it was in that controversy that it first combated a Western heresy with Western methods. The heresy of Pelagius turned entirely upon the problem of the Will ; being vitally interested in morality, and therefore in moral responsibility, he emphasized human freedom in such a way as to make God otiose. With him and his friends (as with Kant) morality came first and religion afterwards ; God does not make us good, but rewards us when we are good ; we are under no necessity to sin, and can resist temptation if we will. As Harnack remarks, " Cicero's words, ' Virtutem nemo unquam acceptam deo retulit,' could be inscribed as a motto over Pelagianism." [1] It may well have been no accident that Nestorius befriended the doctrine and that its condemnation was finally pronounced at Cyril's Council of Ephesus in 431. For its very essence is an extreme individualism which would make havoc of the whole scheme of redemption constructed by the Eastern Church. Atonement through the union of the Divine and Human Natures can have nothing to do with a doctrine that calls on each man to work out his own salvation, or at least his own claim to salvation, in his own strength.

But Pelagianism was useful, and that mainly in three ways. First, a stage of individualism was necessary to allow

[1] *History of Dogma*, vol. v. p. 172.

a sense of individual moral responsibility in connexion
with Christianity to develop, and this Pelagianism and
Semi-Pelagianism provided; secondly, the controversy
brought the whole problem of the will into the fore-
front of theological discussion; thirdly, it was the
occasion of the full doctrinal development and self-
expression of the profound religious genius who was
its chief opponent.

St. Augustine shares with Origen and St. Athanasius
the glory of being one of the three formative powers,
after the Apostles, in early Christianity.   Much about
him was not specifically Western; much that is most
admirable was Neo-Platonic—almost all in fact of that
which afterwards became, through St. Bernard, the root
of Western Catholic mysticism.   But his great contribution lies in his revival of the Pauline experience
of forgiveness and his insight into the nature of the
human will which accompanied it.   His answer to
Pelagianism is, in effect, to pose it with a profounder
problem than its own : " We can resist temptation if we
will," but how are we to will ?   What of his own state
when he prayed, " Give me chastity, but not yet " ?[1]
How is a man to heal that ?   " At last, in the fever
of my delay I made many movements with my body,
which men sometimes wish to do and have not the
power, for that they have not the limbs, or have them
not at their command, being either bound, weakened
with disease, or otherwise hindered.   For instance, if
I tore my hair, beat my brow, clasped my hands round
my knees ; what I willed, I did.   But I might have
willed and not done it, if my joints had not the power
of movement.   So many things then I did, when 'to
will' was not in itself 'to be able'; and I did not
that which I, with a longing incomparably greater,
wished to do, and which soon after, when I willed, I
could do ; because when I should will, I should will
entirely.   For in such things the power was one with

[1] *Confessions,* viii. 7.

the will, and the will with the power ; and yet it was
not done ; and more easily did my body obey the
slightest willing of the soul, in moving its limbs at its
desire, than the soul obeyed itself to accomplish in its
will this great act of will.   Whence this strange conduct? . . . The mind commands the body and it
instantly obeys ; the mind commands the mind, and is
resisted.   The mind commands the hand to be moved,
and is so readily obeyed that the command is scarcely
distinguished from the execution ; yet the mind is
mind, and the hand is body.   The mind commands
the mind to will, that is, its own self, yet it does not
obey. . . . Why is it?   It commands, I say, to will
something, which it would not command it to do unless
it had already willed ; yet that is not done which it
commands.   *Sed non ex toto vult ; non ergo ex toto
imperat. . . . Non utique plena imperat, ideo non est
quod imperat.   Nam si plena esset, nec imperaret ut esset,
quia iam esset.*" [1]

There Augustine touches the root fact.   If our will
were a single and complete faculty bestowed on us at
birth, Pelagius would be right.   But the moral struggle
itself shows that it is a faculty to be slowly built up out
of numberless conflicting impulses.[2]   To speak of the
opposition of the Will and the Desires is, strictly speaking, nonsense, though it may be provisionally useful.
When Augustine prayed "Give me chastity, but not yet,"
he really wanted to be pure, and he also really wanted
to indulge a little longer ; and it was the same *he* who
wanted both.   To say to such a man that he must
strengthen his will is mockery ; his will is just himself,
and how shall a man strengthen himself except by
coming deliberately, when the good desire is uppermost,

---

[1] *Confessions*, Bk. VIII. chaps. viii. and ix. (Hutchings' Translation).   "But it
does not will with the whole will, therefore it does not command with the whole
will. . . . Assuredly it does not command with its whole power, and therefore what
it commands is not realised.   For if its whole power were concentrated, it would not
give command for the thing to be, because it would already be."

[2] Cf. my volume, *The Nature of Personality*, pp. 22-49.

under some external influence? And how shall that good desire ever be uppermost except through the indwelling Spirit or communicated Grace of God?

No doubt Augustine never shook off his Manichaeism completely; no doubt he drew his distinctions too sharply, and held a doctrine of the Church and particularly of Baptism which requires a Manichaean basis; no doubt his form of the doctrine of original sin rests also on such a basis; but he apprehended clearly the nature of sin and the need of redemption; he reached the true conception of the will and its freedom—not fatalism, not libertarianism, but self-determination.[1] And the self which determines is the same as the self that is to be determined; the self which, according to Pelagius, is to make me good is the bad self that needs to be made good. We can be good if we altogether will to be good; for that act of will is itself the being good. But the whole difficulty is that we only will in part to be good; we do not altogether will it. The disease is in the will—not in some part of ourselves other than the will which the will can control. How can the diseased will provide the cure? I can only be brought to will what now I do not will by some external power—and this Augustine calls Grace. It is a free gift, for *ex hypothesi* I cannot deserve it; it is just because and in so far as I am sinful and have no merit that I need it. It is the free gift of God in Christ.

It is to be noticed that hitherto there has been no mention of the Death of Christ in our account of either Eastern or Western Theology. Of course the Fathers dealt with it—chiefly regarding it as a ransom paid to the Devil, by which God bought us back from the just dominion of the Devil under which we had fallen through sin;[2] even in Augustine no inner connexion is shown between the operation of Divine Grace and

---

[1] I am speaking here of the religious experience which finds expression in the *Confessions*, and not of his completed theological system, which was, perhaps, something far less attractive. Cf. Allin, *The Augustinian Revolution in Theology*.

[2] The popularity of this is due to its position in the works of Origen.

the Death (or, for matter of that, even the Life) of
Christ.[1] In their *theories* there is, in fact, no room for
the Cross as the means of Salvation. Among the Greeks
all the emphasis is upon the Union of Natures through
the Incarnation ; [2] with Augustine it is upon the psychological effect of mystical communion with God, mediated
by the sacramental system of the Church. This lack
of emphasis on the Cross is a grave defect in their
doctrines, for it was as clear to them as to St. Paul
and to us that the saving power of Christ is focussed
in His Death, as the rays are focussed in the centre of
a burning-glass. So Athanasius appeals not to the
Incarnation but to the Crucifixion when he wishes to
point to the efficacy of Christianity as compared with
other systems.[3] So, too, Gregory of Nyssa gives us his
sister's dying prayer in his biography of her : " Thou,
Lord, hast for us destroyed the fear of death. . . .
Thou hast snatched us from the curse and sin, having
Thyself become both for us. . . . Thou hast paved the
way of the resurrection for us, having shattered the gate
of Hades and destroyed him who had the power of
death. Thou hast given those who fear Thee the image
of Thy holy Cross for a sign for the destruction of the
adversary and the safety of our life. . . . O Thou
Who didst break the flaming sword, and didst restore
to Paradise the man crucified with Thee who begged
Thy mercy, remember me too in Thy kingdom, because
I also am crucified with Thee, piercing my flesh with
nails from fear of Thee, and fainting in dread of Thy
judgments ! " [4]

That comes from the Eastern Church, but it might

---

[1] But it is true that Augustine had a vivid appreciation of the superiority of
Christianity to Neo-Platonism in that it presented the truth embodied in a Person,
and thus had power over the heart ; much of the truth was in the philosophers, but
ubi erat illa aedificans caritas a fundamento humilitatis, quod est Christus Jesus ?

[2] The Cross can of course be introduced here incidentally. Cf. Hegel, *Pro-
paedeutik*, p. 204 : " Sein Schmerz war die Tiefe der Einheit der göttlichen und
menschlichen Natur im Leben und Leiden."

[3] Ἑλλήνων οἱ φιλόσοφοι μετὰ πιθανότητος καὶ τέχνης λόγων πολλὰ συνέγραψαν·
τί οὖν τοσοῦτον ὅσον ὁ τοῦ Χριστοῦ σταυρὸς ἐπεδείξαντο ; (*De Inc.* L.).

[4] Quoted by Harnack, *op. cit.* vol. iii. p. 180.

almost come from St. Bernard or St. Catherine of Genoa. Yet the Fathers who knew that experience did not know how to make their doctrine express it. Even St. Bernard, though he makes it central, can only repeat the theory of ransom paid to the Devil. The bringing of the Cross into its true doctrinal prominence was the work of St. Anselm and Abelard.

Anselm is the first theologian to approach his subject wholly from the juristic point of view. His scheme is subtle and cannot be fairly represented by an outline. The main steps of the argument, however, are these. God's claim upon us is for absolute obedience, because He created us. This claim we cannot satisfy, because, even if we obey Him for all the future, that is only our bounden duty, and leaves our debt already contracted wholly unpaid ; and if we cannot satisfy His just claim, still less can we make good any claim upon Him (this is the juristic way of putting Augustine's main point against Pelagius—the incapacity of man in his own strength to be pleasing to God). We are guilty and our guilt is infinite, for its degree is that of the Divine Majesty we despise. An infinite restitution must be made ; and this only God can make ; but it must be made by Man, for it is Man that sinned ; hence God must become Man to make the restitution, for otherwise God will have been permanently robbed, which He cannot permit. Being sinless, the God-Man need not die, and His Death will therefore be more than His Duty, and may be regarded as the required restitution ; it is infinite, for it is God Who suffers ; it may be accounted to us, because the Father must recognize the obligation He is under through the infinite offering made, and the Son having all, requires nothing, so that the advantage may accrue to those who by His Incarnation are the Son's fellow-men, if they will approach the Father in the name and according to the precepts of the Son.

Internally the great difficulty of this theory is that it

does not show *how* the death of Christ was meritorious ;
He was sinless, so He need not die ; but that does not
prove that it was *meritorious* to die. Yet the advantages
of the doctrine are obvious. It deals with the whole
subject from the standpoint of guilt ; it is concerned
with the claim of God upon man, not a supposed claim
of the devil upon man, which God has somehow to
buy off ; it brings the Incarnation and the Crucifixion
together, and both into close relation with the
experience of forgiveness, and it leaves a part for the
individual to play.

But it is open to three serious objections. (*a*) It
represents the Death of Christ as the means of appeasing
the anger of God, not as the outcome of His Love and
of that alone. (*b*) And though it insists, and that
beautifully, on the part we still have to play—" Take
Mine only-begotten Son and give Him for thyself "—it
seems illogical in this, for the infinite restitution made
by Christ may, at least, be regarded as covering all
offences. (*c*) Moreover the correlative of restitution is
offence ; but what we need is the assurance, not only
that our offences are pardoned and their penal consequences abrogated, but that the alienation of our wills
from God is at an end.

With this need clearly before him Abelard constructed his theory. For him the Death of Christ is
the main evidence of the Love of Christ, and thence
derives its power ; as proof of that Love it breaks
down our self-will and draws out from us answering love. That is almost the whole of his theory.
It was condemned as heretical at the instance of St.
Bernard, whose objection seems to have been simply
that it included no " transaction." He *needed* a
transaction. He could not escape from the dominant
Western mode of thought—the juristic ; he could only
understand the Atonement if it were a transaction.

The real distinction is this : Did the Crucifixion alter
God's will and purpose for us or our attitude to Him ?

Clearly the latter, and the latter only, though, of course, a change in us leads to a change in His *treatment* of us. His attitude to us has always been Love. But this simple truth was concealed from earlier thinkers by two considerations. In the first place, having no theory of development in these matters they were not at liberty to regard the Old Testament conception of God as incomplete without, and therefore in its peculiar features abrogated by, the revelation of God in Christ ; somehow therefore the Jehovah of Moses and Ezekiel had to be transformed into the God and Father of our Lord Jesus Christ, and the " placating sacrifice " of the Cross was supposed to achieve this. We remember that Marcion had tried to solve the problem by supposing that there were two Gods—the Just God revealed in the Old Testament and the Loving God in the New, and it is a similar instinct which makes St. Anselm personify Justice in the Father and Mercy in the Son. This view depends upon the tacit assumption that justice consists essentially in the awarding of appropriate penalty. If by His justice we mean that God is " no respecter of persons," then no doubt we are right to call Him just ; but if we mean that He accurately balances wickedness with pain, He is not " just " at all. Such " justice " is no virtue ; and if it were a virtue in man, it would not be morally possible in God. It is nonsense to talk about God's justice in this sense of the word.

> O Thou, who Man of baser Earth did'st make,
> And ev'n with Paradise devise the Snake,
> For all the Sin wherewith the Face of Man
> Is blacken'd, Man's forgiveness give—and take !

Punishment which is merely retributive is always nonmoral or immoral ; in the case of the Creator it would also be outrageous.

It is customary to admire the piety of Abelard's theory, but to object that it is too " subjective " and makes the whole sphere of the Atonement " psycho-

R

logical." But what else is it to be? Salvation is of souls, or in other words is psychological. For an occurrence to be "subjective" does not make it any the less real, or, for matter of that, any the less " objective." If my whole will is changed, no matter how that is accomplished, that change is a real and objective fact, though it is, of course, wholly psychological.[1] But there are two real defects in Abelard's theory, though it is the best of the post-Apostolic theories ; one is that it does not show *how* the Death of Christ is a manifestation of Love. If it was a vicarious satisfaction, it was such a manifestation, but (at first sight) not otherwise. Christ was indeed full of love ; but how can that love lead Him to die?[2] The suffering of One so loving may awaken sympathy ; but we need to see how the suffering itself flows from the love—and in this respect the " transaction " theory, whether of Anselm or of Bernard, is superior to Abelard's. The other defect in Abelard's theory is that it gives no expression to the antagonism between sin and God ; it leaves no room for God's " hatred " of sin, and here again the " transaction " theory has the advantage of it.

III. An Attempt to restate the Fact

Our task now is to search for some way of at once retaining the peculiar merits in the various attempts we have reviewed, and finding room for all in our own construction. We have Abelard's exclusive insistence on the Divine Love calling out our answering Love ; we have in Anselm a perception of the impossibility of

---

[1] Cf. Essay VI.

[2] The complaint of subjectivity in this theory seems to betray a confusion. We need, surely, to insist on two points. The Atonement is wrought *for* us, not *by* us ; but also it is wrought *in* us and not *outside* us. At the same time the Cross is, no doubt, something more than a means of producing a certain effect in us ; it is the revelation of the eternal character of God—of His Love and of the agony which sin inflicts upon Him. (Cf. Essay VI. pp. 321-322, 331.)

a Holy God merely condoning evil and of the moral
necessity which He is under of expressing His hatred
of it, and we have also the introduction of the Death of
Christ as the mediating force ; this latter we have also
in Bernard's strong insistence on the necessity of a
"transaction," though the precise form of it which he
took over from Origen and the Greeks is untenable ;
in Augustine we find a recognition of the impotence of
the human will; in the Greeks we find that sense of
corporate union with Christ, and thereby with God (for
Christ is Humanity and Divinity in One), which is the
central fact in Christian experience.

St. John's doctrine of the Logos or "Word" is our
natural starting-point, for now as then it, or something
like it, is what every one dimly believes in. A hundred
and fifty years ago it was generally supposed that God
had made the world and then left it to behave according
to laws He had imposed, interfering now and then by
way of miracle ;[1] God acted, in short, here and there,
now and then. But gradually science explained this or
the other "intervention," and it seemed that the sphere
of the Divine activity was being curtailed. At last men
came to regard all events as instances of "natural law"
—and there seemed to many no need for the hypothesis
of God at all.[2] But in coming to this belief they had
really come to believe in the world as a single system
governed by a single principle—which is essentially
what was meant by the Logos. Religion is learning
again to claim all creation as the sphere of God's
operation ; He works not here and there, or now and
then, but everywhere and always. Science has not
curtailed His sphere ; it has restored us to that belief
in His omnipresent activity which we should never have
let go. But this is to anticipate. What we all instinctively believe in to-day is not, perhaps, God, but only a
World-principle, the Logos of the Stoics.

---

[1] Or of what Insurance Agencies still call "The act of God."
[2] Cf. Laplace's saying "I had no need of that hypothesis."

Political developments have had the same result. Always popular religion is conceived on a basis of unconscious political analogy. When nations were governed by Kings it was natural to extend the analogy to the Universe and think of God as a cosmic Emperor, ruling the world by laws which He imposed on it from without. When (in the eighteenth century) our fore-fathers thought that respectability required a belief in the constitutional necessity of a monarch, but that political prudence required that he should not be allowed to do anything, the analogy was again unconsciously employed, and the strange phenomenon of Deism appeared. Now that democracy has established its claim, a new change is observable ; the only power before which the individual citizen will bend his will is the collective will of the citizens as a whole, and the power of government operates not on the subjects from without but through them from within. It will be right therefore to begin with the conception of God as Indwelling, because that is the conception most easily grasped.

To begin with it—but not to end with it—for what "indwells" in the physical universe cannot be a Person even though it may be Personal in the sense of being the work or activity of a Person ; it must be a principle, therefore it is not the God of religion ; it is It and not He. I might worship It, but could not pray to It ; I might be devoted to It (as a man is devoted to his country, which is a whole "immanent" in its parts, of which he is one), but I could not love It as I love another man. We must follow St. John here strictly ; we begin with the Logos—the world-principle which is the intellectual explanation of all things ; but we go on to the Father ("He Who sent Me"). And this is required by reason ; for if the explanation of the world is a Purpose, that Purpose must be rooted in a Will. To speak of an immanent Purpose is very good sense ; but "an immanent Will" is nonsense. Shakespeare's thoughts and feelings are immanent in his plays—but not Shakespeare thinking and feeling.

Our great concern then is to know the character of this World-Principle. We do not begin with Christ and ask whether He was divine ; we begin with the World-Principle, in which every one believes, and ask what must be its character, if it is to be adequate to its greatest achievement. And if we declare that it is fully revealed only in a Person, we shall at once be involved in the belief that it is something more than could ever be immanent in its fulness in the physical world.

St. John proclaims that the World-Principle was manifest in a human life—the life of Jesus of Nazareth. " The Word was made flesh " ; " He that hath seen Me hath seen the Father." This is his great advance upon St. Paul, who tends to begin with the conception of a supernatural Christ, and as a consequence sometimes represents Christ's life on earth as a period of humiliation ; to St. John that Life, and more particularly that Death, are the revelation of the eternal glory of God—a glory which is moral, not spectacular, and is pre-eminent through sacrifice and not through force. Some of St. Paul's metaphors, as has been already said,[1] might suggest the idea of Heaven as a place or state of enjoyment as we ordinarily understand enjoyment, and that Christ consented to an interval of thirty years' humiliation in the midst of an eternity of such happiness. This would be a wholly distorted view of St. Paul's doctrine as a whole, but St. John takes us beyond all possibility of such misconception by his insistence that in the Life and Death of Christ we see the eternal glory of God.[2]

But this is only credible if we regard the Life of Christ as something more than an isolated event in past history. We are making trial of the belief that in Christ we see the Power by which the world is governed —the Almighty. But the world, if we regard its

[1] P. 219.   [2] Cf. Essays VI. and IX.

present condition in isolation, is most manifestly not governed by any such Power. The Sin and Pain of the world we know cannot be themselves the goal of the Purpose of God, if God is the Father of Jesus Christ. Either then Christ is not the revelation of God, or else the world as we see it does not express its real meaning. Only, in fact, as Christ is drawing men to Himself from generation to generation is the victory over evil won, and His claim to reveal the Father vindicated ; we can only regard Him as Divine, and supreme over the world, if we can regard Him as somehow including in His Personality all mankind. If the Life of Christ is just an event in human history, what right have we to say that the Power which directs that history is manifest here rather than in Julius Cæsar or even Nero ? We can only say this, if He is drawing all men to Himself so that in Him we see what mankind is destined to become. This doctrine of the " representative " or " inclusive Personality " of Christ was expressed by the old theologians in those terms of " substance " which have become meaningless to people of our day who have not had some training in the history of human thought ; we need to find new vehicles of expression.

But would it not be better, some one may ask, to give up the untenable theologies, and simply return to the Historic Christ ? Let us by all means come as near to Him as we can ; but that will not involve a repudiation of theology, for He Himself interpreted His own work and person in terms of " the Son of Man "—the Apocalyptic Messiah. He was " despised and rejected of men," and He claimed to be the glorious Judge of the world. Here already is the problem of Human and Divine.

Let us then try to express in our own language the meaning and value of Christ's Life and Death. St. John is always seeing the Divine in the Human ; their unity is a presupposition of which he is so confident that he makes it unconsciously ; this unity is the theme of the Greek Fathers, and the fact[1] to be explained or articulated has been tersely summarized in the words of the late Dr. Moberly, " Christ is God—not generically but identically. Christ is Man—not generically but inclusively,"[2] or, as we may paraphrase the words, Christ is not *a* God (or *a* Divine Being), but God ; Christ is not only *a* man, but Man.

As we begin our attempt to elucidate this "fact," let us remind ourselves of the impossibility of a completely satisfactory exposition. This fact is unique, and for that very reason cannot be fully set forth in terms drawn from our experience of other facts. We can never reach an adequate Christology, but we can press on from the more to the less inadequate.

Before doing so we may remark that to ask whether Christ differs from us in kind or in degree, as is often done, is to state the problem in a misleading way. The distinction between "kind" and "degree" is in itself so indefinite that no answer can be given until these two terms have been carefully defined. Does beauty differ from ugliness, or a man from a boy, in kind or in degree ? We shall therefore not try to answer the question in these terms, but try to set forth positively the relation of Christ to His Father and to His brother-men so far as we are able to do so. The reader may then employ the terms "kind" and "degree" in whichever way he likes.

Let us take first the Divinity of Christ and try to interpret it not in terms of substance but of Spirit— that is of Will. This will not be a repetition of the attempt of Paul of Samosata, because we shall not distinguish between Will and Substance. For, after all, Will is the only Substance there is in a man ; it is not a part of him, it is just himself as a moral (or indeed "active") being. And a man's will is most

---

[1] This "fact" is no doubt a hypothesis, but if it explains the other "facts," it justifies its claim to be called by the name.

[2] *Atonement and Personality*, p. xx (Contents Table, referring to pp. 81-92). My debt to this great book will be evident to all who have read it.

"free," not when he may do anything and no one can count on him, but just when he is quite dependable and *must* do this or *can't* do that. Consequently in putting all the emphasis on will, we are not, as Apollinaris supposed, driven to accept a " changeable Christ." Christ cannot be other than what He is,— could not for example yield to the three Messianic temptations at the opening of His ministry,—because He *is* Himself, that is, One in Character and Purpose with God. Nothing outside Himself prevented His yielding to the Temptation ; and in that sense it was possible for Him to yield, and the Temptation was real. But, being of the Spirit that He was, He could not yield. The actions of a spiritual Being are not determined from without ; but they are determined from within.[1]

What then is the relation of the Will—that is, the entire active Personality of Christ to the Father ? It is clear that no final answer can be given until philosophy has provided us with a final account of Personality, both Human and Divine. But it may be possible to make some real advance by following the line of thought which has guided us hitherto.

Christ's Will, as a subjective function, is of course not the Father's Will ;[2] but the content of the Wills— the Purpose—is the same. Christ is not the Father ; but Christ and the Father are One. What we see Christ doing and desiring, that we thereby know the Father does and desires.[3] He is the Man whose will is united with God's. He is thus the first-fruits of the Creation—the first response from the Creation to the love of the Creator. But because He is this, He is the perfect expression of the Divine in terms of human life.[4] There are not two Gods, but in Christ

---

[1] Cf. *The Nature of Personality*, pp. 22-32.

[2] To say it is, would be to combine the Sabellian and Monothelite heresies in their most objectionable forms.

[3] Cf. John v. 19, 20, and generally the controversial section of the Gospel, v.-xii.

[4] By the identification of Will and Substance there is, I think, effected a reconciliation of the "Incarnationist" and "Adoptionist" positions.

we see God. Christ is identically God ; the whole
content of His being—His thought, feeling, and
purpose—is also that of God. This is the only
" substance " of a spiritual being, for it is all there is
of him at all. Thus, in the language of logicians,
formally (as pure subjects) God and Christ are distinct ;
materially (that is in the content of the two conscious-
nesses) God and Christ are One and the Same.[1] The
Human Affections of Christ are God's Affections ;
His Suffering is God's ; His Love is God's ; His
Glory is God's.[2]

Our account has already fallen into verbal contradiction. We have said that the whole " substance "—
(" all there is ")—of Christ is identical with God, and
yet that in " subjective function " Christ and the
Father are distinct. No doubt we must expect to have
recourse to paradox if the fulness of truth concerning
such a theme is to be stated.[3] But a large part of our
trouble arises from the inadequacy of our language and
the false suggestions which it conveys. In all experience
there is a subject and an object ; but in the last resort
they are not separable. At any rate the subject is
nothing apart from its object. Will is distinguishable
from Purpose, but apart from Purpose there can be
no Will ; the activity of thinking is distinguishable
from any thought, but apart from thoughts there
is no thinking. We easily fall into the notion of a
self which " has " various thoughts and purposes ; but
in truth the self exists in thinking its thoughts and

---

[1] Cf. Bosanquet, *op. cit.* p. 272. Clearly it is the Logos—the Divine Humanity
—that pre-exists. The " finite centre of consciousness " (Jesus) had a beginning.

[2] Cf. Browning, *An Epistle* :

> " The very God ! Think, Abib ; dost thou think,
> So, the All-great, were the All-loving too—
> So, through the thunder comes a human voice
> Saying, ' O heart I made, a heart beats here !
> Face, my hands fashioned, see it in Myself !
> Thou hast no power nor mayst conceive of mine,
> But love, I gave thee, with Myself to love,
> And thou must love Me who have died for thee ! ' "

Cf. also *Saul*, § xviii.

[3] Cf. Essay IX. pp. 520-521.

willing its purposes, and apart from its thoughts, purposes and the like, it is just nothing at all.[1]

When, therefore, we say that in "subjective function" Christ is distinct from God, we are speaking of something which, while distinguishable in thought, is not in fact a separate "thing" from that "content" which was said to be the whole "substance" of Christ, and in which Christ and the Father are one. After all, the problem is not peculiar to theology; it arises with regard to the relations between ordinary human beings. When two people have the same thought or the same purpose, there is a real sense in which they are "of one mind" or "of one will"; yet they are not simply merged in one another.[2] And in such a case it is to be remembered that the identity extends to a very small part of the content of consciousness, while in the case which we are considering it extends to the whole.

It is not pretended that there are no difficulties in this position—difficulties arising, for example, from the limitations of our Lord's human knowledge. But what we are forced to by the work of Christ in the world is not the belief that He is the Absolute God in all His fulness of Being—("The Father is greater than I")—but the belief that in all which directly concerns the spiritual relation of Man to God, Christ is identically one with the Father in the content of His Being—("I and the Father are one"[3]). And so, while conscious that our formulation is far from adequate—(for, as we have said, no adequate formulation is as yet philosophically possible)—we may proceed on the basis of our statement that in content of heart and will[4] Christ is identically one with God.

But if this is true, something else immediately follows. If God can be revealed in a life of human

---

[1] Cf. p. 231, and Essay IX. pp. 496-498.
[2] Cf. Essay IX. pp. 501-507.　　　　　[3] ἕν : not εἷς.
[4] I.e. the *nisus* and whole method of His Self. Limitations (*e.g.* of knowledge) due to Time and Place seem to be strictly irrelevant.

love, human love must be, and must from all eternity
have been, an attribute of God. Jesus of Nazareth
was born at a certain time and place ; but in Him
there was active in the world the Eternal Spirit of
God, and in Him we touch the divine Humanity which
was always in the Godhead but only then was made
fully manifest.[1] The Everlasting Son of the Father,
the Humanity of God which is eternally obedient to
the Divinity of God—if the expression may be allowed
—took flesh in the fulness of time, that, seeing Him,
we might learn to love God.

It is sometimes asked how the Infinite God can be
revealed in an individual Person, and whether the
whole of God or only a part was in Christ. Before
we answer that question we must remove a source of
misunderstanding. In their strict sense the words
" whole " and " part " are not applicable to what is
spiritual at all, but only to what is material. Quality,
not quantity, is the only relevant category under
which to conceive the spiritual ; and the widely felt
difficulty as to how the Will of Jesus of Nazareth can
be the expression of the infinite God rests upon a
confusion of these two categories.[2]

But while it is thus quite possible that the Will of
the Infinite God should be revealed fully in Jesus of
Nazareth, so that Christ and the Father are one, it is
also true that the Father is greater than He. There
is a sense, no doubt, in which we must say that something less than the whole Godhead is revealed in
Christ. There are other attributes and functions of
the Divine besides those made manifest in Christ ;
but it is these—the Divine Humanity—which would
without Christ be unknown and to know which imports
more than all else. I know God is Infinite in Knowledge, and I am dumb ; I know He is Almighty, and

---

[1] The recognition of this fact is one great advantage of the Catholic over the
Sabellian doctrine of the Trinity. Cf. *The Nature of Personality*, p. 115.

[2] It may also be pointed out that, if spirit is the only substance in question,
" moral " and " metaphysical " unity are one and the same.

I fear ; I know He is All-Holy, and I worship. But what shall make me love ?

> He who did most shall bear most ; the strongest shall stand the
> most weak ;
> 'Tis the weakness in strength that I cry for ; my flesh that I seek
> In the Godhead. I seek and I find it.[1]

But while this line of thought helps us to understand in part the double aspect of the Person of Christ which is familiar to Christian experience by stating it in terms which we employ in other departments, it still fails to satisfy. Some further light may be thrown upon our problem by the experience of the great mystics, who, in the moment of vision, feel that they are utterly lost in God. But the parallel is not complete, for the typical mystic is extremely conscious that there is a self other than God which must be lost, and that he only loses it in the mystic trance ; whereas in Christ we find nothing that must be lost before we confess Him very God, and certainly He is not one who lives in a perpetual trance.

In fact any attempt to state in terms of ordinary thought the whole meaning of the Divinity of Christ must be inadequate. For, in the first place, we know that Logic has never yet solved the difficulty of stating the relation between Universal and Particular, and here (as in the case of a perfect work of art) we have a Particular (Jesus of Nazareth) which is a perfect instance of its own Universal (the Deity)[2]; the difficulty therefore, from a logical point of view, is not peculiar to this subject. It is really the theological form of one of the unsolved problems of philosophy, and is in no sense a "mystery" artificially constructed by theologians. But there is also another reason for

[1] Browning, *Saul*. It is important to realize that the Divinity of the Man Christ Jesus involves the eternal Humanity of God. This truth is what makes plausible and even partially justifies the "Worship of Humanity," which many in our own day have wished to substitute for Christianity.

[2] Cf. also p. 258, where the same point is urged in relation to the inclusive humanity of Christ.

the partial failure of our attempt to which we must return when we have considered the other part of Dr. Moberly's statement which we took as the basis of our inquiry.

How then is Christ " not generically but inclusively " Man ?   Not by way of " substance " ; that would lead us into all the difficulties of Greek Patristic doctrine and its neglect of the moral problem.   Christ's " inclusiveness " is not " substantial " but spiritual, not quantitative but qualitative—that is, it is accomplished through personal influence.   We are in Christ as Christ is in God.   We are ourselves and not He ; but His Influence, His Spirit, has come upon us, and we have (a little) yielded ourselves to it.   We do not surrender our " freedom " ; we love Him (a little) because He is Himself and we are what we are—and we believe that if we loved Him wholly and took His Purpose for our own, with all the pains that must involve, we should find in that the true consummation of our being.   " This is life eternal, that they might know Thee, the only true God, and Jesus Christ Whom Thou hast sent."   But we are also fond of pleasure and we shrink from self-sacrifice ; and we pray " Make me Christ-like, but not yet."   Gradually, as we contemplate that Life and Death, or as we associate with those who have come under its spell, as we commune with the Living Christ, the Influence that streams from Him moulds our own affections and purposes ; gradually we are drawn to return His love and accept His Purpose as ours ; gradually He becomes all-inclusive — not because we are merged in Him but because He is revealed, and we become like Him when we see Him as He is.

We are ourselves, and not He ; but we are social through and through.   Modern thought is only just returning from the exaggerated protest of individualism to a just appreciation of the fact which was the basis of Greek political thought, the fact that we are born members of our families, of our nations, of our race, and that all are linked together in bonds of mutual sympathy and influence. None of us is constitutionally capable of complete indifference to the love of others ; and to the Love of God, perfect in self-forgetfulness and unshrinking in sacrifice, we must, at last, respond. Our hearts and wills are drawn to God, so that we take His Purpose as our own ; as we do so, we vindicate the claim made for Christ that His Personality is representative and inclusive. To say that He represents humanity, as humanity now is, would be absurd ; when we call His Personality representative we mean that in it we see what all men shall become. But He builds us up to the measure of His own stature by drawing our hearts to Himself and filling our souls with His Spirit, so that in His Purpose the issue of our lives is included. His Personality is representative because it is potentially inclusive ; and it is both one and the other because the appeal of His Love is irresistible. To the appeal of that Love, if we understand it, we cannot fail to respond.

It is for this reason that we can rightly "plead the sacrifice" of Christ and say that

> between our sins and their reward
> We set the Passion of Thy Son, Our Lord.

By what right, men sometimes ask, can you plead on your behalf the sacrifice of Another? And we answer that we can rightly do it because that sacrifice itself has transforming power ; we believe that as we come to understand it more fully and to realize more perfectly the Love of the Victim-Priest, " we shall be like Him, for we shall see Him as He is." And so we plead His sacrifice on our behalf because we believe that one day, in the inspiration of that sacrifice, we too shall offer ourselves in like manner " to be a reasonable holy and lively sacrifice " to the Father, even as already, in its power, we offer ourselves in some degree. It is because potentially His sacrifice includes us in itself that we can plead it.

> Look, Father, look on his Anointed Face,
> And only look on us as found in Him.[1]

We surrender ourselves to it freely ; our wills are not paralysed or annulled ; yet in the degree in which that surrender is made our lives are governed by the Lord to whom we have given ourselves, till at last we may say " I live, yet not I, but Christ liveth in me." [2] The Atonement was made when the revelation of God was completed upon Calvary, for then the Atoning Power came fully into the world ; but the realizing of the Atonement in human history and individual experience is the work of Christ's Divine Spirit operating in our hearts.

The Greeks held fast to Christ's inclusive Humanity. Abelard taught that the Atonement is wrought by Christ's love which draws out our love in return. But we find that if we interpret the word "inclusive" spiritually, these two are the same. Christ " includes " us in this sense ; we freely will His purpose, because it is His, and whatever is true of Him is therefore true of us, if and in so far as we are as yet devoted to Him. Thus we may bring into the Greek theory a recognition of the exclusiveness of personality—(*qua* centre of consciousness each is himself and no other [3]) ; and yet retain the Greek theory of Christ's inclusive Personality by considering the nature of spiritual activity—affection and volition ; and, adding to this a doctrine of development, remove the absolute opposition of the Divine and Human while still fully recognizing the evil in the world. Because humanity is not alien from God, but is spiritual as He is spiritual, God can be revealed

---

[1] Cf. Essay VII. p. 344.

[2] St. Paul's "faith" (πίστις) is that whereby this identification with Christ is affected.

[3] But see Essay IX. pp. 501-507.

in a human life ; because men are sinful, it takes all the ages for God's self-revelation to win them to Himself.

We are also enabled in this way to recognize the absolute truth of Augustine's central position. The seat of the problem is our wills ; we could be good, if we would ; but we won't ; and we can't begin to will it, unless we will so to begin—that is, unless we already will it. " Who shall deliver me from the body of this death ? I thank my God through Jesus Christ our Lord." I am told to repent if I would be forgiven ; but how can I repent ? I only do what is wrong because I like it, and I can't stop liking it or like something else better because I am told to do so—nor even because it is proved that it would be better for me. If I am to be changed, something must lay hold of me and change me—not by force or by deception, for then my will is unchanged after all, but by winning my free devotion. And what shall do this if not *illa aedificans caritas a fundamento humilitatis, quod est Christus Jesus ?* [1]

Redemption is by Christ only—that is, by the Spirit of Christ. Christ is Divine, and therefore His Spirit is the Spirit of the Universe. His Spirit of service (which is only perfect in love) is the spirit of all life. Biology, Ethics, Politics, all teach the same lesson ; a species has significance through its assistance in the evolutionary process ; moral advance means widening the boundaries of the sphere of our service till all humanity is included ; political progress is the growth of insistence on the duty of each to serve all. And many may be brought to a high degree of excellence without coming personally under the direct influence of the historic Christ. But in Him alone the Divine Spirit of service to the point of sacrifice and sacrifice to the point of death is fully manifest. Others have the Divine Spirit in their

---

[1] " That charity which builds on the foundation of humility--which is Christ Jesus."—AUGUSTINE.

degree ; He alone is altogether God. When all else fails the Cross must at last prevail.

And so we come to the merit of Anselm's (or even Bernard's) theory, which gave it superiority on one side to Abelard's or the Greek—the central position given by it to the Cross. We saw that the defect in Abelard's doctrine was its failure to show how the Cross is a revelation of love. Following St. John's guidance we can see this. In Christ we see the Father. In Christ's way of meeting opposition and the death His opponents inflict we see the Father. That is to say, the pain our hostility (which is sin) brings to God can only be figured in the Cross and Passion of Christ ; and how does God bear the pain we give Him, or regard us as we inflict it ? "Father, forgive them, for they know not what they do." His love does not wait till we are loveable ; His forgiveness is not withheld till we are reformed. At the moment when we wound Him, He yearns for us. And in the moments when we realize that, we cannot sin ; we should dread to add a wound to One Who bears our wounds like that. We are, indeed, filled with fear—but it is not fear of His anger or of the punishment it will inflict ; our fear is lest we stab with our ingratitude the most loving of all hearts. "There is mercy with Thee ; *therefore* shalt Thou be feared." Christ upon the Cross is the image of God's relation to our sin—what it costs Him and how He regards us as we inflict the blow. "When He was reviled, He reviled not again ; when He suffered, He threatened not." The Agony in the Garden, the longing that the Cup might pass, and the Cry of Desolation on the Cross are the human analogue and expression of the Divine Agony in Redemption.[1] God so loved, and so loves, the world ; He that hath seen Christ hath seen the Father, and in Christ also the response of Man to the Father's love is pledged and the earnest of it given.

[1] Cf. Essay VI. pp. 321-322, 331.

S

But we have imperceptibly fallen back upon the language of devotion : we have no scientific vocabulary that helps us here. The logical difficulty already mentioned confronts us here again : we are dealing with a Particular (Jesus of Nazareth) which perfectly embodies its own universal (Humanity). And we have used language about the influence of Christ upon the souls of His disciples which is almost ludicrously inadequate to the Christian experience of the power of the Spirit and the presence of the Lord. Christ is present in His Church, not merely as Arnold is present at Rugby ; Christ inspires His Church, not merely as Gladstone inspires the Liberal party ; He is present as our most intimate friend is present, and even that is inadequate.

Our analogies break down. We may help ourselves towards an understanding of His Divinity by means of the formula, " The form of His consciousness is Human, while its content is Divine " ; we may help ourselves towards an understanding of His Humanity by interpreting its inclusiveness in the terms of our social nature ; but we know that neither attempt leads us to the heart of the mystery.

But this is what we should expect. If it is only in Christ that we have any clear vision of God, it is also only in Christ that we have any clear vision of Man. Our attempts to formulate the doctrine of the Incarnation are attempts to state a unique fact in terms which are drawn from our ordinary experience ; and that is from the nature of the case impossible. We use terms —Divinity and Humanity—whose meaning is only revealed in Christ, to account for the fact of Christ. We are involved in the mistake against which the opening of this essay protested—the mistake of regarding Christ as the problem, instead of regarding Him as the solution of the problem.

We do not know what Matter is when we look at Matter alone; only when Spirit dwells in Matter and uses it as a tool do we learn the capacities of Matter. The sensitiveness of eye and ear, the delicacy of the artist's touch, are achievements which we should never anticipate from the study of the lifeless. So, too, we do not know what Humanity really is, or of what achievements it is capable, until Divinity indwells in it. If we are to form a right conception of God we must look at Christ. The wise question is not, " Is Christ Divine ? " but, " What is God like ? " And the answer to that is " Christ." So, too, we must not form a conception of Humanity and either ask if Christ is Human or insist on reducing Him to the limits of our conception ; we must ask, " What is Humanity ? " and look at Christ to find the answer. We only know what Matter is when Spirit dwells in it ; we only know what Man is when God dwells in him.

And what do we find ? We find that if a man is thus united to God, Nature is his servant, not his master, and he may (so the story tells us) walk upon the water ; the fetters of social influence cannot bind him, and he may be sinless, though tempted, in a sinful world. The incapacities which we thought inseparable from humanity are accidental after all, just as the stubbornness of lifeless matter is no necessary quality of matter. The machine-like character of the Universe, with its rigid laws and uniformities, is given to it by our unspiritual way of handling it ; to a man in whom God dwells everything is plastic that he may mould it to God's Purpose.

But if so, it is clear at once that neither Deity nor Humanity can be expressed in terms which are drawn from the unspiritual levels of our ordinary thought ; still less then can the unity of Deity and Humanity in Christ be so expressed. Thus we reach a perfectly definite and dogmatic conclusion. But it is a new kind of dogmatism. Allusion has already been made to Archbishop Temple's statement in 1857 that " we are in need of and are being gradually forced into a theology based on psychology," [1] and we have tried to assist the movement which this indicates. We may find in another of his early letters a description of the dogmatism to which that effort leads us ; in 1850 he wrote : "I cannot help thinking that *a* dogmatic theology is yet to be looked for, which will avoid both the difficulties (putrefaction and petrifaction). I cannot help thinking that much of that will consist in distinct refusals to define ; —a dogmatism hitherto never practised by the Church." [2]

"Distinct refusals to define," coupled with repeated efforts to restate and understand as far as may be, must be our method, not because definition is an evil thing nor because the fact is in its nature unintelligible, but because all our language and mental apparatus is constructed to deal with a different class of data. We have to go back to the old story, see God and Man there made manifest, and then reinterpret human history and human psychology in terms of Christ.

Thus we read the narrative again, with the words perpetually in our ears, "He that hath seen Me hath seen the Father." We watch the Lord as He becomes conscious at His Baptism that He is entrusted with a Mission which must be called Messianic if it is to be expressed in words at all ; [3] He goes into the wilderness to meet the Temptations which arise from this conviction. The Temptation to use His Power for His own comfort, even though no one else be injured, is set aside. [4] The Temptation to interpret His Messiahship in the light of the expectation of a Warrior-Christ, such as we find in parts of Isaiah, is set aside. [5] The Temptation to interpret it as a literal fulfilment of Daniel's apocalyptic Son of Man, descending from heaven and upborne by angels, is set aside. [6] Nothing is left but the great

---

[1] Cf. p. 226.   [2] *Memoirs*, vol. ii. p. 513.
[3] Mark i. 10, 11.   [4] Luke iv. 3, 4.   [5] Luke iv. 5-8.
[6] Luke iv. 9-12. The view adopted in this sketch is in substantial harmony, but is not quite identical, with Mr. Streeter's ; cf. Essay III. pp. 99-102, 121-127. For a fuller exposition of my reading of Christ's Messianic consciousness, cf. the first of my lectures on *The Kingdom of God*.

commission to proclaim the Kingdom of God. He
comes proclaiming. It is a message of joy and
emancipation, and He Himself is full of love and
joy and peace. He is absolutely unfettered and
spontaneous. He will have no regulations to fetter
the action of His free spirit. Men are to fast when
they need it, not when it is prescribed ;[1] they are not
even to keep the Sabbath except when it is good for them
to do so.[2] And when all this brings upon Him the
opposition of the Pharisees, He recognizes the necessity
of the breach in words that show appreciation, not
censure, of what He discards. It is the old cloth that
suffers, not the new piece, when new is grafted on to
old ; if the new wine is spilled, the old skins are burst ;
the man who knows the goodness of the old will not
desire the new.[3] So He lives—frank, spontaneous,
generous,—a life reflected in His teaching, in which all
the images are drawn from out-door life or the homes
of simple folk.

But a change came. The indifference and opposition
of men turned the Teacher to whom men flocked into
the Fugitive with His twelve companions, until at the
last we see Him striding on before them with face set
hard to go to Jerusalem, and His disciples following,
wondering and afraid.[4] Three men came to Him on
that journey. One came of his own accord ; he was not
welcomed, but only told that he was choosing to follow
an outcast. Another He calls, and will not let him
wait to see his old father into his grave. And another
who would follow is not allowed to say Good-bye to
his family.[5] Why is He so stern ? Surely because of
the strain He is putting upon His own will and spirit ;
He dare not be tender then. For He sees now what
conception of Messiah He is to adopt and realize. He
points out that in kingdoms of this world rulers

[1] Mark ii. 18-20.   [2] Mark ii. 27.
          [3] Mark ii. 21, 22 ; Luke v. 39.
[4] Mark x. 32.   [5] Luke ix. 57-62.

exercise authority, but not in the Kingdom which He is founding.[1] There the governing power operates by drawing the hearts of its subjects to itself. By preaching and healing, even by living the Life Divine, He has failed ; there is one more appeal—the appeal of the uttermost sacrifice. The Son of Man—the heavenly Messiah—came not to be ministered unto, but to minister, and to give His Life a ransom for many.[2] He says the end is near. Daniel's prophecy regarding the Coming of the Son of Man and the inauguration of His Kingdom is immediately about to be fulfilled ;[3] and before the High Priest He claims that its fulfilment is accomplished —" From this moment there shall be the Son of Man seated at the right hand of the Power of God." [4]

" I, if I be lifted up from the earth, will draw all men unto Me." [5]

We often think of the Love of God as the august pursuit of a purpose of universal benevolence, or we fix all attention on its supreme sacrifice. But we must watch the whole story. The Love of God is the Christ of the early ministry, lavishing benefits on deserving and undeserving alike ; but, under the pressure of hostility and indifference, the sunny, frank, spontaneous, generous affection is changed to the passionate intensity of the tragic Hero who marches before His followers to Jerusalem and who goes out in solitude to die. God so loved, and so loves, the world ; He that hath seen Christ hath seen the Father.

As this image fastens on our mind, our hardness disappears. We become repentant, then receptive ; at last we surrender ourselves freely to the infinite Love ; we take His Purpose as our own ; He becomes to us no longer an imposing and attractive Figure, but an indwelling and inspiring Presence, the breath of our lives. St. John records the gift of the Spirit in the

---

[1] Mark x. 42-44. [2] Mark x. 45. [3] Mark xiii. 30.
[4] Luke xxii. 69 ; cf. Matthew xxvi. 64 (ἀπὸ τοῦ νῦν ; ἀπ' ἄρτι : the agreement of Luke and Matthew against Mark, which lacks the words, may well be the more original). [5] John xii. 32.

words, " When He had breathed on them, He said,
Receive ye the Holy Spirit." Thus slowly we are
all drawn in, till all men have one Purpose, and that
the Purpose of God ; till all men come to constitute
" One Perfect Man, the measure of the stature of the
completion of the Christ."

Then for the first time will the Divinity of Christ
be fully manifest ; then for the first time will the God
revealed in Christ be fully known.

VI

THE ATONEMENT

BY

W. H. MOBERLY

(iii.) It was intrinsically necessary, both in general to the
perfecting of the human character of Jesus, and
specifically to his final conquest of sin . . 310
Further, the work of Jesus Christ was the work of God.
"God was in Christ reconciling the world to Himself." The
recognition of this is necessary not only to any adequate
theodicy, but to the universalizing of the work of Christ ; and
this involves not only the Crucifixion but the Resurrection . 314

IV. THE RELATION OF THE WORK OF JESUS CHRIST TO
OTHER MEN 317-327

(1) Liberalism makes this too slight . . . 317
(2) Conservatism makes it too legal . . . 318
(3) According to the "inclusive" view, salvation must
take effect within us, but must be initiated from outside us.
Christian theology has provided a reasoned account, on these
lines, of the process by which the lifework of Jesus may come
to make a vital difference to all men 319
Thus—
(a) The historical facts of the life and death of Christ
are signs of supramundane realities . . . 321
(b) Jesus is alive and is influencing men to-day . . 322
(c) There is the doctrine of the Spirit . . . 322
Consequences—
(1) Practical :
(a) Though religion must issue in character, character,
in the end, depends on religion . . . 324
(b) The Gospel offer is not only a position of privilege
but an opportunity of service . . . 324
(2) Theoretical :
(a) "Justification" cannot properly be separated from
"sanctification" 325
(b) Our ordinary conception of personality is too
individualistic 326

V. SOME OBJECTIONS AND FINAL SUMMARY . . 327-335

Objections :
(1) We are minimizing the difference between religion and
mere morality 327
(2) We are substituting mere ideas for the historical facts . 328
Answers to these objections 329
Further difficulty as to the relation of the work of Christ to
those who have never heard of Him ; and its answer . . 331
Summary of conclusions 333

VI

THE ATONEMENT

Rex tremendae majestatis,
Qui salvandos salvas gratis,
Salva me, fons pietatis !

Nothing in my hand I bring,
Simply to Thy Cross I cling ;
Naked, come to Thee for dress :
Helpless, look to Thee for grace :
Foul, I to the Fountain fly ;
Wash me, Saviour, or I die.

THIS was once the natural language of piety : to very many it is so no longer. The mental outlook of the average educated man has been greatly transformed in recent years, and, as we all know, this has affected his theology. But nowhere is the change more marked than in connection with the theology of Atonement. For centuries the Atonement was the centre of Christian belief—not only with men of an extreme type such as the Father in Mr. Gosse's *Father and Son,* but with the great mass of sober Christian men. The Forgiveness of Sins through the Death of Jesus Christ was the heart of the Gospel message ; trust in that forgiveness was the hallmark of the individual believer ; and to become a Christian was truly to enlist in a " salvation army." To-day such language no longer rises naturally to men's lips. This does not necessarily mean that the world has grown less religious ; for among religious as well as irreligious men the Atonement has receded into the background.

The reason is not hard to find. The modern mind no doubt has its peculiar weaknesses ; but its strength certainly lies in an unusually resolute effort " to get down to moral values " in its use of religious terms. It asks of any doctrine submitted to it, " What is its cash-value in terms of moral experience ? " Tried by this test, much that is traditional is set aside as unimportant or obscure. On any showing, we do not believe some things that the ordinary patristic or mediæval churchman believed. But such change does not usually come through any formal repudiation of old beliefs, but by a tacit and gradual shifting of emphasis ; the outworn parts of theology quietly drop out of private devotion and practical teaching. Something of this sort seems to have happened in regard to the doctrine of Atonement.

The cause of the change is largely intellectual. When the average man asks himself what the inner meaning of this doctrine is, he is unable to find an intelligible answer. If he considers the explanations of theologians in different ages, he is chiefly struck by their diversity and inconsistency. They are generally metaphorical, but the metaphors differ ; they are sometimes commercial, sometimes military, and sometimes legal, and none of these seem to him to touch the realities of life and moral experience. Nor is this the worst. For, so far as he can understand the doctrine at all, it seems to him actively immoral. Jesus saved men, it seems to teach, from the penalties of sin—in fact from hell—by undergoing those penalties in their place. But such a transaction seems doubly immoral. On the one hand, it postulates a God who would otherwise condemn men to endless misery for their sins. And a God capable of this seems to the present generation no God but rather a devil. On the other hand, if we once entertain " the conception of an Almighty Chief Justice," the notion that the guilty could be acquitted in consideration of the punishment of the

innocent strikes us as involving a trifling with justice
and morality. If men are to be "judged " at all, they
must be judged by what they really are.

On these grounds, our generation tends to drop, or
at least to lay little emphasis on, the doctrine of Atonement. How far, we must ask ourselves, is this tendency
to be acquiesced in ? And there are some things to be
considered which should give us pause.

1. In so far as we insist on going behind signs and
symbols to investigate their inner meaning and value
for life, we are on sure ground. Not to us is *omne
ignotum pro magnifico* ; we cannot worship where we
cannot, at least in part, understand. But it does not
follow that the belief on which our fathers laid so much
stress must disappear. It would be rash to conclude
that, because the intellectual explanations of Atonement
are obscure or even repellent, there can have been no
experienced reality to be explained. On the principle
that smoke proves the presence of fire, the reverse is
more probable.[1] And, though we are right to appeal
to experience, we should not be too narrow or insular
in our reading of experience. We must not take the
kind of experience that is common in a particular
people or a particular generation as necessarily exhaustive. John Bull is not the measure of the spiritual
possibilities of the human race. We shall be slow then
to reject what has played so large a part in the personal
religion of many generations as unreal or obsolete,
because it does not immediately come home to ourselves
or readily find a place in our first hasty conception of
the universe.

2. This general caution is justified by recourse to
the inductive study of religion. William James in his
Varieties of Religious Experience finds something similar
to the Christian conception of Atonement at the heart

---

[1] So Dale (*Atonement*, p. 299) argues that the very difficulties which theologians
have had in explaining the Atonement are themselves a tribute to the vitality of
the Idea.

of all religion. He defines the religious consciousness as consisting in a sense, firstly, of present uneasiness, of something wrong about us as we stand ; and, secondly, of a solution for that uneasiness—of a sense that we are saved from that wrongness by making proper connection with the higher powers. Where religion is moral, man is " conscious that the higher part of him (the true self) is conterminous and continuous with a *More* of the same quality, which is operative in the universe outside of him, and which he can keep in working touch with and in a fashion get on board of and save himself, when all his lower being has gone to pieces in the wreck." [1]

3. If we try to investigate the doctrine of Atonement historically, we shall go back to St. Paul [2] behind the explanations of Schoolmen and Fathers which may seem to us fanciful or incredible. It was he who first formulated the theory ; and on this point he is a modern of the moderns. For his appeal is, first and last, to moral experience. His theology is rooted in the most vivid personal experiences of his own ; and he is no merely hysterical enthusiast, but one of the world's great men.

Redemption through Jesus Christ is to St. Paul no mystery accepted on authority. On the contrary, his theology is a generalization from his own personal experience. The starting-point in his theory, as in his own mental development, is the perplexities of moral experience ; and particularly the overwhelming consciousness of moral failure, inevitable in a man of his high ideals and sensitive conscience. "The good that I would I do not, but the evil which I would not, that I do. . . . Who shall deliver me from the body of this death." It is this discrepancy of ideal and attainment that specially shocks him ; the deadliest sin is sin against the light. Such wilful transgression is universal ; and

---

[1] *Varieties of Religious Experience*, p. 508.
[2] Cf. Essay IV. p. 176.

so are its consequences ; for every sin increases the liability to sin and past sin involves present disability.

And, worst of all, his sins have put him wrong with God. His moral life is not merely weakened and disordered, it is cut off from its natural source of strength and guidance. St. Paul is a Jew ; and the whole outcome of the history of Israel is the branding in upon the Jewish mind of the righteousness and holiness of God. He who would walk with God must be pure in heart ; and that is just what the sincere man knows that he is not. Nor is he capable of mending his ways and becoming righteous. The very fact of sin makes unaided recovery impossible, for the sinner is wanting in will-power and is incapable of sustained moral effort. He cannot wage war successfully : there is a traitor in the camp. The Old Testament sacrifices, and the works prescribed by the Law are no remedy, for it is man's heart that is corrupt.[1]

St. Paul's problem then is the problem of moral corruption and consequent estrangement from God ; the story of Jesus of Nazareth comes to him as the despaired of solution. Jesus is not to him merely the latest of the prophets. The life and death of Jesus appear to him as the supreme and central event in the history of the human race. They make possible what had seemed impossible — moral recovery and the renewal of right relations with God. They are to him the key that fits the lock, the light that dissipates the darkness.

The question which in this essay I shall try to consider is : Has the modern world the same problem as St. Paul ; and if so, can it accept the same solution ?

We must, I think, in dealing with these questions, distinguish roughly between two main divergent lines of thought—the Liberal or Modernist, and the Con-

---

[1] Cf. Essay V. pp. 235-237. St. Paul's revolt on behalf of reality and experience against the Jewish remedies for sin is in many ways parallel to the modern revolt against traditional theories of the Atonement.

T

servative or Evangelical. The position of this essay is
that each contains much truth, but not the whole truth.
And the method adopted is, at each stage, to state the
two sides and then to try to reach some "Tertium
Quid" which shall combine what is true in either.

I. The Problem—The Existence and Nature of Sin

We are met at the outset by a denial that the
modern world has the same problem at all. Sir Oliver
Lodge has said, in words that have become famous :
"As a matter of fact, the higher man of to-day is not
worrying about his sins at all, still less about their
punishment; his mission, if he is good for anything, is to
be up and doing."[1] On this view, the whole Pauline conception of Sin is a nightmare and rests on ideas of God
and Man which are unworthy and untrue. If Christianity is on this point committed to Paulinism, so much
the worse for Christianity ! If not, we must go back
behind St. Paul's legal conception of the relation
between God and Man to the trustful optimism of the
Synoptic Gospels.

This amounts to a claim for superiority for the first
of the two types of religious consciousness, which
James distinguishes as the Once-Born and the Twice-
Born. It is worth while therefore to consider that
distinction.

(1) The Once-Born

The first is the joyous type represented by the 23rd
Psalm. "The Lord is my shepherd ; therefore can I
lack nothing. . . . Thy loving-kindness and mercy shall
follow me all the days of my life : and I will dwell in
the house of the Lord for ever." James himself
describes persons of this type as "sky-blue souls

[1] *Man and the Universe*, p. 220.

whose affinities are rather with flowers and birds and
all enchanting innocencies than with dark human
passions ; who can think no ill of man or God ; and in
whom religious gladness, being in possession from the
outset, needs no deliverance from any antecedent
burden." [1] To such men, absorption in sin, and
especially in past sin, appears to be morbid and to
imply a want of proportion. James quotes Whitman,
as expressing this feeling with some bravado—

> I could turn and live with animals, they are so placid and self-
> contained,
> I stand and look at them long and long ;
> They do not sweat and whine about their condition.
> They do not lie awake in the dark and weep for their sins.

The consciousness of evil, such men feel, should be
blotted out in the glad consciousness of communion.
Within Christianity they would lay more emphasis
upon the joyous side, on peace on earth and good will
towards men.

(2) The Twice-Born

The second type is marked by a consciousness, similar
to St. Paul's, of the divided self. It starts from a
radical pessimism. It only attains to religious peace
through great tribulation ; and even then a minor note
of sadness still persists. James associates this type
with the Germanic, as contrasted with the Latin
character. Where the latter is aware of " sins " which
can be expiated in the confessional, the former is aware
of " Sin," an inward disease of the soul which nothing
external can cure. So James contrasts this as the
religion of the " sick soul " with the religion of
" healthy-mindedness."

James' own conclusion is that there is room and
need in the world for both types. " If an Emerson
were forced to be a Wesley, or a Moody forced to be a

[1] *Varieties of Religious Experience*, p. 80.

Whitman, the total human consciousness of the divine would suffer." [1] But—somewhat to the surprise of the modern reader—it is the second type which James takes as deepest. Such have been the greatest religious leaders ; such is the most forcible ; such alone sounds the depths of the human heart. " No prophet can claim to bring a final message unless he says things that will have a sound of reality in the ears of victims such as these." [2] If this type in extreme cases becomes morbid, the other may easily degenerate into shallowness. In view of the facts of life, the simple reiteration of "God's in his heaven, All's right with the world" is to many minds simply irritating. And if it is true that the sense of sin is decreasing, that may only prove the shallowness of the modern mind ; for the sense of sin is apt to be in inverse ratio to its actual presence. What men need of religion is *power*. And "modernism," it is often felt, is losing the dynamic, world-conquering force of the older gospel. *In hoc signo vinces.* We have lately been warned [3] that we cannot without loss substitute the Manger for the Cross as the symbol of Christianity.

The "Liberal" View of Sin

The distinction between the "liberal" and the "conservative" views of moral evil [4] corresponds roughly to this distinction of religious "types." "Liberalism" builds largely on the conception of Evolution. To it, sin marks a stage in moral progress which is higher than the stage of innocence ; just as,

---

[1] *Varieties of Religious Experience*, p. 487.

[2] The same seems to be the view of a writer so little tainted with ecclesiasticism as Lord Morley (*Miscellanies*, i. p. 344). He criticizes Emerson, as having never really faced "that horrid impediment on the soul, which the churches call sin, and which, by whatever name we call it, is a very real catastrophe in the moral nature of man."

[3] Johnston Ross, in the *Hibbert Journal*, April 1911, *The Cross : The Report of a Misgiving.*

[4] The term "Sin" may itself be felt to be question-begging.

to St. Paul, the stage of consciousness of the Law is itself an advance. We know that " the man who never makes mistakes never makes anything," and sins are the moral mistakes incidental to moral progress. Indeed there is an element of truth in the saying, *Pecca fortiter.* The best man will not be he in whose life it is most difficult to pick holes.

Further, sin is largely ignorance. The Christian conception of human brotherhood is specially congenial to the spirit of this age ; and, in accordance with that conception, the essence of sin is selfishness. But an analysis of the nature of Choice will make it clear that selfishness is always a mistake. The peculiar mark of rational choice as distinct from animal appetite is the conception of the object chosen as affording satisfaction to the chooser. A " motive " is not a mere desire but a desire identified with the idea of personal good.[1] But Plato and Aristotle were right in holding that man is naturally a social being, whose rational life depends on the width of his interests ; hence selfishness is always self-contradictory. Even when we should say he is acting wilfully, the man who chooses the selfish course is making a mistake. He aims like the good man at self-satisfaction, self-expansion, self-expression. But in acting selfishly he chooses what, owing to the constitution of human nature, must in the end fail to satisfy. In Dr. McTaggart's vivid phrase, Sin is like drinking sea-water to quench thirst.[2]

But if sin is largely ignorance, and sinners truly " know not what they do," our conception of the attitude of God towards erring men must be modified. The sinner merits pity and education, not the hostility of God or man. So much is due, had we the skill to trace it, to heredity and environment. *Tout comprendre, c'est tout pardonner.* It may be doubted

---

[1] This is T. H. Green's way of putting it.

[2] To *choose* is always to *choose as good*. This is suggested even by the defiant language of wilful wrongdoing, " Evil be thou my good."

whether the traditional theology has sufficiently purged
itself of elements which belong not to the true Christian
message, but to the barbarism of the peoples among
whom Christianity first spread.   Anything that suggests
"an angry God"—still more a God whose wrath is
quickly stirred and lightly laid by such trivial causes as
move human princes—is rejected as falling below the
best secular morality of to-day.[1]   God is Father rather
than Judge ; and the parable of the Prodigal Son gives
a truer and more Christian view of His attitude to the
human sinner than all the imposing imagery of the
Great Assize.

The Conservative View of Sin

(*a*) By the other school sin is viewed not so much
as selfishness but rather as rebellion.   It is indeed
egoistic ; but its egoism is directed not so much against
society as against God.   It is not due merely to the
survival of the animal in man.   It is positive rather
than negative, and springs not so much from low-grade
and undeveloped personality as from the perversion of
personality at its highest.   Increase of civilization, it is
suggested, does not necessarily carry with it decrease of
sin.   And it has been pointed out that the sins towards
which Jesus was most severe were not such as sensuality,
which spring from animal instincts, but the more
subtle and deadly sins such as hypocrisy, malignity, and
spiritual pride against which culture and intelligence are
no sure defence.   The climax of sin would then be not
the brute but the devil.

(*b*) Further the sin of a responsible moral agent has
the special character of "guilt."   The sense of responsibility is an ineradicable element in moral experience.

---

[1] Dr. McTaggart suggests that theological notions of the propriety of eternal
punishment have at this moment a retrograde influence on our practical treatment
of criminals.   And Mr. Holmes traces most of the evils of our elementary education
to the prevalence of the ecclesiastical conception of the natural depravity of child-
nature.

We must look at sin, it is held, if we are to view it truly, not so much with the eyes of the criminologist who is only an external observer as with the eyes of the sinner himself. If a man who has done wrong is worth anything, if he still retains a healthy sense of right and wrong and any power of being sincere with himself, he does not acquit himself of responsibility for his own sins on the grounds which might satisfy the external observer. His sin weighs on him as guilt, and he feels that it deserves punishment. Human justice, no doubt, is an external and imperfect thing, to which he may or may not be amenable ; not all sins are crimes, and not all crimes are in fact detected and punished. But, though he may escape all human punishment, he cannot escape the inner tribunal of his own conscience ; and, tried at its bar, he knows himself guilty and punishable.

(c) If modern thought denies any validity to the belief that sin incurs the wrath of God, it has overshot the mark. Indeed, its whole estimate of moral values is challenged. The humanitarian movement of the nineteenth century, it is held, has swept us off our feet, and has degenerated into softness and sentimentalism. A certain fierceness against wrong and wrongdoers is involved in a real ardour for goodness : it is necessary for moral health, and, if we have lost it, we need to recover it.[1] This will apply to our conception of God. The mere amiability of " le bon Dieu " of much modern opinion is but one step removed from the moral indifference of Omar Khayyám's " Good Fellow."[2] The use of " anger " or " wrath " in connection with God is only objectionable, in so far as it suggests an arbitrary, private, and personal emotion. But judicial

---

[1] Dr. Holland tells us that the late Dean Church, the gentlest of men, was capable of a white heat of indignation against anything really vile, which recalled the phrase, " the wrath of the Lamb," and was altogether terrifying.

[2] " Why," said another, " some there are who tell
Of one who threatens he will toss to Hell
The luckless Pots he marr'd in making—Pish !
He's a Good Fellow, and 't will all be well."

retribution is impartial and impersonal. "Vengeance is Mine" : this limits, but at the same time consecrates, the notion of retribution. The disinterested infliction of retribution is sometimes a moral necessity. "Indignation against wrong done to another has nothing in common with a desire to revenge a wrong done to oneself. It borrows the language of private revenge just as the love of God borrows the language of sensuous affection." [1] "Be done by as you did," is the law of a moral universe.

The Influence of Metaphor

It is to be noted that the cleavage we have traced between the two conceptions of sin corresponds roughly to a difference in the kind of symbol or image chosen as the vehicle of thought. From the time when the still small voice was recognized as a truer representation of God than the fire or the earthquake, theological advance has largely consisted in the improvement of the mental forms or "categories" in which we think. We are forced therefore to consider the comparative adequacy of different sets of images ; just as the artist or craftsman has to decide not merely how best to execute a design in a given medium, but which medium is best for his purpose. Thus "a knife is properly made of steel ; you can only make a bad one of iron, or copper, or flint, and you cannot make one at all of wax." [2] Sir Henry Maine, in a brilliant chapter in his *Ancient Law*, calls attention to the enormous and largely harmful influence which conceptions drawn from Roman Law have exercised in the history of political thought, and hints that the same might be shown to be true in Theology. In politics, as with the contractual theories of the origin and basis of political obedience, it had a cramping influence, against

---

[1] T. H. Green, *Principles of Political Obligation*, § 183.
[2] Bosanquet, *Essentials of Logic*, p. 50.

which Burke finally protested, when, in language now famous, he declared his inability to "draw up an indictment against a whole people," because "the thing was too big for his ideas of jurisprudence." In Western theology, this influence has been equally strong. In the conception of an universal rule of Justice, and of sin as guilt deserving punishment, we have the moral relations of God and man conceived in terms of criminal law.

This has met with drastic criticism from modern thinkers ; with whom, in theology as in politics, biological are tending to oust juristic metaphors. They feel that the legal imagery makes the relations of God and man, and of one man with another, too rigid and external. They feel further that such ideas imply an exaggerated notion of individual freewill and too sharp a separation between voluntary and involuntary actions. Leslie Stephen even ventures to assert that the conception of God as an Almighty Chief Justice is too antiquated for serious discussion. And some theologians hold that the great obstacle to a satisfactory theology of the Atonement in the past has been the dominance of the popular imagination by the ideas of the Latin, as opposed to the Greek Fathers.

But the older-fashioned thinkers do not so readily surrender. They contend that metaphors drawn from Jurisprudence preserve an important truth which the language of Biology obscures. Law deals with the relations of persons ; while Biology blurs what Coleridge calls "the sacred distinction between things and persons." Moral evil, they insist, like moral goodness, belongs rather to "will" than to "nature" ; the evil from which men need deliverance is "sin" rather than "death" ; and physical metaphors such as "disease" and "medicine," "the infection of sin" and "the infusion of grace," are largely misleading.[1]

[1] Cf. Essay V. pp. 231 ff.

Original Sin

So far we have been concerned with moral evil in the form of voluntary acts ("actual sin"). When we come to "Original Sin," the case is different. There is the same contrast of liberal and conservative, but their use of categories is partially reversed.

Here, too, Sir Oliver Lodge is voicing a widespread feeling when he roundly denies the existence of Original Sin. It is a figment so impossible, he holds, that no one but a monk could have invented it. The following are some of the difficulties which the Liberal finds in the conception of Original Sin.

(1) It is connected with the belief in an historical fall from a primitive condition of perfection. But the conception of a Golden Age in the remote past, though common in antiquity, is impossible to reconcile with the facts of evolution and the knowledge spread by modern science of the early history of the race.

(2) But no doubt the historical side of the belief is not of primary importance. Not the origin but the fact of mutual entanglement in evil is what is really asserted. That the individual does not start free ; that he is hampered by a sinful "nature" and sinful impulses even before his first voluntary sinful act ; that he inherits a bias and predisposition to evil ; that behind individual sin there is corporate sin and corporate liability to punishment ; these assertions are the real nerve of the doctrine. They are met by the Liberal with an emphasis on the distinction between sin itself and what is often called " the matter of sin." Sin is wilful : solicitations only become sin when yielded to. Within the self we are accustomed to the distinction of " person " and " nature." Heredity is chiefly physical, as the mode of its transmission is physical. We are largely interdependent physically and in regard to the " matter " of our moral life ; but spiritually each man is, in the last resort, a free man. And particular

theories of the mode of transmission are inevitably materialistic.[1]

(3) Even if Original Sin were conceivable, Original Guilt would be inconceivable ; for individual responsibility is limited by individual power. To primitive morality it seemed natural that a whole family or clan should suffer for the wrongdoing of a single member, and that the sins of the fathers should be visited on the children. But the world has not stood still ; and the growth of civilization and of moral understanding has been precisely in the direction of greater discrimination. Civilization has moved, in Sir Henry Maine's phrase, from Status to Contract ; *i.e.* from a condition in which a man's fate is determined by birth and other circumstances over which he has no control, to one in which each man is increasingly the architect of his own fate. And when it comes to moral payment each man, an English sense of justice suggests, must settle his own accounts.

> The sin that ye do by two and two
> Ye must pay for one by one.

These are difficulties which we all feel : but, to each of them, the Conservative has, I think, a sufficient answer.

(1) The projection of an ideal into the past is a natural tendency of the human mind. In the history of political theory we know that thinkers were at one time mainly occupied in reconstructing the origin of society in ways which better historical knowledge has shown to be entirely fictitious ;[2] and we have learnt to see that, though historically false, their theories were not necessarily valueless. They spoke of origins ; but they were really concerned with the practical question of the basis and limits of authority in their own time. The same is true here. What is important is not an historical Fall, but the fact of " fallenness." It is the sense of contradiction involved in human experience of

---

[1] See Tennant, *The Origin of Sin.*
[2] *E.g.* the doctrine of an Original Contract.

sin which it is desired to emphasize. I am not, I feel, what I was meant to be : the whole human race is not what it was meant to be. Sin is universal, but it is unnatural, and this is well illustrated by the common phrase, " Be a man ! " [1] There is a feeling of home-sickness in our yearnings for goodness.

(2) Any sharp division between "will" and "nature" is unsound psychology. The self is always a great deal more than the content of consciousness at any given moment. The conscious and the unconscious shade off into one another. There are probably very few conscious acts in most men's lives which express the character of the doer at all fully. But dispositions, as well as acts, have moral quality. And all that lies below the threshold will form part of a final moral estimate of the man.[2]

(3) Behind particular theories of transmission, we find in the Old Testament an impressive consciousness of corporate solidarity in good and evil. A benefit to an individual is a benefit to his whole family ; an injury to an individual is an injury to the whole family. And perhaps we shall be less ready than Maine and his contemporaries, fifty years ago, to assume that this is simply a relic of primitive moral stupidity. It is less plausible now than then to maintain that society is moving towards a sort of glorified individualism. Is it simply an unreal sentiment which makes us hold that, as Englishmen, we have some share in the glory of Trafalgar and Waterloo, and of the abolition of the slave-trade, and some share in the shame of the loss of

---

[1] This is put with his accustomed vigour by Mr. Chesterton. " If I wish to dissuade a man from drinking his tenth whisky and soda, I slap him on the back and say, ' Be a man ! ' No one who wished to dissuade a crocodile from eating its tenth explorer would slap it on the back and say, ' Be a crocodile ! ' "

[2] Cf. Browning—

Thoughts hardly to be packed
Into a narrow act,
Fancies that broke through language and escaped,
All I could never be,
All men ignored in me,
This I was worth to God Whose wheel the pitcher shaped !

America and the South African disasters, even though,
as individuals, we contributed nothing to either?
In truth, neither in its causes nor in its consequences
is sin a purely individual affair. The havoc in our
own lives is often not the worst result of our sins;
and if lack of imagination did not prevent our realizing
the sin and misery our own sins have caused in the
lives of others, we should need no further hell.[1] The
individualist may continue to asseverate his independence:

> It matters not how strait the gate,
> How charged with punishments the scroll,
> I am the master of my fate;
> I am the captain of my soul.

And on such terms a vicarious atonement would be
neither necessary nor possible. But the boast is simply
unfounded. With such individualism we can make no
terms. In the spiritual world, whether we like it or
not, there *is* taxation without representation.[2]

In this section we have distinguished two types of
theology resting on two types of religious experience.
It has already been suggested that neither has the
whole truth; but, for the moment, I do not attempt to
combine them in a synthesis, but have simply tried to
clear the issue. The direction in which they may be
combined may become more clear in the course of the
next section.

---

[1] Cf. *The Bridge of Sighs*—

> In she plunged boldly,
> No matter how coldly
> The dark river ran;
> Over the brink of it
> Picture it,—think of it,
> Dissolute Man!
> Lave in it, drink of it,
> Then, if you can!

[2] At this point, the combatants seem to have exchanged weapons. The Liberals
insist on individual personality as the source and limit of responsibility, and hold
that the moral quality of the individual's own character entirely determines his
status in the eyes of God: while it is the Conservatives who find an exclusively
moral view inadequate to life. This uncertainty of touch accords with our contention that either view by itself is one-sided and inadequate and hence demands the
other for its completion.

II. The Conditions of a Solution

(1) Here too we find the same line of cleavage between a liberal or modernist, and a conservative or evangelical view. Liberal thought, taking a less gloomy view of the problem, is naturally more optimistic as to the possibility and nature of a solution. On the one hand, it is no use crying over spilt milk. The past cannot be undone ; to put the clock back is not only impossible but meaningless.

μόνου γὰρ αὐτοῦ καὶ θεὸς στερίσκεται,
ἀγένητα ποιεῖν ἅσσ᾽ ἂν ᾖ πεπραγμένα.

On the other hand, it holds, we are not in practice enslaved to the past. " Let the dead bury their dead," the future is ours. The secret of redemption, for us as for Faust, is work in the service of man ; " not brooding and lamentation, but putting in so many hours of work per day." In the older view, it is suggested, there is a moral defect, in that it implies an unhealthy pre-occupation on the part of the individual with the fate of his own soul. There are some sins which it is the best policy to forget ; to put them resolutely out of mind, " *getting away from* sin, not groaning and writhing over its commission." The dangers of the opposite course may be seen in some of the more repellent developments of casuistry. Here, indeed, there is place for a judicious pragmatism. The extraordinary power for good often exercised by those who "think no evil" is proverbial. To treat a man as good, and to expect the very best from him, has often proved the surest way of eliciting the best. It may be that we should treat ourselves on the same principle. The greater demands we make on ourselves, and the less we dwell on the possibility of our own failure, the more likely, it may be, we are to succeed. With regard to our relation to God, sin no doubt means remoteness from Him and incapacity for communion.   But all that is needed to bridge the gulf is moral improvement on our part ; there is no barrier between us and God over and above our moral unfitness ; there is no need to propitiate an angry God. God does not change ;   He is always loving, like the Prodigal's father.   Vengeance is not a motive worthy of a moral being ; *a fortiori* it can have no place in the character of God.   Love, indeed, is not inconsistent with discipline ; "whom He loveth, He chasteneth." But this is only a means to an end.   Purely retributive punishment, inflicted with no merciful purpose, would be immoral.   To bring man near to God, all that is needed is to build up his character, and consciousness of sin is not a help to this.   All the Old Testament metaphors of sacrifice are to be discarded.   To express the truth in such terms may not be absolutely impossible, but it is to put new wine in old bottles.   It is unnatural and unreal for a Western world to try to interpret to itself the deepest spiritual truths by means of an Oriental imagery that has no place in the living concerns of to-day.   The process of character-building may very probably involve suffering.   There will be plenty of room, as Sir Oliver Lodge says, in the long struggle *humanam condere gentem* for ennobling self-sacrifice and voluntary suffering in the service of others.   But there need be no *penal* suffering.   The various metaphors of a "burden" which weighs men down, or a "debt" which they must pay antecedent to moral recovery, are pure mythology.   The only burden is the burden of actual imperfection ; the only "debt" which men owe is obedience to the moral law, and that is a debt which nothing can remit.

(2) To the Conservative, such optimism seems too cheap and easy.   It appears to conflict (*a*) with the necessities of the moral government of the world ; (*b*) with the facts of human nature ; (*c*) with the witness of religious experience.

(*a*) We should not lightly assume that the infliction of retributive punishment must be impossible to God. Indeed, if we take the conception of "divine government" seriously, such retribution would appear to be not only possible but necessary. The infliction of punishment may be a duty, because, apart from any ulterior effects, the moral order has to be maintained. Something like this feeling of a moral obligation to punish is familiar to the experience of all who have exercised authority. Private and personal offences may be forgiven, but public wrongs cannot so lightly be dismissed. It is not that repression in the abstract is good ; but such repression is only the other side of the maintenance of a moral order, *i.e.* of a system of rights and duties, the existence of which is itself a good, and which must be supported if necessary by force. *Noblesse oblige.* The ruler is not a free agent, and cannot freely indulge his private wishes, whether for his own pleasure or in indolent good nature towards others. The necessity of retribution rests not on barbarism, but on "a stately and austere conception of order."

This sense of obligation to punish has found powerful expression in literature. Kant, for instance, made the famous declaration that "even if a civil society resolved to dissolve itself with the consent of all its members, so that punishment would no longer be required for deterrent purposes, the last murderer lying in prison ought to be executed before the resolution was carried out. This ought to be done in order that every one might realise the desert of his deeds, and that blood-guiltiness might not remain upon the people." [1] The same feeling of moral obligation pervades the Pope's deliberations on the fate of Guido in *The Ring and the Book* :

> I may die this very night,
> And how should I dare die, this man let live ?

---

[1] *Philosophy of Law*, translated by Hastie.

No doubt there is in all this much that is metaphorical. We cannot without reservation apply to God the necessities of the human ruler. But this is largely true of any terms in which we may think. Does there not, we must ask ourselves, remain a large residuum of truth which must find a place in any theology we can construct?

(b) When we penetrate behind what is conscious and voluntary to the sphere of the natural constitution of the human mind and the natural laws of its working, we may see more reason for a somewhat pessimistic view. Liberalism appears "to be offering a pill for an earthquake." To prescribe inattention as a remedy for sin suggests too readily the adage, "Let us eat and drink, for to-morrow we die!" But the past contains the seeds of the future; and the theology which treats our past sins as a "burden" is not frightening us with bogies, but is merely giving a rather metaphorical statement of actual facts. We have here no invention of priests, but something that is substantially endorsed by modern psychology. "We are spinning our own fates, good or evil, and never to be undone. Every smallest stroke of virtue or of vice leaves its never so little scar. The drunken Rip van Winkle, in Jefferson's play, excuses himself for every fresh dereliction by saying, 'I won't count this time!' Well, he may not count it, and a kind Heaven may not count it; but it is being counted none the less. Down among his nerve-cells and fibres the molecules are counting it, registering and storing it up to be used against him when the next temptation comes. Nothing we ever do is, in strict scientific literalness, wiped out." [1] This conception has abundant support in the world's imaginative literature; conceptions such as that of the Greek "Furies" are really based on this inner, "self-acting" retribution. And those who bear it in mind sometimes show a certain impatience of optimists who appear to have forgotten it.

---

[1] James, *Principles of Psychology*, vol. i. p. 127.

(*c*) Important as are moral character and conduct, they are not the whole of life. The supreme question about a man is not, What is his inner character ? but, What is his relation to God ? And though the two are connected, it is not the inner change but the outer that is primary and causal.

Now religious experience has continually been an experience of individual impotence. To this we have a great body of witness from men who were neither fools nor weaklings. We are caught as in a net : " tied and bound with the chain of our sins." This is the experience not of the few but of the many.

> Not the labours of my hands
> Can fulfil Thy law's demands ;
> Could my zeal no respite know,
> Could my tears for ever flow,
> All for sin could not atone ;
> Thou must save, and Thou alone.

To neglect this because it does not immediately come home to ourselves, would be worse than foolish.

(3) So far we have been collecting evidence : we must now try to formulate our own attitude in view of the evidence. We may perhaps venture to put forward three assertions.

(*a*) We shall, on the whole, agree with the Liberal in holding that the problem is really a moral problem. Our status in the universe—or, in religious language, our relation to God—depends on character. The truth of what we are in our inmost souls, this, and nothing that is comparatively irrelevant or external, determines our fate.

The whole history of religious development supports us in this conclusion. Early mythologies contain truth with an admixture of irrelevant spectacular machinery that " half conceals " as well as " half reveals " the truth it symbolizes. Growth in apprehension takes the form of increasing discrimination between substance and accident, and a consequent elimination of irrelevancies.

The phenomena of primitive sacrifice suggest that the early gods might take pleasure in all sorts of unimportant things. The Jews, however, were gradually educated to understand that character is the one thing that matters to the true God. Because God is good, the only godliness is goodness. To love righteousness and hate iniquity is the only way to find favour in God's sight. "The word God means always Righteousness and Truth, and the Love which is the Love of Righteousness and Truth. Nothing can ever affect God's relation towards us, which does not affect the relation towards us of Righteousness and of Truth. If God loves us, they love us. If they love us not, neither does God." [1] This principle is absolute, and must regulate all our thought.

(*b*) We shall then agree most with the Liberal on the relative value of different "categories." The metaphor of Ruler or Sovereign is on a lower plane, and describes the relation of God to man less truly than the metaphor of Father or loving Friend. In the argument from the obligation of the judge to punish irrespective of the present moral condition of the criminal, solely because he has done wrong in the past, so much obviously depends on human limitations. The human judge has no power to measure repentance and amendment; he has frequently to sacrifice the welfare of the individual to the good of the community. To transfer such limitations to God is to indulge in quite superfluous anthropomorphism. To suggest that the past binds God to act irrespective of changes of circumstances, is to conceive of Him very mechanically. In particular, it seems to leave no room for the all-important distinction between the sinner and the sin which is so prominent in the New Testament. It seems to assume that the sin is always a true expression of the sinner's personality; whereas in truth it never is so. So far as our past sins affect our present character,

[1] R. C. Moberly, *Atonement and Personality*, p. 280.

and no further, will they affect God's treatment of us.

(*c*) But we shall agree with the Conservative that the magnitude of the change demanded in man is much greater than liberalism allows for. It is no reform of superficial qualities in me, which " I " might effect. It is " I " who am to be changed, not superficially, but fundamentally. " How can I, if I have lied, be not a liar ; how can I, if I have murdered, be not a murderer ; how can I, if I have sinned, be not a sinner ? "[1] For my sin is part of myself. It is not like a debt or an illness which leaves me at bottom the same person, whether solvent or insolvent, whether well or ill. So true reformation is intrinsically very difficult, and for myself unaided impossible, because *I* am the obstruction. The far-reaching nature of the trouble and the need is well illustrated by Mr. Temple's distinction of Augustinianism from the Pelagian heresy.[2] " Pelagius's position put shortly was :—I can be good if I will. God rewards me when I am good, but does not make me good ; His reward is, of course, an incentive to goodness, but it is no more. Augustine in effect replies : I could be good if I would, but I won't. And that is the whole difficulty ; I can't move my will. My will moves everything else. But what is to move it, if it is diseased and is set on the things I know are wrong ? What in the world would cure that ? The whole difficulty is, that when the opportunity of wrong-doing comes I always choose it. How am I to cure myself ? "

And because moral revolution is difficult, forgiveness is difficult. If forgiveness meant merely not resenting, dropping the matter, not prosecuting or letting off a penalty, it would be easy enough ; but we are purposely putting aside forensic imagery as misleading and inadequate. And if it means, as it

---

[1] *Atonement and Personality*, p. 36.
[2] *The Faith and Modern Thought*, p. 130 ; cf. also Essay V. pp. 235-237, 256.

must, the full restoration of delicate personal relations
between friends or between parent and child, then it
is exceedingly difficult. How often we hear it said :
Yes, I will forgive him, but I can never feel the same
towards him again ! Such " forgiveness " is a mere
parody of divine forgiveness of sins. But sin is a
barrier to intimacy. And intimacy with the sinner
can only be renewed if the context of the sin is altered,
so that it is seen that it did not really express him.
But if it did ever really express him, even in part,
then he must be altered, and such an alteration is very
costly.

We have then to consider how we can formulate in
terms of our familiar experience the moral transformation which would, if it were possible, constitute an
atonement for sins ; *i.e.* which would in removing the
cause of estrangement remove, as it were automatically,
the estrangement between God and man. And perhaps
the experience of penitence for wrongdoing is the most
enlightening for our purpose. Penitence is a word
which is often abused ; and if it is to serve our purpose,
we must use it with its fullest meaning ; and understand
by it no easy emotion of self-loathing or self-contempt,[1]
but a real change of purpose of heart and of mind.[2] If
this were ideally complete, it would constitute a breach
with the past so fundamental that the man might really
be said to be morally a " new man." What he used to
love, he now loathes ; the principles he used to ignore,
he now strenuously follows. This would be a change
of character—so far we agree with the Liberal. But
it is penitence, not mere obedience or amendment, it

---

[1] It's not enough to say,
    " I'm sorry and repent,"
    And then to go on afterwards
        Just as you always went.

[2] The word " penitence " has perhaps an ecclesiastical flavour which may damage
it in the eyes of some. But I cannot think of any substitute that is better. The
point is its double-facedness, the combination of shame towards the past and new
resolve for the future. And even towards the future it suggests a certain humility,
a certain distrust of self and trust in God, which Liberalism a little misses.

directly faces and contemplates, and does not ignore the past—and so far we agree rather with the Conservative.[1] It is sometimes felt that there is something morbid about this, as when Sir Oliver Lodge prescribes work rather than " brooding and lamentation." And it certainly can be morbid and exclusive. But the man to whom religion is a reality will have learned to distrust these clear-cut antitheses. He knows, for instance, that the antithesis of prayer and work is true for a narrow logic rather than for life. And he may reasonably suspect that the same is true with regard to the antithesis between regret for the past and resolve for the future.

But complete penitence is merely ideal; and penitence which is real in experience is only imperfectly transforming. Complete penitence demands great will-power, and this is just what is not forthcoming. " I can be frightened at my sin ; I can cry out passionately against it. But not the tyranny only, or the terror, or the loathing, but also the love of it and the power of it are *within me*. The reality of sin in the self blunts the self's power of utter antithesis against sin. Just because it now is part of what I am, I cannot, even though I would, wholly detest it. It is I who chose and enjoyed the thing that was evil ; and I, as long as I live, retain not the memory only, but the capacity, the personal affinity, for the evil taste still." [2] Penitence in experience then does but offer a hint of a moral regeneration to which it never attains. It is not ordinarily atoning ; and here we are at one with the

---

[1] This interest in the past, which is the distinguishing mark of the synthetic view as contrasted with Liberalism pure and simple, may seem unprofitable and superfluous. But I believe it is connected with a profound difference in metaphysic between the two. If the ideal were a mere blotting out of past sin, making it as though it had never been, then concentration on the past would be waste of time. But if such a blotting-out is literally incredible, being purely mythological, and having no intelligible meaning for experience ; and if the ideal is not the *abolition* but the *transformation* of the past, not mere happiness but the bliss of the redeemed (cf. Essay V.) ; then we should naturally lay stress on continuity, and our attitude towards our past history would have a very practical importance.

[2] *Atonement and Personality*, p. 42.

Conservative. But again we find ourselves nearer to the Liberal when we consider the reason of this failure. Penitence, we hold, is insufficient atonement for sin, not because it is *merely penitence* (*i.e. only* a change of character), but because it is *incomplete penitence* (*i.e. only* a *partial*, and therefore very probably a transitory, change of character).

We have then at least a glimpse of what salvation would mean. But we see also that the individual cannot save himself. We must therefore consider what are the agencies known to us in experience by which individual effort can be stimulated and supplemented. These range from forcible interference in the form of punishment, through all the different degrees of education, up to the most delicate and spiritual influence, by way of affection, of one person upon another.

(*a*) *Punishment.*—The moral influence of punishment is often denied. It tends, it is sometimes thought, to degrade and brutalize rather than to elevate ; and in any case its results can be only mechanical, and a compulsory morality is no morality. But here again we must protest against too sharp a division between the physical and the moral. Force and persuasion shade off into one another. Between them there is every variety of influence ; at no point is it possible to draw a line and to say, Above this line there is morality ; below it there is none. What begins as non-moral external force need not end there. The true object of punishment, so far as the person punished is concerned, is to awaken in him a sense of disgrace ; that is, to arouse in him such a realization of the true meaning of his wrongdoing as may induce him to repudiate it and to change his ways. " When we kick against the pricks, and it reacts upon us in pain, this pain has subtle connections throughout the whole of our being. It brings us to our senses, as we say ; that is, it suggests, more or less, a consciousness of what the habitual system means and of what we have committed in offending against it.

When one stumbles and hurts his foot, he may look up and see that he is off the path."[1]

Even this may seem too exclusively intellectual. Increase of knowledge, it may be felt, will not by itself make a bad man good. It is his will, not his reason, that needs to be changed. Once again we must deprecate sharp divisions. Reason and will are intimately connected. "The first step towards moral reformation is to rouse reflection in a man or people ; to give them a new insight into the significance of moral alternative. . . . All moral awakening is primarily an intellectual awakening, a repentance or change of mind (μετάνοια). . . . A moral truth does not remain a merely intellectual apprehension ; it rouses the emotions, and demands expression, through them, in action or in life."[2]

(*b*) *Love.* —Though punishment is a genuinely moral agency, it is only a humble one, and deals after all only with low beginnings. The higher we get in the scale the less is there any question of "infliction," the less anything like a collision of wills. But the best chance for the sinner is the existence of a loving friend who has not shared in the moral disaster. There is fine and true psychology in the picture in *David Copperfield* of the attitude of Daniel Peggotty to Em'ly after the catastrophe. There is no passing by on the other side. There is no diminution of affection. There is from first to last no doubt or hesitation, but an attitude of unquestioning love and welcome. In a real sense, the old fisherman may be said to have joined in bearing his daughter's sin and shame just because of the bond of love that existed between them. This instance is illuminating : we may note, firstly, that there is no compromising of moral values nor blurring of the extreme sinfulness of sin. Though Mr. Peggotty's love for his daughter[3] is not in the least diminished by her fall, it is henceforth coloured by the fact of it.

---

[1] Bosanquet, *Philosophical Theory of the State*, p. 225.
[2] James Seth, *Ethical Principles*, p. 9.
[3] Literally " niece," but " daughter " by adoption.

The mental attitude in which father and daughter eventually join is penitential. We have here not only penitence, but vicarious penitence. It is easy to say that the sin was the sin of one, and that it is impossible for one individual to be penitent for the sins of another. But how clearly irrelevant is the objection, and how obviously is life too wide for that kind of logic ! And, secondly, though there is external help and no external imposition of penalty, there is here no question of "getting off easily" or avoiding suffering. To see another bearing the shame of one's own sin is indeed to learn to loathe the sin and to know it as it is. But it is not to escape shame or penitential suffering, but rather to feel these with a keenness otherwise impossible. "There is no agony like the agony of returning animation." [1]

So far Atonement would seem to consist in the thorough-going moral regeneration of the sinner, which would by itself constitute a true "reconciliation" or at-one-ment between himself and God. But we have not yet exhausted the truth of the Conservative contention that no change of character in the individual sinner is by itself sufficient atonement. The time has gone by when we could treat either sin or restoration as a simple transaction between God and the sinner without the intervention of third parties. "A gospel of the Atonement is singularly parochial which covers only the relations of the individual with God." [2] Sin, we have already agreed, is more than merely individual in its causes and its nature : its consequences also are not confined to the individual sinner. The dreadfulness of our own sins lies not merely in their effects on ourselves, but in their devastating effect on the lives and characters of others. But, if this is so, and if the

---

[1] Lodge, *op. cit.* The reality of vicarious penitence in human experience, as illustrated especially in the relation of mother to child, has been very carefully worked out in *Atonement and Personality*, ch. vi.

[2] Dinsmore, *The Atonement in Literature and Life*, p. 219. My obligations to this most suggestive book are very great.

sinner is a man of the smallest generosity of mind, his own restoration to moral purity and to favour with God, while the fate of the victims of his sin is doubtful or worse, will afford him a very partial satisfaction.[1]

We have here not merely an inner, but an outer limit to the atoning efficacy of human penitence at its best. It cannot by itself restore the broken lives and stunted characters of those who have been influenced for ill by the past sins of the penitent. For our complete satisfaction it would be necessary that we should see that our very sins against others and the offences we had induced in them had in the end been turned to their good ; as Joseph's brethren found that their very sin had been an instrument in the providential shaping of Joseph's life. But such a consummation is quite beyond the reach of our own private efforts. An element in Atonement is suggested which is intelligible in terms of our moral experience, and yet is quite outside the range of individual transformation.

On this point many will feel that the traditional theology has been defective. A recent writer has said that, for whole centuries, faith was occupied with self : " To die so as to escape the Devil was an art, the *Ars Moriendi*." [2] In this there is no doubt much caricature, but there is also some truth. It is important to insist that the problem is never simply : " Should I be safe, if I were to die to-night? " Any redemption worth having must be a social redemption.[3]

III. The Work of Jesus Christ

We have been considering the nature of the more fundamental human needs. We have now to ask in

---

[1] Mr. Dinsmore puts this very strongly. He quotes Adam Bede, "There's a sort of wrong that can never be made up for." Arthur Donnithorne is penitent, and Adam Bede has forgiven him, but he cannot do much to repair the consequences of his sin in the life of Hetty. They have passed out of his control.

[2] *Light, Love, and Life*, p. 173.   [3] Cf. Essay IV. p. 177.

what sense the life-story of the Founder of Christianity suggests a satisfaction for those needs. What is the meaning of the offer, "Come unto Me"?

(1) *The Liberal View*

Different views of the work of Christ correspond roughly to different views of his person. The Liberal generally emphasizes the reality of his humanity : a supernatural conception of him is not only difficult to accept on intellectual grounds, but has also the special disadvantage of introducing a magical element which would impair the religious value of belief in Christ. In the same way, the chief work of Christ is, in the eyes of the Liberal, his revelation of the true character of God. The real Incarnation consisted in the demonstration that "God is Love," that His relation to men is more fitly symbolized by the relation of father and child than by the relation of sovereign and subject. In regard to man the chief work of Christ was to provide a pattern of character for imitation. The moral appeal which he makes to the human heart is so familiar that it need not be laboured. By example even more than by precept, he taught that the life of obedience to God and of service to man is the highest life that man can live and the life which most truly satisfies his deepest nature. His mission was to make others what he was himself ; and thus to be the first-born of many brethren.

On this view, too much attention has, in the past, been concentrated on the *death* of Christ. It is his life, not his death, that is really of central importance. It is true that, in an imperfect world, the service of man nearly always involves sacrifice, and the power of self-sacrifice to move men's hearts has been attested over and over again : *Sanguis martyrum semen ecclesiae.* But the difference between the death of Jesus and that of every other martyr to human progress is a difference of degree not of kind. To apply conceptions drawn from the Old Testament to the death of Jesus will then be misleading ; for the old sacrificial system is abrogated in favour of something better. That death is not a sacrifice except in the sense of " Lo, I come to do Thy will, O God." " It is not only permissible but obligatory for us to eliminate from our thought of the reconciling work of Christ every trace of expiation or penalty except as illustrations such as might be given in parables or metaphors." [1] Indeed, to this school, the whole conception of a need of expiation rests, as we have seen, on a false and unworthy view of the character of God.

(2) *The Conservative View*

Its Method. — The Conservative view claims to be inductive and not deductive. It starts from the authority of Revelation as guaranteed by religious experience rather than from *a priori* considerations of what is morally probable or fitting. The fact of salvation through the death of Jesus is our primary certainty and our most practical concern. We must expect to understand but imperfectly its Why and Wherefore. There is here an element of mystery, something not directly translatable into the terms of our ordinary moral experience ; and it is just at the point where our explanations most fail that we are most conscious of the need for worship. We shall be wise therefore to cherish a certain reverent agnosticism. This attitude is well described by Dr. Sanday : " I have the greatest reluctance, even upon what seem to be obvious propositions of morality, to lay down laws for the Almighty. ' Shall not the Judge of all the earth do right ? ' is no doubt a maxim that stands absolutely fast. But it is another thing to say that we shall always be able to see what is right. The lines meet, no doubt, somewhere,

---

[1] Canon J. M. Wilson, *The Gospel of the Atonement*, p. 94.

but that meeting-point may be beyond our ken."[1] If then we criticize the Conservative account of the *rationale* of Atonement, it is only fair to remember that this is put forward as partial and secondary, and that the main grounds of its authors' belief lie elsewhere.

(*a*) *The Death of Christ primary.*—St. Anselm distinguished between Christ's life of obedience, which was only what is due to God from every man, and his voluntary death, which was more than was due. He held that it was in virtue of the exceptional merit of his death that Christ was able to claim from God the remission of the punishment due to man.[2] No one would now hold St. Anselm's theory in its literal form ; but the distinction of the death from the life, and the ascription of an unique value to the former, underlies much that is accepted. The life was within the human sphere ; it is in the death that we reach the supernatural. And the Conservative holds that the death was, or at least set in motion, an event, act, or transaction, in the supersensible world, the results of which are of transcendent importance. This event may be differently envisaged. And the fact is much more certain than any particular imaginative setting.

(*b*) *Its Significance in Military Terms.*—The significance of the death of Christ has constantly been conceived by the popular mind in military terms, as the culminating point in the cosmic struggle between the forces of good and evil. On Calvary was fought the supreme " decisive battle " in the world's history. There the devil and his angels met their Waterloo.[3] Such is the imaginative setting of the death of Christ in many of our hymns and much of our popular devotion.

(*c*) *Its Significance in Juristic Terms.* — The military metaphor has exercised some sway over popular

---

[1] In a review of *Atonement and Personality* in the *Expositor*, April 1901, afterwards reprinted in *The Life of Christ in Recent Research*, p. 238.

[2] Cf. Essay **V.** p. 239.

[3] Cf. Simpson, *Fact and Faith*, p. 56.

thought. But, at least in the centuries since the Reformation, the legal metaphor has exercised a much greater influence, not only over popular thought, but over scientific theology. The sinner is conceived as subject to the "wrath of God," by no arbitrary fiat, but by the necessity of the moral constitution of the universe. In virtue of his personal identity, he is responsible for the past. He needs to be cleansed not merely from the present power of sin, but from its guilt. The problem is, how he can be excused, and how God can remit the penal results of sin consistently with the claims of Justice. The answer is, that it is not possible for one holding a position of responsibility simply to pass over offences. Punishment can only be remitted if the hostility to evil from which it springs is adequately expressed in some other way. In this case, this is done by the voluntary substitution of another for the guilty. The obvious objection to such a theory is that it only proves the nobility of the substitute at the expense of the justice of the judge ; for no just judge could possibly accept the substitution of the innocent for the guilty. In answer to this objection, emphasis is placed on the identity between the judge himself and the substitute as expressed in orthodox dogma. We are familiar with a trivial example of the same principle on the not infrequent occasions on which the magistrate on the bench pays a prisoner's fine for him. His official position makes it impossible for him not to enforce the law ; but the circumstances of the case may have roused his pity, which can only take effect in this way.

(*d*) *Its Relation to God.*—The result accomplished by the death of Christ is greater than any conversion or moral change within man. By it the attitude of God Himself towards men is altered. They had been justly subject to His righteous wrath and hostility. Now, without detriment to His righteousness, that hostility is removed. This is clearly suggested by Dr.

Fairbairn :[1] "What do we conceive Christ accomplished by His death? What was its purpose, its *terminus ad quem* as it were? Is its influence exhausted in what it enables man to do or become? Or does it so concern God that, because of it and through it, He has new relations to man?" The death of Christ makes repentance not only possible to me but acceptable to God.

(*e*) *Its Relation to Sin.*—The death of Christ has a direct relation to the past sins and consequent guilt of men. It is therefore rightly and appropriately described in sacrificial language. And the widespread feeling of the necessity of sacrifice—though it sometimes takes barbarous and horrible forms—is to be taken as a fundamental human instinct and as really sound.

But we must distinguish within the conception of Sacrifice between its primary aspect of sin-offering or propitiation and its secondary aspect as moral self-dedication. In virtue of Christ's sacrificial death in the former aspect, something is done in the eternal world, whose causes we can understand but dimly if at all, but whose effects we can appropriate and enjoy. Apart from the Atonement, men are in a double difficulty : they are not only unable to do right in the present and future, but they are estranged from God by their guilty past. It is this burden of the past that the death of Christ has removed. There must therefore have been in it something which transcended any merely moral work : "Penitence cannot undo, and Christ did."[2]

Further, the essence of Christ's sacrifice, the sin-offering or propitiation, is unique. It is a finished work, done *for* men and not *by* men, "a full, perfect, and sufficient sacrifice, oblation and satisfaction for the sins of the whole world." It is in this thought that the triumphant character of Evangelicalism consists.

---

[1] In Dr. Sanday's *Priesthood and Sacrifice*, p. 129.
[2] Dr. Forsyth in *Priesthood and Sacrifice*, p. 124.

The final salvation of the individual is, indeed, still conditional. There are still moral demands to be made on men ; they are called upon to share the secondary moral aspect of Christ's sacrifice, the life of perfect obedience to God, which involves continual readiness to suffer. But the greatest part of his work they neither do nor could share, though moral effort is still necessary. By Christ's atoning work they are given a fresh start. What is restored to them once for all is freedom of approach to God.

(3) The "Inclusive" View

(a) *A Caution.* — When Evangelicals distinguish between the experienced fact of salvation through the death of Christ and all theoretical explanations of that fact, we shall have much sympathy with them. We are trying to find human analogies which may enable us to translate an old dogma into the language of our own moral and intellectual experience. But we can only expect a very partial satisfaction. It is claimed that the fact we are investigating is unique, in degree if not in kind. *Ex hypothesi*, therefore, we should not expect to match or parallel it at all exactly. The most we can hope is to find such approximations to it in familiar experience as may make it intelligible and credible. If we succeed in this the relation will be mutual. The phenomena of experience will help us to understand the work of Jesus ; and that work, understood by these means, will cast back light on the phenomena by the help of which it is itself understood.

(b) *Neither Liberalism nor Conservatism is by itself satisfactory.*—(i.) We cannot expect to be satisfied with the Liberal explanation of the contribution of Jesus to human welfare ; for we have already seen reason to think that its conception of human needs is minimizing and inadequate. It has thus no room for, and is forced to explain away, much that is central in the religious experience of the past.

(ii.) The Conservative explanations of the Atonement are based on a legal conception of the relations between God and man. And, as we have held, this not only shares the inevitable defects of all human analogies, but is also not the best of such analogies available for our purpose. In particular, there is too much emphasis on the need of "keeping up appearances," and on the risk of misunderstanding. These play a part in the policy of the human judge or statesman ; but they seem demonstrably to belong to human weakness and limitation. To ascribe them to God appears crude. Again, the suggestion of a change in God seems open to grave risk of misinterpretation. God's external treatment of us no doubt may change with changes in ourselves. But we need to insist that His inner mind, the principle on which His treatment of us is based, never changes. That principle is always Love, and Love only ; never an artificial compromise between Love and some other principle such as Justice.

(c) *What we take from Liberalism.*—We shall agree with the Liberal that what is of primary importance is not the death of Jesus, taken in isolation from his life ; but the career as a whole, taken as an exhibition of character. It is character only that has intrinsic value in the sight of God. And character is shown not so much at a single dramatic moment, but is continuous throughout life.[1] That character has two faces, the one towards God and the other towards man. Towards God, his attitude shows the serene confidence of un-

---

[1] The traditional expression for the moral perfection of Jesus is " Sinlessness." There is in modern times considerable dissatisfaction with this expression ; not so much because the moral elevation it ascribes to Jesus is felt to be excessive and incredible, but because it is too negative. It seems to suggest too much the Pharisaic conception of the moral life as a continual anxious avoidance of innumerable slight occasions of stumbling ; or that false puritanism of which Mr. Chesterton speaks as " chopping up life into small sins with a hatchet." We need to emphasize the positive principle which underlies avoidance of sin. Cf. Essay IV. p. 154.

X

disturbed prayerful communion. On this his outer conduct is based. He "walked with God." And because man is meant for God, and only realizes his true nature when in union with God, the life of Jesus was the highest achievement and example of the possibilities of unspoiled manhood. And this Godward attitude issues directly in a burning love for his fellow-men—the love that "believeth all things, hopeth all things, suffereth all things."[1]

(*d*) *What we take from Conservatism.*—Though the Liberal view is true, it is not the whole truth. The death of Jesus is of one piece with his life and cannot be understood in isolation from it, but it is essential to the completeness of his work, and is in no sense accidental or irrelevant. The nature of this necessity we must now try to make clear to ourselves. Why could the cup not pass from him, if mankind was to be saved?

(i.) Jesus was an historical figure and his death had historical causes.[2] As his ministry proceeded it roused opposition and produced a collision of wills. It soon became clear that only at the cost of conflict could he proceed with his mission,—that is, with the furtherance of the Kingdom of God by "doing good," directly to his own countrymen and indirectly to the human race. And conflict, to one who practised non-resistance, meant suffering and death. So far he may be said to

---

[1] This agrees with what we are now told as to the true and original meaning of Sacrifice; so that the traditional Oriental metaphor would seem, after all, to harmonize with modern thought. The chief meaning of primitive sacrifice appears not to have been the idea of an expiatory gift to the god, which might appease his anger and remove the offence; but rather the idea of a common meal or communion for the family, and the god is a member of the family and akin to the worshipper. He is probably the totem animal; and the family or tribe thus eat their god and derive strength from him. "Without shedding of blood," it is said, "there is no remission of sin." But blood is originally a symbol of life, not of death, and the purport of the sacrifice is communication of life-force. It is only, as it were, by an accident, that it is necessary to kill the victim in order to get at the blood. Any suffering is entirely irrelevant; and there is no thought of any antecedent offence. Even in the developed sacrificial system, which involved atoning sacrifices, the *death* of the victim remains incidental. The idea is of atonement through offering of life, not through infliction of death. Cf. Essay IV. pp. 194-98.

[2] Cf. Essay III. pp. 122 ff.

have died as the soldier dies, at the call of duty ; only
the work which he would not abandon was a work of
benevolence, and his death was therefore, in the plainest
way, a death incurred in the service of others.

But self-sacrifice has always power. And it has
this in transcendent degree when it involves the
sacrifice of life itself. " Greater love hath no man
than this, that a man lay down his life for his friends."
There is no appeal to the human heart that can
compare with this appeal. So, again, we rightly feel
that the patriot's death for his country has a creative
and life-giving influence : it is by such means that
nations are forged.[1]

(ii.) The spirit that governed the life and death of
Jesus was the spirit of love. Now, love involves sympathy, sympathy with those in trouble involves sacrifice,
and *sympathy with those in sin demands vicarious penitence*. Here we reach the very heart of our subject ; for
this, in our interpretation, goes to the root of human
need. An atonement for sin is necessary in the shape
of something that will abolish it by doing away with its
effects and transforming the sinner. And the experience of penitence seemed to afford the only indication of how this might be. And here the phrases
of the New Testament—" He bore our sins "—" He
was made sin for us "—seem to suggest such a self-
identification of Jesus with sinners as would make
penitence for the sins of others possible to him.

But before trying to work this out, we shall have to
meet a serious objection. The old trouble, it may be
said, with the traditional theories of the Atonement
was that they seemed unreal and untrue to moral
experience ; a theory which is to satisfy the modern
mind must be morally intelligible. But that is just what
the conception here suggested is not. Penitence is

---

[1] " Here and here did England help me : how can I help England ? say."
Compare Lincoln's speech at Gettysburg—" that from these honoured dead we take
increased devotion to that cause for which they gave the last full measure of
devotion."

certainly an experienced fact ; but in experience it is directly connected with the sense of responsibility. I may feel sorrow, but I cannot intelligibly feel penitence for the sin of another in which I had no hand and which I could not have prevented. "Vicarious penitence" is really a self-contradictory conception.[1] Behind this objection there is a further feeling of dislike for an ecclesiasticism which treats men in the lump and makes them all declare themselves in church to be "miserable sinners," though many of them are, and know that they are, nothing of the kind, unless words are twisted out of their natural meaning. It is felt that there is a certain insincerity about this false humility or Socratic εἰρωνεία ; and when insincerity enters in, there is an end of true religion.

To this objection we may answer : (*a*) If vicarious penitence is unmeaning and impossible, the problem of atonement is insoluble ; for penitence that is not vicarious, the unsupported penitence of the sinner himself, is never complete or whole-hearted. It sounds reasonable in superficial logic to say that penitence can only be proportional to the sinfulness of the penitent ; but this is to ignore moral psychology. We are dealing with living persons, not with dummies or with logical machines. And, in life, the more sinful a man is the less is he capable of the penitence that really cleanses. (*b*) The objection proves too much. For vicarious penitence is not only an hypothesis framed by theologians to account for the work of Jesus, but is, in some degree, as illustrated by the already quoted case of Mr. Peggotty and Em'ly, a familiar experience. The girl was redeemed by her father. Two conditions were necessary to make such redemption possible ; the completeness of his love for her, which enabled him to identify himself with her in her shame, and his own

---

[1] It is this feeling, more than anything else, which has hindered the acceptance of the conception of Christ's atoning work as "penitential," which is the main argument of *Atonement and Personality*. I believe it is sufficiently answered there ; indeed I have nothing to urge which is not there anticipated. But the fact remains.

undimmed goodness and purity which enabled him to bring her also to a true attitude towards her sin and towards the Moral Law.[1]

The individualistic theory on which the objection is based at once breaks down when tested by life. We may then continue to assert that vicarious penitence is the most "saving" thing in experience ; that it is possible, not in direct but in inverse proportion to the degree in which the penitent is himself tainted ; and that the work of Jesus is to be conceived as the same thing raised to a much higher power.

How is vicarious penitence saving ? It is by doing more perfectly what punishment does imperfectly ; namely, destroying the sin-taste in the sinner by "showing up" sin and so producing such an intense realization of the true nature of sin and goodness as must find outlet in action. This happens best in our experience when we come to see our sins through purer eyes than our own, and this is made possible by mutual affection.[2] Thus, when we see the trouble and suffering that our faults have brought on those whom we love, our eyes are most likely to be opened to a true understanding of spiritual values. And this will be so most when the trouble and suffering thus produced is least the accidental or external consequence of sin, but just the shame which mere knowledge of our sins produces in those who love us.

We note (*a*) that such moral regeneration is initiated outside us ; it is the goodness of others which may arouse a beginning of goodness in us. But (*b*) it takes effect within us, and until it does so there is no re-generation. Mr. Peggotty does not bear the shame of

[1] Any one who doubts the possibility of penitence for faults which are those of others rather than of the individual penitent may be referred to Daniel ix.

[2] Cf. Laurence Binyon's lines :
> " O World, be nobler, for her sake !
> If she but knew thee what thou art,
> What wrongs are borne, what deeds are done
> In thee, beneath thy daily sun,
> Know'st thou not that her tender heart
> For pain and very shame would break ?
> O World, be nobler, for her sake ! "

Em'ly's sin in order that she may escape it. She is indeed to escape from sin; but the consciousness of shame is the means of her redemption. It is present first in the father in order that it may be aroused in the daughter. Vicarious penitence is only redemptive when it succeeds in becoming more than vicarious.

The application of this to the death of Jesus is clear. There can be little doubt that He went up to Jerusalem for the last time, expecting, and even courting, death. And it is suggested in Essay III. that the reason for such a martyrdom may have been conceived by him in the light of the picture of the Suffering Servant in Isaiah liii., and of the sacrificial system. The Kingdom of God was to be realized by a voluntary self-offering of one man on behalf of the people. At the same time the Crucifixion was a crime, and a crime committed by those whom he was trying to help. It is he who is sinned against; and yet he rises so far above private feeling or passion as at the moment of greatest stress to identify himself with his persecutors: "Father, forgive them, for they know not what they do." And this is only a vivid example of his consistent attitude to his fellowmen. Vicarious penitence, we said, destroys sin by "showing it up." Was sin ever "shown up" more luridly than here? Christian devotion has rightly insisted on the striking character of the love and selflessness here shown. To most of us ugliness and discord are minor disagreeables : to the artist or musician they are an intolerable pain. But sin is to the saint as ugliness and discord to the artist and musician. Sin is moral leprosy, yet we are here confronted with one who, with the instincts of an Apollo, yet acted like Father Damien.

(iii.) We have not yet fully understood the intrinsic necessity of the death of Jesus. We have seen that it is due to the spirit of self-sacrifice; and that, as the service which men most need, is rescue from sin, this takes the form of vicarious penitence. But it is still not entirely clear why this must have involved death. We can see, indeed, that it involved willingness to die, and that, in a naughty world, such willingness was only too likely to be put to the test. But we do not seem to see any reason why in the nature of things it must have been so. We have, as it were, discovered an historical, but not a philosophical reason for it. Yet we are conscious of a strong instinct in the experience of the Christian worshipper that the death, which is outward failure, is itself the triumph and the Cross itself the throne of glory. To understand the basis of this instinct, I think that we should consider the individual career of Jesus and the way in which his human character was humanly perfected. We must not ignore the fact that he had an individual human life with an individual value. " Our Blessed Lord did not endure temptation in an official capacity." [1] To the perfecting of that character the death was necessary in two ways.

First, we may remind ourselves that the practical outcome of Christianity, strenuously reaffirmed by at least one great modern philosophy, may be summed up in the maxim, " Die to live." " He that saveth his life shall lose it, and he that loseth his life shall save it." And this is the principle of all life. Not only death but all life as well, Nettleship reminds us, is a process of change. The difference between what we call " life " and what we call " death " is that the former is a change into something which we consider higher, better, more developed, etc., while the latter is the reverse. " To 'live,' then, is to 'die,' *into something more perfect.*" Spiritual life consists in self-surrender, and physical death, voluntarily incurred, would be the supreme example of such self-surrender. We are not here merely making the stoical reflection that " death does not count to a man who is within his duty." It is rather true that death " counts " uniquely ; and that,

---

[1] Simpson, *Fact and Faith*, p. 55.

in spite of the apparent paradox, death is the most fruitful experience in life. We all must die ; and it may be that, to all of us, the experience of dying is the greatest opportunity of soul-culture. But martyrdom —which is death voluntarily incurred in the exercise of life—is the form of death of which this is most true. And the death of Jesus is the most conspicuous martyrdom in history.

Secondly, the death has a special relation to sin. This is not easy to see at once. Death is physical and sin is spiritual ; the connection between them seems strained and artificial. Yet it is by a natural and familiar analogy that sin is likened to death—a "spiritual death." And, then, later, the position is reversed. When men consciously adopt the moral or religious scale of values, the soul becomes more real than the body, and sin a more real destruction than that which is physical ; so that now it is physical death which is a pale copy or suggestion of sin. At this stage the notion naturally arises that it may be possible —and if it is possible, it will certainly be well—to sacrifice the lesser good to save the greater. "If thine eye offend thee, pluck it out." This principle is vital to the understanding of the theory of punishment. In punishment the suffering inflicted is the outward symbol of that inner moral decay which is the natural result and the true retribution of sin. But it is also, in intention, the means by which that natural process of decay may be arrested ; the bitter medicine by which the microbe of sin may be exterminated. The symbol is the means of averting the reality ; so that what is outwardly failure is really the rally that precedes success. This paradox goes deep.

> Then, Soul, live thou upon thy servant's loss,
> And let that pine to aggravate thy store,
> Buy terms divine in selling hours of dross ;
> Within be fed, without be rich no more :—
> So shalt thou feed on death, that feeds on men,
> And death once dead, there's no more dying then.

In the light of this principle we can dimly see how
the fact of sin and the requirements of holiness made it
necessary that Jesus should die. Whatever theory of
"Original Sin" we may hold, we cannot doubt that
the fact of sin colours all human life. We are certain
that, whatever else Jesus was, he was fully man. We
are certain that he deliberately identified himself in love
and sympathy with the disabilities and responsibilities
of his fellowmen. His own moral life and holiness
then, to have been really human, must have been
coloured by the fact of sin. The mode of his own
moral perfecting must have been through resistance to
temptation and the overcoming of human tendency to
sin. And this always means pain and self-surrender.

He was tempted at all points like as we are. It
may be doubted whether orthodox thinkers, in their
fear of irreverence, have always emphasized sufficiently
this vital truth. We feel a natural distaste for
attributing to any saint the sort of temptation with
which we are familiar in our own experience. And no
doubt a saint's temptations are more subtle and less
coarse in form than our own ; but they exist. Still
more naturally do we feel it irreverent and presumptuous
on our part to attempt to pry into the inner mind of
Jesus. Yet we can see—and it is a false and not a true
reverence which would prevent our dwelling on it—
that he must have lived under the constant temptation
either to neglect his mission owing to the difficulties
which confronted him, or, still more, to be untrue to his
ideal of its nature, and so to fail in perfect dutifulness
and loyalty and in perfect oneness of will with God.
Now selfishness at least comes near to being the essence
of sin, and self-surrender to God and to the welfare of
man to being the essence of goodness. Hence the call
to the sacrifice of life is the supreme test of the spirit of
self-surrender. It involves the climax of temptation ;
and successful resistance to temptation at its strongest,
we instinctively feel, is itself the means by which the

tempted is finally rendered immune, and carried quite beyond temptation's reach. It is the consummation of goodness.

We have now tried to trace the significance in relation to sin of the life and death of Jesus in their human aspect. But the orthodox creeds assert that he was not only human but divine. Now, we are not concerned here with the exact meaning or formulation of the identity thus asserted between Jesus and God.[1] But it is within our scope to notice certain practical and religious motives for asserting some kind of identity. Moral evil, we have said, is always sin against God ; it is a rupture of personal relations which are vital to our well-being. "Against Thee only have I sinned and done this evil in Thy sight." And the well-being with which sinfulness is inconsistent is a condition of communion with God. Hence all human needs can be summed up into one,—the need of God. "My soul is athirst for God : yea, even for the living God." Only by the action of God Himself can this thirst be slaked.

In the particular case of the Crucifixion, Jesus was the person immediately sinned against. And his death has a regenerative effect, because, though the offence is against him, he identifies himself in love and penitence with the offenders. But that this regenerative effect should be universalized and exercise a healing influence not merely on the principals and accessories of that particular crime but on all sinners of all times, it is necessary that we should feel it to be in a special sense the act of God Himself. "God was in Christ, reconciling the world to Himself" ; it is of this that we need to feel certain.[2] The elaborate Christologies of the creeds are only exercises on this theme. If *our* sins are to be forgiven and destroyed through the death of Jesus, that death must be unlike the death of Socrates, and not merely one more dramatic episode in

---

[1] Cf. Essay V. [2] Cf. Essay IV. p. 175.

the varied history of the world. " If He were not God, the fact that He was good . . . would be a fact of no more moment to me than the fact that Samson was strong, or Solomon wise, or St. Paul intrepid, or St. John beloved. They are, but I am not ; and that is the difference between them and me ; and that is all."[1]

It has often been pointed out—and it is argued in this book[2]—that some doctrine of the divinity of Christ is necessary to any adequate Theodicy, and that the Christian message is first and foremost a message about God.[3] The spectacle of Jesus bearing the sins of his persecutors, and, by so bearing them, initiating their overthrow, is the guarantee that God is bearing the sins of the world ; that sin exists only to be caught up and transmuted in the love of God ; and that such a heart-subduing, world-conquering sacrifice is an eternal " moment " in the Divine Life, an essential part of the activity whereby God is God.

This brings us to an idea which is out of harmony with the general trend of modern thought ; namely, that in the little group of historical events which were the terrestrial sign of these eternal truths, the Resurrection as well as the Crucifixion was necessary to · the scheme of salvation. The exact nature of the Resurrection is discussed elsewhere :[4] we are only concerned with what it stood for. Now the Resurrection is apt to seem to us something of an anti-climax ; as when a " happy ending " is introduced into some story which by all the canons of art should have been a tragedy. So here, we are apt to feel, the lesson should have been " the world well lost " and love and goodness shining out more brightly by contrast with the extreme blackness of the outward circumstances amid which they are set. But what the Resurrection stood for was the approval of God, the fact that the strongest forces in the universe were behind Jesus. And this—the

[1] *Atonement and Personality*, p. 82. [2] Cf. Essay V.
[3] Cf. Essays I. and V. [4] Cf. Essay III. pp. 127-141

triumphant issue of his sacrifice — is essential to a complete Atonement. The moral appeal of Calvary by itself would be insufficient. So much of what is wrong and "out of joint" even within us and still more without is beyond the control of our wills. If we are more than selfish individualists, we need an assurance of the triumph of good in the world at large ; and for such assurance we need to believe that the life and character of Jesus were, in a pre-eminent sense, the life and character of God.

There is one difficulty which may probably be felt at this point. The Jesus who died for the sins of the whole world, it may seem, is a metaphysical figment, or, at best, a superhuman being far removed from ordinary experience. We seem to lose the real, human, historical Jesus. What sense can there be, it may be asked, in saying that Jesus of Nazareth died, *e.g.*, for atrocities perpetrated in Armenia or on the Congo in the twentieth century ? He died, no doubt, from love of God and of his fellow-men. But this love was not an abstract metaphysical affection for the human race, but a love for Peter, James, and John, and the other disciples, and for the publicans and sinners, the poor in the goods of this world or the next, who flocked to him in Galilee and Jerusalem.

There underlies this difficulty a truth which we can accept. We have learned not to be afraid of the frankest recognition of the real humanity of Jesus, or of all that that implies. But the method of counting heads is beside the mark. It was not, directly, for individuals, whether few or many, that Jesus died, but for "the kingdom of God"; and this kingdom has no historical or geographical limitations. The conviction of the modern worshipper, "He died for *me*," is entirely sound in principle.

IV. The Relation of the Work of Jesus
Christ to other Men

When we put aside everything that is merely pictorial
or allegorical and confine ourselves to moral realities, it
is difficult to see how the moral quality—be it what it
may—of a life or death in Syria in the first century
of our era can make a vital difference to the lives
of Western Europeans in the twentieth century. No
explanation of the Atonement which does not face this
difficulty squarely can be worth much. The difference
between Liberalism and Conservatism, which we have
traced throughout, appears once again at this point.
But it need not now occupy us long ; for we have
already seen reason to think that neither view is more
than partial. Here, too, we can accept neither view
simply as it stands ; and, in each case, one-sidedness
brings a speedy intellectual Nemesis.

(1) According to Liberalism, what we find in Jesus is
an example for imitation. In spite of the differences of
detail which changes in civilized life involve, he furnishes
us with a pattern of true human life. And his teaching
is the highest teaching we know about the nature of
God and man, and about their mutual relations. The
effect of his personality on the character of the true
Christian to-day may be summed up in the term
"influence." One man may always influence another.
But to use any stronger term is to travel outside the
sphere of character and moral experience altogether.
For character is not a machine-made product, and
cannot be put into a man from outside. The nearer
we approach to compulsion, the farther we are from
moral values. And as it is character alone which in the
last resort has value, no man can be " saved " except by
himself. There are clear limits to the power of one
man to help another ; he can at best co-operate with
the person he wishes to help. And these limits, being

dictated by the very nature of goodness, apply also to the power of Jesus to " save " men.

The difficulty of this view is that the salvation it allows for seems not to meet human needs. It is not a moral standard or ideal that we need so much as power to live up to it. Our defect is weakness of will. If my salvation depends in any degree upon myself, then it is beyond hope ; for I know that *I* shall always fail when the strain comes. And this view meets with a curious Nemesis. It sets out to exalt the importance of morality ; but it ends by limiting the possibilities of moral influence. There is apparently a residuum of hard fact, a citadel of self, where it cannot penetrate :

> The hold that falls not when the town is got,
> The heart's heart, whose immuréd plot
> Hath keys yourself keep not ! [1]

The inmost Ego is what it is, and nothing can touch it or save it.

(2) The Conservative is at one with some modern philosophers of distinction in insisting that " Religion is more than Morality." The growing moralization of religion through history will have ended in exaggeration if it leaves us with nothing but " morality touched with emotion." So here, though, in the old language, " sanctification " is a natural and necessary supplement to "justification," justification is not sanctification, but something greater and better. It is a great objective blessing, over and above personal sanctification. Our status is changed once and for all, previous to any well-doing or deserving on our part. What is now demanded of us is not so much conduct as faith ; *i.e.* whole-souled adhesion to Christ and his cause. Responsiveness to his personality, as we feel its influence in prayer or mystical communion, is the mark of the religious man. Hence arises the distinctive flavour of the Evangelical type of piety, with its sense of gladness and immediate assurance.

---

[1] Francis Thompson, *A Fallen Yew.*

We are to be perfected in goodness, and we have been put right with God. But it is the latter which is primary and causal. It is the consciousness of this which is the essence of religion : " It will not comfort us so much, in our moments of weakness or dying, to be adjured to remember the dignity of our being, as to be pointed to the scene enacted once for all upon the Cross." [1] This is where power dwelleth.

But here again one-sidedness brings its own Nemesis. The whole intention is to magnify the work of God : " See what God hath done unto my soul ! " But when justification is separated from sanctification, the result is the reverse of what is intended. It is much easier to alter a man's status than to change his character. So far as forgiveness means merely remission of penalty, it is a small thing : it is easy for a juryman to vote for the " acquittal " of a guilty prisoner, if he is never to see any more of him. But if it means, as we have seen it must, a renewal of intimate personal relations, and hence a real change in the character of the sinner (for it is his character which is now the bar to intimacy), then it will be much harder. Mere acquittal is formal ; and hence is, to moral experience, no salvation, or at most a very imperfect one. " It says ' Go,' but leaves the prison doors shut." [2] And the suggestion of the " imputation " to men of a righteousness that is not theirs implies an atmosphere of artificiality and insincerity which is intolerable.

(3) We must turn without further delay to the " inclusive " view, which is to combine the truths one-sidedly expressed by Liberalism and Conservatism. And we can at once lay down two conditions. First, our salvation must involve a change in our character : it must be a change within us. Anything else would be unreal. " The response of the Gospel to the human sense of actual sin and unattainable holiness is not the

---

[1] *Atonement and Personality*, p. 322.
[2] Bushnell, *The Vicarious Sacrifice*, p. 360.

half-grace of forgiveness but the whole-grace of redemption and deliverance."[1] And, secondly, the psychological change required is much more fundamental than any which we could effect for ourselves. For certain purposes, we are accustomed to distinguish between a wider and a narrower use of the term "self." On the one hand, the Self includes everything that is ours, everything which a psychologist might observe in us ; on the other hand, we sometimes treat it as an inner Ego, which presides over the whole kingdom of the self, which contemplates the wider self as an object and sees in it some things which it approves and some which it deplores and therefore *resolves* to change. But the distinction breaks down at this point ; for the inner Ego itself needs to " suffer a sea-change." *Quis custodiet ipsos custodes ?* Though salvation must take place within the self, it must be initiated from without, for it must go down to the very roots of the will.

Bearing these conditions in mind, I believe that we may see that Christian theology has not neglected, but has provided a reasoned account of, the carrying of the lifework of Jesus into effective relation to the lives and characters of men of other races and other times.

It is the remoteness of the life of Jesus in time and place from our own lives and circumstances that constitutes the difficulty in understanding how there can really be a living relation between them. If there is any truth in the view of the possibilities of personal influence which we have already taken, we can understand how his personality might have power to transform and mould the characters of those, such as his own disciples, with whom he came into personal contact ; and we can even see how, in a fainter way, that influence might be mediated through men like the apostles, who were full of his inspiration, and so reach men such as St. Paul, who had never actually seen him. But with every new generation such influence would

---

[1] Du Bose, *The Gospel in St. Paul*, p. 102.

become less, and to speak of a personal influence exercised across the centuries would be more and more fanciful. And now that the whole episode is wrapped in the mists of history, how can *we*, inhabitants as we are almost of a different world, both intellectual and practical, in any intelligible sense share the experience of the early disciples ?

The answer is to be found in the assertion which we have already been forced to make of the divinity of Christ ; by which we meant at least that God was in Christ in such sense that the work of Christ was the work of God, and the character of Christ a clue to the character of God. From this certain consequences follow :—

(*a*) The historical facts of the life and death of Jesus Christ can only affect the whole universe in so far as they are more than merely historical. They have a genuinely " sacramental " character, being, in the words of the Church Catechism, " an outward and visible sign of an inward and spiritual grace." They embody a principle which is a structural law of the universe.

It is easy to see what principles these historical facts embody. It is the spirit of inexhaustible love of men and readiness for self-sacrifice on their behalf. And the practical meaning of the assertion of the divinity of Christ is that these qualities characterize God Himself,[1] and so belong to the very structure of the universe. " What has made Christianity an invincible power in the world has been the conviction that somehow or other the life of love is the best, the divinest, life we can conceive, and, that every one who even for moments knows what it is to lose himself in others is doing what God does eternally." [2]   And this is a basis for the universalizing of the effect of the life and death of Christ on his immediate disciples.   " As the flash of

---

[1] Cf. Essays I., V. and IX.

[2] Nettleship, *Remains*, vol. i. p. 105. (Extracts from Letters.)

Y

the volcano discloses for a few hours the elemental
fires at the earth's centre, so the light on Calvary was
the bursting forth through historical conditions of the
very nature of the Everlasting. There was a cross in
the heart of God before there was one planted on the
green hill outside of Jerusalem. And now that the
cross of wood has been taken down, the one in the
heart of God abides, and it will remain so long as there
is one sinful soul for whom to suffer."[1] The historical
facts were, like all historical facts, limited to a particular
time and place. The timeless facts for which they
stood are equally true for all times and places.

(b) Just so far as we do think in terms of Time it is
a commonplace of theology that Jesus is alive and is
influencing men just as much in the year 1912 as in
the year 29. To Christian theology, he not merely
died on Calvary, but is alive, and has been ever since
the Ascension at the right hand of God in glory. Not
that he is merely glorified; his death for men on
Calvary is not merely a past and distant episode; the
having died is a predicate eternally true of him, and
is part of what he now is. The theology of the
Atonement has been largely expressed in terms of the
Jewish sacrificial system; as, notably, in the Epistle to
the Hebrews.[2] In those terms, it asserts that the
sacrifice of Christ is not merely something that took
place nearly nineteen hundred years ago. It is something which is eternally offered in heaven by the
glorified Christ. "He abideth a priest for ever."

(c) It is also a commonplace of theology that the
bodily presence of Jesus to his disciples was to be
replaced by something at least as real—the presence
of his Spirit. That Spirit is the spirit of universal
love; and the community of followers of Christ, which
ideally should be the whole human race, is the sphere
in which the Christ-spirit comes home to the individual.
The Church so far as it embodies that spirit is the

---

[1] Dinsmore, pp. 232-233.   [2] Cf. above, Essay IV. pp. 193-198.

channel of communication between the believer and the living Christ. (Just as " he who has done it unto the least of these, has done it unto Me," so the community and its corporate life and institutions are the means by which Christ acts on the individual.) We are not concerned with controversial questions arising out of ecclesiastical divisions : we are only concerned with ideals. Ideally the Church is one, on earth and in heaven.[1] The Sacraments, the preaching of " the Word," the personal influence of holy men are means of access to Christ ;[2] ways by which the individual Christian of to-day may be brought into the same personal contact with him as the original disciples.

Theology, then, has not been blind to the provision made for the extension of the saving work of Christ to modern times. Calvary, it has been said, can only be understood in terms of Pentecost. The work of the Spirit in the Church is an essential part of the theology of the Atonement.

But this is not realized. This part of traditional theology is difficult for us to apprehend, because it is expressed in language which does not convey much meaning to the average Englishman, unless he has special ecclesiastical associations. On the one hand, we do not think naturally in terms of the ritual of sacrifice ; and, on the other hand, the imagery of two distinct spheres or regions, a heavenly and an earthly, the latter of which is dependent on and in communication with the former, has become unnatural to us, though we have not any alternative imagery at present by which to replace it. The translation of this branch of theology into modern language, it may be hoped, will soon be undertaken. But what we are now emphasizing is, that there is a fairly coherent theology to be translated.

---

[1] Cf. Essay IV. pp. 196-197, and Essay VII. *passim.*
[2] I use these instances by way of illustration only. I am not here suggesting that they are *necessary* or *exclusive* means.

This has certain consequences, practical and theoretical.

(1) *Practical Consequences*

(*a*) *Inward.*—Religion, to be worth anything, must issue in character. But character—at least for the mass of men and in its highest developments—must be based on religion. For the Christian, as for Christ himself, the secret of power is not self-assertion in any form, but the attitude of conscious dependence on God to which prayer is the chief avenue, and the quiet confidence and trust in which it issues. And, for the Christian, Christ is the way to God. This is the experience of the great saints. The moral inspiration which transforms their lives is directly connected with Christ : " I live ; yet not I, but Christ liveth in me."

The practical moral, then, would be that what men really need is to " find religion " or to find Christ as the first stage on a journey, the ultimate goal of which would be to become Christlike. But this is a mode of expression which is always corrected by the insight of a more advanced religious experience, which substitutes for " I found Christ " the truer assertion " Christ found me."

(*b*) *Outward.*—If man's need is to become Christlike,—to " grow incorporate with " him in Browning's phrase,—with the Christian as with Christ the godly character must issue on its outer side in love and service to men ; and this in a world in which sorrow and sin are so prominent means vicarious sacrifice and vicarious penitence. It is here that Evangelical theory—not Evangelical practice—seems sometimes deficient. It is a deep-rooted religious instinct that insists on the " finished work " of Christ. But it is also a deep-rooted religious instinct which bids us " fill up that which is lacking in the sufferings of Christ." The Gospel invitation is not merely an invitation to unalloyed bliss ;

it is an invitation to each man to "take up his cross" (though the Cross is never merely the symbol of suffering but of victory through suffering). The Gospel gift is not merely a remission of pains and penalties; it is a gift of strength to do and bear something of what Jesus did and bore. The Christian life is a life of service to men based on the love of men, and where the missionary spirit is absent, there is no true Christianity.

Our ordinary, respectable, lukewarm Christianity, then, is in sharp contrast to the heroic fervour of primitive Christianity. And the great outbreaks of spiritual life in the history of Christianity, from the Friars to the Oxford Movement, have been reversions to the ardour of those early days. The real Christianity is constantly breaking out in unexpected places. To those who can read the signs of the times, such as the Student Movement, it may appear likely that the present generation will witness not the least of these outbursts of power.

(2) *Theoretical Consequences*

(*a*) *Justification.*—Justification cannot properly be separated from Sanctification, the "great objective blessing" from its subjective effect. The process of salvation can only be understood as a whole. The only true "justification" is not a mere preliminary acquittal which averts the condemnation merited by past sins, but rather the removal of the power of present sin; it does not consist merely in God's forgiving men, but rather in His making them forgivable; it is not the "imputation" to us of a righteousness that is not really ours, but the imparting to us of an actual righteousness. And therefore it takes time. Acquittal, forgiveness, imputation, might all be the act of a moment; the far greater miracle of a real salvation must be a gradual process, because it involves the fashioning of personal character.

It need not take long to pronounce a verdict, but it takes long years to make, or remake, a man.

On the one hand, then, we shall reject any suggestion of artificiality or make-believe. God is Truth and sees men as they really are. His treatment of them may outrun their present achievement; He may treat them as they are not now, but as they are becoming; but, if so, the man that is to be is more truly the real man than the "thing of shreds and patches" which exists at the moment. On the other hand, we do but magnify the work of God. The gradual moulding of character is wholly the work of "grace." God does not simply adapt Himself to a psychological material which is independent of Him, but slowly fashions a material fit for His purposes.

(*b*) *Personality.*—The experience of the saint, we have said, is naturally expressed as "I live; yet not I, but Christ liveth in me." This carries us some way from the hasty assumption of superficial theory that "impenetrability" is an attribute of personality — as though persons were solid things in space exclusive of one another![1] Yet it is this assumption, latent more often than explicit, which, by excluding all vicarious action or suffering from a moral order, would make the Atonement impossible and unintelligible; since nothing done or suffered by Jesus could make a vital difference to the characters of men. This assumption we unhesitatingly reject, but it is difficult to find a theoretical statement which shall do justice to the facts of religious experience. On the one hand, we want to safeguard personal identity. When the sinner through penitence becomes a saint, it is the same individual with the same natural temperament and gifts who *was* a sinner and *is* a saint. Simon Bar Jonah, who denied his Lord, becomes St. Peter, the rock on which the Church is built. Saul of Tarsus, who persecuted the saints, becomes St. Paul, the apostle of the Gentiles, who laboured more abun-

[1] Cf. Essay IX. p. 498.

dantly than all ; yet in each case it is the same individual who was one thing and became another. On the other hand, in the process from sin to holiness, there is a change of character so complete that the difference between the two stages may seem greater than the identity, and this leads to paradoxical expressions. The religious man seems only to have become a self, in any full sense, by abandoning himself to the inspiration and will-power of another, so that the strength and goodness and purity of that other gradually become his. But even this expression is inadequate, for it suggests an unchanging Ego with changing properties ; whereas it is the very " I " that needs to be changed in the sinner and that has been changed in the saint. There are analogies to this, as we have already suggested, though much lower in degree, in experience that is not specifically religious.[1]

This is what the Greek Fathers were trying to express when they thought of Christ as uniting in himself the substance of Divinity with the substance of Humanity which is present in all individual men. The expression was imperfect,[2] because too materialistic ; but the idea which they were trying to express is vital to any theology of Atonement. Jesus was not merely one among men, separate from all others. He was not only *a* man but Man.[3]

V. Some Objections and Final Summary

At this point two objections must be faced. (1) Are you not, it may be said, leaving out of your philosophy much of what was strongest and most prominent in the old Evangelical position ? After all, Christianity is a religion, not a system of ethics, and are

---

[1] " The times when one feels that one is most truly oneself are just those in which the consciousness of one's own individuality is most absolutely swallowed up, whether in sympathy with nature, or in the bringing to birth of truth, or in enthusiasm for other men " (Nettleship, p. 53).   Cf. Essay IX. pp. 501 ff.

[2] Cf. Essay V. pp. 231-233.   [3] Cf. Essay V. pp. 253-257.

you not, in your anxiety to moralize religion, coming perilously near to reducing it to the consistent observance of a moral code? Dr. Simpson[1] reminds us that St. Paul was a man of lofty character before his conversion, while yet he had the profoundest conviction of sin. If "sin" to him meant merely a low level of morality, the language he uses about himself would be stupid hypocrisy. In fact, it means to him estrangement from God ; and this can coexist with a high level of morality. So also we may think of J. S. Mill and many another, who without conscious religion has lived on a high plane of moral achievement. The fact is that "conversion touches the personality at a point above the level of ordinary morality." The essence of the old Evangelical religion of faith in the Atonement was an influx of new life that raised the whole self to a higher power. Good conduct naturally follows on this. But to make good conduct the primary thing is to invert the true proportions of religion and morality, and it issues in practice in an over-anxious type of piety, which, like the Pharisee, looks for salvation to the laborious acquisition of merit by a long course of good works. This is to trammel the force of grace within "the meshes of a pettifogging morality" ; it is based on the spirit of Martha rather than on the spirit of Mary.

(2) On the one hand, we are accused of confusing religion and morality. On the other hand, we may probably be charged with dissolving religion in a vague religious philosophy and with identifying Christianity with Christian Platonism. To the theorist, it may seem an advance to treat historical facts as illustrations of eternal principles ; but this is not an attitude which will ever commend itself to the practical man. He holds by *facts*.[2] These to him are the data of thought ; and all speculation upon them is more precarious than the data. But Christianity is a religion for the multitude,

---

[1] *Fact and Faith*, p. 68.
[2] Cf. Simpson, p. 10. "At the risk of appearing hopelessly unphilosophic, I am prepared to affirm that a fact is a fact."

and has always successfully resisted efforts to transform
it into a philosophical sect. A nebulous mysticism is
not the religion of power.

Further it may be felt that our method is responsible
for this result ; and that it is too deductive and too
little inductive, too self-confident and too little humble,
that it builds too much on *a priori* theory and too little
on practical experience ; and that it rests on a much
exaggerated assumption of our power to understand the
ways of God to man. Had we gone to school with the
great multitude of holy and humble men of heart, we
should have been less content with a theory which
appeals mainly to the student in a University. What
is really needed and what our method will not supply is
such an understanding of the Atonement as will carry
the plain man through life and death.

To these objections we must try to make some reply.

(1) Here we seem to find re-emerging something like
the old opposition of types which we have traced all
through. Each of these is continually supplementing
and correcting the other. We shall expect therefore
that such a protest will rest on a positive aspect of truth
which must be included. The special attraction of the
view here urged against us is that it seems to make the
Atonement applicable in its fullness to our present
situation as sinful men, rather than to some far-off ideal
of consummation that is very remote from present
reality. But we must ask whether the opposition is as
considerable as it seems. Each is really pressing for
a larger and more living conception of the religious
significance of the Atonement ; the one as against a
legalistic and " pettifogging " moralism, the other as
against an external and superficial view of forgiveness
("not the half-grace of forgiveness but the whole-grace of
redemption and deliverance "). They can really agree
(*a*) that salvation is nothing less than a moral transformation of character, and (*b*) that so far as
" morality " is used in a narrow sense as something

less than the whole reality of personal life, the transformation is "supermoral." [1]

On the other hand, we have tried to guard against certain dangers which the Evangelical view does not entirely escape. In the form which we are now considering, its aim is to find expressions which shall include the whole personality at its fullest, something for which even morality is too narrow. But the conception of the "supermoral," like the conception of the Superman, is very difficult to grasp, and is apt to end in a morality which is not the highest. So here we find metaphors, such as "debt" and "acquittal," which are wholly human but are drawn from the more external and artificial relations of persons instead of those which are more intimate and vital, such as the relation of father and child or friend and friend. But this is a retrograde movement. [2]

No doubt, it is impossible to reach a complete understanding of the process of salvation as an intelligible whole in terms of Before and After. Different stages are separated in Time which can only be understood fully as parts of a single whole. But, as I understand it, the difference between the Evangelical mode of statement and ours is precisely that it claims to treat justification or an objective atonement as complete in itself apart from a subjective issue, while we deprecate any such separation.

---

[1] Dr. Simpson (pp. 151 ff.) has guarded himself in anticipation against this suggestion of a "higher synthesis." The issue, he contends, is a real one, because the two different types of theory issue in practice in two different types of piety; one that dwells more anxiously on observance, and one which is closer to the joyous and almost exuberant Pauline sense of free grace as a present possession. But I cannot detect either in Dr. Du Bose or in Dr. R. C. Moberly, the two writers against whom his strictures are more particularly directed, any lack of the feeling of confidence and vitality which he desiderates.

[2] A statement in extreme caricature of the kind of misconception against which the Evangelical formulae do not seem to guard sufficiently is to be found in the following verse quoted by Newman in a letter to Faber. (*Life*, vol. i. p. 224.)

> "Man is but 'accounted righteous'
> And, though justified, must sin.
> Grace does nought but wash the surface,
> Leaving him all-foul within."

(2) With regard to the other objection, we must deny that our universalizing of the historical facts involves any diminution of their objective reality. In terms of the old pictorial dualistic language, a " fact in heaven " is more and not less of a fact than a " fact on earth." And what we are suggesting is the equivalent, in less pictorial form, of the "fact in heaven." An Atonement that lasts ten thousand years is not a smaller fact than one which lasts three hours. And we are not arguing that the power of the Cross consists chiefly in its appeal to human sympathy and human affection, but in its evidence that—in pictorial language—God is bearing the sins of the world. And the universalizing is necessary. Only by making the self-sacrifice of Calvary a witness to the eternal love of God Who indwells in the world and in all men, and Who is about the path and the bed of every one of us, can we do what at the outset of our inquiry we saw to be essential ; namely, to explain to this generation the significance of the Atonement for modern religion in terms of moral experience. Only so can it be made intelligible ; and what is not intelligible will form no part of personal religion.

Finally, there is a difficulty which affects all explanations of Atonement. Even if it is admitted that the influence of Christ can reach and transform not merely those who " knew him after the flesh " but Christians of all times and places, there is the difficulty which we cannot but feel that Christians are only a small fraction of the human race. How can we possibly believe in a divine scheme of salvation for the human race which " leaves whole continents out of its ken "? If, on the other hand, we hold that the work of Christ is not confined to those who are consciously his followers, are we not abandoning the whole of our explanations ? With what possible meaning can we assert that Christ is the saviour of Confucius and Buddha, of Plato and Caesar ?

To this difficulty we have no complete answer. But we can see the direction in which an answer is to be sought. If explicit consciousness is necessary to religion, *cadit quaestio*. But if it is not, then something in the direction of an answer might be reached by holding fast to the idea which the early theologians expressed in terms of the Logos-theology ; the idea of a bond uniting all men, in virtue of their manhood, to the perfect man. In any case, we shall insist on the truth of the old stanza : [1]

> Many man for Cristes love
> Was martired in Romayne,
> Er any Cristendom was knowe there
> Or any cros honoured.

And this is not all. The Christian does not believe that terrestrial history exhausts even that part of reality which concerns human beings. He believes not merely that there is an unseen world, but that our abiding city is there and not here. The doctrines of the descent into hell and of the communion of saints, as stated in the Creed, stand at least for this ;— that the long task of human perfecting, of building the city of God, is not confined to the few years of a man's life on earth. The Gospel message of salvation may yet reach that great majority which in this life has never heard of it. If, then, we are inclined to believe that the highest possibilities of human character can only be realized through conscious allegiance to Jesus Christ, since only so are men brought to the fullest knowledge and service of God, the limitations in space and time of historical Christianity need form no insuperable obstacle.

The career and personality of Jesus Christ are the revelation of the eternal God. It is this that gives them their universal reference. In the saying, " He that hath seen me hath seen the Father," is summed

[1] Quoted by Dr. Inge in *Contentio Veritatis*.

up the whole Christian Gospel and the whole hope of the world.

The general purport of this discussion should now be clear. In religious as in secular thought there is a modern point of view ; and this we have called "Liberalism." Where Liberal thought prevails, the Atonement has tended to drop out of personal religion. It is natural that the Liberal should not easily accept any distinctive doctrine of Atonement, for he does not feel the need of salvation. "Conviction of sin" is not a prominent part of his religious experience, as it was of the religious experience of his ancestors. In other words, modern thought is favourable to the Once-Born rather than to the Twice-Born type of religion.

But if there is any truth in the argument of this essay, a religion in which there is not a large ingredient of the latter type is fatally impoverished. The issue is one of psychology ; and we have argued that human nature is so constituted as to need a radical change to which individual effort is inadequate. The Liberal is, no doubt, in reaction against much that was morbid in older views. There may be healthy sincerity in his refusal to think of himself as a miserable sinner. But when every admission is made, it remains true that modern optimism is too facile and superficial. Those who are not conscious of deep-seated moral disorder in themselves do well not to make pretences. But even if *we* were comparatively unscathed, only narrowness of sympathy could keep the mass of evil in the world from being felt by us as a personal burden. And such narrowness of sympathy is itself sinful. If we realized more fully that sin consists even more in what we leave undone than in what we do, it would hardly be possible for any man to be without sense of sin. The problem of sin and salvation is as urgent to-day as it was for Bunyan.

But even if the need is admitted, it does not follow that the traditional Christian doctrine will commend itself to-day to the sincere inquirer as being either morally edifying or psychologically sound. The difficulties which men feel in making Atonement a real part of their religion are, at bottom, largely intellectual : they are difficulties of understanding. Moral ideas have not stood still ; and the older explanations of Atonement seem to sink below the level of the best secular morality of to-day. So far as this is so, the "modern mind" rightly rejects them. It will not listen to any theory of the dealings of God with man, which represents Him as actuated by anything but the highest goodness that we can conceive. But the fault is not all on one side. The modern thinker is right in making moral experience a touchstone of the truth of religious doctrine ; and in insisting that, if such doctrine does not altogether correspond to the conclusions of experience, it shall differ from them only by way of development and further illumination. But, in fact, his own ethics and psychology are often crude ; and it is because of this that any belief in Atonement seems to him impossible. In particular, an over-individualistic conception of the nature of personality stands in the way. And the chief object of this essay is to make clear and to criticize the psychological presuppositions with which the modern inquirer is apt to approach these questions. For it is in this region that the case is really determined.

On the other hand, the Conservative thinker is wrong in so far as he relegates to a secondary place the whole method of appeal to moral experience. And he is apt to make the ways of God to man seem unacceptable to conscience and to experience by failing sufficiently to exhibit the process of judgment and salvation as a whole. So far as there is truth in the conception of God's judicial condemnation and punishment of sin, this has always a saving character. It is not as though

God began as Justice by condemning sin and instituting a penal hell ; and then, as it were by a happy after-thought, intervened as Mercy to arrest in part its operation. The condemnation cannot be separated from the salvation : only as intended to lead to it, has it place or justification.

Our method throughout has been to exhibit the Liberal and Conservative views side by side, with the suggestion that they are mutually dependent half-truths. To preach that the way to truth is by reconciliation and combination of opposing views may seem an empty platitude. But the aim has been to show in some points *how* and *why* the two views involve one another. The Liberal thinks in terms of modern ethics and psychology. But these leave us with a problem, for the solution of which we need the dynamic power of the atoning work of Christ, as the Conservative conceives it. The Christian Gospel, then, is the great need of this generation as of St. Paul. And to us, as to him, it is a gospel of salvation and atonement.

VII

THE CHURCH

BY

WILLIAM TEMPLE

SYNOPSIS

PAGE

I. THE CHURCH IN ESSENCE AND FACT . . 339-347

    The Church is the Church of the Resurrection ; it lives the
Risen and Ascended Life of its Lord ; its unity is the unity of
that Life, and can therefore never be broken ; the Church on
earth is a sacrament of that Church 339
    Expression of the foregoing in the Eucharist ; its sig-
nificance 343

II. THE CHURCH MILITANT HERE IN EARTH . . 347-359

    The Church on earth a sacrament ; the organ of the Will
of Christ, and thus the completion of His Being . . 347
    Its unity realised through diversity ; affinities of St. Paul's
doctrine with modern sociology . . . 348
    Practical results ; Christian unity ; the consequent strengthen-
ing of faith ; the need for loyal Church-membership . 350
    The Church entangled in the World . . . 355
    The Fellowship of the Holy Ghost 357
    The perfecting of the Church dependent on the conversion
of the world 358
    " The completion of Him who all in all is being fulfilled " 359

VII

THE CHURCH

"And I saw the holy city, new Jerusalem, coming down out of heaven from God, made ready as a bride adorned for her husband."

I. The Church in Essence and Fact

When the earthly ministry of the Lord was ended, the fruit of it was not a body of teaching or a collection of writings ; it was a little society consisting of those who had been His companions and had been given, by the fact of His Resurrection, an unshakeable conviction that in Him God had taken action and had redeemed the world. This primitive Church is before all else the Church of the Resurrection. The Resurrection was what changed the dispirited disciples into the founders of the Church militant and triumphant ; the Resurrection was the burden of their preaching ; the Resurrection was itself the condition and type of their own lives. For St. Paul claims outspokenly for the Church that it lives the Risen and Ascended life. We are " in Heaven " now. " God being rich in mercy, for His great love wherewith He loved us, even when we were dead through our trespasses, quickened us together with Christ (by grace have ye been saved), and raised us up with Him, and made us to sit with Him in the heavenly places, in Christ Jesus." The Church, the Society of those who are risen and ascended with

339

Christ, is called the Body of Christ,[1]—that is, the
instrument of His will ; and the Bride of Christ,—that
is, the object of His boundless love. It is conceived
as something altogether perfect; its individual members
are, by virtue of their mere membership, " Saints " ; it
is " a glorious church, not having spot or blemish or
any such thing."

To us this sounds remote and unreal. We do not
feel that death and sin are conquered in our lives ; the
vast chaos which for us represents the Church, with
its hateful cleavages, its slow-moving machinery, its
pedantic antiquarianism,[2] its indifference to much that
is fundamental, its age-long ineffectiveness, its abundant
capacity for taking the wrong side in moral issues—
how can this be described in the language of St. Paul ?
His dream was beautiful ; but was it not after all only
a dream ? Or if the early Church could be so described,
has it not long ago forfeited its splendour ?

We are bound to ask these questions. But before
we attempt to answer them we must remind ourselves
that the Church of St. Paul's experience was not free
from grave moral scandals, as is clear from his letters
to the Church at Corinth. The Church which is the
spotless Bride of Christ cannot be simply the group of
believers to whom some of his warnings are addressed.
Is the Apostle then simply painting an ideal which, in
moments of exaltation, he treats as an actuality ? Or
is there something in the Church deeper than all the
phenomena of its history ? Is there an ideal Church
which the actual Church only imperfectly represents ?

The Church, he says, is the fulness, or completion,
of Him who all in all is being fulfilled.[3] A philosophical

---

[1] This phrase, like so much else in the Theology of the New Testament, is
probably taken from the Eucharist—the rite suggesting the doctrine ; cf. 1 Cor. x.
16, 17. Cf. Essay IV.

[2] This happens to be peculiarly out of place. The earth will in all probability be
habitable for myriads of years yet. If Christianity is the final religion, the Church
is still in its infancy. Two thousand years are as two days. The appeal to the
" primitive Church " is misleading ; we are the primitive Church.

[3] Eph. i. 23. Cf. Armitage Robinson, *ad loc.*

conception of God, as is shewn in another essay,[1] requires us to regard the world and its history as essential to the very Life and Being of God. The Church is "a community, whose life is nothing less than the life of God." . . . "In the Christian doctrine the life of the Church is the life of the Spirit, and the Spirit is the Spirit of the Son, whereby he is the Son."[2] From our experience of the Love of God in Christ we are led on to conceive the perfect object of His Love—the Bride of Christ ; and this conception is not disturbed by the imperfection of the Church militant here and now on earth. That is a society only half complete, and consisting of members who are also members of the secular and still half-pagan societies which make up Christendom,—half-pagan, because the standards of our social, commercial, and political life are not even professedly the standards of Christ. Of course it does not realise the ideal of the Apostle's vision. But yet there is in it a life which flows from Christ Himself, and which gives the promise of a completed Church deriving its life from no other source than Him alone. In the sight of God—in the experience of God— that perfected Church is the true reality.

The society which Christ founded to proclaim and carry on His redeeming work does not depend for its distinctive character on the men who join it ; that character is given to it by Christ alone. The Church was founded[3] by the Life, the Teaching, the Death and

---

[1] Cf. Essay IX. pp. 510-512.

[2] Webb, *Problems in the Relations of God and Man*, pp. 230 and 249.

[3] This is true for all modern and practical purposes. The early Christian Church, however, regarded itself as the true Israel—the "remnant" of the Prophets—which answered the Divine requirement, and was now alone the "chosen people," since "Israel after the flesh" had forfeited its claim by rejection of the Messiah (cf. Essay IV. pp. 161-164). Before the coming of Jesus Christ the eternal Church had its representative on earth, just as the "Word" had lightened every man before it became flesh. The Jewish Church was such a representative, and in St. Paul's view Christ did not found the Church but redeemed a Church which was already there. But we cannot limit the pre-Christian Church to Israel any more than we can deny the presence of Christ's spirit in persons and bodies other than Christians and the Church. Abraham and Isaiah, Socrates and Phidias, Buddha and Confucius, must all be reckoned as, *each in his degree*, a representative and organ of the eternal Church.

Resurrection of Christ, and by the consequent outpouring of the Holy Spirit ; it was not made by men ; its first members did not construct it, but joined it ; and if it should happen that, through the infidelity of men, the Church on earth should cease for some years or some centuries to exist, yet even then the first man, who, by reading the New Testament or otherwise, should become a disciple of Christ, would not be a second founder of the Church ; he would merely join the Church—One, Holy, Catholic, and Apostolic—to which all the saints belong. There is, and there can be, only one Church. However multiform its organisation, however varied in degree of adequacy its interpretation of the fact of Christ, still in its adherence to that one fact it is one, with a unity not made by its members but by Christ, when in utter loneliness He bore the Cross from Jerusalem to Calvary.

Christ is the whole life of the Church ; from Him comes whatever is distinctively Christian in its several members ; our function is to receive life from Him, and express His one Truth, realise His one Purpose, according to our capacities. For though we can bring nothing to the Church's life, each of us has part of that life entrusted to him. So St. Paul tells the Corinthians, "Now ye are the Body of Christ, and members each in his part." There is some part of the Church's life which waits till we are willing to live it. And because we are not willing, the language used about the Church by Saints and Theologians seems often to be exaggerated. What a contrast between the life of Christ and the life of the Society which calls itself His Body ! What a contrast between the tiny band of followers at supper with their Lord, and our well-dressed congregations worshipping with impressive ceremonial—and no agony or cross to follow! But that is what we should expect. This contrast reflects discredit upon Churchmen but not upon the Church or its true life. The Church on earth is a sacrament,

an outward and visible sign of the Church Universal,
and criticism of its outward form no more exhausts its
spiritual significance than the geometrical treatment of
curves exhausts the significance of their beauty.

The Catholic Church is universal, not only in space
but in time ; the living and the dead alike are members
of it. " The gates of Hades shall not prevail against
it." Death is no ultimate division in that society.
Just as the old members of a School or College are still
members of it though they have " left " or are " gone
down," so those who have " departed this life " are
members of the Church equally with us which are
alive. Indeed, we who are united by faith to Christ
are even now, as St. Paul declares, in heaven. " God
. . . quickened us together with Christ . . . and
raised us up with Him, and made us to sit with Him
in the heavenly places in Christ Jesus." And when
we think of our Lord's Ascension, we pray that these
great words may be true of us, and that " like as we do
believe . . . our Lord Jesus Christ to have ascended
into the heavens, so we may also in heart and mind
thither ascend and with Him continually dwell."

All of this is expressed in the one great rite of the
Christian Church, the Rite of the Holy Communion,
that is of the Communion of Saints. We come to
receive the Body and Blood of Christ " which are
verily and indeed taken and received by the faithful in
the Lord's Supper." He Himself is veritably there.
Just as there is beauty in a great picture, though a man
of no artistic training cannot see it, so Christ is truly
present in His Sacrament. Two men may look at the
same picture ; in one sense both are looking at the
same object—the same lines and colours ; but it may be
that only one of them sees the beauty. Yet the beauty
is there ; he finds it there, and does not put it there.
So the faithful find Christ at His own Table. But we
find Him there, not because our worship draws Him
down to us, but because as we worship He draws us to

Himself. His sacrifice is perpetual ; His will is wholly given to the Father.[1] Once in the history of men the whole nature of that sacrifice was set forth ; but the sacrifice itself, which is His obedience and the submission of His Will, is eternal. And if we use aright the Eucharistic and Sacrificial Feast of the Lord's Supper, we there lift ourselves "in heart and mind" into the heavenly region where Christ dwells and wherein unceasingly His eternal sacrifice is offered :

> And now, O Father, mindful of the Love
> That bought us once for all on Calvary's Tree,
> And having with us Him that pleads above,
> We here present, we here spread forth to Thee
> That only Offering perfect in Thine eyes,
> The one, true, pure, immortal Sacrifice.
>
> Look, Father, look on His anointed Face,
> And only look on us as found in Him.

The elements upon the altar, the Bread and Wine which we receive, are signs and vehicles of the Life which is obedient unto death, and which we receive that it may become our own. But as in heart and mind we are lifted into that heaven where the Ascended Christ eternally offers the sacrifice of Himself, what is the congregation in which we find ourselves? It is not the few people assembled in Church at the moment ; it is the whole Communion of Saints. We hear the Absolution and the Comfortable Words ; we lift up our hearts unto the Lord ; and thereupon it is "with Angels and Archangels and with all the company of Heaven" that we laud and magnify His glorious Name. Patriarchs and Prophets, Apostles, Evangelists and Martyrs, and all who have tried to put their trust in the God and Father of Jesus Christ—these are the real congregation in the service of the Holy Communion or Holy Fellowship, into which we enter as we receive into ourselves the Life of Christ.[2]

[1] Cf. Essay V. pp. 250-251.
[2] Cf. Van Eyck's well-known picture, "The Adoration of the Lamb," where people of every type and period unite in worship.

Moreover, the proof that we receive that Life is our incorporation into its Fellowship. The climax of the service is our dedication of ourselves ; in the strength there given to us we say, " Here we offer and present unto Thee, O Lord, ourselves, our souls and bodies, to be a reasonable, holy, and lively sacrifice unto Thee." A man whose life is not offered to God in practical service has certainly not received into himself the Life of Christ. But if that Life of Love and service and sacrifice has taken, or is taking, possession of us, we are thereby knit to all others who share it, whether in this world or in that beyond.

Our faith is so feeble that this great company is usually hidden from us. We think of Christ as present only in the consecrated elements, or only in the souls of those who faithfully receive them ; we think the worshippers are just the few who are present with us in the same building. But this is plainly wrong. Christ is present wherever God is present ; and that is everywhere ; " Heaven and earth are full of Thy glory " ; only we need aids and helps if we are to realise His Presence and appropriate His gift of Life ; the congregation at His " Service " is the whole Communion or Fellowship of Saints, and the "Service" itself is the Service of the Holy Fellowship or Holy Communion. It is not the movement of our bodies up the chancel, but it is the accompanying movement of our attention and care from selfish or worldly aims to the Purpose of God—it is our ascension " in heart and mind " to the Heaven which is ever about us— that gives the " Service " its significance.

We have spoken of our approach to Christ ; but in truth we can only come because He draws us. It is the whole point of the Sacrament that Christ gives and we receive. No other " aids and helps " can ever take the place of these, because they are the means appointed by Himself, and carry us back to the moment of His supreme revelation of the Father in the Passion. The sacrament is a communion because it is a memorial. Christ's Human Nature is the veil which hides from us His Divinity unless we pass through the veil by receiving that Human Nature as our own ; but as we share His Human Life we find, as the beloved disciple found, that it is the Life Divine. But prior to our coming to Him must be His revelation of Himself to us. The Word was in all the world from all eternity ; but only when it became flesh did men behold its glory. As in the Incarnation, so in the Eucharist, He comes unto His own, and only because He comes to us can we be sure that we may approach Him. It is all His doing, not ours. He gives, and we receive; when we approach, it is because He draws us. But the realm to which He draws us is not merely the sanctuary of a Church, nor an Upper Chamber in Jerusalem ; it is the presence of God Almighty, where He is worshipped by the heavenly host with hymns that are never silent, and thanksgivings that never cease.

For we "are not come to a mount that may be touched," nor to an altar that may be seen with bodily eyes, "but we are come . . . to innumerable hosts of angels, to the general assembly and church of the firstborn . . . and to God the Judge of all, and to the spirits of just men made perfect, and to Jesus." [1]

Thus the one great "Service" of the Christian Church emphasises the true nature of the Church. We have lost sight of a great part of this truth in England. Abuses and errors had become associated with parts of the full doctrine, and in the abolition of the abuses the truth itself suffered. Prayers for the dead dropped out of use ; but they represent a spontaneous and generous impulse of the human heart, and the right to offer them is implicit in the doctrine of the Communion of Saints. The Invocation of Saints passed out of use, because men not only asked the Saints to present their prayers, but prayed to the

---

[1] Hebrews xii. 18, 22. Cf. Essay IV. pp. 196-198.

Saints themselves instead of God ; but if " with Angels
and Archangels and with all the company of Heaven
we laud and magnify God's glorious Name," why
should we not ask that company to assist our prayers
as much as our praises ?

For the Church is one, and the gates of death do
not prevail against it. The Church as it exists for the
Omniscient Love of God is the all-embracing communion of His children, the worthy object of His
Love, the Bride of Christ.

II. The Church Militant here in Earth

Of this spiritual Communion the Church as visibly
organised on earth is a sacrament, and its organisation
should express at once its sacramental character and the
character of that whose sacrament it is.[1]   But it is also
the instrument through which the Holy Spirit works
in the world, as He builds up in successive generations
the Body of Christ.

We have already alluded to the problem involved
in the fact that the body contains imperfect and even
vicious members.   That difficulty will always be the
greatest obstacle to the Church's life and work, but it
is not unanswerable.

The answer is that the Body itself is still imperfect;
and therefore the Power of Christ that works in it is
still imperfect.   In the final exposition of St. Paul's
doctrine on this point, which is contained in the
Epistle to the Ephesians, this is made perfectly clear.
The Church is the completion ($\pi\lambda\eta\rho\hat{\omega}\mu\alpha$) of Him who
"all in all is being fulfilled" (i. 23).   And only
when this process of development has reached its goal
will the full measure of the Power of Christ be known;
it is when we are all come to a perfect man that we
shall also come to the measure of the stature of the

---

[1] Cf. Essay VIII. pp. 391-394.

completion of the Christ (iv. 13). For all humanity is to be gathered in ; Christ has broken down " the middle wall of partition " (the symbol of all exclusiveness), " that He might create in Himself of the twain one new man " (ii. 14, 15) ; and the whole community thus constituted is so closely knit together, by the one Divine purpose which controls it, that it may be called " one new man," or "a perfect man " ; each of us individually being members or limbs of that one Body.

All possible diversitie᷈ are required : " If the whole body were an eye, where were the hearing ? If the whole were hearing, where were the smelling ? " (1 Cor. xii. 17). And so " He appointed some to be apostles, and some to be prophets, and some evangelists, and some pastors and teachers ; for the perfecting of the saints . . . unto the building up of the Body of Christ, till we all come . . . to [constitute] a full-grown man, the measure of the stature of the completion of the Christ . . . from whom [meanwhile] all the Body fitly framed and knit together, through that which every joint supplieth, according to the working in due measure of each several part, maketh the increase of the Body unto the building up of itself in love."

It may be worth while to call attention to the affinities between this great conception and the leading features of modern sociology. (*a*) The unity of the whole is realised, not despite but through, the diversity of the parts ; (*b*) the conception is dynamic, not static ; (*c*) the social unity is spiritual ("in love "), not mechanical. Perhaps it may be well to show this in more detail.

(*a*) Students of the subject are familiar with the idea that in primitive tribes the unity of the whole overrides all individuality ; this is the condition of " Communism," in which the rights and claims of the individual are simply ignored. As social life develops the individual citizen gains more liberty, and the differences between individuals are more fully allowed for. This may proceed so far that "individualism" threatens to break up, or at least to thrust into the background, the unity of the nation. The result is a partial reaction which endeavours to realise the unity of the nation not through the elimination of all differences but by the harmonising of them. This aim becomes conscious in "socialism." [1] The "Communist" unity is like that of a jelly-fish, different parts of which are barely distinguishable from each other; the "Socialist" unity is like that of a human body, where the single life of the whole absolutely depends on the diversity of the parts alike in form and function.

(*b*) Again, whereas the social ideal of early political thinkers was fixed and static, however long and gradual the process by which it was to be reached, modern thought is not content with the hope of a fixed perfection. Mr. H. G. Wells claims that his *Modern Utopia* is the first work which recognises that growth must be an inherent element in the ideal itself. So the members of St. Paul's ideal society labour for "the increase of the body, unto the building up of itself."

(*c*) Thirdly, the recognition of the diversities of the individuals and of their "freedom" involves the necessity that the citizens should not be merely held together in the state, but should consent to being so united ; that is, they must be united in a community, because each in his own will desires such union with the others. But this is not far from the "love" which St. Paul recognises as the uniting power in the Body. In short, his inspired insight has leapt at once to the most modern conceptions of ideal social relationship.

But we are only now emerging from an age of

---

[1] It may be well to point out that this may be autocratic, aristocratic, bureaucratic, or democratic. Germany is on the whole the most socialist state in Europe, but its socialism is, as yet, not democratic.

individualism, and many find it hard to sympathise with the conception that the society is, or may be, prior to its members. Yet we know it well enough of our own families ; a man is not first himself, and afterwards a member of his family ; he is born in it, and membership of it is a part of what he himself is. So, too, the member of a school knows perfectly well that while the members make up the school, its life is something continuous, into which successive generations enter, and from which each derives far more than he can ever contribute to it. And, in moments of patriotism at least, every citizen knows that this is true of himself and his country. So, St. Paul insists, the Church is the Community of those who have been drawn to Christ and in which His Spirit lives. Those who are " members incorporate " in that Body will be governed in all their lives by the Spirit which thus takes control of them.

This conception has many practical results. The first of these is that, however various the manifestations, we should "give diligence to watch the one-ness of the Spirit in the bond of peace " (iv. 3).[1] We must realise that all diversities of spiritual gifts and activities are required for the life of the Body. The Prophet will not despise the Pastor, nor the Pastor depreciate the Prophet ; and if we see devils cast out, we shall not say that it was done by Beelzebub, on the ground that those who did it either are or are not members of an episcopalian body. It has been partly through forgetfulness of the immensity of its task, that the visible Church has had so fatal a tendency to take its eyes off the one-ness of the Spirit, and to quarrel about the diversity of gifts and methods, till it broke into little pieces. Now that we realise again to some extent the greatness of the Church's task, in converting

[1] τηρεῖν means "to watch" rather than "to keep" ; in any case it would be nonsense to bid people "keep the unity of the Spirit," because it cannot be either broken or lost ; St. Paul's point is that we are to keep before our minds the fact that the Spirit is one however diverse may be its modes of operation.

the world and conforming the practice of the Christian nations to the standard of Christ, we are again conscious of the need for Christian unity ; and we are beginning to realise that it must come by " comprehension " and not by " compromise," and that we are therefore required at once to insist on what we have found to be true, and to search earnestly for what is good or true in the practice or belief of others.

Still more important perhaps is St. Paul's contention that when the one Body is fully built up, we shall be " no longer children, tossed to and fro and carried about with every wind of doctrine " (iv. 14). For it is only when all men agree in faith—when " we all attain to the unity of the faith " (iv. 13)—that the faith of any individual will be secure. Our doubts come very largely from the fact that some men do not believe at all, and that those who believe interpret their faith so differently. Much of the unbelief of our own time rests on no reasoned arguments, but on the knowledge that many men—and some of them able and learned men—have rejected entirely or in part the traditional faith. If our individual faith were supported by the faith of all mamkind doubt would be almost impossible ; in any case there would not be divers winds of doctrine, by which we could be tossed to and fro.[1]

A purely individual faith is bound to be precarious, partly because of doubts suggested from without, and partly because the whole Spirit of Christ can only operate in the whole Body and not in a single member. No one person and no one group of persons could claim to have exhausted the unsearchable riches of Christ. There is amazing confusion of thought on

---

[1] Cf. Cicero, *De Natura Deorum*, lib. i. cap. 6. " Profecto eos ipsos, qui se aliquid certi habere arbitrantur, addubitare coget doctissimorum hominum de maxima re tanta dissensio."

No doubt the chief cause of perplexity is that Christians seem to be no better in conduct than many of their neighbours. Men notice, with Spinoza, that Christians differ from others not in faith or love, or any of the fruits of the Spirit, but only in opinion (*sola opinione*). (Spinoza, *Ep.* lxxiii.)

this subject. In no other department of life does any individual suppose that his experience contains all the data necessary for the solution of its problems. We obey the laws of our state and follow the conventions of our civilisation without insisting that we personally should see their necessity. But for some reason people resent the idea that in relation to the most difficult of all problems we should admit that the wisdom of the community is likely to be greater than our own, because of its experience being wider. The conflict between an individual and the Church in matters of belief is not a conflict between reason and faith, but between the reason of an individual working upon certain facts of experience and the reason of a whole community working upon other facts of experience ; it is always possible that the Church is wrong, but the weight of probability is always on its side.[1]

And so it is just silly to reject an article of the Creed or a traditional custom of the Church because " it is no use to me," or " I do not see the use of it." If we consider, after full examination of the evidence, that an article of the Creed is false or a custom of the Church injurious, we must, of course, reject. But we must still remember that the facts we have considered have probably been considered by the Church, which may well have had other evidence which has not been before us. The accumulated experience of Christendom is the basis on which the belief and practice of the Church is grounded ; it may be the duty of an individual to set himself against the belief and practice current in his day —every true prophet does so to some extent. At any time the synthesis already made is bound to be inadequate, and progress is won through the perception of this inadequacy by the individual man of genius ; but he can only appeal to principles already accepted, and

---

[1] This takes account only of points where the Church is united ; the divisions of Christendom, of course, fatally weaken the authority of the Church with regard to all points which they affect, and in consequence with regard to all points.

when he differs from the Church he must realise the initial probability that the Church is right.[1]

There may be some parts of the Church's whole belief which are not part of the religious life of this or that individual believer, and are yet a necessary part of the whole Christian doctrine, and will be needed by others ; and thus, because only in the whole Body can the whole Spirit live, they become indirectly part of the support of his own faith. What comes home to me will only be part of the whole truth : I may be the eyes, sensitive to light but not to sound ; I may be the ear, sensitive to sound but not to light. The whole fact of the world is known, if at all, only when each of the senses has received its own impression and contributed to consciousness what it can tell ; the whole fact of Christ is known, if at all, only when all men have found in Him the satisfaction of the need of each, and have brought to the total experience of the Church the manifold experience of all disciples.[2]

From this various conclusions follow. In the first place a man must be a loyal member of the Church if he is to come under the full power of the Spirit of Christ. In his own soul he will find something of that power ; but only in the whole Church will he find it in its fulness—only indeed in the whole Church when the Church includes all mankind. It is through the Church that the power of Christ reaches the individual Christian. It is by other Christians that he is taught, and they again were taught by others. The Church is thus the medium of salvation—in this sense at least ; but it is so in a further sense also. Just as the spirit of a school is not to be found in its entirety in a single member of the school or any group of members ; just as the temper and life of a nation is not fully represented in any one citizen or group of citizens, but only in

---

[1] Cf. Essay VIII. pp. 377-378. The more united the Church becomes, the more necessary is it that individual members should have and exercise freedom of criticism, otherwise there will be no progress.

[2] Cf. Essay VIII. pp. 392-394.

2 A

the whole history of the people, so the Spirit of Christ can only operate in its full power through the one Church of all lands and all ages, and only in its fellowship therefore can the individual's salvation be complete.[1]

Again, in teaching we are bound to present the whole Christian doctrine, and not only those elements in it which are of vital importance to ourselves. No doubt we shall teach the latter with far greater force ; that is inevitable. But we can never be sure that what matters most to us will also matter most to those whom we teach. To one the Forgiveness of Sins will be almost everything ; to another the Communion of Saints or the Holy Catholic Church. Logically, no doubt, they all stand together ; but in experience they will affect different people in very varying degrees ; and a man has no right consciously to endanger the fulness of another's life because of the limitations of his own ; but, conversely, it is not to be demanded of every individual that he should here and now obtain a personal hold upon the whole Christian doctrine.

Above all, we find that the primary duty of the Christian is not (of course) the saving of his soul ; nor is it the saving of some one else's soul. The primary duty of the Christian is the building up of the Body of the Christ, which, as we saw, will carry individual salvation with it. We are therefore confronted with problems in relation to the various branches of the Church, to the whole life of Christendom, and to the unconverted peoples ; and all of these problems are inextricably intertwined.

The prayer in which the Lord Jesus dedicated Himself for the final sacrifice is a prayer for the unity of His disciples. The Master and eleven disciples stood in the Temple Court in the darkness of night. And the Master was about to be withdrawn ; upon those eleven men hung the hope of the world. If

[1] Cf. Essay VI. p. 298.

they began to quarrel, all was lost. And He prays, not chiefly that they may be good, but that they may be united, for that is what is vital for the spread of the Gospel. " Holy Father, keep them in Thy name which Thou hast given Me, that they may be one, even as we. . . . Neither for these only do I pray, but for them also that believe on Me through their word ; that they may all be one ; . . . that the world may believe that Thou didst send Me." The conversion of the world is the Church's task, and only a united Church can accomplish it.

The problem of Re-union lies outside the limits of our discussion.[1] But we may refer to the general principle that, as a rule, men are right when they assert and wrong when they deny. Those who have insisted on the value of liturgical worship are right ; so are those who have insisted on the value of *ex tempore* and open congregational prayer. Those who have insisted on a ministry of order are right ; and so are those who have insisted that the wind bloweth where it listeth, and the spirit of prophecy may light on any man.

But while only a united Church can accomplish the Church's task, even a united Church will fail if it is a mere fragment of the nations from which its members are drawn. The possibilities of our spiritual achievement are limited by our whole spiritual environment. A Christian Church whose members are also members of an almost pagan society will not achieve very much. Only when England is Christian will the Church of England be altogether so. While trade and business are dominated by competitive selfishness, and while the community is possessed by the spirit that leads to industrial wars, no effort for the world's evangelisation will come to very much. The members of the Church are also members of " the world," and cannot escape from " the world's " influence. I am, as I hope, a Christian Englishman ; but then I am only an English

[1] Cf. Essay VIII. pp. 403-407.

Christian, and my character is moulded not only by the Spirit of Christ but also by the spirit of contemporary England, which is not the same. And this is inevitably true of every member of the Church, and therefore of the Church itself as an active force in the world. The Church cannot be more than a limited distance ahead of the society in which its members live.[1] The early Church tolerated slavery ; the contemporary Church tolerates sweating.

Not only is loss of power involved. But the heathen world is watching the so-called Christian nations to see what Christianity works out at; and what they see does not attract them. There is a Hindu journal which lately published from time to time accounts of the slums of our great towns, and added on each occasion the refrain—"This is what Christianity has done for England ; do you want it here ?" The civilian, the trader, or the soldier, who is selfish or contemptuous, is taken by those among whom he lives as a representative of Christianity ; and rightly so, for his character is the measure of the Church's failure. Moreover, our Western nations are full of students and others from the unconverted lands, who carry back reports of what they found in "Christian" England. English Christianity can do little to convert the world till England is Christian, not only in profession but in life. To this end those who are members of the Church must do what they can to live by Christ's principles of utter self-forgetfulness and complete indifference to wealth. In the conflict with the devil and the flesh, "Christian" society upon the whole is on our side ; in our conflict with the world it is decidedly against us. It is here that the real issue lies. "Blessed are the poor in spirit, for theirs is the kingdom of heaven."

---

[1] This is the justification of monasticism. But monasticism ignores the facts that economically, at least, "the saint lives off the sinner" (cf. Essay I. p. 16), and that by his withdrawal he loses his influence over the sinner.

It is the fact that we are members both of the Church and of our half-pagan nations which makes our Christianity and the Church's work so ineffective. We read with amazement Christ's praise of poverty and disparagement of wealth, because it seems to us that the best things in life—the society of refined people and even the affection of our intimate friends—are dependent on at least a moderate supply of this world's goods. If a man loses all his money, he must, in our day, lose most of his friends as well : they will not deliberately leave him ; but he will have to live where expense can be avoided, and they will not follow him. If we had the true spirit of fellowship, such as ought to bind together the various members of Christ's Body, this would not be so. The sting of poverty is often the worldliness of a man's friends ; and poverty can only deserve the blessing which Christ pronounced upon it when the sense of fellowship between His disciples is strong enough to overcome the worldliness of men.

How are we to acquire that sense of fellowship ? It is the gift of the Holy Spirit. The best way to bridge class-divisions and the like is always to bring men together under the inspiration of a common ideal. And strongest of all such bonds ought to be that which arises from common devotion to the greatest of all causes—the growth of the Kingdom of God. But for most of us there is no link with other men to be found in our religion ; we have no fellowship of (or in) the Holy Ghost, no sense that we belong to one another because we all belong to Him. If some stranger came up to me and claimed a somewhat intimate acquaintance on the ground that he worshipped the same God in the same Church, I might regard it as an outrage. That is all wrong. We allow people to claim our acquaintance on the ground that they were at the same school or College ; that is recognised as a real bond of union ; but merely to be worshippers of the same God is not enough to draw us to one another—because our worship is something laid over the surface of our lives, not something bursting from their inmost depths. We go to Church in families, and sit in our own pews ; we say our own prayers, and pay our respects to our own God ; and then we come out again and go to our own homes, to eat our own luncheons or our own suppers. We do not concern ourselves with the people in the next pew, unless they sing out of tune, when we brace ourselves for the extreme measure of turning round to look at them. How can we hope to realise our fellowship with the whole company of believers in the Communion of Saints when this is our attitude to those who worship at our side ? We know some little fragment of the Grace of our Lord Jesus Christ and of the Love of God ; of the Fellowship of the Holy Ghost we know virtually nothing.

But if we have failed hitherto, where is the power that can enable us now to succeed ? It is in Africa, in India, in China, in Japan. As Bishop Montgomery has said, " the Body of Christ is a torso." Only when the glory and honour of all nations are brought into the Kingdom will the true greatness of the Kingdom be known. A meeting of devout Christians a little while ago was startled to hear a well-known missionary say something like this : " What are the characteristic virtues of a converted Englishman ? Honesty, manliness, truthfulness, trustworthiness. And what are the characteristic virtues of the converted Hindu ? They are love, joy, peace, long-suffering, gentleness, goodness, faith, meekness, temperance." But what will be the result when the mystical and spiritual nations of the East, and the affectionate and childlike peoples of Africa, are quickened by contact with the perfection of their own virtues in the Person of Jesus of Nazareth ? Inevitably the whole Church will be filled with a new spirit of devotion and selflessness.

Stage by stage, then, the Church must build itself up, its work at home rendering possible more work abroad, and the work abroad bringing new inspiration for the work at home ; until at last the one Purpose of God will govern all mankind, and the measure of the stature of the fulness of the Christ is made known.

For the Church is the Body of Christ ; and its growth is the growth of the Body of Christ. He is the Head—the source of all its purpose, the guiding and dominant fact. But a head without a body, or with a maimed, imperfect body, is ineffective ; its purpose may be excellent, but its achievement will be small. So Christ in Himself is complete ; in His earthly Life the whole character of God was manifest. But in power over the world He is incomplete until the Church, His Body, the instrument by which He accomplishes His will, is complete. For it is His Body, "the completion of Him who all in all is being fulfilled." As Origen remarks in commenting on this phrase : " We may conceive of a king as being filled with kingdom in respect of each of those who augment his kingdom, and being emptied thereof in the case of those who revolt from their king. . . . Wherefore Christ is fulfilled in all that come unto Him, whereas He is still lacking in respect of them before they have come."[1] And our task is not only to extend the power of Christ over the nations who do not know Him, but thereby to develop to its completion that power itself.

It is not the historic Life of Jesus, cut off from its historic consequence, but it is the work in human history of Jesus and His Church, that brings men's souls to God and establishes God's Kingdom on the earth.

" To Him be glory in the Church
and in Christ Jesus."

---

[1] Cf. Armitage Robinson, *ad loc.*

VIII

THE PRINCIPLE OF AUTHORITY

BY

A. E. J. RAWLINSON

I. AUTHORITY AND TRUTH.
II. AUTHORITY AND CHURCH ORDER.
III. AUTHORITY AND REUNION.
APPENDIX.—*The Historical Origins of the Christian Ministry.*

SYNOPSIS

PAGE

I. AUTHORITY AND TRUTH.

The modern opposition of "authority" and "the Spirit" rests on a misunderstanding. The idea of authority has been interwoven with that of inspiration and stereotyped by legalism. If "authority" be taken in its classical sense (*i.e.* as *auctoritas*) it will be recognized as a principle on which men ordinarily act in every sphere of human interest : why not, therefore, in that of Religion ?   365

Discussion of the inter-relation of religious "authority" and "inspiration." An inspired authority not necessarily infallible. Infallibilist view of authority developed as the logical corollary of an over-mechanical view of inspiration. Problem of the "seat of authority" the nemesis of this. An appeal made successively (*a*) from the "prophet" to the Bishop (as custodian of tradition) ; (*b*) from the individual Bishop to the Synod ; (*c*) from the Synod to the Council. Authority conceived as vested in officials. Papal Infallibility the logical outcome of a one-sided development   367

Repudiation of the idea of authority by Protestantism equally one-sided. Historically, Protestantism untrue to itself in substituting infallible Book for infallible Church. Modern Ritschlianism reverts to the position of Luther in falling back upon "witness of the Spirit" : inadequacy of Ritschlian view .   371

An attempt at restatement must start from the classical meaning of "auctoritas" and from a study in the light of this of actual religious psychology. Three phases in the life of the educated Christian :—

(*a*) Tutelage or "bondage to authority"—the stage proper to childhood. The failure of "simple believers" to transcend this stage impoverishes their intellectual but not necessarily their religious life.

(*b*) The stage of "abstract freedom," *i.e.* the assertion of the right to criticize and, if necessary, to deny : leading on to

(*c*) The final stage of "concrete freedom," *i.e.* voluntary assent on grounds of reason to what was formerly believed "on authority." The final stage represents an ideal progressively realized but never completely attained   .   .   373

The critical stage is the second : the conditions of a true solution of the individual problem are lacking if the authority of the Church is ignored. But by the authority of the Church must be understood *the corporate witness of the saints to the validity of the spiritual experience on which their lives are based* : and what is guaranteed by the *consensus sanctorum* is rather a life than a theology 377

Nevertheless the hypothesis of the validity of spiritual experience must inevitably involve dogmatic implications : and the truth of the spiritual and moral values of the Christian life will be found in the long run to carry with it the substance of traditional " orthodoxy " 379

II. AUTHORITY AND CHURCH ORDER.

Conceptions of the Christian Ministry are of two types, "Catholic" and "Protestant," "priestly" and "prophetic" : these terms defined: they determine controversies of Church Order, which are misrepresented when treated as disputes about origins 381

Inconclusiveness of argument from history :

(*a*) Ambiguity of historical evidence as such.

(*b*) Nature of our Lord's Messianic outlook as affecting the problem.

(*c*) Legitimate appeal on Protestant side to post-Reformation experience 383

I. Statement of "Protestant" view of Ministry and Sacraments 387

Some criticisms of this from "Catholic" standpoint . 389

II. Statement of "Catholic" view of Sacraments : the "Catholic" view of Ministry as corollary of this—("One Bread, One Body," therefore *ideally* One Ministry) . . 391

Catholicism compared and contrasted with Congregationalism 394

The historic Episcopate defended :

(i.) As embodying principle of continuity with the past.

(ii.) As expressing the idea of an authority wider than that of the *local* Church.

(iii.) As magnifying the office rather than the man.

(iv.) As required for the mediation of the "Catholic" type of piety 394

On the other hand, Episcopacy need not imply either—

(*a*) a vicious "clericalism," or

(*b*) prelacy, or

(*c*) autocracy, or

(*d*) a magical view of Orders 397

The Ministry of Sacraments and the Ministry of the
Word : the latter requires in the minister a personal endowment, the former (on the Catholic theory) an ecclesiastical
commission. That the minister of Sacraments be also a
minister of the Word is desirable but not essential. Need in
Catholicism for more general development of lay preaching . 400

The discussion has been of abstract principles : existing
Christian "denominations" are neither consistently " Catholic "
nor consistently " Protestant." Probable narrowing of issues
in the near future. Is a synthesis possible ? . . . 402

III. AUTHORITY AND REUNION.

Reunion can only be possible on a basis of comprehension
and synthesis. Protestants will not abandon Protestantism
nor Catholics Catholicism. Each must learn from the other . 403

What Catholicism has to give to Protestants . . 404

What Protestantism has to give to Catholics . . 405

The individual, like the Church, should aim at a synthesis . 406

The existence of Anglicanism is evidence of the possibility
of comprehending Christians of both types within one fold . 406

Right and wrong ways of seeking to forward the cause of
Reunion 406

APPENDIX

THE HISTORICAL ORIGINS OF THE CHRISTIAN MINISTRY . 408

Solidaire de Dieu et des autres pour être et pour vivre, on est aussi
solidaire de Dieu et des autres pour savoir ce qu'on est et ce qu'on doit
faire en vivant.

LABERTHONNIÈRE.

Ad discendum item necessario dupliciter ducimur, auctoritate et ratione.
Tempore auctoritas, re autem ratio prior est.

AUG. De Ord. ii. 9.

VIII

THE PRINCIPLE OF AUTHORITY

I. Authority and Truth

Ego vero evangelio non crederem, nisi me catholicae ecclesiae commoveret auctoritas.

Aug. *Contra Epist. fundamenti*, § 6.

It is the fashion in modern books to oppose the religions of authority to the religion of the spirit, with the object of discrediting the former. The idea of authority is out of favour, largely because it is misunderstood : more particularly because it is popularly confused with infallibility. It suggests to the modern mind the notion of an irrational despotism, imposing by external and arbitrary fiat belief in what is incredible. The "religion of the spirit," on the other hand, is taken to mean a nebulous atmosphere of religious idealism which refuses to embody itself as a concrete faith in anything in particular. The early Christian standpoint was very different. "The Spirit" in the New Testament is not the antithesis of authority, but its source : "authority" is not the tyranny of an ecclesiastical despotism but the witness of the Spirit to the truth of God.

Ecclesiastical history — and more especially the history of the Western Church—exhibits a gradual modification of the conception of authority as the Church's system hardened and crystallized and became more and more effectually dominated by the legalism of

the Latin mind. The immense edifice of Roman law—
the one considerable legacy of the decaying civilization
of the Western Empire to the new barbarian kingdoms
which arose upon its ruins—was taken over and absorbed
into the mind of the Catholic Church of the West, the
heiress by default of all the great ideas for which
Imperial Rome had stood. The legal spirit reacted
with transforming effect upon the conceptions alike of
authority and of inspiration. It would be an interesting investigation—though one which would require
more space than an essay affords and greater learning
than the writer can command—to trace fully the course
of this modification. From the first the two conceptions
have in Christian thought been intertwined.

In itself the word authority signifies primarily a
statement or an opinion for the truth of which some-
body is prepared to vouch : more particularly an
expression of responsible and competent opinion. This
is the classical meaning of the Latin word " auctoritas "
—" auctoritas Patrum," for instance, means properly
not " the authority of the Senate " in the modern sense
of the words, but rather what we should call a resolution
of the Senate, the expression of the considered judgment
of the Fathers upon a question submitted for their
deliberation, with the further implied suggestion that
such an expression of opinion carries with it a certain
weight. The weight to be attached to any " auctoritas "
varied with the assumed competence and knowledge
of the " auctor " who vouched for it. " Authority "
attaches in general to the utterances of " authorities,"
that is to say, of persons of wide experience and expert
knowledge in the spheres, of whatever kind, in which
they *are* " authorities " : and that upon a perfectly
sound principle—*cuique in sua arte credendum.*

In all spheres of human interest this is the principle
upon which men act. Artistic appreciation is trained
and developed not by indulging immature and Philistine
preferences, but by sitting at the feet of recognized

masters and asking not whether, but why, they are good. A youth desirous of becoming a doctor studies medicine under skilled guidance, and does not dream, so long as he retains the consciousness of being a beginner, of questioning the diagnosis of an experienced physician. In like manner if we would become good (so Aristotle teaches in the *Ethics*) we must begin by doing good actions suggested to us by " the legislator," even though our actions be not, properly speaking, virtuous, until rationalized by that insight into the principle underlying them which only subsequent reflection can give.   Is it so very paradoxical a contention that in matters of religion we must go to school with the saints, that in the religious as in other spheres there are experts, who as such are entitled to speak with authority ? [1]

Thus far upon grounds of mere reason most persons would in the abstract be prepared to go ; for it is but applying in a particular relation a principle of universal acceptance.   The case is complicated, however, when we proceed to apply the principle concretely in the sphere of religion, by the considerations hinted at above. The notions of authority and inspiration have reacted inextricably upon each other : they can hardly in their relation to Christianity be studied apart : and both have been injuriously affected by that spirit of legalism, begotten ultimately of the Roman imperial system, from the cramping tyranny of which in one form or another the whole of Christendom still suffers.

Authority in religion, for all believers in the guidance of the promised Spirit, becomes the witness not simply of the expert but of the inspired expert ; and there has been a persistent tendency both to take the inspiration of religious " authorities " for granted, and also to assume that the effect of inspiration is such as to render their witness infallible.   The nature of inspiration is discussed elsewhere in the present volume.[2]   Here it

---

[1] Cf. Essay II. pp. 62-63.   [2] Essay II. pp. 56-57.

may be sufficient to remark that we have no more reason, *a priori*, to look for infallibility in the sphere of intellect, as the result of that operation of the Divine Spirit which we call inspiration, than we have to look for impeccability in the sphere of conduct, as the result of that parallel operation of the same Spirit which we call grace. In practice, as a matter of fact, we find neither the one nor the other : the Church, the school of saints, is yet the home of sinners : the Church, the pillar and ground of the truth, has yet been endowed with no miraculous exemption from liability to human error. Nevertheless, just as we may believe, in spite of immoral popes and worldly bishops, nay, in spite of the sins which form the matter of our own daily confessions, that the heart of the Church has beaten true upon the whole, and still beats true, to the moral ideals of her Divine Master ; so we may believe, in spite of Robber Councils and Erastian Confessions, and the chaos of sects and parties in modern Christendom, that the Church has been, and is being, guided into an ever-deepening apprehension of divine truth. A morally stainless Church, it may be, would grasp intuitively the whole truth of God without admixture of error or taint of inadequacy ; though here, again, we may well refrain from any too confident assertion, as we remember that even He, Who though not formally impeccable [1] (for He suffered being tempted), was yet actually sinless, nevertheless was in nowise exempted from such intellectual limitations, or even (within the spheres of science and history) from such erroneous conceptions of fact, as were inseparable from the use of the mental categories of the age and generation among whom He came.

Considerations such as these, however, if they were ever in any form entertained in the Church (which may

---

[1] It was not that our Lord *could* not sin, but that He *would* not. The reality of the moral struggle in Him and the fact of His actual sinlessness are both equally vital to the truth of the Incarnation. Cf. Essay V. p. 248.

well be doubted), dropped early out of sight. The notion of inspiration was taken over by the New Israel from the Old uncriticized and at its crudest, pretty much in the form which it had assumed in late Jewish speculation. Any utterance, of course, which is taken as inspired is as such in some sense the voice of God : the true prophet speaks with a certain measure of divine authority. Moreover, inasmuch as the ultimate truth of things is the truth as God sees it, the " authority " of God would be absolute, could it be adequately ascertained. Inspiration having been for the most part taken as plenary, and no degrees being recognized, it was all too readily assumed that the divine authority in this absolute sense belonged to the prophetic witness, whether as manifested by individuals or by the Church corporately in her prophetical office. Already in the *Didache* we find it laid down that when once the Christian prophet has successfully surmounted certain tests of his genuineness and been recognized as inspired not of Satan but of God, to question henceforward his lightest word amounts to that sin against the Holy Ghost which has never forgiveness : " A prophet that speaketh in the Spirit ye shall neither test nor discriminate : all sin shall be forgiven, but this sin shall not be forgiven." [1] Already, in other words, the intrinsic appeal of prophetic inspiration to the light that is in man, to the eye which, if it be not deliberately darkened, must recognize the truth, is in process of being externalized into the dogma of a mechanical infallibility which stands superior to reason and must be accepted without criticism at its own valuation.

The process, however, which we here detect in its beginnings, received an early check in its development, arising from the practical difficulty of a conflict of authorities. Prophets with equal claim to the divine

---

[1] πάντα προφήτην λαλοῦντα ἐν πνεύματι οὐ πειράσετε οὐδὲ διακρινεῖτε· πᾶσα γὰρ ἁμαρτία ἀφεθήσεται, αὕτη δὲ ἡ ἁμαρτία οὐκ ἀφεθήσεται (*Didache* xi.). The date of the *Didache* is disputed, but most critics assign it to about 100 A.D. The authorship is unknown.

afflatus were discovered to be contradicting flatly each other's message. It was necessary in these circumstances to set up a criterion of inspiration in the shape of an appeal to tradition. The depositaries of tradition were inevitably the bishops, and more especially the bishops of those sees which claimed to be of apostolic foundation. It is probable that this, rather than the doctrine of order, was the original significance of the emphasis which so early as Irenaeus[1] we find laid upon the apostolic succession of the bishops. As original prophecy declined and was discredited, men fell back more and more upon the authority of settled Church order and the norm of the common life in faith and practice. No doubt, as the canon of the New Testament gradually took shape side by side with that of the Old, the ultimate appeal in matters of doctrine tended to be to Scripture, or, more strictly, to Scripture as interpreted by apostolic tradition ; but of this tradition the bishops continued to be the natural depositaries and custodians. The bishop, it came to be held, possessed as such a spiritual gift or " charism " of truth ;[2] if in spite of this his teaching was questioned, the appeal lay to the synod of his brother-bishops—ultimately, in later times, to an ecumenical council of the bishops. These questionings and developments in any case affected not so much the general conception of authority and inspiration in the Church as the problem of its rightful seat. That an inspired authority existed no one doubted ; nor was it doubted but that inspired authority was tantamount to infallibility.

The increasing concentration of the authority and witness of the Church in official—that is to say, in episcopal—hands must undoubtedly be regarded as due, at least in part, to the influence of the legalist temper, increasingly operative as the Church at once conquered, and was conquered by, the Empire. The tendency to claim for the hierarchy the exclusive custody of revealed

---

[1] Irenaeus wrote probably about 180 A.D.
[2] Cf. Iren. *adv. Haer.* III. iii. i.

truth, and a plenary inspiration for the determination of disputed points of doctrine and practice, grew with the growth of their administrative authority. Already by the time of Cyprian[1] the belief existed, if not in an infallible Pope, at least in something like a collectively-infallible episcopate. The right to speak with authority in spiritual things was conceived as vested no longer in the saints, or corporately in the Church considered as the school of saints, but in the Church's administrative organs acting in virtue of their apostolic commission ; and hence the rise of an ecclesiastical authority more and more despotic in its form, conceived more and more not as representing and voicing, but as dictating, the convictions of the spirit-bearing community ; as not merely speaking the truth in all things, but as mechanically infallible in its utterances, the truth of which was supposed to be externally guaranteed by the mere fact that they had been dogmatically imposed. The process finds its logical culmination in modern Romanism of the ultramontane type, and may be said to have reached its historical climax in 1870 with the decree of Papal infallibility.[2]   It is not extravagant to suggest that this represents a one-sided development of the idea of authority, which however explicable historically is none the less disastrous in its outcome.

Equally one-sided, however, and as we are constrained to think, equally disastrous, is the logical issue of that repudiation of the idea of authority in religion which is the characteristic aberration of Protestantism. There is a sense, indeed, in which the so-called orthodox Protestantism, which for three hundred years dominated Northern Europe and in which our fathers for the most part believed, was not Protestantism at all, but only mutilated Catholicism. Its intellectual basis, that is to say, was equally authoritarian with that of Rome, from

---

[1] Martyred A.D. 258.

[2] It is perhaps fair to observe that in the numerous qualifying clauses inserted in this decree the influence must be traced of a moderate party within the Papal Curia itself which was opposed to the more extreme claims of Ultramontanism.

which it differed merely in the substitution of the infallible Book for the infallible Church : a substitution which in itself was by no means an improvement.

Such, it is only fair to say, had not been the position of the original Reformers. Luther, for instance, found the seat of authority not in the letter of the Bible, but in the self-authenticating witness of the Spirit of God speaking through its pages and discerned by the spiritual man ; he proceeded upon this basis to exalt such of the Biblical books as particularly appealed to him and to depreciate others. Such a conception of religious authority, however, was too subtle for popular theology, and was, moreover, defenceless against the perils of an arbitrary subjectivism such as Luther's own. Historical Protestantism as a whole lost sight of it and fell back upon infallibility and verbal inspiration. In so doing it was, however, as above hinted, untrue to itself ; and the shattering to pieces by the criticism of the last century of this particular mode of conceiving the ground of Christian faith is but the working out after three hundred years of that principle of religious individualism which was a large part of the inner significance of Protestantism from the first.

Both infallibilities, we may say, are to-day discarded : the infallible Book has gone the way of the infallible Church. It is not surprising that under these circumstances there should be in some circles a reversion to the position of Luther. The claim to be in the true Lutheran succession and the only logical Protestants is made for themselves in Germany by that school deriving ultimately from Ritschl, of which the most notable living exponent is Professor Herrmann of Marburg, whose book, *The Communion of the Christian with God*, is readily accessible in an English translation.[1] Space forbids discussion of it in detail : it must suffice

---

[1] Crown Theological Library, vol. xv. (Williams and Norgate, 1906). The late Auguste Sabatier, in his *Religions of Authority and the Religion of the Spirit.* sets forth a view which is substantially identical with that of Professor Herrmann.

to say, somewhat dogmatically, that while it contains positive teaching of very great value, the general view of religion which it is designed to expound appears to be lacking in objectivity, and is in any case too difficult a doctrine to be made intelligible to the plain man. Such, conceivably, might be the religion of university professors; such, assuredly, could never be the faith of the millions ; and its patent inadequacy in the latter rôle might even suggest a doubt whether, in the last analysis, its spiritual atmosphere might not turn out to be too rarefied even for the soul of a professor.

What is needed is rather a restatement of the principle of authority which shall avoid either confusing it with infallibility or legalizing it as despotism. Our suggestion in this essay is that such a restatement may profitably find its starting-point in a return to something nearer akin to the classical meaning of the word "auctoritas." When St. Augustine writes "evangelio non crederem, nisi me catholicae ecclesiae commoveret auctoritas," is not his meaning much more nearly represented by some such rendering as "corporate witness,"[1] or even "inspired witness" of the Catholic Church, than by the paraphrase "infallible voice" ?

Meanwhile not a little may be learnt from a consideration of the course of actual religious psychology in the normal individual life. Authority (in the sense of "auctoritas") is the form through which all truth, and a fortiori all religious truth, reaches us in childhood. We accept implicitly what we are told by parents, pastors, and masters, as being the teaching of "authorities" who would not willingly deceive us, and of whose competence to speak we have no doubt. Our teachers represent to us, however informally, the authority of the Church Catholic in her teaching office : we accept their utterances, as a general rule, in unquestioning faith and docility. In this, as a matter

---

[1] Cf. the famous saying, "securus iudicat orbis terrarum" (Aug. Adv. Petilianum).

of fact, we are but following the law of all life. Every living organism is born into a specific environment and inherits a specific tradition, which it disregards only at its peril. For a child to manifest a precocious independence by refusing to avail himself of the knowledge and experience of older people, as a protest against the authoritative form in which alone he is as yet capable of receiving it, would be generally recognized as a piece of culpable folly. "A fool despiseth his father's instruction ; but he that regardeth reproof is prudent." If we describe the status in question as that of tutelage, we are constrained to admit that tutelage has its rightful and inevitable place, at least as a stage proper to childhood, in the development of all our lives.

But we must go a step farther. If we are to be true to the facts of experience we must recognize that the status of tutelage (we may, if we like, paraphrase it as "bondage to authority") is one which even in adult life is never transcended by the mass of mankind. Academic theology is always being tempted to overlook the obvious fact that only a minority of Christians can ever be fitted by opportunity, training, and habit of mind to work out an individual reconstruction of the traditional theology which forms the intellectual vehicle of their spiritual life. The average man, if he is religious at all, accepts his religion " on authority"— whether the authority in question happens to be that of the parish priest, the nonconformist preacher, or the " naked Bible "—as inevitably as he imbibes his political views from the leading articles of his favourite newspaper. It is of the last importance, in view of these facts, to recognize that tutelage, though representing a lower intellectual level than that of " thinking for oneself," by no means necessarily involves a lower level of religious life. A man's creed—i.e. the intellectual expression of his faith—is but a single element (though admittedly an element of regulative importance) in the rounded whole of his religion ;

and the religious value of this element is in any case largely independent of the particular form of mental process by which it was attained. It is as much the exaggeration of Protestantism (or, more properly speaking, of intellectualism in religion) to despise the faith of " babes in Christ " and to aim at making every charcoal-burner a theologian, as it is the error of Romanism to aim at making tutelage universal, to treat the charcoal-burner as the type of all.

Nevertheless, normally all educated persons[1] ought in their measure—in religious as in secular matters—to emancipate themselves from tutelage *pari passu* with advancing knowledge and experience, inasmuch as growth ought to be harmonious upon all sides of a man's nature, and the attempt to combine intellectual maturity in all other relations of life with a theology stereotyped in childhood is only too apt to lead to shipwreck as touching the faith. To criticize becomes in such circumstances at once a right and a duty. A stage is reached in the inner life of the spirit at which the individual claims, and is bound in the name of intellectual honesty to claim, the right to question, and, if need be, to deny, the validity of inherited and traditional dogma. It is this which is the underlying truth represented by the much-abused Protestant principle of the right of private judgment—which should perhaps be more accurately described as the private right of judgment. We may designate this claim " the abstract freedom of denial." It is the phase or moment of scepticism, and stands for the assertion of the individual self-consciousness over against the social whole.

The legitimate assertion, however, of such an

---

[1] The implied dichotomy of mankind as either " educated " or " uneducated " is, of course, adopted merely for clearness of exposition, and is in no sense intended to suggest the notion of an exclusive aristocracy of intellect outside whose magic circle tutelage compulsorily reigns and original thinking is forbidden. As it is possible to combine the desire that all the Lord's people should be prophets with the admission that not all, in effect, are such, so is it possible to combine the pious wish that all should be capable of giving a reason for the hope that is in them with the recognition of the facts set forth above.

abstract freedom to deny need not necessarily involve actual concrete denials, and ideally it should not do so, except in cases where the previous dogmatic teaching has been faulty or untrue. In any case the stage in question ought not to be more than a temporary phase mediating the transition from the simple faith of childhood to the mature convictions of manhood, thought out and justified at the bar of reason, and knit into the texture of a living and growing spiritual experience. We may name this final stage " the concrete freedom of voluntary assent." It is of the nature of a return to the faith of childhood, the same in substance but transformed. The content of belief at this stage is in no necessary antithesis to the teachings of authority, but it is no longer "upon authority" that it is believed. Whereas formerly a creed was held true because authority imposed it, it is now increasingly perceived that "authority" imposed it only because (as experience and reason combine to assure us) it was and is true. "Ye shall know the truth, and the truth shall make you free." So, too, the claim of the individual to religious self-realization is found to be in no necessary antithesis to the claims of the Church upon individual loyalty, because it is discovered to be only in and through the Church that the individual is capable of religious self-realization. ("Ανθρωπος φύσει πολιτικὸν ζῷον—"it is not good for man to be alone.")

That the foregoing sketch represents not unfairly the intellectual development of the average educated Christian in its broad outlines will hardly, I think, be denied ; though, of course, in concrete cases the stages may be less clearly defined. The final stage, in particular, is never, strictly speaking, complete ; for as experience continually broadens and deepens, so ought the intellectual aspects of the faith to be grasped with an ever surer insight and the theological synthesis to be growing in adequacy, even to the end.

This, however, is a process which may safely be

left to take care of itself. It is in the critical intermediate phase, the stage of transition from tutelage
through abstract to concrete freedom, or as Carlyle
would say from the "Everlasting No" to the "Everlasting Yea," that the problem becomes one of practical
urgency. No one can have any experience, however
slight, of educational work from the religious standpoint,
whether among undergraduates or public school boys,
without becoming thoroughly familiar with the phenomenon of intellectual "unsettlement" resulting from a
species of spiritual growing-pains. In such cases little
can be done beyond urging the importance of preserving even in scepticism the religious temper, the spirit of
reverence, and something of the humility of the child.
But as regards the outcome of the struggle (for a
struggle it usually is) not a little may turn upon the
attitude taken up in relation to authority.

The individual, indeed, must in such cases in honesty
justify his faith at the bar of reason : the vocation to
do so is the meaning of the trial. But the judge,
nevertheless, is not to be confused with the evidence ;
and individual experience by itself may well prove too
narrow a basis of evidence to work upon. The true
Christian apologetic, after all, is to be found in the lives
of the saints ; if, looking upon these, we are to
pronounce them grounded in the last analysis upon
illusion, we may reasonably ask what in human
experience is to be pronounced trustworthy. "I had
almost said even as they, but lo! then should I have
condemned the generation of Thy children." It is a
sobering reflection, and one which may reasonably lead
to the recognition that, after all, authority and tradition *prima facie* hold the field, in religious as in
other matters. The corporate witness of the Church
(regarded as the summed experience of the saints)
constitutes a weighty "auctoritas" which is at least
a provisional justification of the venture of faith : an
"auctoritas" from which it is not the part of wisdom

lightly to depart. Criticism of tradition there must indeed certainly be ; but it should be criticism from within and not from without, and inherited orthodoxy should serve at least as a guiding-line, a preliminary orientation of the mind as it embarks upon its voyage of individual discovery and construction. Broadly speaking, it may be taken as an axiom that the community is wiser than the individual, and that authority attaches to the corporate witness and the common mind of the spirit-bearing Church as against individual aberrations.[1] It should be the individual's aim (under the guidance of the Holy Spirit of truth), both during the transition period and subsequently, to appropriate and make his own, in so far as he may, the whole complex fact of the Christian life as historically manifested in the experience of the Church—the living concrete whole of which the formal pronouncements of official "authority" (creeds, and conciliar decisions, and judgments as to the inspiration of Scripture) are the intellectual symbols ; not necessarily concluding that such elements as he has already been able personally to assimilate and justify represent all that is of truth and value, and that the rest is husk and dross. Religious teachers are, as a rule, right in what they affirm, wrong in what they deny : inasmuch as systems are partial, and no one of the convictions in the strength of which men live but has something of essential truth behind it.

Throughout the constructive part of this essay authority has been understood in the sense of the witness of the saints, individually and corporately, to the validity of the spiritual experience upon which their lives are based. The question may reasonably be asked how much, strictly speaking, this witness covers. Admitting, that is to say, the legitimacy of the appeal to authority so interpreted, how far do we stand committed to the *theology* of the saints—to the intellectual concepts and thought-forms by which they have

[1] Cf. Essay VII. pp. 351 *sqq.*

interpreted their experience—or to what extent is it true to say that the aegis of this authority of theirs covers only the moral and religious values which their lives exemplify ? We are here entering upon admittedly difficult ground. Primarily, no doubt, the experience of the saints is testimony rather to the essential validity of a certain way of life than to any particular mode of formulating or attempting to formulate its intellectual implications. Nevertheless, the modern tendency to distinguish sharply between fact and interpretation, theology and religious experience, may easily be carried too far. In the concrete the two are often hardly separable. Doubtless we are not committed in detail to the systematized theologies of the past, or absolved from the obligation of formulating our own by our conviction that behind them was a solid basis of reality. Doubtless, too, the notion of authority has often been stretched unjustifiably, and made to cover intellectual deductions and historical judgments for which, as we now perceive, religious experience afforded no warrant. But it by no means follows from these admissions that the hypothesis of the validity of the Church's spiritual experience will not be found to involve dogmatic implications as to the nature of the universe or of God, or even to carry with it certain judgments of fact in matters of history.[1] It is difficult, for instance, to see how the spiritual and moral values of the Christian life could be regarded as independent of the existence of God, of freedom, and of immortality ; or, again, of the historical existence of our Lord, the fact of His resurrection, or the truth of His divinity ; and, speaking generally, it may be said that in each of the dogmatic statements of

---

[1] " Although it may be rightly said that belief in particular historical facts is *morally* indifferent, this is not the same thing as to say that for *Religion*, when it has come to reflect upon itself, its historical circumstances might just as well be other than they are. In the simplest language used by religion itself, the way in which God has chosen to manifest Himself must be the best ; in more philosophical phraseology, we shall not in the last resort be content to ascribe to the universal a complete indifference to the particulars in and through which alone it has its being " (C. C. J. Webb, *Problems in the Relations of God and Man*, p. 101).

the historic creeds we are to see the intellectual reflex of an experienced fact, which we are at liberty to express (if we can !) in other terms, but to whose validity we must in any case do justice.

Christian theology may perhaps be defined as the process of drawing out and formulating in intellectual terms the inferences, historical and metaphysical, which are legitimately involved in the present and past experience of spiritual persons ; and more especially, no doubt, in the experiences—" classical and normative" for Christianity—of the apostolic age. Forms and habits of thought change from age to age, and thus in a limited sense new theologies are required ; but unless we are to suppose the Christian thinkers of the past to have done their work wholly amiss, we ought not to expect to find the new theologies turning out to be radically at variance with the old. Human nature, after all, varies but little from age to age, and " Jesus Christ is the same yesterday, to-day, and for ever."

Summing up, we may lay it down as the function of authority in religion neither to compel assent nor to override reason, but to testify to spiritual experience. Its province is not to define truth for the intellect, but to guide souls into the way of peace. Nevertheless it is bound to assert that that which has been discovered has also been revealed : that the way of life and peace is equally the way of truth ; and of the underlying truth of every dogma, whether ecclesiastical or biblical, it should be the aim of each of us to take account.

Towards the Church with her wider life and her age-long experience the individual must ever stand related as a disciple towards his teacher, and he who would teach a new truth or reject an old (and to do so is a vocation to which in every generation some men are called) must both expect to meet in practice with the persecutions by which true prophets are assailed, and must also face the *prima facie* likelihood that his own prophecy may turn out false.

II. Authority and Church Order

Qui maior est in vobis, fiat sicut minor, et qui praecessor est, sicut ministrator.

Evang. Sec. Luc. xxii. 26.

Prophet or priest—which? Is it by virtue of a delegated commission to act for the Church, or by virtue of a prophetic vocation to speak for God, that a man becomes a minister of Christ? If from the problem of Authority and Truth we pass to that of Authority and Church Order, from a consideration of the corporate " auctoritas " of the Christian Society as bearing witness to spiritual values, to that of the nature and sanction of executive and administrative authority within the Christian Body itself, we find ourselves confronted, upon the very threshold of our inquiry, by a radical divergence of view as to the very nature of that Christian ministry which forms the subject of discussion. " By what authority doest thou these things, and who gave thee this authority? " The question asked of the Master is the question still, and men debate the old antithesis—" From heaven, or of men? "—in many cases without having considered whether it may not, after all, be a false one, and whether the true answer should not be " From both."

It is well to begin by a definition of terms. By " prophet," accordingly, shall be meant, for the purposes of the present discussion, *a man called and empowered of God to preach the Gospel*; by " priest " *a man ministerially commissioned and authorized by the Church to act for certain purposes as the organ of her corporate life.* It will be obvious at the outset, that amid all the diversities of doctrine and practice with regard to the ministry which characterize existing Christendom we may distinguish two broadly-contrasted types—we may call them " Protestant " and " Catholic " respectively—of which the one tends to regard the ministry as primarily prophetic, the other as primarily sacerdotal. Doubtless in practice this antithesis is never quite absolute : that is to say, the " prophet " or pastor is commonly " set apart " by some form of " ordination," while in the candidate for priesthood evidence of vocation is required. Nevertheless, it is from a divergence of respective emphasis upon the prophetic and the priestly elements in the ministry that whatever is distinctive in the two great historic Christian positions proceeds. Upon the one hand we have the ministry of Sacraments subordinated to that of the Word ; a tendency to depreciate " forms and ceremonies "; and the interpretation of ordination not primarily as the bestowal of an endowment or commission, but as the " recognition " of a gift already bestowed from on high. On the other we have the ministry of Sacraments given the primary place ; stress laid upon institutions as the media of the Spirit's operation ; the conception of ordination, not as the recognition, but as the bestowal of an office, and therewith of the " charisma " or gift of grace needed to sustain it ; and the strict requirement that men shall not take upon themselves the discharge of functions in the Church to which they have not been formally commissioned.

It will be necessary later on to develop this antithesis at somewhat greater length ; but before doing so it may be well to point out that if discussions upon the subject of the Christian ministry have hitherto resulted in little that is determinative, the reason is to be found in a failure to recognize the real point at issue. Essentially, as we have said, what really underlies the dispute is a radical divergence in the conception of the ministry itself ; but in a majority of controversial discussions of it, the case has been represented as depending on the alleged form assumed by the ministry in the first age of the Church. Writers upon the one side have sought to show that the continuous succession of the bishops from the original Apostles is in the strictest sense a literal historical fact : to demonstrate, either that the threefold ministry in something like its present form goes back to the beginning, or (at the least) that there has from the beginning existed in the Church an ordained hierarchy commissioned by recognized ecclesiastical superiors in regular succession, and that from the beginning no "valid" ministry, at least of Sacraments, could be exercised in the Church except by ministers so ordained and commissioned. Writers who represent the opposite standpoint have sought to disprove this assertion on historical grounds, and to account for the existing evidence upon some alternative hypothesis.

Now, it may fairly be said, with regard to this whole method of approaching the subject, that the resultant position is one of stale-mate. In its strictest and most traditional form the theory of an original Apostolic succession has perhaps broken down ; but the liberalized restatement of it, which is to be found in the writings of Duchesne and Batiffol abroad and the present Bishop of Oxford at home,[1] is at least a tenable interpretation of the evidence as viewed in the light of certain antecedent presuppositions. It is not, however, likely, in the nature of the case, to carry conviction to those who do not approach the evidence with the presuppositions in question ; for though a view with which the facts are compatible, it is not one which they necessitate.[2] The same, *mutatis mutandis*, may be said of the goodly variety of competing theories which divide with those of Bishop Gore and Catholic investigators abroad the

---

[1] Duchesne, *Histoire Ancienne de l'Eglise* and *Origines du Culte Chrétien* ; Batiffol, *L'Eglise Naissante* ; Gore, *The Church and the Ministry* and *Orders and Unity*. See also Hamilton, *The People of God*, vol. ii.

[2] The point of controversial weakness in Bishop Gore's treatment of the subject is the position assigned to the itinerating "prophets and teachers" who appear in the *Didache* as taking precedence, at the celebration of the Eucharist, over the local "bishops and deacons." The Bishop apparently identifies them with the "apostolici viri" of Tertullian (Tert. *De Praescr. Haeret.* xxxii.), and describes their office as "quasi-Apostolic." It is not made clear, however, in what way these men received their authority, or upon what ground of principle they are to be differentiated, for example, from the Irvingite "Apostles" of modern times.

world of scholarly opinion on this subject. All are
more or less legitimate interpretations of the evidence :
no one is certainly demonstrable : and none is likely,
so far as can be seen, to win its way to universal
acceptance. It follows that the attempt to reach
precise agreement upon grounds of history alone is a
fundamentally mistaken one, and that the problem must
really be decided, as we have already hinted, in a quite
different sphere.[1]

This apparently unsatisfactory conclusion may serve
in passing to illustrate the nature of historical evidence
in general. There is always in its interpretation a
certain margin of ambiguity. It is no doubt perfectly
true that " the facts happened in one way, and in one
way only "; but when to this remark is added the
dictum that " History is a science, no more and no
less," it becomes important to enter a *caveat* as to the
sense in which this holds good. History is indeed a
science in the sense that it employs scientific methods
of criticism and research, and has by so doing in our
own day won many notable triumphs and gained in
some cases assured results. It is again scientific in
having as its *aim* the recovery of objective truth
undistorted by prejudice. But inasmuch as " history
never repeats itself," historical conclusions, unlike those
of the physical sciences, are unverifiable. They can
never be subjected to the test of experiment, and
consequently they can never be " proved." They
represent the individual historian's guess at truth—
a guess made, of course, only after weighing and
estimating the evidence by the best methods available ;
but still at best the intuition of an individual, and as
such impatient of objective tests ; a probable judgment,
not a " scientific " certainty. What we have ventured
to call the margin of ambiguity can never, therefore,
be entirely eliminated ; and this margin is necessarily

---

[1] A brief indication of the writer's personal attitude upon the historical question
will be found in the Appendix to this essay, pp. 408 *sqq.*

at its maximum where, as in the case under discussion, the available evidence is fragmentary and disputable. There is another and an even more fundamental objection to the determination of this question upon grounds of history, and it is this. A close critical examination of the New Testament documents is making it more and more difficult to conceive of the Master as having definitely and explicitly *legislated*, upon this or any other matter, with regard to His future Church. If the view of His self-consciousness as Messiah, advocated elsewhere in the present volume,[1] is at all well grounded, He must be regarded rather as Prophet than as Legislator ; and it is at least probable that His vision of the future (like that of the prophets generally) was preoccupied, to the exclusion of other considerations, by the single dominant thought of the manifestation of the Kingdom in ultimate triumph, conceived as a thing ever upon the immediate verge of accomplishment. It is doubtful, to say the least, whether anything resembling the long course of Christian history which has actually supervened was *explicitly* contemplated by our Lord under the conditions of His earthly life. If therefore we are debarred from considering the form of the ministry as constituted and determined for all time by actual legislation proceeding from our Lord's own lips,[2] its authority must on any view be regarded as mediated through the Church, by which under the guidance of the promised Spirit it was evolved. To those who are interested in controversies of Church Order primarily as they bear upon the practical problem of Reunion, this is a consideration of capital importance. For what the Church has determined the Church might conceivably alter. There is no longer any rigid necessity, at any rate in theory, for the future to be determined by the past.

[1] See Essay III.
[2] The suggestion that dominical legislation, of which no record has survived, may have taken place upon this subject during the " forty days " of Acts i. 3 can hardly be taken seriously.

2 C

Strict Catholicism regards it, indeed, as beyond the competence of a section of Christendom to vary in this respect from the institutions of Christendom as a whole; but that Christendom as a whole, supposing the Church to be reunited and agreed upon the point, would be theoretically competent to vary the form of the ministry, the strictest Catholicism might allow. It follows, therefore, inasmuch as the ideal of a reunited Christendom involves and postulates ultimately some corporate action of Christendom as a whole, that any requirement of a particular form of Church Order as a term of eventual reunion must be justified upon its intrinsic merits, and not based merely upon antiquarian precedents.

It is to be remembered, moreover, that the argument from history can by no means be regarded as making wholly for one side. The first few Christian generations may be capable of ambiguous interpretation, the un-broken reign of episcopal institutions may be undisputed from the third century to the sixteenth, but the non-episcopal communions which date from the Reformation can now point to some three hundred years of vigorous spiritual life and Christian experience, and may claim, not without reason, to be regarded as something more than a temporary anomaly. No one of the existing Christian communions, in view of the past, is in a position to throw stones at its brethren; and it is unreasonable to expect either the disappearance of Protestantism, or the unconditional repudiation by Protestants of the significance of their spiritual history. The ministries of the various Protestant denominations may quite legitimately point to the witness of the souls they shepherd, and with St. Paul exclaim, "The seal of our apostleship are ye in the Lord"; and it were well if the further bandying of epithets like "valid" and "invalid" could be abandoned by consent, as the *damnosa hereditas* of an age of legal metaphors and embittered controversy.

Recurring therefore, in the confidence that our starting-point is the right one, to the point from which we digressed, we proceed to draw out in detail the principles which underlie severally the diverse conceptions of the ministry which characterize the two great schools of Christian tradition : a clear grasp of the antithesis between them, and of the truths for which they respectively stand, is an essential preliminary to any future synthesis.

I. For Protestantism,[1] then, the supreme and determining principle, to which all else is subordinate, is simply " the Gospel." By this term is meant, of course, not any particular written or oral statement, but the glad tidings of the love and grace of God, as made known in the Christian revelation : that evangelical message of salvation and forgiveness which the Apostles preached and the Church received. We may perhaps in this connexion paraphrase the word as " a revivifying message of Divine grace and power." " Grace," writes Dr. Bartlet, " comes through the Gospel as written in the Bible, preached in faith, and visible in Christian lives, rather than through special sacraments or orders." This notion of the Gospel or Good News is, it is claimed, the centre of the New Testament perspective and emphasis ; and that it should be so is more than accidental, for Christianity is essentially the appeal of personality to personality, and the Word as proclaimed by the preacher is therefore its characteristic and normative expression. " Christ sent me not to baptize, but to preach the Gospel." " It was God's good pleasure through the foolishness of the proclamation to save them that

---

[1] In what follows I am indebted to my notes of an opening speech contributed to a conference on this subject by my friend Dr. Vernon Bartlet, of Mansfield College, Oxford ; though Dr. Bartlet must not be held directly responsible in details for what is thus indirectly ascribed to him. See, however, his essay, " The Protestant Idea of Church and Ministry as rooted in Early Christianity," in the volume entitled *Evangelical Christianity : its History and Witness,* published under the editorship of Dr. W. B. Selbie, Principal of Mansfield.

believe." All the New Testament language, so it is urged, is in terms of this type of piety, and the place of Sacraments is in such a setting subordinate. Baptism and Eucharist are to be retained indeed, but it is in the light of this conception of "the Gospel" that they are to be understood : they are seals, covenant rites, "verba visibilia" ;[1] they must be defined in terms of personality and not of any lower category. It is "by the hearing of faith" rather than through Sacraments that the Spirit is received ; and not Sacraments, but Christians, are the true "extension of the Incarnation." In the last resort, therefore, it would even be possible to dispense with Sacraments altogether —the spiritual vitality of the Society of Friends is a proof of this.

In harmony with these ideas the Christian community is not to be sought primarily in any outward and visible network of ecclesiastical organization, but is a purely spiritual entity begotten of, and constituted by, "the Gospel," and the working of the Spirit *in human hearts*. Where Christians are, there is the Spirit : and where the Spirit is, there is the Church.

The *genius* of Christianity, therefore (so it is claimed), inevitably makes the Word primary and the Sacraments secondary and derivative ; and this emphasis is preserved in the Church polity contemplated in the *Didache*, according to which (see the note on p. 383) the "prophets and teachers"—the supreme organs of the Word—take precedence over the local bishops and deacons. Later on the emphasis gradually shifts as Christianity develops upon Greek and Roman, that is, upon foreign, soil : the ministry of the Word is thrust into the background and the Sacraments usurp the primary place. The grace of the Sacraments, moreover, comes to be viewed under quasi-physical, or at least *sub-personal*, categories : the original personal emphasis is lost. But the new emphasis must be judged by its

---

[1] The phrase is St. Augustine's.

conformity to the New Testament type, and not *vice versa*. It is no true development, but an aberration of the original Christian idea.

There can be no doubt that this position, as stated, is a strong one ; and full justice must be done to it. With the positive stress which it lays upon the Gospel it is impossible not to be in warm sympathy ; and to criticize the entire position in detail is not our present purpose.

Nevertheless, from the " Catholic " standpoint it inevitably appears somewhat one-sided : it has the look of basing everything upon personal religious experience (the " mystical element ") to the virtual negation of what is "institutional," if not also of what is "intellectual."[1] This latter criticism must not be misunderstood · it does not, of course, mean either that the Protestant position cannot be intellectually appreciated or that it does not require to be intellectually grasped : but there exists in modern Protestantism a widespread tendency (traceable, no doubt, very largely to the influence of Ritschl) to deny to the intellect the rights which legitimately belong to it within the religious sphere ; a tendency to deprecate " theology " and to eschew " metaphysics " : a refusal to face the duty of thinking out the implications of religious experience and formulating them as positive dogmatic truths about God, and Christ, and the world,—which in extreme cases comes near to reducing Christianity to a mere inward glow or fervour of subjective piety, not consciously related to any definite belief whatever.[2] No doubt in the past the intellectual element in religion has from time to time been given an unbalanced predominance : that is to say, orthodoxy has been pre-

---

[1] The conception of religion as a synthesis of three " elements "—institutional, intellectual, and mystical—is especially associated with the name of Baron von Hügel. See the Introduction to his great work, *The Mystical Element in Religion*.

[2] Cf. the remarks upon Professor Herrmann's book in Part I. of this essay (pp. 372-373).

ferred to charity. But this does not justify the modern reaction which rejects the dogmatic principle as such. The paradox of Ritschlianism, which would eliminate metaphysics from religion, is the evil genius of contemporary Protestant thought.[1]

The root fallacy of this modern Protestant position (which in its most logical and consistent form involves the rejection, upon grounds of principle, of sacraments and dogmas alike) lies in the fact that it is at bottom an attempt to isolate the Spirit from the forms by which it is mediated. Carried out in strictness, this would involve the reduction of all religious activity to what the mystics call " the prayer of quiet " : that is to say, to an energy of inner contemplation which claims to dispense equally with vocal speech and with discursive thought. Except at such a cost neither dogma upon the one hand, nor institutions upon the other, can ever really be eliminated either in principle or in fact ; for they are the indispensable vehicles of expression, without which there can be no corporate religion. The antithesis which is not uncommonly set up between matter and spirit is therefore a false one : the criticism of dogmatic or institutional forms as in themselves " unspiritual," " external," or " mechanical " is beside the mark. Beings of flesh and blood can share no spiritual experience *in common* which is not materially mediated ; there is a material side (though the fact is often forgotten) to the ministry of the Word itself; for in the appeal of the preacher spirit speaks to spirit not otherwise than through the medium of sound-wave and nerve-shock, whereof physical and physiological science have their several accounts to give. The true antithesis is therefore not between matter and spirit, or

---

[1] These remarks, of course, apply exclusively to modern educated Protestantism. It certainly cannot be charged against the great schools of Protestantism in the past that they eliminated dogma and metaphysics from religion, or failed to attach a due value to orthodoxy. In refutation of such an idea it is only necessary to think of Calvinism, which, as the great intellectual system of Protestant dogmatics, occupies a position on the Protestant side somewhat analogous to that occupied by the *Summa* of St. Thomas Aquinas in Catholicism.

between spirit and form, but between a spiritual and
an unspiritual *use* of the material vehicles of worship.

II. These principles, if conceded, form the bridge
which may serve to carry us over from the Protestant
to the Catholic doctrine of Sacraments. Certainly no
Catholic would be prepared to admit that in the
emphasis upon Sacraments which is characteristic of
Catholicism there is a lapse from personal to sub-
personal categories ; rather would he describe the
Sacraments, with the late Canon Bright, as " points of
personal contact with Jesus Christ." [1] Moreover, in
the very challenge to the superficial reason which is
involved in the seeking of God, not vaguely in the
void, but here and now, in this definite way and through
these definite concrete means—a challenge of which he
is at least as conscious as his Protestant brother ; in the
appeal to a faith that can pierce the veil of sense and
find in seeming " outward things " the medium of the
spirit's access to the Presence, and the vehicle of Divine
grace and power ; in these very stumbling-blocks of
the natural man he seems to himself to experience in
unique fashion the touch of God upon his soul.

> Sensus, visus, gustus in Te fallitur :
> sed auditu solo tuto creditur :
> credo quicquid dixit Dei Filius :
> nil hoc verbo Veritatis verius.

In a sacramentalism so conceived is the true democracy
of the spirit, in which kneeling expectant at the altar-
rails prince and pauper together may become " as little
children."

Fortified by convictions and experiences such as
these, the Catholic is bold to identify himself, where
the Protestant hesitates, with the main stream of
Christian thought and devotion in the past ; and greets
his spiritual kin across the centuries or across the

[1] Cf. Essay VI. p. 323.

ocean, wherever the Sacrament of the Body broken, the Blood shed, is offered, received, and pleaded. Crude ways of stating the Sacrifice and cruder theories of the Presence count for little as compared with the richness of a common underlying experience which such doctrines are struggling to interpret, and which the negative cautions of Protestantism appear to Catholic minds unduly to minimize. For there, somehow, in the Eucharist—so in all ages Christian worshippers have felt—heaven meets earth and earth heaven ; and the Lord's Body discerned by faith, is That by which man is made one with God and God with man. The Sacrifice is one and eternal : the sacrifice of a perfected obedience offered perpetually in heaven, where is the true Altar, of which our earthly altars are the types and shadows : and from that heavenly Altar in Holy Communion we are fed ; it is "in the heavenly sphere" that our worship is enacted.[1] The keynote of the whole is in the Collect for Ascension Day : "Grant, we beseech Thee, Almighty God, that like as we do believe Thy only-begotten Son our Lord Jesus Christ to have ascended into the heavens ; so we may also in heart and mind thither ascend, and with Him continually dwell, Who liveth and reigneth with Thee and the Holy Ghost, one God, world without end."[2]

It is to a religious consciousness of the type which finds the devotional traditions of Catholicism congenial, that the requirement in the minister of the sanction of an authoritative Church commission tends to present itself as at least *ex parte hominum* essential. For if the Eucharist is one, not many : if it is a question, not of a plurality of commemorations independent each of each, but of an approach through appointed media to a single spiritual reality of tremendous significance "within the Veil": if as the Eucharist is one, so also the Church is one, according to the thought of St. Paul, "one Bread, one Body" : it follows that in each

---

[1] Cf. Essay IV. p. 196.   [2] Cf. Essay VII. pp. 343-344.

particular eucharistic celebration not merely the "two or three" gathered in bodily presence, but the whole Church in earth and heaven is ideally implicated, and a ministry representative in claim and commission of the "whole state of Christ's Church" is by natural consequence desiderated. To the question "Who is sufficient for these things?" the answer is, that no individual and no sectional community is sufficient : that as the eternal Priest is Christ, and none may derogate from His royal priesthood, so nothing short of the whole Church as ecumenically manifested is the adequate Vicar of Christ upon earth.[1] Only in a united Church would there be possible a perfect Sacrament ; and the goal of unity lies in the future, not in the past. The "babes in Christ" have bickered from the beginning with all the quarrelsomeness of children, and the process of growing out of the childishness of individualism and schism "into the corporate oneness of the full-grown Man" is still far indeed from its accomplishment. Nevertheless the episcopate, and the ministry episcopally commissioned, represents *in idea and principle* an authority wider than that of the merely local Church, an authority which *in claim and potency* is that of the Church Universal. Behind the stubborn insistence of Catholicism upon a ministry commissioned in the historic succession lies the instinct, deep if seldom articulate, that the minister of Sacraments must exercise his function not in virtue of any personal endowment or individual prophetic gift which he may possess, but as the "living instrument" (ἔμψυχον ὄργανον) of the Christian Body : that in every act of ministerial priesthood it is never the minister as such, but the Church through the minister, and Christ through the Church, Who baptizes, blesses, absolves, offers or consecrates : it is required of such ministers only "that a man be found faithful."

It is in a sense no small paradox that the point of

---

[1] The Vicar of Christ is properly the Holy Spirit operative in the Church.

view which in one way most nearly approaches that of Catholicism, though in another it diverges from it most widely, is that of Congregational Independency. Both are at one in conceiving the Church as primarily a mystical and religious entity, eternal in the heavens, a spiritual communion of the elect people of God which is of a higher order than space and time ; and both agree in conceiving the assemblage of Christian people for worship as a manifestation visibly upon earth of this invisible or ideal Church—*ubi tres, ibi ecclesia*. Their difference is, that whereas for Congregationalism *each or any* " two or three," gathered in Christ's name, is an *independent and autonomous* manifestation of the " Jerusalem that is above," Catholicism conceives that not the local community in its independence but the " whole congregation of Christian people dispersed throughout the world " is the manifestation of Christ's Body upon earth, and that the unity which already invisibly and ideally subsists between Christ's members, ought to seek and at last to find for itself a visible sacramental analogue in an outward unity of world-wide organization and corporate life—" sacramental," in the sense that the external unity of Church Order is at once the effective vehicle, and the " outward and visible sign," of the unity already ideally subsisting. The historic ministry is valued, because in it the *principle* of such world-wide organization and authority, in those who are the vehicles of the corporate life of Christ's Body (as mediated by the Sacraments which they administer), finds proleptic if inadequate expression: an expression whose completeness and adequacy would postulate a perfect Church, united in organization as in charity, and fulfilled, by the ingathering of all men, " unto the measure of the stature of the completion of the Christ."

What, then, in brief is the precise nature of the plea which we would put forward on behalf of the historic Episcopate ?

(i.) The Episcopate represents and sacramentally embodies the principle of continuity with the past. It forms a concrete link between the Church of to-day and the Church of mediaeval times and of primitive Christendom. The pure Protestant, discarding such links, may yet indeed claim spiritual kinship with true Christians always and everywhere ; but in practice inward and outward tend to react each upon the other. It is difficult not to think that those Christian communions which at the Reformation broke off from the historic succession of the ministry[1] have suffered (with whatever compensating advantages) an impoverishment of Church-consciousness and a weakening of the idea of Churchmanship. "The Church" has *tended* to be conceived as national or sectarian, rather than as ecumenical; the "Reformation" has been thought of, not as a crisis or paroxysm in the continuous life of Christendom, but as a fresh beginning of everything *de novo*.

(ii.) The Episcopate, as it has already been pointed out, is historically representative of an authority wider than that of the merely local Church. It stands in idea and claim[2] (and therefore in promise and potency) for the authority of the whole Church Catholic dispersed throughout the world. It therefore secures that the ordained man shall be regarded not as the minister of a sect but of the Church. Acquiescence in anything less is only not intolerable to Protestants because they do not really conceive the minister institutionally at all, but prophetically : that is to say, not as the organ of the Church, but as the spokesman of God.

---

[1] Historians of the Reformation tell us that in many cases the breach was made only with extreme reluctance. Non-episcopal theories of the ministry of the early Church did not determine it, but were rather evolved controversially to justify it after the event.

[2] Not, of course, at present altogether in fact. The Roman Church disallows Anglican ordinations and regards those of the Greek Church as irregular. The attitude of the Greek Church towards Anglican orders is non-committal. Protestants (with the exception of the " High Church " party among the Scotch Presbyterians) regard the whole conception of validity of orders as unmeaning. Cf. the remark *supra* that only in a united Church would there be possible a perfect Sacrament.

(iii.) Ordination in the historic succession embodies a guarantee which is at least subjectively necessary for both priest and layman. The latter in seeking the ministry of communion or of absolution claims, and has the right to claim, that the priest from whom he seeks these things shall act not in virtue of any personal fitness of his own, but as one bearing the commission of the Church ; the former in presuming to minister requires to be able to feel that he has not taken the office upon himself, but is merely fulfilling a commission which he has received. Herein is the great safeguard against " clericalism "—an abuse to which, paradoxically enough, the prophetic view of the ministry is liable in proportion as it takes itself seriously.[1]

(iv.) Episcopacy, and the ideas which have historically gone along with it, is alone, probably, capable of mediating a certain specifically " Catholic " type of Christian piety. The suggestion of a variation of type and spiritual flavour as between Protestant and Catholic saints respectively will seem to many at first sight fanciful : and no doubt the two shade off into each other in concrete cases by imperceptible gradations : the attempt to distinguish them will be necessarily impressionistic. Nevertheless the impression is at least difficult to resist that the two types are really very different, and that the Church would be the poorer for the loss of either. Uprightness, strength, and veracity we look to find in Protestantism ; a certain peculiar tenderness and humility in Catholicism. The most conspicuous examples of saintly character in Catholicism have been built up and fostered not only by the sacramentalism of the Mass but also by the spiritual discipline of Confession ; and from this point of view it is of real importance to retain an ordinal which includes the charge based upon St. John xx. 22-23.

---

[1] Cf. the striking passage from the *Didache*—quoted in Part I. of this essay, p. 369—in which to question the prophet's word is regarded as sin against the Holy Ghost.

The words in question are no doubt capable of varying interpretations ; and they were not inserted into the Latin ordinal (of which the present English rite is an adaptation) until a comparatively late period. But it does not follow that their removal, when once they have been inserted, would make no difference. Private penance itself is a comparatively late usage, which appears to have grown up as a mitigation of the severer primitive discipline of public penance. In spite of the abuses by which it has from time to time been attended it may be said, upon the whole (when not suffered to become mechanical by being made compulsory), to have been justified by its fruits : the liberty of recourse to it is certainly among the things " in any wise to be retained in the Church." As things stand at present, those ordained to the priesthood in the historical succession are bearers of a definite commission to mediate forgiveness of sins on behalf of Christ through His Church, and are differentiated thereby from the ministries of denominations in which confession is either unknown or is only informally practised : as, for example, in the " class meeting " of old-fashioned Wesleyans or the " enquiry room " of a Revival Meeting.

On the other hand, it is well to bear in mind certain cautions, and to distinguish what is genuinely involved in the episcopal principle from certain parodies of episcopacy, and from coincident abuses by which from time to time it has been attended.

(a) Episcopacy does not or need not involve the notion of a clergy whose priesthood is vicarious in a vicious sense, that is to say, as transcending that of the Body whose organs they are. As the Father sent our Lord, so our Lord sent the Apostles, not to lord it over God's heritage, but to preach the Gospel to every creature. " Go ye therefore and teach all nations "— the mission of the Church to the world must not be converted into a mission of the Apostles to the Church.

Neither the Pope nor the clergy but the Church is the
Vicar of Christ upon earth. An uncritical application
of Old Testament analogies (which begins as early
as Clement of Rome[1]) has no doubt worked untold
mischief and is largely responsible for the abuse of
"clericalism." But it is possible heartily to eschew a
vicious clericalism, and yet to retain the conception of
an official priesthood, who shall be (in the classic phrase
of the late Dr. Moberly) ministerial organs of the
priesthood of the Church. Kings, like priests, were
frequently regarded in mediaeval thought as set over
the people by God and responsible to Him alone :
subjects and lay people had but to render a passive
and unquestioning obedience : our own annals exhibit
the dominance of this theory in its most exaggerated
form so late as the age of the Stuarts. The divine
right of kings has disappeared from modern political
theory, but not so the kingship as an institution. In
modern England the King rules as the representative
and organ of the people, with whom the ultimate
sovereignty is admitted to reside. The clergy in like
manner are the organs and representatives of the spiritual
people of God, with whom resides the ultimate priesthood. The essence of priesthood, which is the
dedication of life to God's service on behalf of
others, is the privilege and duty of every Christian ;
if for certain purposes the Church exercises her
corporate priesthood through ministerial channels, it
is without prejudice to the priestly character of the
Body as a whole.

(*b*) Episcopacy is not the same thing as prelacy.
The Puritans of the sixteenth century objected with
far more vigour, and with greater reason, to the
notion of "*lord* bishops" (as they called them) than
to that of bishops *per se*. It is an accident which is
not of the essence of episcopate that bishops should in
this country inhabit "palaces" and be addressed by

---

[1] Clement wrote about A.D. 96.

complimentary titles ; it is a more serious matter, and one which approximates to a scandal, that by reason of the unwieldy size of their dioceses they should be " unknown by face " to the majority of their laity, and comparative strangers even to their clergy ; the modern diocese should undoubtedly be drastically subdivided.

(c) Nor, thirdly, need episcopacy mean autocracy. The principle laid down by St. Ignatius [1]—that the flock should " do nothing without the bishop "—was in early times rightly supplemented by the rule that the bishop did nothing without the counsel and support of his presbyters. The laity, in like manner, must claim and exercise that due share and voice in Church affairs which belongs of right to every member of the *laos* or " people " of God.[2]

(d) Lastly, it is not necessary to interpret magically the grace of orders. It is not a question of episcopal hands being charged with virtue in a quasi-material sense. There is even no abstract necessity for ordination to take place through *tactual* laying on of hands at all. Laying on of hands must be regarded simply as the means used by the Church to show that she is making the appointment and bestowing the authority ; some such " outward and visible sign " to mediate the commission is doubtless required, but not necessarily this particular sign. What the doctrine of " grace of orders " really stands for is the recognition that the work of the ministry is such as no man could undertake in his own strength, and the belief that in response to the prayers of the Church those commissioned by the laying on of hands are endued with the needed strength

---

[1] Martyred about A.D. 110.

[2] See the Rev. R. B. Rackham's dissertation, " The Position of the Laity in the Early Church," in the volume of *Essays in Aid of the Reform of the Church*, published in 1898 under the editorship of the present Bishop of Oxford, and the speech delivered by the late Bishop of Salisbury upon the proposal to establish a Representative Church Council, at a Joint Meeting of the Convocations of Canterbury and York, 1903 (Report published by the Church Historical Society). It should be obvious that the rights of the laity must include an effective voice in the selection and appointment of Bishops and other clergy.

and power from on high ; upon the principle that no Christian man is rightly called to fulfil duties of any kind without a corresponding endowment of grace sufficient for his needs.

In all that has been said about episcopacy we have been thinking primarily—perhaps exclusively—about the ministry of Sacraments. The ministry of the Word stands, surely, upon a different footing. Effective preaching requires a personal gift. The preacher is born and not made—or rather he is a man raised up and empowered by the Spirit of God to utter a message, and his gift is independent of institutional channels. It must be admitted that Catholicism in the past has been unduly suspicious of the liberty of prophesying. It has indeed allowed in theory that there is no reason in the nature of things why the layman should not preach ; but in practice lay preaching has been but meagrely and grudgingly recognized. In point of fact, the distribution of the " charisma of the Word " cuts transversely across the distinction of clergy and laity, and many laymen are excellent preachers as certainly as many of the clergy are exceedingly poor ones. Admittedly, men with a certain preaching gift are, other things being equal, the most suitable recipients of ordination ; and many besides the sixteenth-century Puritans have felt a prejudice against " non-preaching Prelates." Bishop Gore,[1] for instance, would conceive the ideal Christian ministry as synthesizing, in the conception of Pastorate, a complex of functions, regal, priestly, and prophetic. Nevertheless there are " diversities of gifts," and there is no *a priori* reason why they should not, in some cases, lead to " diversities of ministrations." From a Catholic point of view there need be little or no difficulty in recognizing the Protestant pastor as a "godly minister of the Word " ; though it might appear difficult or impossible

[1] *Orders and Unity*, p. 35.

to recognize him, apart from ordination, as *in the Catholic sense and for Catholics* a qualified minister of Sacraments.

It will be urged, doubtless, that Catholicism as we have interpreted it is a late development, not to be found in the earliest Christian records.[1] The contention is one which might easily be disputed, for Catholicism equally with Protestantism claims to find its starting-point in the Church of New Testament times ; the germs both of sacramentalism and of institutionalism are to be found within the pages of the New Testament,[2] nor is any attempt here being made to plead for a loftier doctrine of the Church than that which is set forth in the Epistle to the Ephesians. The point of the present argument is not to represent the Catholic type of piety as the only primitive one, or as the type to which all Christians must conform ; but, rather, in the first place, to claim for it the consideration to which it is legitimately entitled as representing one whole side of the historical working out of the Christian idea ; and in the second place to exhibit its dependence upon the conception of a commissioned ministry ideally representative of the authority of the Church as a whole, and upon the existence in the Church of certain specific sacramental or quasi-sacramental institutions.

The aim, in short, has been to exhibit two contrasted principles in sharp antithesis, and to show the

---

[1] See the statement of the Protestant case outlined above, pp. 387 *sqq.*

[2] Professor Kirsopp Lake—a critic who certainly holds no brief for Catholicism —discovers a strongly Catholic sacramentalism already developed in the writings of St. Paul, and considers that the appeal to primitive Christianity in support of the Protestant view of Sacraments has failed ; though he adds the interesting remark, " The Catholic advocate, in winning his case, has proved still more : the type of doctrine which he defends is not only primitive, but pre-Christian." Christianity, in other words, was preached by St. Paul, and certainly understood by St. Paul's converts, as a sacramental system analogous to the " mystery religions " with which the ancient world was familiar (Lake, *The Earlier Epistles of S. Paul*, p. 215). See further, Essay IV. pp. 181 *sqq.* It is perhaps worth remarking that the fact of certain elements being common ground between Christianity and other religions may be regarded not as discrediting those elements, but rather as proving their essential congruity with a universal instinct of religious humanity.

manner in which they determine respectively the Protestant and the Catholic view of the ministry. For the sake of clearness the discussion has been made abstract : few, if any, of the existing denominations of Christendom are either consistently "Catholic" or consistently "Protestant." Even the Church of Rome recognizes "spiritual communion" as conferring a grace equivalent to that of the Sacrament where the latter is not to be had ; even the Society of Friends, which has abolished Sacraments, cannot entirely eliminate from its worship the mediation of spirit through form : it does not limit religion to the "prayer of quiet" ! Broadly, we have taken the issue as being between the Catholic episcopate and the various types of non-episcopal ministry. This is not to ignore the fact that there are non-episcopal denominations—the Presbyterians of Scotland and the English Wesleyans may be cited as examples—which in some respects approximate more nearly to Episcopalian than to purely Protestant ideas of the ministry. But it may well be doubted whether, in the period of general criticism and reconstruction which is upon us, existing lines of denominational cleavage and distinctive denominational conceptions of the ministry within the general unity of Protestant Christianity will prove capable of survival ; and whether, therefore, the alternative possibilities will not in the future be narrowed down to a broad choice between Protestantism and Catholicism much as we have defined them. Is a synthesis possible between the two elements of this residual antithesis? Or is the future reunion of Protestant Christians among themselves to have for its result merely the driving deeper of the line of cleavage which already separates Protestants from their brethren in Christ?

III. Authority and Reunion

Ecce quam bonum et quam iucundum habitare fratres in unum.
Psalm cxxxiii. 1.

Charitas hoc facit suum quod amat in altero ;
Proprium sic singulorum commune fit omnium.
PETER DAMIANI, *De Gloria Paradisi.*

The Christ-Spirit has manifested Himself historically in divers forms and in divers manners ; the divisions of contemporary Christendom represent severally the various partial embodiments and aspects of His working. No proposed scheme of Christian unity can be regarded as satisfactory (as assuredly none has any prospect of ultimate success) which fails to comprehend and to do justice to them all. If reunion is ever to come about it can only be by Protestants seeking to appreciate and to make their own the truths for which Catholicism specifically stands, and by Catholics in like manner seeking to appreciate and assimilate the positive truths of Protestantism. Each has to reckon with the "auctoritas" of the other.

Nay, just as every individual Christian is called to make his specific contribution to the life of the Church as a whole, so we may believe that each smallest sect exists to bear witness to some neglected fragment or aspect of Christian truth which is vital to the balance of the whole. Each has something to teach, and each has a great deal more to learn. If the Pope must learn to appreciate and value the Methodist prayer-meeting, the Puritan in his turn must learn to worship with insight and devout intelligence in St. Peter's at High Mass. The temper of mutual suspicion and unchristian prejudice, and the attitude of mind which proceeds upon the naïve assumption of a speedy conversion of all opponents to one's own sectional standpoint, are almost equally inimical to the cause of real reunion. Protestants can no more expect Catholics to abandon the specifically Catholic institutions which are to them as the very breath of their nostrils, than Catholics can expect Protestants to submit to an intellectual strait-waistcoat or an unreformed ecclesiastical discipline. The essential prerequisite of any true *rapprochement* is a teachable spirit and a readiness to find the truth of God lurking beneath the crudest exterior or in the most unexpected corners. The Church can afford to leave no element unrepresented in the final synthesis.

The precise form which that synthesis will take, time and experience alone, no doubt, can show ; and yet it is not difficult to single out certain elements as likely to form part of the specific contribution of the one side or the other. Thus we have seen that Catholicism stands in an especial sense for institutional religion : for the use and value, that is to say, of rites and sacraments as being neither dead forms nor illogical excrescences upon a religion otherwise wholly spiritual, but as being themselves spirit and life, the natural and normal media of the operation of the Word-made-Flesh. So, again, Catholicism witnesses to the glory of Churchmanship, the sense of spiritual kinship and unity, not with a section of Christendom, but with the whole ; to the idea of worship, as prior in religion to that of edification ; to the communion of quick and dead in Christ's mystical Body, as not to be denied its natural outlet in mutual prayer ; to the legitimate place of the " religious " life as one among the manifold workings of the Spirit in the unity of the Body ; to the possibility of a science of the soul and a specific type of Christian sanctity, most characteristically mediated by the Confessional and the Mass.

These things are inseparable neither from the abuses with which in the past they have been entangled, nor from whatever has been ill-advised in the forms of their expression : they represent elements of historic religion which neither Protestantism nor the Universal Church of the future can afford to lose. " Except these abide in the ship, ye cannot be saved." Yet we have argued that their retention is hardly conceivable apart from the retention, in some form, of the institutions by which historically they have been mediated : it follows that Protestants must not discard institutions, but rather, wheresoever they have been too hastily abandoned, recover them.

But if Protestantism has thus many things to learn from the Catholic witness, it bears in turn a specific witness of its own. At its best it stands for the power of personal religion, for the spiritual freedom of the individual as answerable in the last resort to his Maker alone, for the prophetic word as the dynamic which alone can vitalize the ritual of the priest, the word of God which is not bound, the wind of God that bloweth where it listeth. Protestantism has borne splendid witness to the truth of evangelicalism and the liberty wherewith Christ hath made us free. It has warned us impressively, and not always unnecessarily, of the deadness of the letter, except as expressing and mediating the Spirit. The Catholicism of the future certainly cannot afford to disregard the truths of the Protestant witness, and must to a certain extent reinterpret and revalue (without abandoning) its institutionalism in the light of them.

Each of the two great Christian types has need to be at once the scholar and the teacher of the other. The final unity (which must assuredly be outwrought in God's good time) will come not by way of compromise, but by way of comprehension. Truth is a synthesis, not an elimination, of differences, and the claims of conflicting " authorities " must be harmonized by being included and justified, not negated, in the ultimate whole. There shall not be one lost good ; for " Wisdom is justified of all her children."

"The law shall not perish from the priest, nor counsel from the wise, nor the word from the prophet."

As with the Church, so also with the individual.

The aim should be a comprehension and a synthesis. Varying temperaments, doubtless, will result inevitably in variations of individual emphasis upon this side or upon that. What is inexcusable is the recognized and conscious one-sidedness of outlook which springs from asking not purely and simply what is true, but what is taught respectively by Paul, or Cephas, or Apollos. No loyalty is in the last resort due to any lesser authority than that of truth ; and only the whole truth will ultimately satisfy the hunger of the soul of man.

To-day men's minds are turning to the thought of unity with a new urgency and a new longing ; is the unity they look for to be pan-Protestant or pan-Christian ? It is distinctive of that portion of Christendom which is in communion with the see of Canterbury, that alone among existing bodies of Christians it combines within a single fold representatives of both the two great Christian types. We trust we are under no illusions with regard to the Church of England : the time is past in which it was possible for Anglicans to speak or write of her with any smugness of self-satisfaction. Nevertheless, with all her defects and shortcomings, with all her insularity and legalism, and with all her sins and blunders, the English Church, as holding both principles together (albeit juxtaposed for the present in somewhat unstable equilibrium), seems not to her own sons merely, but also to not a few external observers, Catholic as well as Protestant, to bear within her bosom the promise of a reconciliation and of an eventual synthesis, such as in the providence of God may one day be the means of peace not only within her own borders, but (as we dare to hope) for Christendom at large. The way and means thereto is assuredly not hastily to seek the readiest compromise or to sacrifice the whole to the part. Neither by the empty interchange of facile compliments, nor by alleging " unity of spirit " as an excuse for acquiescence in actual disunion, nor again by the effort to " break down denominational boundaries" by irregular and spasmodic acts of intercommunion which represent no real or abiding unity of principle—not by any such impulsive attempt to "heal lightly the hurt of the daughter of My people" is true unity to be won.

Rather by thought and prayer and study ; by the slow interchange of opinions, and the perhaps slower spread of charity ; by the intellectual toil of scholars and theologians, and the eventual leavening of the popular mind by their results ; by the dissipation of prejudice and the mutual learning of each from each ; after many days, in the appointed time, the "Vision of Unity," which it has been given to our generation to see afar off, shall come, and shall not tarry. Meantime we need to remember that slow advances are the surest, and that he that believeth shall not make haste. We men, as Bishop Butler said, are for precipitating things ; but it is the lesson of history that the mills of God grind slowly.

> Jerusalem is builded as a city
> That is at unity in itself.
> O pray for the peace of Jerusalem !
> They shall prosper that love thee.

APPENDIX

THE HISTORICAL ORIGINS OF THE CHRISTIAN MINISTRY

IF we adopt the views set forth above (p. 385) as to the nature of our Lord's Messianic consciousness and outlook, and if we consequently regard it as improbable that He made explicit provision or gave direct instructions as to the form of the ministry in His Church, we shall find it difficult not to see, in the view which reads back the hierarchical system in something like its modern form into the actual beginnings of Christianity, the working of an historical mirage, the same in kind if not in degree as that which reads back into the age of Moses the legislation of the Levitical Code, or crowns S. Peter with the triple tiara of the modern Popes.

No doubt the germs of institutionalism were present in the Church from the first: no doubt the Apostles in particular enjoyed a large measure of prestige and personal authority, both as being the authentic witnesses of the Lord and also as being the "begetters in Christ" of their own spiritual children. Nevertheless, speaking broadly, it is probable that we ought to see in early Christianity what we may roughly call a *pre-institutional* phase or moment, a great prophetic outpouring of the Spirit, which overflowed all regular channels, and had as yet no fixed and uniform organization or institutional embodiment. The crystallization of what was at first formless or only loosely institutional into fixed and definite Church Order and regular form was a later, though an early and an inevitable, development.

It does not follow that we ought to-day in the light of history to seek to undo the past by reverting to the primitive conditions. No solution of the problem of ecclesiastical unity will ever be achieved along the lines of a self-conscious and artificial archaism which ignores the work of the Spirit of God in the facts of history subsequent to Apostolic times. The "institution" is in effect the divinely-constituted heir of the "charisma," and "if the claim of Apostolic Succession as commonly understood be questionable, that of general ecclesiastical continuity remains unassailable."[1]   There is here, in fact, a suggestive parallel to be drawn between Christianity and Judaism. Of both religions it would be true to say that, speaking broadly, the Prophets came before the Law, and that the Law gathered up, embodied, and conserved the results of the work of Prophecy. In both, again, as the result of the operation of the "historical mirage," legalism has been traditionally read back into the prophetic beginnings.

What follows does not claim to be more than the writer's individual impression of what was probably the actual course of events. It will be convenient to distinguish two questions which have too frequently been confused together, viz. (*a*) the form of the ministry, and (*b*) the mode of its appointment.

A. The Form of the Ministry in the Primitive Church

By the end of the first century of our era there were scattered throughout the Roman Empire—more especially in the large cities, in the seaports, and along the Roman roads—a number of small groups of men and women united in religious fellowship. They consisted of people who in one way or another, usually by the preaching of some missionary Apostle or Evangelist, had been brought to believe in Jesus the Messiah, in the Gospel of salvation from sin as the result of His Cross and Passion, in the possibility of redemption from the power of evil through the gift of God's Spirit in their hearts.

Believing these things they had been admitted by Baptism into the Messianic Remnant of the true Israel. They conceived of themselves as the People of God, elect before the foundation of the world, and they met together in assemblies which in each locality where they assembled were the manifestations or embodiments of the ideal and eternal Church. They waited for God's Son to come from heaven and redeem them from this present evil world ; and meanwhile their life was marked by a kind of enthusiasm, and enriched with various gifts and

---

[1] Tyrrell, *The Church and the Future*, p. 133.

manifestations of aptitudes and powers, which they called *charismata*, and which they referred to the operation of the Spirit.

None were devoid of "gifts," though the gifts of some were more striking than those of others ; and all gifts were intended to be used for the service of the whole Body ; they were given "for the perfecting of the saints unto the work of ministering" (or service), that is, "for the building up of the Body of Christ" (Eph. iv. 12). Every Christian was thus in his degree a minister or servant of the rest. Those who had (*e.g.*) the gift of prophecy freely exercised it : the rest "discerned," and recognizing the Spirit accepted the utterances of the prophets as the inspired word of God and did their bidding accordingly. But there were others whose "gifts" were rather those of administration and government : and these gifts, too, were recognized, and the work of administering was entrusted to such. (Cf. 1 Cor. xii. 4-11 ; Rom. xii. 4-8.)

If we ask precisely where and how in the life of such a little community the need would arise for something like a "regular" ministry as we understand the term to-day, must we not say that it would arise almost at the very outset, and that quite inevitably, in connexion with that which was the central and characteristic action of their common worship ? If a Cup was to be blessed and Bread broken in common, clearly some one individual must perform those actions on behalf of the Church as a whole : and moreover, inasmuch as whoever did so was virtually taking the place of the Lord and distributing the gifts at His Table, inevitably he would tend, *ipso facto*, to become "chief man among the Brethren" : that is to say, the celebrant at the Eucharist,[1] representing the Lord at His Table, would be also, under Christ, the shepherd of the flock, and overseer or "bishop" of the whole of its corporate life.

So long as he remained to labour among his converts the functions of presidency at the Eucharist and general oversight of the flock would naturally be exercised by the Apostle or Evangelist who had founded the local Church : when he moved on to another sphere of missionary labour, it is natural to suppose that he would designate one or more of his converts, with the consent of the brethren, to have general charge of the

---

[1] It is not inconceivable that originally there may have been nothing *in theory* to prevent *any* leading Christian from discharging the duty of presidency at the Lord's Table *in case of need* ; but in practice it is fairly clear that in any given Church the celebrant in normal cases was always either the same individual or one of a small and definite group of individuals.

community in his absence—as in practice every missionary, of whatever "denomination," does to-day upon the mission-field. We have here the origin of what we may call the "local" ministry in the primitive Church, as opposed to the "general" ministry of Evangelists and Apostles.

It was in accordance with Jewish analogies and also with a very natural symbolism that upon such local pastors the Apostle or Evangelist should, before his departure, have laid his hands in blessing, and prayed that they might be equipped by the Holy Spirit with the gifts of wisdom and ghostly strength needed for the exercise of their ministry : and in this we may discover the germ of ordination.

The local pastors, thus appointed, came to be called *bishops*, that is, those who exercised oversight. To assist them in their work, and especially, it would seem, to distribute to the people the eucharistic gifts after the Bishop had blessed or consecrated them, certain "servants" of the Church (*deacons*) were appointed ; the Bishops with the deacons, their assistants, thus came to form the regular ministry in the local Christian "Churches."

Apart from this nascent "clergy" those of the faithful who possessed the gift of prophesying were, of course, allowed to use it in inspired preaching and exhortation for the edifying of their brethren. Sometimes, no doubt, a Bishop possessed and exercised the prophetic gift himself : this was, however, by no means necessarily the case, although in virtue of his position he would naturally teach, admonish, and exhort the several members of his flock.

We have spoken thus far of "bishops" and "deacons" : the Church's traditional hierarchy, however, is not twofold, but threefold : and the title *presbyter*, which has come to be appropriated as the technical name for an order of ministers intermediate between the episcopate and the diaconate, occurs already in several passages of the New Testament writings. It is necessary, therefore, to raise the question whether or not its usage is already technical, whether, that is, we are already confronted in New Testament times with a twofold or a three-fold ministry.

The solution of this problem is by no means clear or obvious. Various passages both in the New Testament and in the sub-apostolic writings make it evident that bishops were, or might be, also called presbyters. It has been too readily assumed that this proposition may with equal truth be inverted.

Until quite recently the majority of scholars, at least

in this country, have regarded it as established by Bishop Lightfoot's celebrated *Dissertation on the Christian Ministry* (in the Appendix to his commentary on Philippians) that the terms "bishop" and "presbyter" were originally synonymous. According to Lightfoot the local "churches" were governed not by single pastors, but by colleges of "presbyter-bishops" having joint authority. "Presbyter," he thought, was a Jewish-Christian, and "bishop" a Gentile-Christian term for one and the same official. The theory of an originally plural episcopate he based upon the references to "bishops" in the plural in Philipp. i. 1, and Acts xx. 28 ; and with these passages he compared Acts xi. 30, xiv. 23, xx. 17, where similar reference is made to presbyters. Other passages of Scripture are easily capable of being harmonized with this hypothesis, and in the sub-apostolic literature the language of Clement of Rome and the references to "bishops and deacons" in the *Didache* may be interpreted as pointing in the same direction. The problem for Lightfoot was to account for the rise of a "monarchical" out of a "collegiate" episcopate ; and this development he considered to have first taken place in Asia Minor, where it is evidenced by the Epistles of S. Ignatius.

In all this Lightfoot was virtually endorsing the conjecture of S. Jerome, who wrote as a presbyter in the interests of his own order to confute the arrogance of the Roman deacons, one of whom had argued from the prior institution of the diaconate (of which he took the appointment of the Seven in Acts vi. 1-6 to be the origin) that deacons ought to take precedence over presbyters, or at least that deacons and priests were on an equality. In common with other scholars, Lightfoot accepted on the authority of S. Jerome and later writers (presumably more or less dependent on S. Jerome) the statement that at Alexandria down to the time of Heraclas and Dionysius (232-265) the Bishop was chosen by the presbyters from among themselves without any special form of consecration ; and he saw in this a survival of the primitive system in one of the leading churches of Christendom at a time when it had disappeared everywhere else. There is, however, considerable difficulty in this suggestion of a late survival at Alexandria of what, from the standpoint of Christendom at large, must needs have been regarded in the third century as a serious anomaly ; and it has been suggested with high probability by Mr. C. H. Turner that Jerome was misled by evidence which came to him from Arian sources, and had its ultimate origin in the attempt of "certain heretics" to discredit the episcopate of Athanasius.[1] It is probable that in a few localities there *was* at first something like a "plural episcopate" : so much may reasonably be inferred from the evidence of Philippians and of Clement of Rome. If the Bishop is originally the "celebrant" at the Eucharist, it is not unintelligible that in populous cities, as the Church grew in numbers and the Christians, finding themselves in possession of no one room or building large enough to accommodate their entire community, were constrained by force of circumstances to organize two or more eucharistic assemblies side by side, the president or celebrant at *each* may have come to be regarded as "bishop" in relation to his own flock.

The admission of a plural episcopate in certain localities, however, is not the same thing as the admission of an identity between bishops and presbyters ; and the latter theory is open to very grave objections, and is to-day seriously challenged by scholars of such standing as Sohm and Harnack.[2]

According to these writers we must distinguish between "*appointed* presbyters" (καθισταμένοι πρεσβύτεροι) or "rulers" (ἡγούμενοι), who are probably to be identified with "bishops," and *other* πρεσβύτεροι or "elders" who were *not* definitely "appointed" to specific office. In several of our oldest documents both within and without the New Testament Canon (*e.g.* 1 Timothy v. 1, Titus ii. 2-6, Clem. *ad Corinth.* i. 3, iii. 3, xxi. 6, etc.) we find a rough antithesis between οἱ πρεσβύτεροι and οἱ νέοι or οἱ νεώτεροι—the "older" and "younger" Christians—older and younger either in years or more probably, perhaps, in the faith. Obviously it would be undesirable to advance a young convert to the Bishop's chair, though he might quite well become the Church's servant or "deacon." It has been suggested, therefore, with considerable plausibility, that the Bishop was normally appointed out of the ranks of the πρεσβύτεροι, and the deacons from among the νεώτεροι.

At the same time it is probable that the presbyters were a rather more clearly-defined body than the νεώτεροι. There was for one thing the analogy of the Jewish synagogue with its council of elders.[3] There was again the natural reverence for

---

[1] Turner, *The Organization of the Church*, in the *Cambridge Mediaeval History*, vol. i.

[2] Harnack, *Constitution and Law of the Church* ; Sohm, *Kirchenrecht*. A convenient statement in English of the views of Sohm will be found in Mr. Walter Lowrie's *Church and its Organization*, to which book I am greatly indebted especially for the light which it throws upon the influence of the Eucharist on the form of the ministry.

[3] It is this analogy which is often held to constitute the real strength of Lightfoot's position. The assumption is made that the early Church must have organized itself

the old which exists in any well-ordered society—the patriarchal principle, as we may call it ; in the ancient world this was even stronger than it is to-day.

Moreover there was the analogy of the Last Supper in connexion with the Eucharist. The Bishop corresponded to the Lord : who corresponded to the Apostles ? It would seem that certain of the "seniors" of the flock were given the privilege of πρωτοκαθεδρία (cf. Hermas, *Vis.* iii. 7, *Mand.* xi. 12), or in other words the right to sit with the Bishop at the Table of the Lord, as the Apostles had sat at the Last Supper ; and that such privileged seniors thereby acquired what may best be described as *a semi-official status,* and became the Bishop's advisory council in matters of administration and discipline.[1] Out of their number a new Bishop was appointed when the see was vacated by death : doubtless in the Bishop's absence one of their number was temporarily deputed to act in his stead (cf. Ignatius, *ad Smyrn.* viii.: "Let that be considered a secure or valid Eucharist—βεβαία εὐχαριστία—which is under the Bishop *or him to whom the Bishop entrusts it* ").

As the Church in each city expanded in numbers, more and more of the Bishop's functions came to be delegated in this way to the Presbyters : when the faithful became too numerous all to meet together in a single eucharistic assembly, one or more of the presbyters would be deputed to act virtually as what we should now call priests-in-charge of branch congregations—an arrangement which very early came to be more usual than the alternative expedient of having one or more additional "bishops" independent or quasi-independent of the first. The rule held probably in most localities from the beginning—though we have found reason to suppose that it was not at first quite universal—that there was in each city only one "bishop," as originally there had been but one congregation.[2]

---

on the model of the Synagogue. It is, however, exceedingly unlikely that the early Christian communities *deliberately* organized themselves " on the model of "*anything*. They did not evolve a ministry in order to resemble other religious communities, whether Jewish or Pagan. They evolved a ministry because they needed one for the orderly discharge of certain definite functions of a specifically Christian and religious kind. The synagogue analogy can be allowed at most a secondary influence on their development.

[1] This stage of development is perhaps already reached by the time of the Pastoral Epistles. Cf. 1 Tim. v. 17, " Let the presbyters that rule well be counted worthy of double honour, especially those who labour in the word and in teaching." It is not clear whether these presbyters who " ruled " and " taught " were " Bishops," or whether they were only members of the Bishop's " council."

[2] An alternative view is that originally the faithful met in small groups (" house-

By the deputing of presbyters to act for the Bishop the original congregational episcopate was transformed and expanded into a diocesan episcopate in our modern sense of the words—though of course the ancient diocese was small and manageable. The presbyters, from having been as it were semi-official counsellors and advisers of the Bishop, eventually developed into a separate and distinct grade in the hierarchy of ministers, intruded between the Bishop and the people, and cutting off the Bishop from immediate personal contact (except at rare intervals) with large portions of his flock. At some stage of this development—in Asia Minor, probably before the time of S. Ignatius—a specific ordination to the presbyterate was introduced, that is to say, the presbyterate became a definitely "appointed" office and no longer merely a quasi-official status.

The deacons meanwhile continued to be the personal subordinates and immediate attendants of the Bishop : in later times the chief of the deacons, or Archdeacon, who came to be known as the Bishop's "eye" (*oculus episcopi*), or, as we might say in more modern metaphor, his "right hand man," frequently became his successor in the see. In large and important dioceses, especially at Rome, the deacons as forming the Bishop's immediate *entourage* became exceedingly arrogant, and claimed equality with or superiority over the presbyters. We have already referred to the fact that it was this claim which S. Jerome was concerned to refute in his attempt to prove that presbyters were in origin and essence identical with Bishops.

With the above sketch of the probable course of development such pieces of evidence as have come down to us from sub-apostolic times are in general harmony. The *Didache* shows us the local ministry of bishops and deacons still dependent or quasi-dependent upon the "general" ministry of itinerant Apostles, Prophets, or Evangelists to which it owed its origin. It appears to be laid down that an "Apostle" on his arrival should normally celebrate the Eucharist (cf. *Didache*, xi. 3—"Let every apostle who comes to you be *received as the Lord*"), and "prophets" are allowed liberty in giving thanks "as much as they desire" (*Didache*, x. 6) : they are to be the

---

churches ") to hold a common meal which was at once Agape and Eucharist, and that the president of each house-church was a "Bishop." When the Eucharist was separated from the Agape, an attempt was made to mass together all the believers for a common Eucharist, and the one Eucharist brought with it as a corollary the single Bishop.

recipients of "tithes and offerings" like the Jewish high priests of old (*Didache*, xiii.)—perhaps rather in trust for the poor than for their own use, for they are to have "the ways of the Lord" and to be ascetic in their personal life. Still, the local ministers (bishops and deacons) are not to be despised : "they also perform unto you the service of the prophets and teachers. Therefore despise them not : for they are your honourable men along with the prophets and teachers" (*Didache*, xv.). There are, moreover, hints of "false prophets" or "Christ-traffickers" who endeavoured to take advantage of the gullibility of the local Christian communities by claiming hospitality and maintenance to which they were not entitled. It is clear that in spite of the predominant position accorded in the *Didache* to the members of the "general" ministry, actual respect for them is flagging and their decline is imminent. We hear nothing of them in later writings, and their disappearance presumably left the local ministry in a position of virtual independence.

In the West our earliest witness is that of Clement of Rome, who wrote about A.D. 96 on behalf of the Roman Church to rebuke the Church in Corinth for having deposed from their functions certain persons who had "offered the gifts of the bishop's office unblameably" (Clem. *ad Cor.* xliv.)—a proceeding which Clement appears elsewhere in his Epistle to regard as part of a general sedition of "young" against "elders." "Presbyters," "bishops," and "deacons" are all mentioned by Clement, but little light is thrown on their respective functions. The most that can be said is that there *appear* to be indications of a plural episcopate at Corinth, and that what is said about presbyters is consistent with the theory of the relation of presbyters to bishops set forth above. It is interesting to notice that the essential and characteristic function of the episcopate is discovered to consist in the "offering of the gifts" ($\pi\rho\sigma\sigma$-$\phi\acute{\epsilon}\rho\epsilon\iota\nu$ $\tau\grave{\alpha}$ $\delta\hat{\omega}\rho\alpha$) at the Eucharist.[1]

When all is said, it is Ignatius (*circa* A.D. 110) who gives us the clearest picture which we possess of the ministry in sub-apostolic times. In the churches of Asia Minor with which he was familiar the threefold hierarchy is plainly established, and the system of Church government implied may be described as that of *congregational monepiscopacy*.

The language of S. Ignatius with regard to the ministry has appeared to many commentators to be almost blasphemous.

---

[1] The language of Clement with regard to the appointment of ministers is discussed below.

"We ought to look upon the Bishop," he writes, "as upon the Lord Himself" (*ad Ephes.* vi.) ; and again he speaks of "the Bishop presiding after the likeness of God, and the presbyters after the likeness of the council of the Apostles, with the deacons also, who are most dear to me, having been entrusted with the diaconate [1] of Jesus Christ " (*ad Magnes.* vi.). It has not been recognized that this language becomes intelligible only when we realize that Ignatius has the picture of the eucharistic assembly in his mind.

The early Christians were accustomed to meet in whichever of their private houses afforded the largest space. " It is now the general opinion that the well-known type of Church building which emerged in the time of Constantine (the so-called basilica) was derived from the peristyle of the better class of Greek dwelling, or—what comes to the same thing—the peristyle-atrium of the Roman house." [2] The " sanctuary " of the Church (corresponding to the *tablinum* of the dwelling-house) was " usually semicircular in plan, raised a few steps above the floor of the nave, and roofed by a half dome—hence called the *apsis*. At the back of the apse was the cathedra of the bishop : and on either side of this, following the curve of the wall, a bench for the presbyters.[3] In front of them (that is, between the clergy and the congregation) was the Holy Table. About this the deacons *stood*, as the original character of their office required."

Such at least was the later arrangement of the basilica, and the language of Ignatius is explained if we suppose that roughly the same arrangement already obtained in the house-churches of his day. It is practically a literal reproduction of the conditions of the Last Supper ; we may illustrate it by Leonardo da Vinci's well-known picture.[4] The Bishop is compared to our Lord or to God, precisely because he sat in the Lord's seat ; the presbyters to the Apostles, because they flanked the Bishop on either side like the Apostles in the Upper Room.

---

[1] This is explained by S. Luke xxii. 27—" I am among you as he that serveth " (ὡς ὁ διακονῶν).

[2] Lowrie, *The Church and its Organization*, p. 285. For a full discussion of the evolution of the basilica from the dwelling-house, see the same writer's *Christian Art and Archæology*.

[3] Cf. Ignat., *ad Magnes.* xiii.—" the fitly-wreathed spiritual circlet of your presbytery."

[4] The basilicas at Ravenna and that of S. Clemente at Rome are the most striking examples of the survival of this arrangement continuously down to our own times. A second-century fresco in the catacomb of Priscilla depicts a celebration of the Eucharist after the fashion of the Last Supper (Lowrie, *Christian Art and Archæology*, p. 228).

The deacons were the ministers who carried the eucharistic gifts from the Holy Table to the people.

Ignatius rightly or wrongly regards this arrangement as universal. He speaks of Bishops as being "settled in the farthest parts of the earth" (*ad Ephes.* iii.). Enormous stress is laid upon the importance of preserving unity : no eucharist ought to be celebrated except by the Bishop or by some one— doubtless a presbyter—to whom the Bishop had delegated it : and the faithful are urgently enjoined to render due obedience to the Bishop and presbyters.

It is unnecessary to pursue further a survey of early evidence, because no one questions the fact that a threefold ministry more or less after the Ignatian model is shortly afterwards apparent throughout Christendom. The attempt has been made in this section to bridge over the gap between Ignatius and the New Testament, and to explain how and why it was that the Church wherever it was established came naturally and inevitably to organize itself in the precise way in which it did.

B. The Mode of Appointment to Ministerial Office and the Idea of Apostolic Succession

The foregoing discussion should have made it clear that the evidence for the form and functions of the ministry in the primitive Church, although scanty and in many respects ambiguous, is yet capable of being made the basis of a self-consistent and intelligible theory. With regard, however, to the form and manner of ministerial appointment and the sense, if any, in which what is called Apostolical Succession may legitimately be asserted as a literal fact of history, the evidence is almost, if not quite, non-existent.

It has already been laid down as a probable supposition that the *first* "local" ministers (bishops and deacons) were in most cases appointed in each place by the member or members of the "general" ministry of itinerant Apostles or Evangelists to whose preaching the local community owed its existence. We have seen, however, that the itinerant or "general" ministry eventually disappeared, and that the result was the virtual independence of the local "clergy." In the utter absence of any evidence to the contrary it is impossible to rule out the supposition that in not a few places the local communities at this stage of their development may have both appointed and also ordained or set apart their own clergy. The local Bishops, advised by their council of presbyters and ministerially assisted by their deacons, fulfilled the functions of pastoral oversight and governance in the Churches : and it is at least probable that when the Bishop died the local presbytery, with the consent of the people, elected a new one from among their own number and ordained him with laying on of hands. (Cf. 1 Tim. iv. 14.)

It is noteworthy that the *Didache* contains the injunction, addressed apparently without qualification to the community at large, " Appoint for yourselves bishops and deacons worthy of the Lord " (*Didache*, xv.): the Epistles of Ignatius, though implying clearly a threefold ministry of bishops, presbyters, and deacons, each several grade of which is evidently already a definite office to which there was presumably some specific form of appointment, throw no light upon the question of what that form of appointment was : [1] while the evidence of Clement of Rome, to which appeal is commonly made as conclusive, breaks down at the essential point.

The views of Clement would not in any case necessarily represent more than the local tradition and custom of the Church in Rome : but apart from this it is worth while asking precisely what that local tradition and custom as interpreted by S. Clement was. Bishops and deacons, he tells us, were originally appointed by Apostles, and since their day they have been appointed by " men of repute " (ἐλλόγιμοι ἄνδρες) " with the consent of the whole Church." The appointment is for life, and consequently it is irregular to depose a duly-appointed ministry. The Apostles, he considers, had foreseen that there would be likely to be disputes over " the dignity of the function of oversight," [2] and it was on that very account that they had in the beginning made definite appointments. The Bishops were originally from the Apostles as the Apostles were from Christ and Christ from God.

Clement's letter is thus clear evidence that in his view :—

(*a*) All things should be done decently and in order—as is plain from the orderliness of Nature and from the analogy of the Old Testament hierarchy.

(*b*) The episcopate is an office held for life, and the deposition of duly-appointed bishops who have " blamelessly offered the gifts " is unjust and a sin against charity.

---

[1] The silence of Ignatius is here especially significant in view of the great importance which he attaches in general to the Bishop's office.

[2] ἐπὶ τοῦ ὀνόματος τῆς ἐπισκοπῆς.

(*c*) Originally bishops and deacons were appointed by Apostles.

(*d*) The Episcopal office is to be a permanent one in the Church, and the Apostles intended it to be such. *In this sense,* therefore, there is and must necessarily be a " succession " of bishops from them.

His letter throws, however, no clear light at all upon the mode of appointment to the episcopate, the forms (if any) of ordination, or the question who was or might be the minister of ordination. The phrase " men of repute " is far too vague to admit of any certain inferences being drawn from it.

The possibility, therefore, that in many parts of Christendom during the first half of the second century the local communities may have been ecclesiastically independent cannot be excluded on historical grounds, though it is improbable that such local independence was of long continuance.

It should be remembered that no Christian community in early times ever regarded itself as an isolated unit, but always as the expression or manifestation in a particular place of the " people of God," that is, the Church. Liability to common persecution, brotherly intercourse, mutual intercessions, the frequent exchange of correspondence and of hospitality, together with the general duty which each community recognized of building up its neighbours in the faith, prevented the isolation of the several local Churches from being more than relative and partial. Upon matters of such moment as the appointment of clergy it would be natural that where possible (now that the " apostles and prophets " were gone) they should consult one another ; representatives of neighbouring Churches would be present and assist at the election and ordination of new ministers.

The so-called *Apostolic Church Order*—one of the two early sources distinguished by Harnack as lying behind the *Apostolic Canons* (the *Apostolic Canons* in their present form date from about A.D. 341)—contains the provision that " in the case where there are only a few men and less than twelve persons in a single locality who are competent to vote at the election of a Bishop, a letter must be sent to one of the neighbouring Churches where there is one well established, in order that three selected men may come from there and carefully examine the one who is worthy, etc." (This surely illustrates the words of Clement of Rome about the appointment of Bishops since the Apostles' time by " men of repute.") Later it came to be the rule that these delegates from neighbouring Churches must themselves be Bishops. The fourth Canon of the Synod of Nicaea provides that the new Bishop must be consecrated by at least three neighbouring Bishops—the system still in vogue—and thus the local ministry was linked on with, and commissioned by the representatives of, the ministry of the Church Universal.

Not the local community in its independence, but the whole assemblage of Christian people dispersed throughout the world, was the manifestation visibly upon earth of that "people of God" whose citizenship was in heaven. The local ministries were no longer merely local, but ecumenical in sanction and commission. It was in a sense a return to the original state of affairs, except that the ecumenical and local ministries were now one and the same ; the unordained ministry of men charismatically gifted had died out, and all ministry had become "institutional" in type. Of course we must not fall into the mistake of regarding the institutional and the "charismatic" ideas as mutually exclusive. Ordination was itself understood to convey a "charisma" or gift of grace for the discharge of ministerial function : but henceforward no man, however charismatically gifted, might discharge ministerial functions except he had been formally commissioned to do so through ordination.

A final word must be said about the idea of succession from the Apostles. We have found something like it already in the Epistle of Clement of Rome. In addition we have certain lists of the Bishops of particular sees—notably that of Rome—which purport to have been kept from the earliest times. Thirdly there are certain well-known statements of Irenaeus, who speaks of Bishops as possessing a *charisma veritatis* in virtue of their office, and appeals to the existence of an unbroken tradition of Christian doctrine, handed down through the successive occupants of those sees which claimed to be of Apostolic foundation, as the guarantee of orthodoxy.

It is to be observed, however, that such a claim in itself tells us nothing as to the mode of the appointment, ordination, or consecration of the Bishops in question, and consequently throws no additional light upon our problem. The successive presidents of a modern college at either of our universities are the depositaries of what we may call a continuous college tradition, in spite of the fact that they are not inducted into office by the heads of other colleges. This may appear a frivolous analogy, but it is intended to bring out the point that Irenaeus' language, while emphasizing the importance of an apostolic tradition of doctrine, tells us nothing as to either the existence or the non-existence of an Apostolical Succession of Bishops from the beginning, in the sense in which those words have been commonly understood.

CONCLUSION

Summing up the entire discussion we may say :—

(a) There is clear evidence that from the beginning of the Church in her specifically Christian character, there has existed in each locality a definitely-appointed minister or ministers to whom was entrusted under normal conditions the "steward-ship" of the sacramental "mysteries"; and from the first it is probable that such ministers have been appointed by laying on of hands.

(b) This ministry appears to have very early assumed the form of a bishop, presbyters, and deacons to each eucharistic assembly. The modern diocese is virtually an expansion of the primitive congregation by means of the delegation to presbyters of functions originally episcopal.

(c) It is probable that originally local ministers were appointed by Apostles, Prophets, or Evangelists ;

But on the other hand :—

(d) It cannot be shown that in the sub-apostolic age there was not, at least in some localities, a stage of congregational independency due to the isolation of local communities from one another and the lack of any provincial organization.

(e) Apostolical Succession in the literal sense cannot there-fore be asserted as more than an historical possibility : and consequently,

(f) Any defence of the principle for which the idea of Apostolical Succession stands must be based upon other than strictly historical grounds. An attempt to defend the principle independently of any appeal to history has been made in Part II. of the foregoing Essay.

Books. In addition to those already quoted mention should be made of Moberly, *Ministerial Priesthood* ; Lindsay, *The Church and the Ministry in the Early Centuries* ; Hort, *The Christian Ecclesia* ; Allen, *Christian Institutions* ; Hatch, *The Organization of the Early Christian Church.*

IX

GOD AND THE ABSOLUTE

BY

W. H. MOBERLY

SYNOPSIS

PAGE

INTRODUCTION 426-431

Religion must make terms with Philosophy . . 426
The present situation ; breakdown of traditional basis, and
existence of great body of new knowledge forming material for
a new Christian philosophy. Hence, this is a moment of
transition, justifying tentative attempts at reconstruction such
as present Essay 427
Problem of Essay defined — relation of "Absolute" of
philosophy and God of religion 430

PART ONE—THE CONCEPTION OF THE ABSOLUTE . 432-480

I. Inadequacy of the old "proofs" of the existence of God
illustrated. The "demonstrative" method unsound . . 432

II. The modern "critical" method builds on experience.
Coherence is the ordinary test of truth 434

III. Acceptance of the "critical" method implies that the
Absolute is knowable and that thorough-going agnosticism is
untenable. Agnosticism is common and plausible, but self-
contradictory. The positive basis of this criticism is the conception of ultimate Reality—the Absolute—as a rational system,
which is the ground of, and is in part revealed in, all finite
realities 438

IV. It is possible to arrange our "categories" in an order
of adequacy of truth. The Absolute is most truly conceived
in terms of mind or spirit 446
Consideration of objections 454

V. The Absolute is good.

A. This seems to be a postulate of moral experience 461
B. Objection that, even so, moral experience may not
be a sure guide to truth of fact 464
C. The pragmatic answer to this objection : all real
thinking is determined by practical wants . . 466
D. Further objection : charge of confusion between
way in which men *do* think and way in which they
ought to think 469
E. Final reasons for asserting goodness of Absolute,
in spite of objections 472

PAGE

VI. Preliminary indication of religious bearing of the
philosophy of the Absolute 477

    Note.—Some modern philosophers . . . 480

PART TWO—OBJECTIONS TO IDENTIFICATION OF THE ABSOLUTE
WITH GOD 481-493

    I. "Absolutism" proves too much.

      (1) It is too ambitious for the religious mind . 482
      (2) Its high claims defeat their own end . . 483
      (3) It ignores the fact of evil 483
      (4) It unduly contracts our horizons . . . 484

    II. It proves too little.

      (1) It is not truly "idealistic" . . . 485
      (2) It is empty 485
      (3) It is only for the few 486

    III. It explains away human personality . . . 487

    IV. It explains away the personality of God. This urged
both from the orthodox and from the unorthodox side. It has
no room for the religious conception of God, as (*a*) transcendent, (*b*) exercising will, (*c*) taking action. All these rest on
the issue of personality : is there a "living God" ? . . 488

PART THREE—TENTATIVE ANSWER TO OBJECTIONS . 494-522

    I. The difficulties rest largely on a conception of personality
which is untrue to experience. This conception is due to—

      (1) Misinterpretation of experience through use of
inadequate categories 495
      (2) Insufficient attention to the higher types of
experience 501

    II. This conclusion is confirmed by attention to specifically
Christian ideas.

      (1) Spirituality of God 507
      (2) The Trinity 508

    III. The view suggested is not "pantheistic" . . 512

    IV. Nor is it inconsistent with orthodox Christianity.
Attempt to justify difference, in this point, from views of
philosophers followed in Part One ; and to meet the charge of
intellectual dishonesty 515

CONCLUDING REFLECTIONS 522-524

IX

GOD AND THE ABSOLUTE

In these days, we have small excuse for forgetting that religion is more than creed and reality richer than thought. It is equally important to remember that religious devotion is directed towards an Object, and cannot continue unless that Object is believed to be real. In most of the higher religions, the object of devotion is One God, believed to be ruler, if not creator, of all men and of the world in which they live. Religion is therefore bound up with certain beliefs about the nature of things,[1] and hence must always settle accounts with the body of beliefs about the world which men derive from other sources. In other words, Religion must make terms with Philosophy; for Philosophy is only the most careful and accurate formulation of those beliefs. Truth is one, from

---

[1] Cf. C. C. J. Webb, *Problems in the Relations of God and Man*, pp. 10, 142-3. "Religion involves a kind of apprehension or awareness, whose object is always, however, in such a sense the whole of reality, or at least the heart and centre of reality, that it is in the long run impossible for Religion to remain contented, as the aesthetic consciousness can, with an object which is merely *its* object, without placing it, so to say, in the centre of things, and relating to it everything in itself and in its environment, and hence committing the religious man to what the Germans call a *Weltanschauung* correspondent to his religion." "The religious sentiment is a sentiment for an object which is regarded as not merely its object, but as somehow the fundamental or ultimate reality." Mr. Webb admits that this last statement has a paradoxical air in view of the apparent variety of objects of worship. But he maintains that it is essentially true. "Is there not from the first in our sentiment towards the object of worship something which from the first would not be excited, except by something which is imagined as holding in itself that mystery or secret which, as the worshipper's horizon widens, we come at last to realize is the mystery of the ultimate ground of all things?"

whatever source it is derived. " To tell a thinking man that he need not interpret to his reason what religion tells him of God is like saying to him, ' Be religious if you will, but you need not let your religion influence your conduct.' " [1]

This has always been so. From St. Paul and the writer of the Fourth Gospel to the framers of the oecumenical creeds, Christian theology was formulated in the language, and in some relation to the problems, of the philosophy of the time. And the elaboration of the grounds in reason on which it rests, and of the consequences which may be deduced from it, was accomplished by the Schoolmen in terms of the Scholastic Philosophy. In our own time the same work has yet to be done.

But the most salient fact in the present situation is the breakdown of the traditional basis. We have to remember that the collapse of mediaevalism which we associate for most purposes with the Renaissance and Reformation is, in the special sphere of " Natural Theology," delayed till the time of Kant. Descartes and Locke changed much ; but in this sphere they mostly retained the demonstrative methods of the Schoolmen. Each thought it possible to give a demonstrative proof of the existence of God, analogous to the proof of a geometrical proposition. But these have now little or no living influence. " That vast literature of proofs of God's existence drawn from the order of nature, which a century ago seemed so overwhelmingly convincing, to-day does little more than gather dust in libraries, for the simple reason that our generation has ceased to believe in the kind of God it argued for. Whatever sort of being God may be, we *know* to-day that he is nevermore that mere external inventor of ' contrivances ' intended to make manifest his ' glory,' in which our great-grandfathers took such satisfaction." [2]

---

[1] Aubrey Moore in *Lux Mundi*, p. 89.
[2] William James, *Varieties of Religious Experience*, p. 74.

In this rejection there is a tone of assurance which implies the possession of a clear and positive view of the nature of the world. This assurance is not without justification. When Mr. Blatchford of the *Clarion* began his hostile examination of the Christian religion with a chapter entitled, "What I can and what I cannot believe," his intellectual arrogance was generally and rightly condemned. But had he written "we" instead of "I," he would have been putting forward a canon which, though undoubtedly subject to abuse, is, in some degree, both legitimate and necessary. It implies the assumption that the opinion of modern times is worth more than that of antiquity. But if we believe in intellectual development, we must admit an element of truth in such a position.

Certainly *Securus judicat orbis terrarum* ; but this maxim can only help us if interpreted by a theory of Evolution. It does not proclaim a democracy of opinion, to which all times and places are alike. That way lies chaos. Thus the apologist appeals in favour of the religious view of the world to the *consensus gentium*. But the sceptic retorts that the unanimity is only verbal, not real. The believer in Jehovah is a witness against Baal, and the believer in Baal is a witness against Jehovah. The same diversity prevails in the sphere of reasoned argument. "There is not a single proof of natural theology of which the negative has not been maintained as vigorously as the affirmative."[1] The edge of this scepticism can only be turned by the familiar conception of Development. If different and inconsistent religious beliefs are viewed, not as on a level with one another, but as different stages in the development of one thing, it is possible to reduce the material to some sort of order. The history of religions will present a picture, not simply of chaos, but of "order dawning on chaos." In that case, the meaning of the whole process is to be sought in its maturest

---

[1] Leslie Stephen, *An Agnostic's Apology*, p. 13.

products. The "heirs of all the ages" can pronounce some decisions with an authority which was impossible for their ancestors. Error is long-lived, but it is not eternal ; and with the progress of thought some errors cease even to be plausible. Fetichism and ancestor-worship no longer challenge our serious consideration.

This consensus of opinion is felt when we consider the nature of God. It defines and limits our problem. God, if there be a God, must at least be a Spirit, and the God of the whole earth. "The only Deity we can believe in, nay, we might say the only Deity we can disbelieve in, or seriously deny, is a universal God, a spiritual principle manifested in all nature and all history."[1] "Whatever else 'God' means, it means the highest we can think of—something in which all that we love and adore in human beings and nature exists without any alloy."[2]

What then is the present situation? In modern times we have acquired a great body of new knowledge of the physical world and of human nature. Everywhere this has transformed men's conception of the universe ; and the new outlook has found its way somewhat tardily into metaphysics. Hence it is that theological systems constructed in an older age have little reality for the modern mind. And modern apologists seem to be fighting a rearguard action, because they are always trying to adapt to new ideas an intellectual scheme which really depends on a quite different set of presuppositions.

The old religion then needs a new theology. We need it not merely for defensive purposes, but for our own fuller understanding of the truth. It is not merely that the preacher of the Gospel must have the gift of tongues ; and that, as he would not speak to Parthians or Medes in Aramaic, but in their own tongue, so he must speak to modern men, not in terms of the

---

[1] E. Caird, *The Evolution of Religion*, p. 63.
[2] R. L. Nettleship, *Remains*, p. 105.

philosophy of the Middle Ages, but in terms of the philosophy of our own day. But further, if we believe in Development, we shall hold that the theology which incorporates the knowledge of the twentieth century will be not merely different from, but better than, the theology of the thirteenth, just as it in turn will be absorbed in the fuller theology of later ages. "The work which Aquinas did for the Church of his day—the fusion of the highest speculative thought of the time with its profoundest spiritual convictions, the reconciliation of the new truths of the present with the kernel of truth embodied in the traditional creed—is a task which will have to be done again and again so long as the human mind remains progressive, and religion remains a vital force with it. . . . But in one respect the work of Aquinas is built on the solid foundation on which all such efforts must repose—the grand conviction that religion is rational, and that reason is divine, and that all knowledge and all truth must be capable of harmonious adjustment." [1]

We are now at a time of transition. The modern theologian has a rich quarry for his working, but its capacities for serving his purpose are as yet largely unexplored. We do not at present know how much of the new thought can be absorbed, and how far it will enrich or modify the old ; nor, on the other hand, how far the old will correct or even reject the various elements of modern thought. *Solvitur ambulando.* It is a time for intellectual ventures, necessarily tentative. The present Essay is an attempt, conceived on these lines, to consider some of the problems which confront modern theologians when they wish to formulate the central belief in God in the light of modern philosophy.

It may be worth while to define the particular problem of this Essay a little more closely. In their view of the Being and Nature of God, religion and philosophy attack the same problem from different angles,

<hr />

[1] Rashdall, *The Universities of Europe in the Middle Ages*, vol. i. p. 367.

and move along different lines. Religion starts with a private and particular relation between the worshipper and his god. It gradually grows in perception of the necessary purity, unity, and universality of God.[1] Philosophy starts with the conception of the universe or the whole of reality. It gradually grows, as I should hold, towards a more spiritual interpretation of the nature of that reality. " Philosophy demands unity, whether personal or impersonal ; Religion demands a personal object, be that object one or many."[2] They have travelled so far on converging lines, but they have not yet met. The God of Philosophy is not yet the God of Religion. To the one, unity and universality are cardinal ; to the other, personality. The philosopher speaks of " The Absolute " ; the religious man speaks of " God." The question for us is—Will the lines meet ? In the process of further development, will the convergence continue till the two conceptions are fused ? or is there some essential difference between the two, which must always prevent identification ?

The Essay is divided into three parts. In the first part, I shall consider how far an argument for the existence of God and a positive conception of His nature can be derived from modern philosophical thought. In the second part, I shall state some of the principal objections to the acceptance of the results of Part One as an adequate basis for Christian Theism. In the third part, I shall make such suggestions as I am able towards bridging the gulf between the conclusions of Part One and of Part Two.[3]

---

[1] The development of the Jewish conception of God, within the Old Testament from the worship of a merely tribal deity to true Monotheism is an instance of this.

[2] Aubrey Moore in *Lux Mundi*, p. 64.

[3] There is hardly a line that is original in the following Essay ; and my borrowings are too numerous to admit of detailed acknowledgment. There are, however, two recent books which I have used so constantly that I should wish to express my gratitude for them. These are Dr. Bosanquet's recent Gifford Lectures, *The Principle of Individuality and Value*, and Mr. C. C. J. Webb's *Problems in the Relations of God and Man*. Of course, Dr. Bosanquet and Mr. Webb are in no way responsible for any crudities into which I may have been betrayed, either in my endeavour to be brief or through failure properly to understand and to apply their conceptions.

PART ONE

I. Inadequacy of the so-called "Proofs"

The conclusions of the demonstrative school are now unconvincing, because the demonstrative method, considered as a method of reaching first principles, is vicious. I have not space to work this out in detail, and to do so would be to "slay the slain." But it is easy to illustrate the unsoundness of some of the old arguments. Thus the most common "demonstrative" proof of the existence of God was the Cosmological Proof. This was an argument from the world as a procession of linked events, each one the effect of some previous cause, to the necessity of some "First Cause" of the whole series which is really originative, and is itself the effect of no previous cause. In the Cartesian form of the argument, this Cause must contain in itself perfection at least equal to all the perfection found in any of the effects.

> If Mary is so beautiful,
> What must her Maker be?

> He that made the eye, shall he not see?

This "proof" suffers from obvious defects :—

(1) In the form of an argument to a "First Cause" in time, it may be represented as merely expressing the inability of the human mind to go on thinking backwards indefinitely. But the point at which it stops is purely arbitrary. No positive argument can fairly be based on this incapacity.

(2) With Descartes at least the argument was circular. It obviously assumes, as an unconditional necessity, the principle that everything that is derives its existence and its essence from something else, and that the nature of the "cause" must be sufficient to account for the nature of the effect. This principle

itself is, to Descartes, a self-evident intuition. But, when pressed as to his certainty that the human mind does not deceive itself, and that it has a right to trust its intuitions, he falls back on his trust in the goodness of God, who would not condemn his creatures to error. That is to say, the assumption of the validity of the intuition presupposes certain beliefs about the ultimate nature of the universe, and about the place of man and of human reason in the universe, and cannot therefore be fairly used to justify those beliefs.

(3) This is an argument from the Finite to the Infinite, or from what holds good in experience to what transcends experience. There is more in the conclusion than can be got out of the premisses. The superstructure is too big for the foundations.[1]

This last objection suggests the flaw that is fatal to all demonstrative reasoning about ultimate reality. The thinker is himself a part of Reality, and can never get outside it to see it as a whole. Hence he must either describe it in purely negative terms, in which case he really says nothing ; or he must describe the whole in terms of the parts, in which case there is always a margin of error in his statement. It is impossible for Him in whom " we live and move and

---

[1] The Teleological and Ontological Proofs are, equally with the Cosmological, now discredited. Thus the Teleological Proof is at best a supplement to the others. It only suggests an architect or sculptor shaping material which he does not make, not a creator, and still less an infinite being. And its popular appeal, which depends largely on apparent adaptation and design in Nature, has been greatly weakened by the Darwinian insistence on Natural Selection as a cause in evolution. The Ontological Proof has never been popular. The very idea of God, it urges, is the idea of an absolutely perfect being. But existence is a perfection and its absence would be an imperfection. It follows, therefore, from the very notion of God that God exists. But *prima facie* this argument assumes the very leap from thought to reality which is in question. If we think of God, we must *think* of Him as existing ; but it does not follow that He *really* exists.

I am not suggesting that these arguments cannot be stated in a way which frees them from the obvious objections. I think they can ; and I would refer to Mr. Webb (*op. cit.* pp. 159-188) for a very illuminating exposition of the truth that underlies each of them. But the process of purification involves a very radical transformation, and it may be doubted whether, *for purposes of popular exposition*, the true arguments are not rather obscured than clarified by a laborious tracing of their ancestry. I believe that the substance of what remains of the traditional " Proofs " after a treatment like Mr. Webb's will be found in what follows.

have our being " to be comprised in the conclusion of a syllogism. Not only did the application of this method actually fail; it was bound to fail, for the method was itself a false one.

II. The Modern "Critical" Method

Modern Idealism [1] has abandoned the old *a priori* demonstrative methods. Though not in the restricted sense of Mill and Spencer, it is a true " philosophy of experience." In what sense this is so may best be made clear by an analogy. It is sometimes disputed whether Aristotle's procedure in his *Ethics* is inductive or deductive : it is, in fact, a mixture of the two. He did not approach the problems of Ethics with ready-made ideas of Right and Wrong, Good and Evil. He started by an examination and comparison of the moral ideas and practices which he found actually existing in the Greek society of his day. He asked how men did actually behave and think about behaviour. But his aim was to discover in this mass of moral experience and half-instinctive moral judgment certain central constitutive principles on which the rationality of particular judgments depended. In the same way the modern idealist starts by the examination of the actual conscious experience of ordinary men. He asks how and on what grounds they actually distinguish truth from falsehood. Thus Kant asked the question : " How is Experience possible ? " If it should prove on analysis—as Kant thought it did—that certain funda-

---

[1] I use the term " Idealism " in the widest possible sense as applying to the whole line of great philosophers from Plato and Aristotle downwards, who have assigned a pre-eminent place in the constitution of the universe to the things that are not seen rather than to the things that are seen. Many persons will hold that the type of philosophy—lately known as " Absolutism "—which I try to expound below, is only one of many competitors to the succession of the great idealists of the past, and that it is one which recent developments have made old-fashioned and out of date. Nevertheless, in spite of the fashion of the moment, I believe that it is, philosophically, the soundest, and therefore the one of which Christian theology has really to take account. Cf. below, p. 480, Note to Part One.

mental principles are so embedded in the structure of conscious experience that only by the assumption of their truth can experience be made rational or intelligible at all, then these principles are not only true but necessary ; they not only are but they must be. This is what Kant meant by his " Transcendental Deduction of the Categories."

Our starting - point, then, is ordinary experience. What criterion do we actually use when we distinguish fact from fancy, truth from error, waking from dreaming ? Why does any one say : " I must have dreamt that " ? The answer is that we reject as fiction or as dream whatever will not fit in or cohere or form one rational whole with our ordinary waking experience. Thus men of the Victorian era disbelieved in witchcraft or " possession," because these seemed to " contradict " the facts of science, and so could not be fitted in or placed in any niche within their rational experience. With a wider experience, men of the twentieth century are perhaps less ready simply to reject the tales of more credulous ages as fables, because there is more in their experience with which these tales, if taken as true, would cohere. We are sometimes in doubt whether certain experiences which we seem to remember belong to the world of actual waking reality or were part of our dreams. We finally place in the category of dreams certain weird and discontinuous experiences, in which persons whom we know act " out of character," personal identity is blurred (for one man suddenly turns into another), or we see persons whom, in our waking moments, we know to be dead or in distant parts of the world. Here we use the same criterion. We receive nothing as real which will in no way cohere with the rest of our experience.

If this is typical, certain conclusions follow :—

(1) Doubt implies a background of certainty. Scepticism or agnosticism is an irrational attitude except within a limited sphere. It is true that illusion is

frequent. Both our senses and our reasoning faculties are fallible. We are continually finding that "things are not what they seem." Yet we cannot make the fact of error the basis of our philosophy. Dreams can only be known as dreams against a background of waking reality : they are a fractional part of experience condemned in the light of the whole.[1] To ask whether the *whole* of experience is a dream is to ask a meaningless question. Those who would throw doubt on the whole of our knowledge because of the imperfection of our faculties[2] really refute themselves. For it is by the use of, and by trust in, these same faculties that they reach their sceptical conclusion. We only doubt or reject the immediate witness of our sense-perceptions because of our trust in human reason as exhibited in the sciences. To the ordinary eye, to-day just as much as before the time of Copernicus, the sun seems to go round the earth. We reject the apparent evidence of our own eyes because of our trust in human reason as exemplified (*a*) in the science of Astronomy, which teaches us that only the opposite hypothesis can account for the facts, (*b*) in the science of Optics, which shows how much of what we seem to see directly is really due to inference, and hence how the mistake has arisen.[3] Moreover, even if it is said that we may doubt all existing theories because of their internal imperfections and their failure to hold together, without having any theory of our own to put in their place, what is this but to affirm that the real world certainly is coherent and harmonious?

(2) This principle holds good not only in ordinary life but in regard to the deepest issues of philosophy. For philosophy is only common sense, applied to the

[1] If, like Du Maurier's Peter Ibbetson, we had a dream-life as continuous and coherent, in spite of interruptions, as our waking life, we should have no reason to consider it wanting in reality.

[2] As is suggested by the title of an article by Mr. H. G. Wells in *Mind*, entitled *Scepticism of the Instrument*.

[3] Cf. Essay V. p. 215.

highest and widest problems : it is vital to it to establish its continuity with the experience of the ordinary man. The only test of a theory of the universe is that it should make the facts of the world intelligible, and that philosophy is the truest which makes most sense. In the language of Logic, each philosophical theory is an hypothesis, and the only kind of proof of which it is susceptible is verification. The question is always— Does it work? It professes to explain. Does it explain?

This procedure is seen also when we reject a theory. " You endeavour to refute your opponent by showing that his error carries some other error with it, that this second error carries still another, and that ultimately his whole rational experience is imperilled by his clinging to his false idea. You give him the highwayman's choice— 'Your error or your intellectual life.' 'Deny this,' we say, 'and nothing remains, for behind this, nay incorporated with it and implicated in its fate, is the whole system of your associated thoughts.' " [1]

It is important to insist that this procedure is true to life. It represents the living action of the mind. In concrete issues, which touch life at many points, it is only a multitude of converging considerations which produces real conviction. As Mr. Chesterton reminds us in his *Orthodoxy*, a man is partially convinced of a thing when he has thought of an argument and has found that *something* proves his conclusion ; but he is really convinced only when he finds that *everything* proves it. A man may be silenced by an argument which he cannot answer, but he is only convinced and converted when his position is not merely refuted but absorbed. When Lord Morley said, " We will not refute Christianity, we will explain it," he proclaimed a true ideal of method. So what is labelled " dream " is not merely rejected ; it is explained and given a real, though lowly, place in experience. Thus the Protestant

[1] Henry Jones, *The Problem of Immortality in Tennyson and Browning.*

urges against the Catholic that he himself accepts in the region of spirit those truths which the Catholic expresses in a bodily and external way. The Catholic, on the other hand, urges against the Protestant that he himself gives ample scope for the individual devotion which the Protestant values, while doing justice to the social nature and interdependence of men which the Protestant ignores. Both use more directly "offensive" argument; but it is only on grounds such as these that conversions are made.

III. This Method implies that Absolute Reality is Knowable and that Thoroughgoing Agnosticism is Untenable

(1) *Agnosticism is common.*—Agnosticism is to-day widely diffused, not so much as an explicit creed but rather as a temper of mind. There is a widespread suspicion that the region of reality to which religious beliefs refer is beyond our ken. Hence such beliefs are unverifiable : it is unprofitable to build on them.

This attitude is not due merely to the hardness of men's hearts or to mental sloth, though both of these contribute to it ; but rather to two more respectable causes :—

(*a*) The "note" of post-mediaeval as contrasted with mediaeval thought is humility. The great advance of scientific knowledge and, more particularly, the Copernican theory impress the imagination with the contrast between the vastness of the universe and the littleness of man. This naturally results in a growing distrust of the power of human faculties to comprehend the mighty and inscrutable world. And the moral for the sensible man is that he should accept his limitations and "cultivate his own garden." "The proper study of mankind is man," and only that corner of the

universe of which he has direct daily experience and
which constantly affects his well-being. This frame of
mind is clearly voiced by Locke. He hopes " to prevail with the busy mind of man to be more cautious in
meddling with things exceeding its comprehension ; to
stop when it is at the utmost extent of its tether ; and
to sit down in a quiet ignorance of those things which
upon examination are found to be beyond the reach of
our capacities." [1] It is then of the first importance to
discriminate between the verifiable and the unverifiable,
the natural and the supernatural, the experienced and
the transcendent ; and to confine our attention and
energies to the former. " Were the capacities of our
understandings well considered, the extent of our knowledge once discovered, and the horizon found which sets
the bounds between the enlightened and the dark parts
of things, between what is and what is not com-
prehensible by us, men would perhaps with less scruple
acquiesce in the avowed ignorance of the one, and
employ their thoughts and discourse with more satisfaction in the other." [2]

(*b*) The other reason that moves men strongly towards
agnosticism about ultimate reality is the age-long failure
of philosophers to arrive at any agreement. In this, as
in other matters, men would probably defer to the
expert, if only the experts were agreed. But " when
doctors disagree," how is the layman to decide ? And,
like Kant, he is painfully impressed by the contrast
between the continual recurrence of the same disputes
within the ranks of the philosophers and the assured
achievements of the physical sciences. The theologians,
indeed, sometimes speak dogmatically enough ; but
then they do not appear to be impartial, for they set
out to prove a foregone conclusion; and, if their

1 *Essay concerning Human Understanding* (Fraser's edition), vol. i. p. 28.
2 Locke, *op. cit.* i. pp. 31-32. In the nineteenth century Darwinism gave
a new impetus to this tendency; for it accentuated still further the age and
vastness of the physical universe and its independence and carelessness of human
purposes.

reasonings are closely investigated, their agreement turns out to be much more apparent than real.[1]

> Myself when young did eagerly frequent
> Doctor and Saint, and heard great argument
> About it and about : but evermore
> Came out by the same door wherein I went.

Leslie Stephen makes powerful use of this difficulty in his *Agnostic's Apology* : "State any one proposition in which all philosophers agree, and I will admit it to be true ; or any one that has a manifest balance of authority, and I will agree that it is probable. But so long as every philosopher flatly contradicts the principles of his predecessors, why affect certainty ?" In face of such facts, it is suggested, the only way of escape from pure scepticism is to recognize frankly the inexorable limits of our reasoning powers, and to restrict our mental activities within the frontiers of experience. In short, we must abandon all "Ontology," and confine ourselves to the phenomenal sphere : over-ambition has been the cause of our intellectual barrenness. On such a view, Comte would be right in holding that the future progress of the human race depends on the abandonment of the trackless wastes of Religion and Metaphysics in favour of the sure path of Science.

(2) *But it cannot survive criticism.*—Agnosticism, though common, is untenable.[2] For

(*a*) It is, in the long run, psychologically impossible.

(*b*) It is self-contradictory.

(*a*) It is futile to advise the human intellect to "fling away ambition." Whatever may be the case with most of us at some times and with a few men at all times, the human race cannot permanently restrain itself from pursuing such "obstinate questionings," however clearly their vanity may seem to be demon-

---

[1] Thus Mansel and, in some moods, Newman provide some of the strongest arguments for Agnosticism.

[2] This statement is to some extent qualified below, p. 445.

strated. As Henry Sidgwick said, the man in men will never consent to this abandonment. No one has stated this more strongly than Hume himself. " 'Tis almost impossible for the mind of man to rest, like those of beasts, in that narrow circle of objects which are the subject of daily conversation and action." Questions continually recur. " Where am I, or what? From what causes do I derive my existence, and to what condition shall I return ? Whose favour shall I court, and whose anger must I dread ? What beings surround me, and on whom have I any influence, or who have any influence on me ? " [1] " *Naturam expellas furca, tamen usque recurret.*" And our nature is such that we cannot avoid these questions, however we may desire to do so.

(*b*) The distinction of spheres as " knowable " and " unknowable " is quite unscientific. And to assert the " existence " of a Reality which is nevertheless " unknowable " is to fall into hopeless contradiction. For to establish a " frontier " implies some knowledge of a " Beyond." To deny this — as I think Mr. Chesterton somewhere puts it—is as though one were to say, " Since all my faculties are totally confined to my own garden, I cannot tell whether the roses next door are in flower." In fact, no line of demarcation can be drawn between metaphysics and common life. Every moment of our waking life we are making the most tremendous metaphysical assumptions.[2] We are

---

[1] Hume, *A Treatise of Human Nature*, Book I. Part IV. § vii.

[2] If philosophy dealt merely with what is remote, it might be reasonable for the average man to treat philosophical questions with unconcern. But philosophy deals also with what is very near ; and it is not possible to avoid taking sides philosophically. Our fortunes are bound up with the truth of certain philosophical contentions and with the untruth of others. Thus a possible philosophical theory is Solipsism—the theory that I am the only reality and that everybody and everything else only exist, like dream-creatures, in my head ; but men, generally, stake the whole of their practical lives on the existence of other men and things. So, again, most science and a great deal of life consists in asking the question, Why ? Yet the rationality of the question and the possibility of an answer depend on the assumption that the ultimate structure of things is such that everything must have a cause. Finally, the rationality of all life depends on the assumption that our faculties are, in general, trustworthy ; yet to make this assumption is to take sides in philosophy.

therefore committed, whether we like it or not, to a metaphysical venture. The agnostic does not escape metaphysical assumptions; but his assumptions are particularly deadly, for he is unconscious of them and refuses to think about them : he is, in effect, a dangerous obscurantist. As Mr. Bradley puts it,[1] he allows us—for he cannot help himself—to think about these matters but not to think strictly : which is absurd. Certainty, then, must be a relative term ; and none of the certainties of common life are independent of metaphysical beliefs.

But it may be said : Are you not misconceiving the true purport of your argument ? You want to invest your metaphysical principles with all the certainty of everyday facts ; but what you are really doing is to evaporate the certainties of common sense and to assimilate them to the shadow-world of metaphysics. If you succeed in proving that there is no half-way house between metaphysical dogmatism and pure scepticism, it may be you will force us all to become sceptics.

Such an objection is natural but baseless. For pure scepticism is, as we have already seen, self-contradictory. To say that Reality is unknowable is itself a claim to know Reality ; for the only sufficient ground for such an assertion would be a knowledge that the positive character of Reality is incompatible with its being known. And even to assert failure is to imply some positive notion of what success would be. But in our assertion of a philosophical method, we have already covered this point.[2] It is only in virtue of a general trust in our faculties that we can criticize or condemn any of their particular deliverances. Without a positive criterion of truth we cannot think at all. And to raise the question of the relation of thought as a whole to Reality is futile ; for it is thought itself which must

[1] *Appearance and Reality*, p. 4.
[2] See above, p. 436.

decide the question. Thought is not only the prisoner
at the bar, but also the judge and the jury.

(3) *The positive basis of such criticism.*—We not
only can see as a fact that Agnosticism is irrational :
we can to some extent understand why it should
be so. Agnosticism is irrational because the universe
is, by necessity of thought, a "Cosmos," a rational
system, all the parts of which are related to one
another, and are governed by one set of principles.
The phrase " necessity of thought" must be understood in the light of what we have said above. The
universe is necessarily a Cosmos, because, on reflection,
we find that we have assumed, and do assume, that it is
so in *all* our thinking. This does not, of course, mean
that the assumption was explicit and conscious ; but
only that we now see that its denial would invalidate
all our previous results, and reduce to chaos the world
of the modest agnostic no less than the world of the
transcendentalist. We now see that it is logically
involved in what we have always assumed, and cannot
be logically denied without its following that we have
been wrong all along. So we use the muscles in
walking, and depend on respiration and the circulation
of the blood in every moment of our physical life,
though normally unconscious of the fact. So again,
though it is probably only the man who has had some
education in Logic who ever formulates to himself the
abstract Law of Contradiction—(" it is impossible for
the same thing at once to be and not be ")—yet we
all are using it all our lives ; and any doubt cast on
its validity would threaten the whole results of our
waking thought, and consequently our sanity.

The fact that, in all our thinking, we are working
with the assumption that the universe is a rational
system, may be illustrated from the special case of our
use of the conception of cause and effect. It is the
presupposition of inductive logic that, when two things
are related as cause and effect, they are necessarily

connected, and where one is the other must be : it is on
this that it bases all generalizations. But many modern
philosophers are inclined to distinguish the actual relation of cause and effect in the real world from the
logical relation of ground and consequence. The latter
suggests a theoretical ideal to which the former rarely
comes up. A true ground would contain everything
necessary and nothing superfluous to the production of
the consequence ; and the necessity which links ground
and consequence would be so thoroughgoing that complete knowledge of the ground would include knowledge of the consequence. A real cause, in any sense
in which we practically use the term, is generally only
an incomplete logical ground : it does not contain
everything necessary and nothing superfluous to the
production of the effect. On the other hand, the
complete logical relation does not hold between concrete things or events, where we hardly ever get a
"pure case," but only between qualities, which are
never found in isolation, and can only be separated by
abstraction. The hypothetical judgment (if A is B, it
is C) would be the true type of the logical relation of
ground and consequence ; and scientific laws, when
applied to concrete things, should, on this view, be
expressed hypothetically, and qualified by an "as such"
or "so far as" ; e.g. though the circumference of the
circle is in a fixed ratio to the diameter, which mathe-
maticians symbolize by the Greek letter π, this ratio
does not hold absolutely of any given pint pot, but only
"in so far as" it approximates to a perfect round.

But the hypothetical judgment itself has a ground in
concrete reality ; and this ground is the whole system
within which the hypothesis holds. "If a picture
measures 6 foot by 7 foot, it cannot be hung in a
space on the wall measuring 5 foot by 6 foot." Here
the true "ground" of the judgment is the actual
nature of space as a system, within which the judgment
is true. "If the boat in the right foreground of the

picture were erased, the judgment of the distances would become confused." Here the ground of judgment is the nature of the picture as an aesthetic whole. But it is only relatively that space or the picture as a work of art are wholes in themselves. We can make judgments about each of them considered as members of a wider system. And, in the last resort, the universe, which is the only completed system, is the 'true ground of every hypothetical judgment. The much-quoted " flower in a crannied wall " would then represent the ideal of knowledge.[1]

This conception at once dictates and limits agnosticism, and that is the reason for this digression. We have not absolute knowledge ; we are not as gods ; and any philosophy which suggests the contrary is at once convicted of unreality and untruth to life. But all knowledge short of absolute knowledge is imperfect. What we know always implies a *more* to be known. And, because all reality is in thoroughgoing relation, what we know is always liable to be modified by what we know not yet.[2] But such agnosticism is very different from the agnosticism of Leslie Stephen. There is here no distinction of spheres ; no impassable frontier or boundary-line. The unknown is not the unknowable. On the contrary, it is continuous with, and in vital relation to, the known. " For knowledge the only unknowable is the unintelligible or contradictory, and to suppose that real existence is unintelligible or contradictory is to belie the nature of knowledge."[3] Reality may be in part unknown ; but it cannot be incompatible with the nature of knowledge.

---

[1] The substance of the last paragraph is taken almost bodily from Dr. Bosanquet's *Logic*, vol. i. pp. 257 ff.

[2] Cf. Locke, vol. ii. p. 262. "The great parts and wheels, as I may so say, of this stupendous structure of the universe, may, for aught we know, have such a connection and dependence in their influences and operations one upon another, that perhaps things in this our mansion would put on quite another face, and cease to be what they are, if some one of the stars or great bodies incomprehensibly remote from us should cease to be or move as it does."

[3] T. M. Forsyth, *English Philosophy*, p. 124.

Professor A. E. Taylor well compares our partial ignorance of Reality to the proverbial deceitfulness of the human heart. We are largely ignorant of ourselves. But between knower and known there is no unbridgeable gulf, and so there is no limit to the possibility of knowledge.

Our doubts, then, as well as our certainties, our questions as well as our answers, the limits as well as the positive extent of our knowledge, all presuppose that the Universe is a Cosmos, and that Absolute Reality is not a mere Beyond, nor again a mere Substratum, beneath but different from all finite realities, but a rational system whose character is the ground of, and is in part revealed in, all finite reality and all actual experience.

IV. Absolute Reality is most truly conceived in Terms of Mind or Spirit

So far we have tried to vindicate our right to think of the Absolute Reality, in which we live and move and have our being, as a "Cosmos" and as the "regulative" principle of all our knowledge, "the master-light of all our seeing." But this, it may be felt, does not carry us very far, and is, indeed, little more than a platitude. What it really imports us to know is the positive character of Reality and its relation to human life and human interests. And it may be suggested that, by our own method, we have debarred ourselves from giving to this question not merely the answer we desire but any answer at all. The light by virtue of which we see cannot itself be seen. We cannot characterize the Whole except in terms of the parts. But such predicates must of necessity be inadequate to, and misrepresent, the Whole. Knowledge in such terms will be "appearance" and not "reality."

To this we may fairly reply that—

(1) We do right and not wrong to characterize

Reality in positive terms, provided we use the best available.

(2) As between different descriptions, we are already committed to the principle that the truest is that which explains most, which makes the whole body of our knowledge most coherent. "The fuller is the more real."

(3) Applying this criterion, we should say that descriptions in terms of life are truer than merely mechanical descriptions, and descriptions in terms of Mind or Spirit are truer than those that are merely on the level of biology.

(1) The position we have now reached has, admittedly, a positive and a negative side. We can have some knowledge of Reality, but all the terms which we can apply to it are crude and fall short. The question is : Do we do more service to truth by emphasizing the positive or the negative aspect? I believe we convey more truth to our own minds and to those of others by making the best positive assertion we can compass than by restricting ourselves to barren negations. The homeliest analogies are the most helpful. If we want to take the truest attitude towards a kind of knowledge that is at present beyond our grasp ; if, that is, we want to shape our thought in the form which, though inevitably crude, will carry us farthest towards a fuller apprehension and leave us least to unlearn when we reach it ; we should consider the way in which we deal with minds capable only of an inferior kind of knowledge to our own. We can see that the theological conceptions of the child or the savage are crude and materialistic as compared with our own. But we rightly continue, in our intercourse with them, to use symbols and images which they will understand in a more literal sense than we. We do not merely say, " Heaven is not a place. It is not in space at all. It is like nothing that you can conceive." We continue to use the old childish language, because we hope that by doing

so we shall suggest a conception of Heaven which corresponds in their intellectual "world" to the fuller conception in ours. We shall thus convey some truth and the best that they are capable of receiving. Whereas, if we restrict ourselves to negations, we shall convey nothing at all. Of course this method is liable to abuse. It is wrong just so far as we continue to use cruder conceptions where better ones are available. We do well to bear in mind the limitations of our "categories" and to be constantly criticizing them. There is always room for an element of agnosticism, provided it is subordinate. But when we have decided which among the categories we have is the best, we convey more truth by affirming it than by simply saying that the truth transcends all our conceptions. To tell a blind man that scarlet is like the sound of a trumpet is no doubt on the verge of meaninglessness. The gulf between sound and sight is so great that the analogy is all but useless. Yet even here, I think, we feel that it is worth while. *A fortiori* we do right in theology in persevering with our best conceptions, until we can improve them. If, for instance, it should appear that a description of the Absolute in terms of personality is the truest open to us, we shall not be deterred from it by the general consideration that, like all possible descriptions, it contains an element of metaphor.

(2) The real problem, then, is to arrange our different categories in an order of truth ; or to decide which among the finite realities known to us in experience can least inadequately represent Reality as a whole. Such a scale of degrees of truth is possible. "Because no approximation is more than approximately the truth, it by no means follows that all are equally wide of the mark."[1] And the title of an early Essay by Professor Pringle-Pattison, *Philosophy as Criticism of Categories*, happily describes the true task of the thinker.

[1] A. E. Taylor, *The Elements of Metaphysics*, p. 38.

But we are already committed to a principle of discrimination. Coherence, we have said, is the test of truth : that philosophy is the truest which explains the most. If then, as we hold, the universe is a system which is the ground and explanation of everything in it, then, as between finite realities, we shall agree with Mr. Bradley that the fuller (*i.e.* the more inclusive and self-explanatory) is the more real, and that a description of the Whole in such terms is the least inadequate.

We can easily see why this should be so ; for the whole Universe, we hold, is a Cosmos. Hence, while everything finite is, in more or less degree, determined and explained by what is beyond itself, the Universe is a self-contained whole. It holds in itself the answer to all the questions that can possibly be asked about it. It, and it alone, is a perfect individual.

But, if so, it will be best understood in the light of those finite realities whose nature approximates most closely to its own. In other words, individuality is the criterion by which we may estimate the comparative truth of different conceptions of the universe. For Reality is completely individual, and the more individual is the more real.

(3) The task of philosophy would then be to arrange the different kinds of things we know in experience in a logical order[1] or rank, according to their different degrees of fulness and individuality. This was done in the most complete and ambitious way by Hegel ; and, though we may not accept his system in detail, the broad principle remains that, as we turn our attention from inorganic matter to living organism and from this to self-conscious and self-directing mind, we are on an ascending scale of individuality and concreteness.

In illustration of this principle, Professor A. E. Taylor[2] takes the instances of a cluster of mass-particles, a machine, a living organism, and a human mind engaged

---

[1] This will not necessarily correspond to the chronological order of development.
[2] *Elements of Metaphysics*, book ii. chap. iii.

in the conscious systematic pursuit of truth. All these constitute individual wholes, but they do so in different degrees. To understand how they came to be what they are and the cause of the changes that take place within them, we have, with the earlier of these, to go much more outside them ; the further we get, the more do we find the answer to such questions within the subject about which the questions are asked. Thus the mass-particles are very much the same, whether in or out of this particular cluster ; the fact that they form a collection is more or less accidental to their nature. But the changes in an organism are to some extent due to the needs of the organism. There is a sense in which the organism may be said to dictate its own detail to a much greater degree than the cluster or even the machine. When we come to the stage of mind or spirit, this is much more true still. There is less in the character of a thinking man than in the character of a plant that is simply determined by the accident of environment. And within the sphere of spiritual existence itself this feature is increasingly prominent, as we turn our attention from lower to higher, from the more rudimentary to the more developed.

There are two sides to this criterion which tend to coincide, though, at our level of experience, they do not coincide absolutely. On the one hand, the higher includes more. In a real sense there is *more* in a man than in a mountain. This is illustrated by the fact that, in order to understand him, we have to invoke the aid of so many more sciences. There is not only a physical and a chemical, but also a biological, a psychological, and an ethical side to his being. On the other hand, what there is of him is also more highly organized. There is much less that is irrelevant : the character of the whole much more dictates its own detail. He is more of a unity, more of a microcosm, more of an *imperium in imperio* ; and so he is more of an individual.

It takes more to explain him; but the explanation, when we get it, is more of an explanation.

The nature of this distinction between different degrees of truth may be made more clear by an analogy from the region of spiritual experience, that has often been used for this purpose. An aesthetic whole, such as *Hamlet*, is expressed in language, and the language is subject to the rules of grammar. It would be possible to write an account of the play from a purely grammatical point of view; and the account would be true so far as it went, even if not very illuminating. But if we want really to understand *Hamlet*, we are carried enormously nearer to our goal by a criticism such as we find in Professor A. C. Bradley's *Shakespearean Tragedy*, which is chiefly in terms of meanings and motives. The suggestion of our argument then would be that even physical nature is most truly understood as being part of a spiritual order; and that a merely physical explanation of the universe is abstract and inadequate in the same sort of way as a merely grammatical explanation of *Hamlet*.

On these lines, a man is more individual, and therefore more like the Absolute, than a watch. A watch is explained mainly by its relation to human purposes; a man is explained more by the statement of what sort of fellow he is. And our argument may seem to suggest that a mountain, when fully understood, is to be assimilated in this respect to a watch. But, at this point, we shall probably take alarm. A watch is an artificial object, made by a human watchmaker for the use of a human purchaser. But this is precisely the difference between artificial and natural objects. We cannot, now, easily believe that the fruits of the earth were made by a divine artificer simply for the use of human beings; still less that God made the Matterhorn simply for the enjoyment of mountaineers.

But the view we are advocating is not the old-fashioned teleology which made Nature simply the plaything or the servant of Man; but only that the highest we know in ourselves is a clue to the deepest nature of all reality. Whether this is sound or not, it is not anthropomorphic [1] in the old objectionable sense. We are not trying to reduce Nature to a dependency of Man, but saying that the deepest character of both is akin; and that, though the interpretation of the physicist is true for certain purposes and within certain limits, such an interpretation as the poet Wordsworth's carries us nearer to ultimate truth.[2] It is not necessary to hold that the whole universe centres round, and depends on, members of the zoological genus *homo*, in order to affirm with Mr. Bradley that "Outside of spirit there is not and there cannot be any reality, and the more that anything is spiritual, so much the more is it veritably real."[3]

The great obstacle to our reception of such a view lies in our obsession by certain inveterate prejudices, which all the great philosophies carry us beyond. We tend to think of the universe as primarily spatial; and we picture Space as a sort of gigantic box, with the human race, like a colony of insects, occupying a tiny corner inside it. And, whatever the qualities of the insects, the box is what it is, independently of them. Or we picture Time as a line, stretching infinitely in either direction; and all spiritual experience as comprised in human history, which occupies only a small section of the line. And, in this way, we get a totally inadequate conception of reality. We think of it as that which occupies space and can be tested by the senses of sight and touch. Or, at a slightly more advanced stage, we

---

[1] I would suggest that the fault of "anthropomorphism" lies, not so much in forgetting the littleness of man in comparison with the immensity of the physical universe, as in taking our average experience rather than our highest for a clue to the nature of ultimate reality.

[2] We are not so much saying that Nature is the creature of Man, as that what is deepest in ourselves is also deepest in Nature. It does not follow that the Matterhorn, as a separate entity, has "a soul"; but only that it is not independently real, and that its reality consists in its membership of a world of which the deepest nature is spiritual.

[3] *Appearance and Reality*, p. 552.

think of it as a series of events in Time. And so we make a sharp division : everything is either real or unreal, according as it has or has not occurred in Time, and there is no room for degrees of reality. But we need to realize that this is simply prejudice. It has the authority neither of general experience nor of the philosopher. (*a*) It is, according to Dr. Bosanquet's important distinction,[1] " common sense theory " not " common sense." Our first theorizings are very much poorer than our actual experience ; and it may need a genuine seer to discover the true philosophy of common sense. So here, Nature—the woods and the flowers, the rainbow and the sunset—is to naturalist, poet and painter very much more than a mere collocation of atoms or whatever may be the purely physical account of it. That account represents the experience of the average man as little as does Mr. Gradgrind in Dickens's *Hard Times*, who dismisses everything but pure selfishness and materialism in human life as sentiment and moonshine.[2] (*b*) All the great thinkers, though disagreeing in much, carry us beyond this first unreflective formulation of experience. We have ample authority for the assertion that it is only low-grade realities of which physical tests can be the main tests or reveal the essence. Of such things, indeed, appearance in space and time may be the chief test, for they contain little more. But the higher we get, the less relevant do these become ; and it is not quantity but quality, not extent in space or time so much as intensity and spirituality,[3] which are the criteria of reality.[4]

---

[1] *Individuality and Value*, p. 261.

[2] Not that the physical account is untrue ; but it is so far from the whole truth that, if taken as the whole, it becomes relatively untrue.

[3] The term "spiritual" is sometimes used in a narrower, and more definitely pietistic, sense than here. At this stage of our argument, at least, we should not be justified in using it with this meaning. Here "the more spiritual" means simply that which, having a psychical side, is the more developed and individual.

[4] For philosophical statements of the argument of this section, see Bradley, *Appearance and Reality*, chaps. xxiv. and xxvi. (pp. 486-499), and Taylor, *Elements of Metaphysics*, book ii. chap. iii.

Objections to this View

Though there is a certain weight of philosophical authority behind this sort of argument, there can be no doubt that it sticks in the throat of the ordinary man. Not only does the result seem too good to be true, but the argument, by which it is established, seems too glib to be sound. It is only candid to admit that it leaves on our minds the impression of a conjuring trick, a feat of logical legerdemain. Hence, even if we see no flaw in the argument, we are apt not to be really moved by it; but rather to feel of it, as Hume felt of Berkeley's argument, that "it admits of no refutation and produces no conviction."

It is difficult, if not impossible, to allay such a suspicion by argument. I believe that it is strongest at a first hearing, and that the more the reasoning is studied, the less does the impression of trickery remain. It is impossible within the limits of this essay to discuss the question properly. But it may be worth while to try to make the nature and the bearing of the argument a little clearer by considering two of the most obvious objections.

(1) It will be felt that our whole procedure is anthropomorphic; and that we are guilty of a "provincialism" in trying to interpret the Universe as a whole from the standpoint of our own corner of it. We may be pointed to the temper of Spinoza as exhibiting that detachment and power to rise above a personal point of view, which is essential to the apprehension of truth, and which is in sharp contrast to our glorification of what is human.

Thus, if intelligibility is to be our criterion of what is real, it is natural, it may be said, that an interpretation of Reality as Mind, after the analogy of the thinking subject, should appear the truest. But nothing is more deeply rooted in men's minds, and nothing is more

continually attested in experience through surprise and
disappointment, than the contrast between fact and
what we think about fact. Thought is one thing and
Reality is another. What right have we to assume *a
priori* that the nature of the world is what would suit
our purposes best either in practice or in speculation ?
A world of which Mind was the heart would be the
easiest for Mind to comprehend. But does it therefore
follow that the real world has this character ?

It is worth while to formulate this difficulty,
because we all feel it. But it involves a misappre-
hension of the argument which it criticizes. It rests
on assumptions :

(*a*) of which the history of philosophy shows the
futility,

(*b*) which we have already set aside as misleading,

(*c*) of which the origin and fallacy can be detected
and exposed.

(*a*) The great English thinkers of the seventeenth
and eighteenth centuries tried to work with the
distinction between " reality " and " the work of the
mind." This ended with Hume in Scepticism, and
the distinction broke down. In their effort to use
it, they found themselves more and more forced to
attribute everything that we ordinarily think real to
the work of the mind ; while " the real " became
more and more remote till it finally vanished altogether.

(*b*) The antithesis is one which, in our rejection of
agnosticism, we have deliberately set aside. If our
method is sound, the ordinary distinction between fact
and fancy is relative ; for it arises within experience.
It is true that the Absolute has not the same kind of
reality as a stone or any other finite thing : it has not
a particular place in space and time. But this is only
because it is the presupposition of all other realities ;
and their reality consists in relation to it. Error, no
doubt, is a fact of experience : it actually does occur.
But if it is argued from this that we can never be sure

of anything as we must always allow for the abstract possibility of error, the inference is unsound. All thought is *prima facie* an apprehension of reality. And though some thought may be doubted or even labelled as error, it is not possible with clear understanding of the issue to doubt that the totality of things is a rational system ; for it is only the assumption of this that gives meaning either to certainty or to doubt about the existence of finite reals.

Whatever then we are forced to think by the very constitution of the mind, is true of reality. The "laws of thought" are laws of reality.[1] There is no alternative. "Reality" means this or it means nothing.

(*c*) The antithesis arises from the fallacious notion that "thought" is an idiosyncrasy, a part of the psychological furniture of an individual mind. Thought, it is said, begins at home ; the immediate data of thought are our own ideas ; the question of their correspondence or non-correspondence with any reality beyond ourselves is a matter to be settled by subsequent inference. If this were true, "necessities of thought" would not be a certain guide to the nature of reality, for I have a well-grounded sense of " my " littleness and a consequent distrust of " my " intellectual competence.

But it is false. It rests on a double confusion :—

(i.) There is a confusion between two different aspects of "idea." An idea is really complex. It is at once an act of awareness and a content of which we are aware, a process and an object of thought. It is active and passive ; a thinking and a thought. Now to say, with Locke, that all our knowledge begins with ideas, is to say something ambiguous. If it means merely that we cannot apprehend anything without a movement, as it were, of our mental machinery, it is true.

---

[1] This may sound fanciful, but the ordinary man really agrees with it. He does not think of the proposition $2 \times 2 = 4$ as being merely a way in which men are psychologically impelled to think. He believes that twice two *is* four.

If it means that that about which we think must be intelligible, or capable of being thought about, it is again true. But it is apt to mean something which is different from either of these and which is not true ; namely, that the immediate objects of our knowledge are " subjective states " as distinct from real objects outside us. The second aspect of idea—the passive object of thought—is first isolated, and then it is invested with qualities which only belong to the first aspect, *i.e.* it is treated as being a part of the individual thinker. The nature of the fallacy may be made clear by an analogy. " It arises, perhaps, from a confusion between the standpoint of one person perceiving objects and that of another person watching the image on his retina while he is perceiving objects. The watcher drifts into the notion that this image *is* the object that his companion perceives." [1] Owing to this confusion between the *instrument* and the *object* of thought, the latter is invested with a limitation and a subjectivity that do not properly belong to it.

(ii.) Another, but very nearly related, confusion is the confusion between experience and " *my* experience." A " note " of modern thought is its determination to criticize all assumptions and to get back to the bedrock of actual experience. " Experience is the beginning and the end of philosophy. . . . This does not mean that we beg the question of philosophy, that we assume what we ought to prove and exclude a sceptical result. We merely state what is the matter in question. All questions must be answered, all doubts resolved, out of experience itself, as within experience the questions and the doubts arise." [2] Experience then is the datum which we must assume and cannot go behind. Now resolute criticism is always good, unless it is half-hearted ; but for an arbitrary mixture of criticism and uncritical assumption there is nothing to be said. And

[1] A. C. Pigou, *The Problem of Theism*, p. 6.
[2] W. Richmond, *Personality as a Philosophical Principle*, pp. 4-5.

yet we are guilty of this if we suppose that this insistence on actuality and on real experience as the basis of thought necessarily involves "subjectivism." If I say that to begin with experience means to begin with "*my* experience," I am at once making an enormous assumption and am sophisticating experience by reading into it the confused and uncritical conception of "myself" with which I ordinarily operate.

Even if, on an analysis of experience similar to Kant's, it should turn out that all experience involves a conscious centre by which it is experienced, it is quite unscientific to identify at once this centre with the historical individual, whom the biographer and the historian commemorate, who is limited to a particular corner of space, and whose days are only threescore years and ten. Whatever the conclusions of philosophy, we must not tamper with its premisses in this way. And yet it is as a result of some such misreading of premisses that philosophy comes to wear a sceptical or agnostic appearance.

Something like this confusion was the chief defect of Descartes and his English successors. They all started from the point of view of the isolated individual. And the inner logic of the whole movement from Descartes to Kant was the gradual getting rid of this assumption as its implications became clearer. Few thinkers would to-day care to commit themselves to most of the details of the Kantian system ; but it remains the permanent merit of Kant that he refused to look at thought or knowledge purely from the psychological end ; and that he insisted that in thought there is something of a universal character, which lifts the individual thinker, so far as he is true to its laws, above the limitations of his private corner and enables him to become, in some measure, a spectator of all time and all existence. It is the old pre-Kantian fallacy, in a more or less concealed form, which is really at the root of the prejudice against the acceptance of· the canons of thought as a sure

GOD AND THE ABSOLUTE

guide to reality ; and we may fairly speak of it as
" exploded." [1]

(2) There is another difficulty, arising out of our
method. "Suppose," it may be said, " that we accept
your whole argument at its face-value, how much does it
amount to ? You have argued that our first principles
are just hypotheses which work, and that the only kind
of proof to which they are susceptible is verification.
And, on those lines, you suggest that the conception of
the universe as an intelligible system, best described in
terms of mind or spirit, is that which best fits the facts
and explains most ; and hence that you are justified in
assuming its truth. But even if we admit the cogency
of your argument, you seem to us to be in danger of
overestimating your results. A working hypothesis is
not a certainty ; and it is always liable to be displaced
by an hypothesis which works better still. Both Logic
and the analogy of the Sciences suggest the expediency
of a certain healthy scepticism."

(*a*) Logicians warn us that verification is not proof.
The discovery of a fact inconsistent with our hypothesis
would indeed be a sign of error ; and the knowledge
that a wide range of facts is consistent with our theory
makes no doubt in favour of its truth. But though
inconsistency is a mark of error, consistency is not an
absolute guarantee of truth. Indeed, logicians have
formally classed among the fallacies [2] the confusion of
verification and proof.

(*b*) The Sciences get at their widest generalizations
in just this way. But it is notorious that precisely
these widest principles are most liable to change. The
physicist appears to the layman to be always inventing

[1] A distinctive feature of Modernism in theology is its appeal to religious
"experience." It is widely distrusted because it seems in this to do away with
objective fact, to make the psychology of individuals the ultimate court of appeal in
all religious issues, and to make religion a matter of nice feelings rather than of our
relation to the Power behind the universe. This distrust is justified, just so far as
the Modernist makes the confusion here suggested between " experience " and " my
experience."
[2] The " Fallacy of the Consequent." Cf. Joseph, *Introduction to Logic*, p. 555.

new hypotheses as to the ultimate constitution of matter. But the science of physics survives such changes without difficulty. Even so enormous a revolution as the change from the Ptolemaic to the Copernican system of astronomy is not incompatible with a real continuity in the science. This analogy then would be unfavourable to any claim for axiomatic certainty on behalf of philosophical first principles arrived at by our method. In fine, a working hypothesis may claim a provisional acceptance. But we shall not stake much on it ; it will have no martyrs.

The reality then of the Absolute and its interpretation in terms of mind are, it is suggested, merely convenient " assumptions " or " postulates." The sting of this suggestion lies in the word " merely." For the use of this term implies a contrast with some superior kind of certainty, to which our knowledge of the Absolute does not attain. But this is an illusion. That "assumption" on which all other beliefs depend is not a *mere* assumption. Its certainty is at least equal to any other certainty in the world ; and therefore, since pure scepticism is irrational, is the highest conceivable certainty. Our method is more living and more elastic than the old demonstrative method ; but its fundamental principles are not less certain.

Hence the analogy of the Sciences is misleading. Even the greatest scientific changes leave us with one identical world, though we now see certain aspects of it to be different from what we previously thought. But to deny the systematic character of the Universe as the one absolute ground of all that is, or its determination by such laws as are inherent, not in the psychology of an individual thinker, but in the very nature of thought itself, would be—if we understood what we were doing— to dissolve the whole world in destruction and chaos, and to put an end to all continuous mental life and sanity.

V. The Absolute is Good

For religion it is not enough to prove that the world is a Cosmos ; it will not be satisfied unless that Cosmos is of a character which justifies an attitude of worship. Is the Absolute properly to be called God? Is it such as to vindicate our notions of moral and religious values? This is the real issue between the religious man and " the fool who says in his heart, ' There is no God.' "

A. *The Argument from the nature of moral experience.*—We have so far argued that whatever is necessary to the validity of experience is *eo ipso* true ; and that the existence of the Absolute is in this way necessary. In the same way, it is suggested, the goodness of the Absolute is necessary to the validity of moral experience. The association of morality and religion is for us traditional. Religious beliefs, we have probably been taught, are the source of the binding force of moral obligations. Hence it may easily appear that we cannot abandon the beliefs without relaxing the obligations.

Yet we now learn from anthropologists that morality and religion were surprisingly independent in their early developments. And to-day our " Ethical Societies " witness to a renewed tendency to assert the independence of morality from all scientific, religious and philosophical beliefs about the ultimate nature of the universe. Thus it is argued (*a*) that, in the nature of the case, " good " and " real " are quite different and disconnected predicates ; (*β*) that a morality which is independent of metaphysics is morally the highest ; and that goodness shines brightest when it is quite independent of reward and even when the whole universe conspires to crush it.

This protest embodies a real nobility of temper. And yet it is directed mainly against a caricature ; though one for which some of those who would connect morality and theology are largely responsible. Thus the optimistic view of reality has been maintained on false grounds, and, more particularly, in two senses which I should wish to disavow before stating what seems to me the real strength of the argument.

(*a*) Hardly any one would now support the naked position of Locke and Paley, that morality is only binding as being the command of an authority which can punish resistance. Such a view was stated in its baldest terms by Locke : " The true ground of morality can only be the will and law of a God who sees men in the dark, has in His hands rewards and punishments, and power enough to call to account the proudest offender." [1] Such a position is rightly condemned in the name of morality itself. God's will can be morally binding on men only because God wills the good, not because He is a supremely powerful being.

(*b*) There is another argument, which is certainly on a very different level to the last, and which yet, I confess, is to me unconvincing. It is said that the sense of *obligation* which characterizes conscience implies man's responsibility to a personal Author of the moral law, for law implies a lawgiver. This line of argument, it seems to me, has been undermined by the spread of democracy. To men's minds to-day, neither the origin nor the validity of human laws implies a monarchical lawgiver. We look upon laws as deriving authority not merely from a sovereign but from the consent of the general body of those whom they are to direct. Ancient fancy thought that the source of the laws of Athens or Sparta could only have been an individual legislator, a Solon or Lycurgus. To us, this is mere mythology.

Now Morality implies a standard or ideal of life. And the true argument from moral experience is not that this ideal needs an external certificate or guarantee, but that in its intrinsic nature *as moral ideal* there is implied an optimistic view of the character of ultimate reality. A moral ideal claims to be more than a matter

---

[1] *Essay concerning Human Understanding*, vol. i. p. 70.

of private taste. But the very meaning of this claim to validity is the assumption that the ideal is grounded in the deepest nature of things.

If I ask, "Why should I be moral?" I do not necessarily want to be pointed to rewards attached to goodness by a *deus ex machina* ; but I do want to be assured that the nature of the universe is not such as to make the pursuit of morality mere vanity. As Kant argued with force, " Ought implies can." A true ideal must be realizable : an obligation, to be binding, must admit of fulfilment, otherwise morality would be self-contradictory. Again, I may ask what is the content of the good ? Is the moral ideal self-realization, or do self-sacrifice and asceticism enter into it? If they have some place, how far are they to be cultivated ? It is impossible to answer such questions except by reference to some positive convictions as to the true nature of man and his relation to the universe in which he has his being. An ideal to be true even as an ideal must be founded on reality. " Man cannot permanently live on fictions." [1]

Moreover, a tacit appeal to reality is, in the end, the standard of our moral judgments. It is true that we often admire and commend the rebel. We admire Prometheus' defiance of Zeus, Mill's defiance of the God of popular Calvinism, Huxley's call to man to withstand the cosmic process. But what is the difference between these rebels and the anarchist, who rebels against all social institutions and all restraint on the gratification of impulse, or the suicide who rebels against life itself ? Is it not just this,—that, where we commend the rebel, we believe him to be appealing to a deeper and more enduring, though more intangible, reality behind the tyrant of heaven and the process of the physical world ?

The moral consciousness not only demands a certain backing of fact if it is not to be stultified, but it makes

---

[1] Cf. Essay I. p. 12.

a draft which can only be honoured by reality in its most ultimate and absolute form. This is shown by the "infinite" character of the moral demand, which moralists have so often noted, as in the case of Carlyle's "shoeblack," who would require for the permanent satisfaction of his soul nothing less than "God's infinite universe altogether to himself." And—though this is perhaps more debatable—it may be doubted whether moral experience does not postulate a certain kinship between man and the heart of the universe such as is expressed in the old pictorial sayings, "God made man in His own image," and "Be ye holy as I am holy."

In any case, some such claim does seem to be made. There appears to be a disinterested demand on the part of goodness itself that the universe should justify it, that the stars in their courses should fight for righteousness. This demand has nothing in common with the desire for personal reward. It is a quite impersonal feeling. "How completely the dignity and glory of the world depend on our finding this moral colouring in the ultimate background of all being is nobly expressed in the words of Socrates, 'If the rulers of the universe do not prefer the just man to the unjust, it is better to die than to live.'"[1] In fine, men naturally reject the notion of an evil universe as incredible ; "witness the attempts to overcome 'the problem of evil,' the mystery of pain. There is no problem of good."[2]

B. *Objections.*—Even if it be admitted that moral experience seems to postulate the goodness of the Absolute, it may still be felt th such a postulate does not settle the question of fact. Morality may lose its speculative justification unless the Universe is moral, but that does not prove it to be so.

(1) In fact, the experience of pain, sin and death

---

[1] Martineau, *Types of Ethical Theory*, vol. ii. p. 105.
[2] James, *Principles of Psychology*, p. 312.

seems to contradict any such postulate. Is there not, we may feel, something paradoxical, in making the very experience of these things itself an evidence for the view that they are not ultimate or permanent ? To make the experience of disappointment itself an argument against the possibility that the universe, when fully understood, may turn out to be disappointing is, we may feel, audacious but hardly common sense. Does it amount to more than a childish refusal to face the facts ? Our experience is in fact chequered and parti-coloured ; is it not the part of courage and sincerity to accept it for what it is ? (We all know the natural instinct to refuse to listen to bad news : " It can't be so ; I won't believe it," we say ; but it is so none the less.) We cannot regard the mere fact that we wish for reassurance as being itself the reassurance required. In short, an *a priori* theory that the universe must be good does not fit the facts ; its very boldness condemns it. Even if optimism were a possible conclusion, even if we could come to hope that " at last, far off, at last to all " the universe should be revealed as good, so sweeping a judgment cannot be a starting-point.

(2) It is true that we have made satisfaction of the mind the test of truth. But if it is argued that the notion of an incompletely good Universe fails to satisfy the mind and is therefore untrue, we may naturally suspect the argument of some looseness of thought. Terms such as " incoherence," " unintelligible," " problem " sound plausible, but are they not used in more than one sense ? We ought, it may be said, to distinguish intellectual from practical satisfaction. The Universe must necessarily be rational and intelligible, but it need not therefore be the sort of universe we should like. In this connection, the illustration has been used of a physician's diagnosis of an incurable disease. In discovering the cause of his patient's symptoms he gains intellectual satisfaction, and the fact that the diagnosis explains the symptoms is an

evidence of its truth ; yet it completely frustrates his practical aim, which is to cure the patient. So it is, it may be, with the theory of the universe. That it should explain the facts of the world is a test of its truth, but not that it should explain them as being of such a nature as to further our purposes.

(3) As a general principle it may be felt that arguments from desires are inadmissible. They commit the fault of arguing from a corner of the universe to the whole, and this is a provincialism. The savage's conception of God is compounded of his hopes and fears, and should be a warning to the civilized thinker against the same mistake. As thinker or rational being, a man may be able to rise above his individuality and to attain an impartial position, but he only does this, and he only thinks truly, in so far as he frees himself from private prejudices and idiosyncrasies. His desires belong to that particular psychological constitution from which he is to free himself. Why should he assume that the universe is constructed to meet his own particular needs and likings any more than an insect's ? Perhaps it may be with human morality, in relation to the Universe, as it was with the starving man in the old story who stole a loaf of bread. " Il faut vivre," he pleaded ; "je n'en vois pas la nécessité," replied the magistrate.

> So runs my dream : but what am I ?
> An infant crying in the night,
> An infant crying for the light,
> And with no language but a cry.

C. *A familiar line of reply.*—To these difficulties there is a familiar line of reply. It is said that to preach such an intellectual asceticism is to condemn the actual thinking of mankind, in general, by reference to some impossible rationalistic ideal, which vanishes before a more exact analysis of the complex processes of actual thought. The appeal is from the schools to real life, from a bloodless academic criticism to the beliefs of the millions. We all know the special danger of academic minds ; their proneness to a one-sided development of criticism with a corresponding atrophy of the constructive powers. A morbid fear of error is apt to produce a mind and character of which Hamlet is the supreme type in literature, and which is unable to make either practical or theoretical decisions. The suggestion is that the negative tendency of such arguments as those of the preceding Section are due to a hyper-criticism of this kind.

Thus James insists that men do, in fact, assume that reality must be such as to satisfy their wider and more permanent needs. He appeals in support of this to a sort of survival of the fittest. Outside the study and in the stress of real life, no pessimism can maintain its ground. Men *will not* in the long run accept any philosophy which runs counter to their dearest desires, and which would put a check on the realization of their practical purposes. Thus neither Solipsism nor Materialism, for both of which there is much to be said in theory, have ever gained even the serious attention of the mass of men. But the more optimistic views are justified by the historical fact that it is those who hold them who make the most of life. " If we survey the field of history and ask what feature all great periods of revival, of expansion of the human mind, display in common, we shall find, I think, simply this, that each and all of them has said to the human being : the inmost nature of the reality is congenial to the powers you possess." [1]

---

[1] James, *Principles of Psychology*, ii. p. 314. The whole of chapter xxi. is full of assertions of the influence of the will and the emotions on our actual beliefs. " A nameless *Unheimlichkeit* comes over us at the thought of there being nothing eternal in our final purposes, in the objects of those loves and aspirations which are our deepest energies. The monstrously lop-sided equation of the universe and its *knower*, which we postulate as the ideal of cognition, is perfectly paralleled by the no less lop-sided equation of the universe and the *doer*. We demand in it a *character* for which our emotions and active propensities shall be a match. Small as we are, minute as is the point by which the Cosmos impinges upon each one of us, each one desires to feel that his reaction at that point is congruous with the demands of the vast whole ; that he balances the latter, so to speak, and is able to do what it expects of him. But

Hence, it is suggested, a refusal to accept all beliefs for which formal logical proof cannot be adduced is a mistake. We should rather begin from the other end, and take those concrete beliefs of which we are most certain and then analyse the way in which we arrived at them. The methods by which such beliefs are actually reached are much more complex and subtle than our ordinary canons allow; but it is the canons which need revision. The method by which real assent is reached is described by Newman. The mind, he holds, "passes from point to point, gaining one by some indication; another on a probability; then availing itself of an association; then falling back on some received law, next seizing on testimony; then committing itself to some popular impression, or some inward instinct, or some obscure memory; and thus it makes progress not unlike a clamberer on a steep cliff, who, by quick eye, prompt hand, and firm foot, ascends how he knows not himself, by personal endowments and by practice rather than by rule." [1] This really amounts to a defence of democracy in thinking. We can no more, it is suggested, go behind the actual procedure of the mind in dealing with moral issues than we can go behind its procedure when we find it, in all thought, taking contradiction to be a test of error and conceivability a mark of truth.

Intellectual objections will be met with a *tu quoque.* If exact logical proof is to be demanded, not only the conclusions of the theologian but all beliefs, including those of the scientist, will be condemned. Mr. Balfour takes this line in *The Foundations of Belief.* All knowledge, he holds, and not merely the optimistic conception

---

as his abilities to " do " lie wholly in the line of his natural propensities, as he enjoys reaction with such emotions as fortitude, hope, rapture, admiration, earnestness and the like, and as he very unwillingly reacts with fear, disgust, despair or doubt, a philosophy which should legitimate only emotions of the latter sort would be sure to leave the mind a prey to discontent and cravings.

[1] *University Sermons,* XIII.

of the universe, is based on non-rational foundations. Everywhere the working cause of belief is "Authority"; by which seems to be meant a kind of inherited instinct, much stimulated by common social life. There would then be no reason for treating the beliefs of religion about the character of the universe with less respect than those of science.

D. *Further objections.*—A defence of theistic belief on these lines is always open to the objection that it is beside the mark. It may be true that we have a natural propensity to believe in that which we should like, but it does not follow that this natural propensity is a guide to truth. An analysis of belief such as is given by Newman or James, however penetrating, is, it may be felt, at best a matter of psychology, not of logic. It gives us a "grammar of assent" but not a criterion of truth, and it would apply not only to true beliefs but to all beliefs which are actually held. Leslie Stephen makes this objection to Newman. Newman only gives us, he says, "a theory of the methods by which men are convinced, not of the methods by which doctrines are proved; and an account of the assumptions upon which creeds in fact rest, rather than an account of the marks by which we may recognize the verified assumptions entitled to be regarded as established truths." [1] The real problem, on the other hand, "is concerned, not with what certain persons do, as a matter of fact, believe, but with what is really true, and, therefore, *ought* to be believed. The fact that, under the immediate spell of an experience, men are forced psychologically to adopt a particular theoretic conclusion is not a proof of that conclusion so cogent that it can be proclaimed *a priori* irrefutable by any conceivable objections." [2]

Further, if this line of defence is pressed to its

---

[1] Leslie Stephen, *An Agnostic's Apology*, p. 209.
[2] A. C. Pigou, *The Problem of Theism*, p. 48.   Cf. Bradley, *Appearance and Reality*, p. 151.

logical conclusion, the result would be favourable not to orthodoxy but to scepticism ; and apologists who use such weapons are often warned that they are handling a two-edged sword and, indeed, incur some suspicion of controversial dishonesty. It is no doubt conceivable that there may be a final contradiction between what we see to be true, when we use our reasoning faculties, and what we are impelled to believe by an irresistible non-rational instinct as soon as we cease to reason ; just as Hume admitted that, as soon as he left his study, he found himself at once accepting the common beliefs of other men, which nevertheless, as a philosopher, he thought he had proved to be mistaken. But if all beliefs depend in this way on fortuitous circumstances connected with the likes and dislikes of individuals, that is only to say that we have no means of distinguishing truth from falsehood, and, if so, it would be mere hypocrisy to contemplate the possibility of a "Natural Theology." In ordinary life a belief which is shown to be congenial to the moral and emotional needs of the believer is so far discredited, because we have found a reason why it should have come to be believed even if it were not true. We always suspect an "interested party." "To assign the conditions of a belief is often to prove its error. If we show that belief in a criminal's fault is associated with dislike of his person, the verdict of a jury loses its force." [1]

Lastly, the practical moral which such apologists preach, it will be felt, is execrable. William James has well shown how, in a case such as the suggestion of witchcraft where men's instincts of revulsion are aroused, the very vividness of their sensations compels belief. But this is the most fertile source of superstition and error. To advise us to trust such instincts is the worst kind of obscurantism. It is deliberately to take prejudice for a guide. The way to truth is through

---

[1] Leslie Stephen, *op. cit.* p. 225.

keeping our minds clear of such disturbing influences.
Aristotle long ago warned us in deciding questions of
conduct to beware especially of pleasure. The very
fact that we have a natural wish to do what is pleasant
with a clear conscience should cause us rather to
suspect our judgment when it is in favour of such a
course. James himself, who asserts that " every exciting thought in the natural man carries its own
credence with it," goes on to say that " the greatest
proof that a man is *sui compos* is his ability to suspend
belief in the presence of an emotionally exciting idea.
To give this power is the highest result of education ;
in untutored minds the power does not exist." And
Leslie Stephen commends to us Locke's famous canon :
" There is one unerring mark by which a man may
know whether he is a lover of truth in earnest, viz.
the not entertaining any proposition with greater
assurance than the proofs it is built on will warrant." [1]

E. *Final reasons for asserting the goodness of the*

[1] A most moving illustration of the possibility of dissociating truth from the
objects of the most sacred longings is to be found in the poignant passage at the
end of Romanes' *Candid Examination of Theism* (p. 114) : " So far as the ruination of
individual happiness is concerned, no one can have a more lively perception than
myself of the possibly disastrous tendency of my work. So far as I am individually
concerned, the result of this analysis has been to show that, whether I regard the
problem of Theism on the lower plane of strictly relative probability, or on the
higher plane of purely formal considerations, it equally becomes my obvious duty to
stifle all belief of the kind which I conceive to be the noblest, and to discipline my
intellect with regard to this mattter into an attitude of the purest scepticism. And
forasmuch as I am far from being able to agree with those who affirm that the
twilight doctrine of the 'new faith' is a desirable substitute for the waning
splendour of 'the old,' I am not ashamed to confess that with this virtual
negation of God, the universe to me has lost its soul of loveliness ; and although
from henceforth the precept to 'work while it is day' will doubtless but gain an
intensified force from the terribly intensified meaning of the words that 'the night
cometh when no man can work,' yet when at times I think, as think at times I
must, of the appalling contrast between the hallowed glory of that creed which once
was mine, and the lonely mystery of existence as now I find it,—at such times I
shall ever feel it impossible to avoid the sharpest pang of which my nature is
susceptible. For whether it is due to my intelligence not being sufficiently
advanced to meet the requirements of the age, or whether it is due to the memory
of those sacred associations which to me at least were the sweetest that life has
given, I cannot but feel that for me and for others who think as I do, there is a
dreadful truth in those words of Hamilton—Philosophy having become a meditation,
not merely of death, but of annihilation, the precept *know thyself* has become
transformed into the terrific oracle to Oedipus—
      " 'Mayest thou ne'er know the truth of what thou art ! ' "

Absolute in spite of all objections.—We have already argued that the intellect does not normally work in abstraction from will and emotion, and that it is, in fact, a natural tendency of the human mind to assume that the Absolute must conform to the ideal of human character as well as to the ideal of human thought. But we have to face the difficulty that this fact is not allowed to be evidence for the validity of any such process. We have not only to show that we have such and such intuitions, but that we have good reason for trusting them.

Now we have already had to face a similar question in regard to the validity of any of our thought. In the development of mind, the first stage is credulity and the second scepticism. But any philosophy that we can accept must, as we have seen, combine these two ; yet in such a way that the element of scepticism is secondary. Though error does actually occur, we nevertheless believe it possible to distinguish between truth and error, between what is merely individual and subjective and what belongs to the necessary constitution of the mind and is therefore objective. But some philosophers, who uphold this general conception of the relation between thought and reality, would yet argue that our mental demand for goodness in the Absolute is not *necessarily* sound, on the ground that it is departmental, arising only from one province of experience, and so may be modified and corrected by wider considerations, while its rejection will not imperil Experience as a whole ; and that it is not *in fact* sound, on the ground that we fall into contradictions when we try to think of the Absolute in such terms.

I do not think that this modified scepticism is itself tenable, for I believe that the isolation of the pure intellect which it postulates is a vicious abstraction.

(1) *Pure thought is not the best instrument for the apprehension of all kinds of truth.*—It is suggested that to take account of our moral and emotional needs is to

import prejudice into the search for truth. Against
this an ideal of intellectual asceticism is held up to us.
The intellect works best, we are told, when most
thoroughly disentangled from the other functions of
our being.   But when such a demand is made, it
becomes important to notice that this is not equally
true everywhere.   An abstract science, such as Mathe-
matics, may be best pursued by an abstract method, but
when it is knowledge of persons that is in question and
of the concrete issues which arise out of personal
relations, another method is required.   For true knowledge of a person not only intellectual discernment but
emotional affinity and power of sympathy are necessary.
This is admittedly true even in historical judgments ; it
is still more clearly true when we are dealing with
living persons.

> God be thanked, the meanest of His creatures
> Boasts two soul-sides, one to face the world with,
> One to show a woman when he loves her.

Love is here not a hindrance to, but a necessary condition of, knowledge.   The best judge will not be he
who is most completely remote from the common
passions of human nature.

In dealing with moral problems, purely intellectual
beings, such as the Martians in Mr. Wells's *War of the
Worlds*, would be completely at a loss.   " There has
been, suppose, dishonesty in a boys' or girls' school.
There are difficult questions of evidence as to facts
and the interpretation of facts and the interpretation of
character to unravel.   You need ready wit and keenness
of intellectual discernment.   But intellect, however
keen, which is intellect only, intellect which is not the
intellect of a moral consciousness, will not disentangle
aright—will not even understand—the most crucial
parts of the evidence.   Parts of the evidence there
may be which it will discern perfectly.   But the most
determining evidence of all will be in a region to which

it has no access, in a subject matter of which it has no knowledge and upon which (so to speak) its utmost keenness of edge cannot bite at all. Why was A close to the scene of the theft at that moment? Why was the money found in B's pocket? Why did this child blush, or tremble, or hesitate? Why was that one pale? or another so voluble and self-possessed? Every one of these things may have been the direct result of innocence or the direct proof of guilt. What is the moral value of a blush or a tremor, a hesitancy or a readiness to explain? The keenest intellect of the mere reason could not measure or answer at all."[1] The possession of certain moral qualities is a condition of knowledge even in philosophy. Indeed, it is impossible to exaggerate the need of super-eminent truthfulness in the thinker's search for the truth about life. There are so many subtle temptations to partisanship, and to slight exaggeration for the sake of effect, that only an unusual degree of the moral quality of single-mindedness can keep the thinker straight.

There are, then, some cases at least, and notably questions about persons and their character, in which knowledge is only possible as one aspect of a relation between persons which is more than mere knowledge, and this no doubt is what St. Paul meant by "faith." But if so, to rule out a priori from the philosopher's quest of the truth about the whole universe all influence of faculties other than pure intellect is to beg the question. If the deepest being of the universe were of a nature akin to the personal, the concrete would be better than the abstract mode of apprehension. It might indeed be the only possible method. We cannot afford, therefore, to assume beforehand that it must lead to error rather than to truth ; for to do so would be arbitrarily to foreclose the whole question, and to rule out in advance the whole theistic line of thought.

(2) *The moral and emotional demands of our nature*

[1] R. C. Moberly, *Reason and Religion*, p. 30.

*need, no more than the intellectual, be merely a personal fad
of the individual.*—It was suggested that to give way to
such demands in our interpretation of the universe was to
quit the position of impartiality and to judge the whole
world from the standpoint of a particular corner of it ;
and thinkers like Mr. Bradley [1] and Professor Taylor [2]
support this view by emphasizing the difficulties and
contradictions into which we are led, when we try to
take the moral or religious conception of the world as
ultimate.   But the case is no different here than with
the pure reason.   In each case, error is not only
possible, but is a frequent fact of experience.   In each
case, a charge of anthropomorphism may be, and is,
founded on the fact of error.   But, here as there, we
may rightly refuse to take the fact of error as the
corner-stone of our philosophy ; here as there, the
practical difficulty of disentangling truth from error
does not carry with it a belief in the speculative
impossibility of such a distinction.   In each case, the
idiosyncrasies of the individual mind may lead the
thinker astray, but, in the one case as in the other, we
may believe that it is possible to eliminate what is
merely idiosyncrasy and to leave something which is
universal and objective.

(3) *The judgments of the mass of men may be rational,
though they are not reasoned.*—The intellectual critic is too
ready to despise the argument from authority, *i.e.* from
the actual thinking of the majority of ordinary men.
The popular antithesis between instinct or authority on
the one hand and reason on the other is misleading.   It
obscures the true relation between the philosopher and
other men.   The philosopher is really related to his
fellows just as the artist is.   He is one who can express,
rather more than others, what most men obscurely feel,
and what they recognize when the genius expresses it for

---

[1] *Appearance and Reality*, ch. **xxv.**
[2] *The Problem of Conduct*, passim.   But Professor Taylor has made it clear that
this does not represent his present view.

them. The artist appeals to men's sense of the beauty that is in the world ; in the same way, the philosopher appeals to men's sense of the reason that is in the world. And with the philosopher as with the artist, the superiority of the expert to the mass of men is only relative. He can only express himself a *little* better than others. He pursues an ideal that eludes him. " The sight never beheld it, nor has the hand expressed it. It is an ideal residing in the breast of the artist, which he is always labouring to impart and which he dies at last without imparting." [1]

It does not follow from this, as the obscurantist would hold, that clearness and directness of thought are unimportant. Their absence is really a mark of imperfection, and the genius is just he who, in some measure, gets beyond this stage. The evil of not thinking out first principles is frequently manifest even in politics, where opportunism is sometimes preached as " the one thing needful " ; it is more dangerous still in religion. But it does follow that what is unmetaphysical in form is not *eo ipso* valueless. We need not accept Dr. McTaggart's pessimistic conclusion (" No man is justified in a religious attitude except as a result of metaphysical study "). The philosopher, like the artist, depends on, and makes his appeal to, the corporate consciousness of his time. It is a great mistake to ignore or minimize the continuity between this consciousness and his own more scientific expression: " that which is unreasoned is not always irrational." [2] To sacrifice richness of material to clearness of expression is the besetting sin of the student, whether freethinker or religious apologist. It is not much more rational in theology than in politics to rule out all opinion which is not metaphysical in form.

Here, as in the metaphysical examination of experience with which we began, there is a sense

---

[1] Joshua Reynolds, quoted by Palgrave in *The Golden Treasury*.
[2] Aubrey Moore in *Lux Mundi*, p. 67.

in which we cannot go behind the common consciousness of mankind. We can analyse it ; but, when
analysed, it is authoritative ; and there is no reason
for attaching less importance to moral experience than
to any other kind. Hence Optimism is ultimately a
philosophical necessity. The faith that evil is somehow[1] "appearance" is of one piece with that trust
in our faculties which alone enables us to reason at
all. Reality must be the source and justification of
our most general moral concepts as well as of our
intellectual axioms. If Reality is to be rational, it must
also be good.[2]

VI. The Bearing of the whole Argument upon Religion

So far our discussion has been abstract and remote
from the concrete religious life. It may be worth

---

[1] I am of course aware that, by the use of the word " somehow," I am shelving
some of the biggest of all questions. But I strongly hold that we cannot say less
than this ; while to say more with any confidence would require a whole treatise,
and, possibly, more of the knowledge which prophets and kings have desired than
seems at present to be granted to mortal man. Cf. Essays V. pp. 219 ff., VI. pp. 294
(footnote) and 298, and below, pp. 514-515.

[2] We are arguing that Reality must be such as to satisfy all sides of our nature,
not only the intellect in isolation. There is of course a danger, on the other hand,
that we may too hurriedly assume that *our* ideas of what is right must be the law
of the universe. We are arguing for a concrete, as opposed to an abstract, criterion,
and must, therefore, be careful not to fall from one abstraction to another. There
is a sense in which " Morality" is less than the whole of life. So far, it would be
only one province in the kingdom of the spirit, and it would be a usurpation for it to
claim absolute control over the whole.
The practical moral then would be twofold. It is not only that we must consult
our ideas of value to gain knowledge of what is real ; we must also consult our
knowledge of reality to gain knowledge of what is good. We may not only have to
modify our ideas of reality, to make them correspond to the demands of goodness ; we
may also have to modify our ideas of goodness, to make them correspond to the
nature of things. We need the warning of the late Prof. Wallace : " Let us not
be in a hurry to suppose that a discovery of the harmony of the universe, its
rationality and rightness, will reconcile it with our aspirations or our ethical needs,
at least unless we first make our ethical needs and our aspirations righteous."
No one has emphasized this more than Mr. Bradley. Yet it is he who asserts
that, " Higher, truer, more beautiful, better, more real—these, on the whole, count
in the universe as they count for us. . . . For, on the whole, higher means for us a
greater amount of the one Reality, outside of which all appearance is absolutely
nothing" (*op. cit.* p. 550). Our ultimate conceptions of value, then, like our more
purely theoretic axioms, are part of the self-revelation of the Absolute pulsing
within us.

while, in a fragmentary way and on only one or two points, to indicate its relation to the religious consciousness.

(1) *The mode of approach.*—We have argued that the Absolute is the necessary presupposition of all experience. And we claim that the argument is not open to the objection urged against the old Demonstrative "proofs," that they put more into the conclusion than is to be found in the premisses; for we do not attempt to build upon the experience of the finite as upon a firm foundation. It is not what the finite is, but rather what it is not, that drives us to accept no description of Reality as true except the fullest. No doubt, on reflection, we see that this means that a sense of the Absolute was inherent in experience from the beginning; and it is for that reason that a rational being can never stop in his quest for Reality until he finds a conception of it which gives complete intellectual satisfaction. He has not grasped Reality, until he has found that which is all-embracing and all-explaining.

Now such a process of thought is parallel to the familiar road by which the soul attains its consciousness of God. Again and again, men have turned to God, because of the felt emptiness and inadequacy of all finite objects; *ex umbris et imaginibus in veritatem.*

> If goodness lead him not, yet weariness
> May toss him to My breast.

It is the experience "*Inquietum est cor nostrum donec requiescat in te*" which leads up to the confession "*Fecisti nos ad te, Domine.*" So far, then, the philosophical argument finds confirmation in the familiar nature of religious experience.

(2) *The conception of God.*—(*a*) *Necessity.*—If God is conceived on the lines of the Absolute of modern philosophy, His existence is in the highest degree certain and necessary. He is not a "possible" or "probable" God; not "a powerful spiritual being,"

existing somewhere in Space and Time ; not one among objects, but the presupposition of all objects ; not *a* God, but *the* God. This would correspond to that absoluteness of certainty in the religious consciousness, which has received classical expression in Emily Bronte's " Last Lines."

> O God within my breast,
> Almighty, ever-present Deity,
> Life that in me has rest
> As I, undying life, have power in thee.
>
> .   .   .   .   .
>
> If earth and man were gone,
> And suns and universes ceased to be,
> And thou wert left alone,
> Every existence would exist in thee.

(*b*) *Universality.*—We are led to a conception of God, not as one who is here and not there, but as one who is everywhere. This harmonizes with the view of Religion as not being a special department,— nor "religious experience" a specific kind of experience,— but rather a certain organization of the whole of life. It is not then to be thought of as parallel to aesthetic or scientific experience, but as properly inclusive of these.[1] It is "the expression of our ultimate attitude to the universe," "the summed up meaning and purport of our whole consciousness of things."[2]

(*c*) *Intimacy.*—Our rejection of agnosticism was largely based on a refusal to think of the Absolute as being related to experience merely as background, underlying substance, etc., and as being essentially complete in independence of all finite beings and finite experience. The true conception of the Absolute, we held, was rather as a Being of which things finite are real and essential, though partial, expressions. Translated into religious terms, this suggests that the relation of God to the World and to Man is not one-sided. He is not complete apart from them. He is essentially

---

[1] Cf. Essay II. p. 61.
[2] E. Caird, *Evolution of Religion*, I. p. 30.

self-manifesting, and Revelation is not arbitrary, but a necessity of His nature.[1] Thus the Christian doctrine of the Logos is considered by idealistic philosophers a great advance upon abstract monotheism. The ideal of thought would be to "see all things in God."

NOTE TO PART ONE

Perhaps this is the place to notice an objection which will inevitably be felt by many. "You are writing," I shall be told, "in a book which professes to deal with the modern situation. And your special part is to consider the relation of contemporary philosophy to the Christian doctrine of God. But what you have given us, as an analysis of the better mind of modern philosophy, is not really modern at all : it is simply Hegel and water. This might have done duty twenty-five years ago, at the time when *Lux Mundi* was written, and when the influence of T. H. Green still dominated the English Universities. But you are now hopelessly out of date. Much has happened since then. There is one vigorous school which draws its inspiration from William James, and which totally rejects the first principles of Neo-Hegelianism. Less revolutionary, but perhaps for that very reason more important to the theologian, is the line of thinkers of which Eucken in Germany, and Professors J. Ward and Pringle-Pattison in England and Scotland, are distinguished representatives. This school draws more from Lotze than from Hegel, lays special stress on Will in its conception, both of human personality and of the Absolute Being, and defends individuality against the conception of an all-devouring Absolute. And—most important of all—France possesses in Prof. Bergson a great original genius, who, whether we agree with him or not, is in the centre of the philosophic firmament. It would help us much more to have a critical account of the relation of the Bergsonian philosophy to Theism than to have yet another academic exercise on your well-worn theme."

To some slight extent, the contentions of the second of these schools will come under review in what follows, though limits of space forbid any real philosophic criticism. With regard to James and Bergson, I can only state a personal[2]

---

[1] See below, Part Three, pp. 509-512.
[2] I am here speaking for myself alone. The other contributors to this Volume are not committed to the same view.

conviction that they are moving on bye-paths,[1] while it is the great idealistic thinkers and their disciples who are on the high road of philosophic progress. Hence it seems to me that it is with the type of philosophy known as "Absolutism" that the theologian has really to reckon. It is from this that he has most to learn ; and from this that, when he is forced to differ, he will differ with most searching of heart.

No doubt the dogmatic expression of an unfashionable opinion, by a writer who has no status which would entitle his opinion to any value at all, is a very unsatisfactory substitute for reasoned argument. But an Essay is not a complete philosophic treatise, and it is impossible to make it into one. It is impossible, for reasons of space, to attempt a controversial treatment of alternative philosophies. (For a critical examination of many of the positions both of James and of Bergson, I would refer to Dr. Bosanquet's recent Gifford Lectures, *The Principle of Individuality and Value*.) But I believe that I can be of most service by examining that type of philosophy which seems to me to be the truest.

PART TWO

When the type of philosophy sketched above is put forward as giving an intellectual basis for the Christian religion, it often fails to satisfy the religious man. It seems at once to prove too much and too little for his purpose. And, in particular, it seems to compromise, if not to destroy, the personality both of God and of man ; and the existence of a personal God and of human persons, with the possibility of personal relations between them, seems to be an absolute condition at least of the Western type of religion.

I. It proves too much

This philosophy appears to be too optimistic in its

---

[1] Of course I do not suggest that there is *nothing* new to be learnt from these thinkers. "Wisdom is justified of all her children."

beliefs as to the intelligibility and the goodness of the world in which we find ourselves.

(1) *The tone of this philosophy is too ambitious to be congenial to the religious mind.*—Another sort of language is more congenial to the religious mind. Human knowledge, as we feel in our saner moments, occupies a position intermediate between omniscience and nescience. "Probability is the guide of life." We have knowledge enough for practical purposes—"to show us which side to take." But we cannot expect to reach demonstrative certainty or necessary truth. "We have but faith, we cannot know." The humbler method of analogical argument is the only one open to us. Here we are not as gods; we "see through a glass darkly." "It is only a very small part of reality that we know. . . . The task of our philosophy is not vast and cosmic, but modest and terrestrial."[1] This sort of language seems to ring truer, just because its promises are less extravagant.

This intellectual modesty seems to consort better with the humility of true religion. There is something in "gnosticism," whether theological or philosophical, which jars on our sense of reverence. "Some theologians," says Leslie Stephen, "define the nature of God Almighty with an accuracy from which modest naturalists would shrink in describing the genesis of a blackbeetle." We instinctively contrast this with the spirit of our typically English theologians; with Church who said : "It was the saying of an old Greek in the very dawn of thought that men would meet with many surprises when they were dead. Perhaps one will be the recollection that, when we were here, we thought the ways of Almighty God so easy to argue about;"[2] and with Hooker: "Dangerous it were for the feeble brain of man to wade far into the doings of the Most High; whom although to know be life,

---

[1] Lotze, *Microcosmus* (E.T.), ii. pp. 715, 718.
[2] *Life and Letters*, p. 338.

and joy to make mention of his name ; yet our soundest knowledge is to know that we know him not as he is, neither can know him ; and our safest eloquence concerning him is our silence, when we confess without confession that his glory is inexplicable, his greatness above our capacity and reach. He is above, and we upon earth ; therefore it behoveth our words to be wary and few." [1]

To such a temper of mind, knowledge in the form of a comprehensive system of philosophy will be unexpected and improbable. Such knowledge as we may hope for is more likely to take the form of aphorisms.

(2) *Its high claims defeat their own end.*—This philosophy purports to be necessary truth. But it has had its say and failed to convince, a fatal confession in regard to a " necessary " system. It has never met with any real acceptance outside academic circles ; and, even within those circles, it is far from being the last word. In short, the argument from authority is against it : for Christian theologians to build on it would be too precarious. " In spite of the confident tone and high claims of the Transcendentalist, he (*i.e.* the theologian) hears too little volume of voice on their side to feel a call upon himself to abandon bettertrodden ways of Theism." [2]

(3) *It ignores or makes light of the fact of evil as it appears to the religious consciousness.*—This philosophy seems to treat evil as unreal, as being merely a phantom

---

[1] *Laws of Ecclesiastical Polity* (Everyman's Library Edition), i. p. 150.

[2] Caldecott, *The Philosophy of Religion in England and America*, p. 37. Cf. also Dr. Scott Holland's Romanes Lecture on Bishop Butler : " With us too, as for him, the metaphysical stop is off. Metaphysics are in suspense. The five or six experts who still hand on the good tradition can be heard crying in the night to one another. But no one listens ; and they alone understand each other, and carry on faithfully, in a tiny knot, the historic debate on the existence of the Absolute. Let them hold on to their high faith. Some day their cause will re-emerge. It cannot be that men will ever surrender the heritage won by the heroic endeavour that opened with Plato and closed with Hegel.

" But the Vision is not yet. And, in the meantime, we are engaged in a debate on the lower plane. We are scientific. We are psychological. We are empirical. We are pragmatic. . . . Our entire thought is concentrated on Experience."

due to the partial knowledge and limited views of finite minds.

> All partial evil universal good,
> All discord harmony not understood.

And this is because it is essentially Hellenic not Hebraic in spirit, and so is inclined to purchase aesthetic completeness at the cost of firmness of grasp on moral facts. This of itself makes it a philosophy of the study. It may do for the class-room or the cloister, but never for the market-place. Whereas what we need is a philosophy by which we can live. And such a philosophy must " build broad on the roots of things," and not only be valid in " hours of insight " but also on "days of gloom," not only "on the Sundays of speculation " but also "on the weekdays of ordinary thought." [1]

(4) *By its very claim to completeness, it unduly contracts the world.*—This philosophy appears to claim, that in the terrestrial world of science and of history it can see the embodiment of the world-spirit. By this satisfaction with the world of ordinary experience it contracts our horizons, and leaves no room for the apocalyptic element in religion. To Christian thought, the true centre of the universe has always been in an " other " and unseen world, where the wrongs and anomalies of this present life are righted, and which is the sphere of the future of the human race. Terrestrial history, on the other hand, deals with only a fragment of the real spiritual world. " Alles vergängliche ist nur ein Gleichniss." The Church Militant is only a minor outpost of the Church Expectant and Triumphant.[2]

---

[1] Cf. Hume, *Enquiry* (Selby-Bigge's edition), p. 101 : " These enlarged views may, for a moment, please the imagination of a speculative man who is placed in ease and security, but neither can they dwell with constancy in his mind, even though undisturbed by the emotions of pain or passion ; much less can they maintain their ground when attacked by such powerful antagonists." A very great thinker, when recently visiting Oxford, startled his hearers during a philosophic discussion by saying, with an emphasis rare and refreshing in academic surroundings, " The unreality of Evil ? It's rubbish ! *rubbish !* I wish it were true, but it isn't."

[2] Cf. Essay VII. pp. 342-347.

II. It proves too little

(1) *It is wanting in true idealism.*—This philosophy purports to be an idealism ; to hold, with Plato, that the good is the real, that right is might, and that matter is not opaque to spirit but is only " the living garment of the Godhead." But such a view is ambiguous. It should mean that, in spite of appearances, facts really correspond to our highest ideals. But, in face of the apparent unreality of any such assertion, it too easily comes to mean, that we fit our ideals to the facts and drop whatever the facts do not seem to bear out. Thus we cease to see visions or to dream dreams : we do not conquer the world, but are conquered by it. A towering idealism soon lapses into the positivism which holds that " whatever is, is right." So we have heard that Hegel, the father of modern idealistic philosophers, was apt in practice to confuse the kingdom of Heaven with the kingdom of Prussia. So Mr. Bradley, in his early work [1] which most nearly represents the same school, sums up the content of the moral law in the expression—a little reminiscent of unprogressive conservatism—" My Station and its Duties " ; and announces that, " to wish to be better than the world is to be already on the threshold of immorality."

(2) *It is empty.*—Our type of philosophy is often held, in William James's phrase, to be " thin " and not " thick " ; *i.e.* to have little practical value for the moral and religious life. It is not so much untrue, as truism or platitude. The religious view of the world, whether true or not, is at least intelligible and important. But the philosophical view here expounded might be accepted as it stands, without making much difference : it leaves us cold. Even if it is admitted to be vaguely optimistic and spiritualistic, and to be, on the whole, " on the side of the angels " in its view of the world, it yet carries us a very little way. If this is all that

[1] *Ethical Studies*, p. 180.

philosophy can do for us, we are apt to feel that
Tolstoy is justified in his assertion of its futility : " By
a long and intricate route of scientific philosophy, they
are brought to the simple position accepted by every
Russian peasant—even by those who are illiterate—
that one must live for one's soul, and that, in order to
live, one must know what to do and what not to do
for that purpose." [1]

Hence results a certain irritation on the part of the
plain man who is seeking a speculative justification of
religion. He feels that he is being put off with words,
that the philosophers teach, as the Scribes, without
the directness and authority of the true prophet, and
that plain issues are being burked. Is there a God?
That is, to him, the vital question. When, in answer,
he is invited to contemplate the " Absolute " of philosophy, he does not know what to make of it. "God,"
he may say, " I know, and No-God I know ; but
what art thou ? " [2]

(3) *In any case, it is only for the few.*—At best this
view is difficult to grasp. An intricate philosophical
argument, not really intelligible except to the philosopher, is represented as being of the essence of
intelligent religious belief. Hence we provide no
justification for the religious belief of the plain man.
This is to substitute philosophy for religion ; to open
up a gulf between exoteric and esoteric Christianity ;
and so to disfranchise the vast majority of Christians.
But such a step is sharply opposed to the genius of
Christianity which has always been democratic : " I
thank thee, O Father, Lord of heaven and earth,
because thou hast hid these things from the wise and
the prudent, and hast revealed them unto babes."

---

[1] In a posthumous fragment in the *Hibbert Journal,* April 1911.

[2] There is a subtlety that over-reaches itself. Our tacticians are now all for
outflanking manœuvres as against frontal attacks. But victories gained by these
methods are sometimes more apparent than real. Some critics of Lord Roberts'
march to Pretoria would say that the failure to fight a pitched battle, though
apparently giving a bloodless victory, really meant the prolonging of the war.

And here again men will revolt. "We have heard," they will say, "that narrow is the way and strait is the gate ; but we have never heard that it is only the wise and the learned that shall walk therein."

III. IT LEAVES NO ROOM FOR HUMAN PERSONALITY

The "Absolute" of philosophy is the all-inclusive and the all-pervading. It is reached by way of the unreality and insufficiency of all finite things, none of which, including finite personality, can have independent existence. But in thus depreciating human personality, we are putting forward a view, it may be held, which is (*a*) untrue to experience, (*b*) incompatible with morality, (*c*) incompatible with religion.

(*a*) It is untrue to experience, because in the experience of each of us, consciousness of self is absolutely fundamental. If, indeed, we analyse the self into a number of separate faculties—reason, will, and feeling—each of these may appear incomplete and be considered as a mere emanation from the Absolute. But what is fundamental in our experience of self is no one of these, but rather a selfhood, an immediate self-existence, the fact of being a *centre* of experience, to which all these are related as adjectives to a noun, as attributes to a substance. And this is not so readily to be explained away.

(*b*) To merge human personality in the Infinite and to make its seeming independence an illusion appears incompatible with moral responsibility. And a religion which is not based on morality is not the religion for us. Indeed, as the development of religion has been steadily towards a growing moralization, to loosen our grasp now on the moral element in religion, would be to abandon the slow gains of ages. Such a world-view might possibly accord with a religion of oriental quietism, which preaches merely a dreamy, self-forgetting contemplation. It will not accord with a religion of action, which seeks to build the walls of Jerusalem.

(c) Religion is essentially a relation of wills. It implies such a conception of the human and the divine as that there can, in a real sense, be co-operation between them. If the religious consciousness and religious experience are to be more than "appearance," human persons, even though created by God, must, when created, have some independence.

> You know what I mean : God's all, man's nought :
> But also God, whose pleasure brought
> Man into being, stands away
> As it were a handbreadth off, to give
> Room for the newly-made to live,
> And look at him from a place apart,
> And use his gifts of brain and heart
> Given, indeed, but to keep for ever.

"Our wills are ours to make them thine." But, as it has been said, unless they are really ours, there is no meaning or value in the surrender.

For all this our philosophy, in its insistence on speculative completeness, appears to leave no room. It would so identify God with the whole universe, as to leave nothing in the universe, not even man, the power to enter into real relations with God. In our effort to magnify God, we are decrying man. And this meets with an appropriate nemesis. For we can only reach our conception of divine personality, by analogy from our experience of personality in ourselves. And if the latter is denied, the former will not long survive. If real personality is not allowed to man, it will soon cease to be predicated of God. And this, as we shall see, is what actually happens.

IV. It leaves no Room for Divine Personality

If our philosophy is put forward as a proof of Theism, it seems to commit the fallacy, known as

Ignoratio Elenchi ; for, if it proves anything, it proves not Theism but Pantheism. It proves only an impersonal Whole of things, animated at best by a spiritual principle or law, but not controlled and directed by a living God. The religious apologist who trusts to this weapon of defence is playing with fire.[1]

This, we shall be told, is recognized by the clearer thinkers of our own school, who see that the logic of our argument involves a frank abandonment of Theism in the old sense. Thus Dr. Bosanquet explicitly rejects " the entire doctrine of theism in the Kantian sense, as involving a personal creator and governor of the world."[2] And Mr. Bradley[3] classes orthodox theology with " our commonplace materialism " as implying the mutilation of our nature. Both " vanish like ghosts before the daylight of free sceptical enquiry." It may seem strange to class William James with Dr. Bosanquet and Mr. Bradley in this connection. But he claims that, on this point, the monistic idealism which he rejects and the pluralistic spiritualism which he advocates are at one ; and that both are alike incompatible with the older orthodoxy. " The older monarchical theism is obsolete or obsolescent. The place of the divine in the world must be more organic and intimate. An external creator and his institutions may still be verbally confessed at church in formulas that linger by their mere inertia, but the life is out of them, we avoid dwelling on them, the sincere heart of us is elsewhere."[4] On this showing, the Absolute has room for religion, just as it has room for art and science. But none of these, in the end, represents it fully. Theology is picture-thinking and must be transcended. Religion, as with

---

[1] This result is due to just that transformation of the old "proofs" which we thought necessary to make them valid. Descartes thought that he was demonstrating the existence of the God of contemporary theology. But the inner logic of his philosophy resulted in its development into the system of Spinoza; and the absolute Substance of Spinoza is quite incompatible with the personal God of Christianity.

[2] *The Principle of Individuality and Value*, p. 156.

[3] *Appearance and Reality*, Introduction, p. 5.

[4] *A Pluralistic Universe*, p. 30.

Hegel, must give place to Philosophy. If the familiar language of religion is kept, it will only be by way of accommodation to the popular mind; and such language would be conscious parable or allegory for the modern philosopher as much as for Plato.

It is then the Absolutists of the "Left" who are alive to the meaning of their own system. Those of the "Right" are only muddled. They attempt to make the best of two worlds at once; but there is a fatal ambiguity in their position, as James points out in a critique of Emerson. "The Universe (according to Emerson) has a divine soul of order, which soul is moral, being also the soul within the soul of man. But whether this soul of the universe be a mere quality like the eye's brilliancy or the skin's softness, or whether it be a self-conscious life like the eye's seeing or the skin's feeling, is a decision that never unmistakably appears in Emerson's pages."[1] In this ambiguity there lurks a real danger of dishonesty. And the theologians have sometimes got a bad name on this score. They are suspected of using a philosophy so far as it is controversially useful, without any attempt to understand it seriously and to follow out its implications to the bitter end.

This attack comes not from the orthodox, but from the unorthodox camp. But very many orthodox thinkers agree that it is justified; and, for that reason, they decline to make our type of philosophy the basis of their apologetics. Absolutism, they hold, sweeps away ideas which are vital to religion.

(a) Absolutism may lead to a fuller understanding of divine immanence, but it leaves no room for the transcendence of God, which is equally important to religion. The necessity of the world and of man to God, in the sense in which it is asserted, is incompatible with a truly religious conception. Absolutism teaches that it is meaningless to look for an existence of God

[1] *Varieties of Religious Experience*, p. 33.

"in Himself," apart from His manifestation in the world and in man. But the instinct of worship is always to hold that God has an existence of His own, of which we know little or nothing ; and that He is what He is, apart from human or earthly history. It is the manward side of God that is revealed in Christ, but this is only one aspect of His nature. He is infinitely more and greater than what is revealed or known of Him. In short, Absolutism has overshot the mark in its wholesale rejection of agnosticism ; and has, in consequence, identified God with the Universe. It invites us to "worship Nature, not the God of Nature" ; and it leaves us no God, nor any place for Him, but only Nature itself, rather fancifully conceived.[1]

(*b*) We miss the emphasis on Will and Activity which is so characteristic of the religious conception of God. Thus the history of Jewish religion is a history of the development of consciousness of God. And if we take the result of that development, which we find in the greater prophets and in some of the psalms, as classical, we shall recognize that the God of religion is conceived as World-Creator and World-Ruler much more than as either the Whole of things, or a Rational Principle pervading the universe, or a Universal Mind contemplating it. We confess in church a God who is "Maker of heaven and earth" ; but we cannot integllibily apply such an expression to the Absolute of philosophy. Yet this recognition of God as *Creator* is essential. The religious consciousness is never content with an impersonal "Strength and Stay upholding all creation" ; it demands something much more living and concrete.

But here is the finger of God, a flash of the will that can,
Existent behind all laws, that made them and, lo, they are.

---

[1] Cf. Caldecott, *op. cit.* p. 41. "Englishmen will not be ready to acquiesce when they are told that they must not think of God as having His own existence, His own character, His own majesty and glory, over and above all that can be seen or known."

So also James points out that we are not *part of* the God of Christian theology, as we are supposed to be of the Absolute of philosophy. " He and we stand outside of each other, just as the devil, the saints, and the angels stand outside of both of us." [1] Anything else would be incompatible with the religious conception of God as creating, " taking sides " in moral issues, standing in a personal relation towards men. In fact, James asserts that he can conceive of nothing more different from the Absolute than the God of David or Isaiah.

Here then is a chasm which is not to be bridged and which cannot be covered by vague phases. " O *living will* that shalt endure " could not possibly be an address to the Absolute. We are apt to use words to gloss over the differences of things. But, as Aubrey Moore epigrammatically puts it, " The motto of Oxford University *Dominus Illuminatio Mea* altogether changes its meaning if we read it *Illuminatio Dominus Meus*." [2]

(c) Religion, it may be said, does not demand a God who is the same everywhere, who is never here and not there, who never does anything in particular, never interposes at the difficult minute. It demands miracle and intervention in the older sense ; in fact, what William James distinguishes as " crass " from " refined " supernaturalism. Theology may make too great sacrifices, in order to achieve philosophic " respectability."

All these objections may be summed up under one head ; namely, that our philosophy explains away the personality of God. Its God is not merely, as we have always thought, the centre, but the whole of reality ; not a person, but the inclusive unity of all persons and things. It may be described as supra-personal,—if we can derive any comfort from the word " supra " ; but *a person* it certainly is not. In short, the Absolute is not God at all, but rather, as it were, " the peace of God which passeth all understanding," a sort of mystical

[1] *A Pluralistic Universe*, p. 110.   [2] *Lux Mundi*, p. 83.

unity, in which the identity and individuality of God and all other persons are lost. And if personality is abandoned, "God may still exist for us as the keystone in the arch of knowledge, but He is no longer, except as a metaphor, 'Our Father which is in Heaven.'"[1]

But here no compromise is possible. Doubtless by insisting on the Transcendence of God, religion escapes the danger of an undue anthropomorphism. Yet God must be so far like men, that He can have dealings with them and they with Him. Such a personal relationship is the lifeblood of religion ; and it implies real personality on both sides. We cannot in the end view the Object of religion as Principle or Law or Force or Substance or System, but only as Living Person. We speak of the Absolute as "It" ; we speak of God as "He." Which is the truer ? Masculine or neuter ? This is a difference which can be glossed over in words, for the philosopher sometimes uses concrete, the theologian abstract, terms. But, in fact, the issue is vital. And a belief in the personality of God, a belief that the use of the masculine pronoun is not a mere accommodation to sentiment but literally truer, is the *articulus stantis vel cadentis ecclesiae.*

The lines then can never meet. If the last step involves dropping the assertion of the personality of God, Christian theology can never take it ; for "in this consists the whole difference between a religion purified and a religion destroyed." Any philosophy on which Christianity can build must be more frankly anthropocentric. We must be ready to be more venturesome. The effort to retain theoretic certainty has resulted in our letting go everything that religion holds most dear.

---

[1] Aubrey Moore, *Lux Mundi*, p. 65.

PART THREE

I. THE DIFFICULTIES RAISED IN PART TWO REST LARGELY ON A CONCEPTION OF PERSONALITY WHICH IS NOT BORNE OUT BY EXPERIENCE

Our problem is now clear. We have to satisfy ourselves that we are not betraying our own cause. Our purpose is to justify the claim of moral and religious experience to a pre-eminent and determining place in the experience of the race as a whole. But, it is suggested, we are really giving away the cause we should defend. For we are abandoning what is most characteristic and important in the experience of religious men ; and this in deference to the supposed demands of *a priori* philosophical theory. We leave no room, it is said, for the personality either of God or of man ; and, without these, all moral and religious experience would be stultified.

This amounts to an appeal to experience, and particularly to "religious" experience. We answer by accepting the challenge. And we must try to show, not only that the philosophy to which we adhere does not explain away actual experience, but that experience positively demands it. The contrary opinion rests on a double mistake. On the one hand, it is supposed that personality, as we know it in human experience, is something clear, fixed and intelligible; and so a standard by which we must judge the legitimacy of the ascription of the term to God. And this is untrue. The modern development of a philosophy of personality has been valuable ; but it may be doubted whether it has not been, by now, slightly exaggerated. "Personality" is sometimes treated as though it were a magic key to unlock all doors, a test to be applied unthinkingly to all things in heaven and earth. It has thus tended to become a formula which dispenses with thought rather than a real illumination. And modern thinkers are apt, without much justification, to adopt a patronising attitude to the Greeks who did not possess so clear a conception of human nature. On the other hand, a sharp distinction between Self and Not-Self is assumed to be vital to personal experience. And this also is a superficial view.

These mistakes are due to two causes :—

(1) The crudeness and inadequacy of the intellectual categories by which we commonly interpret experience.

(2) The direction of insufficient attention to the higher types of experience and to what constitutes the difference between higher and lower.

(1) *Misinterpretation of experience through inadequate categories.*—(*a*) *Substance.*—We have become accustomed to distinguish in anything between kernel and husk, between an element that is permanent, essential, and individual and an element that is changing, accidental, mere attribute. And we too easily assume that some such sharp division is of universal application. We, half unconsciously, bring this distinction with us to the understanding of personality. We assume that, behind all particular qualities and functions of soul, behind will, reason and emotion, behind all a man's interests and relations to others, behind all that changes and grows, there is something fixed, stable and static, which is *he*. His loves, his doings, his knowledge, all tend to be treated as external and comparatively accidental to his essence. And selfhood is assumed to consist just in this inner core of being which is impervious to all external influence.[1]

Such an assumption, if its implications are made clear, produces grave difficulties. This may be seen in

---

[1] " Each self is a unique existence, which is perfectly *impervious*, if I may so speak, to other selves—impervious in a fashion of which the impenetrability of matter is a faint analogue" (Professor A. Seth (Pringle-Pattison), *Hegelianism and Personality*, p. 216).

some advocates of Free Will, who distinguish sharply
between self and character, and thereby make all moral
growth external to the real self. But the assumption
is in itself baseless : it embodies the old fallacy into
which, as we have suggested, the agnostic falls in his
conception of the universe. A better philosophy is
tending to replace the conception of Substance by that
of Activity, and to conceive things dynamically rather
than statically. What anything *is* consists in what it
does. So also there is no " soul-substance " apart from
soul-life. And soul-life consists always in action and
reaction with environment. The soul lives by what it
feeds on. The self cannot be isolated from its interests,
its relations to the world and to men. These *are* its life.

(*b*) *Possession*.[1]— The Western mind is obsessed
with the idea of property and ownership. The mischief
which this obsession has done in the field of social
ethics is beginning to be generally recognized : we are
aware that the mind which runs only in the groove of
" Proputty, proputty, proputty ! " has a narrow and
impoverished view of life. But it is less generally
recognized that the mischief has extended to philosophy
and psychology ; and yet this extension has actually
occurred. Just as we are reluctant to recognize that
any material thing is *res nullius*, so for experience, by
analogy, we look for an owner. Thus man *has* a
character and a religion, "just as he ' has ' an edition
of Plato in his library, a Morris paper in his drawing-
room, and an ornamental knocker on his front-door." [2]

From this mental tendency two sharp distinctions
result. On the one hand, the proprietor is quite
distinct from his property. Accordingly, we think of
God as the " proprietor " of the world, and so as
entirely separate from it. On the other hand, the
dominance of private ownership in our civilization leads

---

[1] The following section is almost entirely based on an essay entitled " The
Universe as Philosopher," in Mr. Jacks' *The Alchemy of Thought.*
[2] Jacks, *op. cit.* p. 96.

to "pluralism" in philosophy. We insist on no distinction more strongly than on the distinction between *meum* and *tuum*. Round his soul, as round his estate, the Englishman sets up a ring-fence with a notice-board, " Trespassers will be prosecuted." So ingrained is this mental habit in us that it is only by an effort that we realize how strange it must appear to an impartial observer. And yet reflection makes this clear. " The philosophy which emanates from the well-furnished studies of Britain, and proclaims at the outset that experience also is ' my own,' must be a sore perplexity to those whose fee-simple in the world extends only to a loin-cloth and a beggar's bowl." [1]

The influence of this prejudice on our conception of personality is aggravated by the legal associations of the word *persona*. By "person" we are apt to mean, primarily, a subject of rights and duties like a property-owner and rate-payer. Now the legal relations of men are very external. Though they unite men, they also hold them at arm's length from one another : they touch life at few points. But if legal relations are far from being the highest or most central of human experiences, man must be conceived as more than "a person." Or, if we retain the word, we must be careful to slough off its legal associations and to transcend their limits.

But the concept of "possession" has only to be made explicit, to lose all plausibility as seriously applied to the philosophy of personality. This is made clear by Mr. Jacks. " According to them (the philosophers), man *has* a place in Nature ; he *has* a relation to the Universe and to God ; he *has* duties to his neighbour and to himself ; he *has* an end to accomplish ; he *has* experience in all its varieties ; he *has* right impulses and wrong ; he *has* individuality which he is told to guard lest it be taken from him ; he *has* virtues of which hostile powers would ' rob ' him ; he *has* vices which

[1] Jacks, *op. cit.* p. 91.

2 K

he had better get rid of; he *has* an ego which is his
very own ; he *has* a soul which he may sell—and so on
through a veritable auctioneer's catalogue of man's
effects. But who is the owner of these job-lots? He
is behind the scenes ; but if you seek him there you
will not find him. When you think you have got him,
he turns instantly into one of his own possessions. It
helps us not a whit to refer us to a *higher* self : for this
higher self also turns out to be something man *has*.
Who, then, is Man? Is he the selfless owner of
himself? We flounder in a realm of nonsense, trying
once more to cook the hare we cannot catch." [1]

(*c*) *Materialism.*—We are familiar in children and
savages with a level of thought inferior to our own,
which perhaps can only conceive of its gods as visible
and tangible, because it is aware of no other form of
reality. We can see clearly the crudity and fallacy of
this. And yet, if we reflect, we may see cause to
suspect that, in our ordinary conception of ourselves
and of our relation to other men and things, we have
fallen, in our degree, into the same type of error.
When we try to understand the nature of personality—
what it is to be a self—we are apt to picture to ourselves the relation of self and not-self in experience as
equivalent to that of one solid body in space to another.
Such bodies are mutually exclusive ; they cannot occupy
the same portion of space at the same moment. We
think of the relation of self and not-self after this
analogy ; for, on one side of our nature, we are bodily
and have bodily attributes. But we do not really believe that this side of our nature is exhaustive or even
central. And to transfer such a conception to the self
as it is in knowledge, will and affection is a piece of the
crudest picture-thinking. [2]

---

[1] *Op. cit.* pp. 93-94.
[2] The nature of this fallacy is illustrated by the metaphysical difficulties of the
problem of knowledge. Metaphysicians now insist that the relation of knower and
object known cannot be treated—as too often in the past—as though it were one of
the relations between things known which themselves are objects of knowledge.

We do not avoid the fallacy of materialism by simply substituting a psychical for a physical " material." Though popular thought has got beyond pure physical materialism, and distinguishes clearly soul from body, it has not at present escaped this kind of error. It interprets " the soul " in a crass way, as a " soul-substance " which has spiritual qualities, but which is itself distinct from the qualities which it has ; like the " spiritualist " who seems to think of the soul as a sort of " ghost," something with quasi-physical attributes, but much more subtle and impalpable than matter.

All these intellectual prejudices lead to the ascription of a fixity and exclusiveness to personality which is unwarranted. If we discard them and try to see things as they are, we must admit that human personality, as we know it in ourselves or in others, is an enigma, a problem to be solved rather than an obvious clue to anything. It is full of contradictions, of suggestions to which no achievement corresponds. Is self-consciousness a mark of personality ? Undoubtedly it is. And yet how little we know ourselves ! and how full of surprises to us our own hearts are ! So very little of the sum-total of me is consciously active at any given moment; during the greater part of life my mind is nine-tenths asleep. True self-consciousness would seem to necessitate at least that grasp of the whole history and character of one's own life, which the drowning man is popularly supposed to have. But, ordinarily, memory extends to the merest fraction of our lives. Is purposiveness a mark of personality ? Again we should naturally answer Yes. And yet that confusion and contradiction of purposes, which Aristotle called ἀκρασία and St. Paul " the body of this death,"

We cannot properly understand the specific relation of knowledge by reference to the nature of relations generally. For the knowledge-relation is *sui generis*, and must be understood by close inspection not by analogies. Mr. Webb points out that the older idealists, such as T. H. Green, were really making the same point in their insistence that the self as subject, and so the presupposition, of consciousness cannot properly be treated as merely one of the objects of consciousness.

is the most common phenomenon in experience. Further, the human person is very imperfectly individual. To understand him, we have to go outside him ; he is not self-explanatory. "Personality that lives only under material conditions in a world of dying, personality whose existence and origin are alike wholly independent of its own thought and will, and which only by degrees discovers a little as to the conditions of its own being—whatever rank it may hold in relation to other present phenomena—is plainly a most limited and imperfect form of personality."[1]

Yet this very criticism of personality as we know it in experience shows that, in spite of present imperfection, we have some positive idea of what personality should be. As always, consciousness of imperfection itself carries us, in a sense, beyond the imperfection. Thus Wallace, while insisting on the incoherence of personal experience—" Even in the recesses of his own being, he seems to meet with a strange, dark substance which is in him, but is not he "—notes also that the ideal of personality here implied is " the thorough appropriation of every particle that is mine by the full reality of me."[2] Though we know personality, like the Venus of Milo, only in an imperfect form, we can yet to some extent reconstruct the true design. And the ideal to which experience points would seem to be not negative but positive, not the hard, impervious, exclusive atom, but coherence, individuality, organization, power. To be at unity within oneself would be the climax of personality.

From this combination of actual imperfection with hints of something better, there results a paradox. " To be ourselves, we must be more than ourselves." Hence the conception of personality is far from being a simple one. It is a term of changing and growing meaning. And this is due not to shiftiness on the

---

[1] R. C. Moberly, *Problems and Principles*, pp. 8-9.
[2] *Lectures and Essays*, p. 278.

part of the philosopher, but to the nature of the case.

(2) *Insufficient attention to the higher types of experience.* —The value of the appeal to experience will depend partly on the kind of experiences which are selected for examination. And the chief place should undoubtedly be given to the higher experiences. We should take as our standard " what a man recognizes as of value when his life is fullest and his soul at its highest stretch." We may no doubt be asked how we know what is " highest." And in a complete metaphysic this would need demonstration. But, for practical purposes, there is sufficient agreement as to what is higher and lower, at least among those who are sufficiently interested in Christianity to " wish it true." And, if we concentrate our attention principally on what most men will agree are our best moments, the criticism that personality, human or divine, involves an exclusiveness, a separation of self and not-self, for which we leave no room, becomes less and less plausible.

All our reasonings on this subject must be based on the twin facts—that all our experience of personality is experience of exceedingly imperfect personality, and that, nevertheless, we have experience of different degrees of imperfection. And as we get higher, the barrier between self and not-self seems to become less. Increase of unity and power, we find, goes with increase in expansiveness. As T. H. Green and others have impressed on us of late years, man is a social animal. The individual only comes to his full stature by playing his part in society and in the world. " The times when one feels that one is most truly oneself are just those in which one feels that the consciousness of one's own individuality is most absolutely swallowed up, whether in sympathy with nature, or in the bringing to birth of truth, or in enthusiasm for other men." [1] Thus the secret of life is self-giving. " He that loseth his

---

[1] Nettleship, *Remains*, i. p. 53 ; also quoted in Essay VI. p. 327, footnote.

life shall save it." All successful life, as Dr. Bosanquet
reminds us, is one in logical structure with self-sacrifice.
A certain self-transcendence is thus a " note " of all our
higher experiences ; and the boundary-line between self
and not-self is continually shifting.

But for our fullest enlightenment, we should go to
the highest of all social experiences, namely love. We
are apt to think of love as an intermittent psychical
activity of a permanent self, and as thus being less real
than the individuals whom it unites. But, in the
highest examples, the balance is reversed. The love
is something which inspires, sustains, and moulds the
personality of the lovers. This antithesis is suggested
by the titles of two of Browning's poems—" Love in a
Life," and " Life in a Love."

Here there is, no doubt, still distinction between the
lovers, but the distinction is subordinate to the unity.
It is not a sense of contrast, so much as the feeling of
unity and reconciliation, which is dominant in consciousness. No doubt it is only the few in actual experience
who ever attain these heights ; and the power of sympathy, even in the best of men, is so contracted, that it is
only towards one or two that such intensity of feeling is
ever experienced. Yet, ideally, there is no limit. We
do not want to be merely fanciful ; but there is no
finality in our present experience, and at least some of
the religious geniuses seem to point us beyond.

Some recent thinkers have insisted that self-realization and self-sacrifice do not always coincide in life.
And we may perhaps agree that philanthropy is not the
road for all men. There is need in the kingdom of
heaven for a Goethe as well as a St. Francis. But a
certain self-transcendence is characteristic also of the
higher artistic experiences. "You scarcely recognize yourself when, for the moment, Shakespeare or Beethoven
has laid his spell upon you." [1]

The same principle holds good when we turn to the

[1] Bosanquet, *op. cit.* p. 260.

more specifically "religious" experience of conscious relation to God. It is important to notice this, because the criticisms which we stated in Part Two, claimed to be based largely on this. But the supposed need of separation between God and man is hardly borne out by experience. Between one man and another there may indeed be some place for exclusiveness and reserve. Anything like hypnotism we resent as an intolerable intrusion by another into our inner sanctuary: "*Secretum meum mihi.*" Such a creation and domination of one person by another, as is suggested in the relations between the Jesuit and John Inglesant in Shorthouse's novel, we feel to be something of an outrage on the dignity of personality. Even here it is probable that we are much more likely to go wrong by erecting too many barriers than too few. But, in any case, such barriers cannot be imported into religion. Whatever may be the case in morals, in religion there is no room for Aristotle's μεγαλόψυχος. The notion that the relation of man to God should be like the relation of a feudal vassal to his overlord, that "the high contracting parties" should treat on terms of mutual respect, is utterly alien to genuine religious experience.

On the contrary, we find that the language of indwelling is natural to the saint. "I live ; yet not I, but Christ liveth in me." No doubt there is here an element of metaphor. But the metaphor stands for something. It is futile to criticize such metaphors by purely external *a priori* considerations, unless we are sure that we are including that which such language was meant to express.[1] Of course, such experience is

---

[1] Cf. Webb, pp. 250-251. "It is not, I venture to think, those who with earnest intention use such language as 'God in us and we in Him' that are guilty of a mis-use of spatial metaphor, but rather those who, instead of seeking the meaning of such an expression in some real experience, which they who use it are intending to describe, proceed on purely general, or what Aristotle would have called merely dialectical grounds, and starting from the general notion of spatial inclusion, go on to contend that one consciousness cannot include another consciousness, and that there is no more to be said. This is surely no proper criticism of language used, not for the sake of talking, but to express a real experience. At this rate one would have to dismiss the reality of the musical experiences denoted by such phrases as 'thrilling,'

comparatively rare ; but so are the highest achievements of saintliness. On the general principles which
should guide our relation to genius, as laid down in
Essay II., we should, so far as we ourselves do not
share the experience of the saint, be prepared to accept
it as due to a further development of what we know in
our own experience.

Hence (*a*) our argument is not, that, because man is a
person, therefore the Absolute also is a person. It would
be almost as true to state the exact opposite, and to say
that, because man is not, therefore the Absolute must
be a person. We argue, with Lotze, from the paradoxes
of human experience to a superhuman experience, in
which is the full fruition of the personality we know, without its contradictions. Nothing short of the Absolute
would have the coherence and comprehensiveness necessary to the ideal of personality. Human personality,
then, is not the standard which we follow when we apply
the term to the Absolute. It is incapable of being so,
for it is always growing towards a goal which is never
reached. Yet the direction in which it lies is clear.
So far is it from being impossible for the Absolute to
be personal, that it is rather true that nothing else could
be fully personal.[1]

(*b*) The sharp antithesis of self and not-self, on
which the objection to the attribution of personality
to the Absolute rests, tends to diminish as we get
higher in the range of spiritual experience. Growth in
excellence and in spiritual life consists largely in a losing

---

'penetrating,' 'stirring,' 'moving,' because the instruments do not get inside our
skin, nor their noise shove us out of our seats. But surely there is a genuine experience which these phrases are used to describe ; and if we ask *how* the manipulation
of musical instruments can do these things, the answer would be, 'In the way in
which all who are musical know that they do.' "

[1] Some may prefer to say that the Absolute is supra-personal, on the ground that
we can never get sufficiently away from the legal associations of "personality." They
will then say, with Wallace, that "the truth of personality is subordinate to the truth
of spirituality." The question here is one of terminology, and no great issue depends
on it. But it will only be legitimate to decline to assert the personality of the Absolute, on the ground that it is so much more than personal, if we recognize that man
also, in his degree, is already more than a person.

of ψυχή,[1] a getting away from impenetrable individuality. The theory that personality is impervious is here a hindrance ; for growth in grace is growth away from separateness. But if separateness decreases with increase in the living personal relation to God, which is what the religious consciousness really clings to, it can hardly be vital to that relation.

It is sometimes said that the language of union with God, used by and of the saint, is only "moral," not "ontological." This distinction really depends on a half-hearted idealism of the kind we have already rejected in Part One. But in any case, the objector cannot have it both ways. We are considering the objection to "absolutism," which bases the necessity of separation on moral and religious interests. The objector is basing a metaphysical argument on moral experience. Our reply has been, that these interests are not sacrificed, but rather secured, by "absolutism," and the objector must not run away from the tribunal which he has himself set up. In view of the fact that the objector appeals to experience against logical theory, it is important to insist that religious experience, when unsophisticated, tells in the opposite direction. It is not the absolutist here who has to put a forced interpretation on the facts. It is not personality, but a false conception of its nature, which is inconsistent with our type of philosophy.

The belief in a God who is less than the Absolute is unsatisfactory, not only from the point of view of philosophy,[2] but also from the point of view of religion. For the religious consciousness demands, in the object of its worship, both a stability and a certainty that are to be found in nothing short of the Absolute. It is not

---

[1] Cf. St. John xii. 25, where the hating of ψυχή in this world is proclaimed to be the road to ζωὴ αἰώνιος.

[2] John Caird points out that the conception of a transcendent God goes with a metaphysic, in which thought has access only to the outer relations of things, not to their inner nature and essential being. And such a metaphysic we have already rejected.

satisfied with a god who is merely a great deal bigger
and stronger and better than ourselves, an indefinitely
magnified man. For we cannot, in the end, rest with
this. Such a conception is inevitably followed by the
conception of a "twilight of the gods"; as the
anthropomorphic ruler of the Greek or Latin pantheon
was dwarfed by an impersonal Fate in the background.
The religious consciousness seeks to find peace by
uniting itself with the absolutely abiding : it needs the
assurance that "underneath are the everlasting arms."
Again, it is satisfied with nothing less than absolute
certainty in its object. It is true that we begin with
religion as a psychological experience of *ours*. It
satisfies a want of *ours*, like electric light and other
resources of civilization. And we think of theologies
as being theoretic hypotheses to account for this
experience of want. This is the stage represented by
the following quotations which William James [1] makes
from Professor Leuba and from W. Bender : "Not
God, but life, more life, a larger, richer, more satisfy-
ing life, is, in the last analysis, the end of religion."
" Not the question about God, and not the inquiry into
the origin and purpose of the world is religion, but the
question about Man. All religious views of the world
are anthropocentric." But this is only true of a low
level of religious development. There is nothing
hypothetical about the object of the genuinely religious
consciousness. Religion cannot for a moment endure
the thought of "a probable God." God is not a more
or less justifiable inference from religious experience ;
religious experience is directly awareness of God. This
way of putting it is the truer to the experience itself.
So again prayer begins as anthropocentric—"Give us
what we want." But it is very imperfectly religious,
until it has become theocentric—"Thy Will be done." [2]

---

[1] *Varieties of Religious Experience*, p. 507.
[2] The answer to the prayer, "We would that Thou shouldest do for us whatso-
ever we shall desire," is, "Can ye drink of the cup that I drink of?" Mark x.
35, 38.

The development then of the religious consciousness is, in this, in tune with philosophy.[1]

The religious man needs, for his satisfaction, to feel himself completely and perfectly the instrument of God. The frequent prejudice against the admission of this and the refusal to go beyond the language of "co-operation" with God are largely due to the characteristic English liking for compromise, which, in another direction, prefers the average respectable churchgoer to the saint. I own that this attitude reminds me unpleasantly of the attitude of the cautious lover to his mistress :

> 'Tis but decent to profess oneself beneath her,
> Still one must not be too much in earnest either.

The truly religious frame of mind is always theocentric, not anthropocentric. Not the fact that we have need of God, but the fact that God has need of us, is ultimate to the religious consciousness.

II. This Conclusion is Strengthened by Attention to Specifically Christian Ideas

(1) *Spirituality of God.*—Growth in religious apprehension may not unfairly be said to consist in an increasing grasp of the truth that "God is a Spirit." But, if so, our popular theology is clearly defective. And perhaps this is because it is too Judaic, and too oblivious of the fact that Christianity was not merely superimposed on a Jewish foundation, but involved a radical transmutation of Jewish beliefs. In particular, it transformed the whole conception of the Divine.[2]

May not the popular demand for a transcendent God be partly a relic of the materialistic imagery of Jewish thinking? The popular insistence on God as Creator and Moral Governor rather than as indwelling

---

[1] Cf. the argument against the "psychological" view of experience in Part One, pp. 454-459.
[2] See Essay V.

spirit is due to a feeling that anything else is derogatory
to His reality and greatness. But it is very dangerous
to trust this sort of feeling. The hostility of the Jews
to Jesus was due largely to the fact that they insisted
on judging His teaching and claims by their antecedent
ideas of the majesty and dignity of God. Are we not
in danger of making the same mistake? This side of
Judaism was developed by Mahomet. The Mahom-
medan thinks of God, so far as he thinks of Him
positively at all, as a sort of Oriental potentate, "the
Sultan of Heaven." But he so emphasizes the separation of God from man and the unapproachableness
of God as to seem to deny Him all positive attributes.

> Whatever idea your mind comes at
> I tell you flat
> God is *not* that.[1]

But Christianity is on this point sharply at issue
with Mahommedanism. "The veil is rent away which
in days of ignorance hid God and made Him an
unknown God; clad Him in thick darkness and terrors
of the mount, saw Him invisible in excess of light,
heard Him whispering indistinctly in the separate
events of history—a factor incalculable, mysterious,
awful." [2]

(2) *The Trinity.*—No part of Christian theology
means less to the man in the street than the doctrine
of the Trinity. And yet it clearly corresponds to a
philosophical necessity. Personality, as we know it,
is marked by a consciousness of self and not-self in
partial relation; and the ideal of personality should
include this relation in its completeness. But when
the theologian suggests to the philosopher, that orthodox
Christianity possesses in the doctrine of the Trinity
what he (the philosopher) is looking for, the philosopher
is rather irritated than conciliated. He feels that some-

---

[1] Rhyme quoted as current in Egypt by W. H. J. Gairdner, *The Reproach of Islam*, p. 151.
[2] Wallace, *Lectures and Essays*, p. 50.

thing, which bears a superficial resemblance to what he wants, is being flung at him unintelligently without any real appreciation of his problem. And no one has yet succeeded in formulating a Christian metaphysic, based on orthodox Trinitarianism, which this age can accept. And yet, though it is just here that we are most out of our depth, and that anything we can say must be specially tentative, there are certain positive truths which we seem to see.

Thus the doctrine arises historically out of reflection on the Incarnation and Atonement, and should be understood in the light of them. Very much of the best thought of our time is agreed in insisting that the Incarnation and Atonement are in no sense accidental, but are vital to the perfection, and therefore to the being, of God.[1] Dr. Du Bose is voicing a widespread feeling in the following fine passage : " It is only in Christ that God not merely manifests what He is, but in His activity and self-expression through creation *becomes* what He is. . . . We speak of the incredible self-lowering or self-emptying of God in becoming man or in undergoing the death of the cross. Is the act in which love becomes perfect a contradiction or a compromise of the divine nature? Is God not God or least God in the moment in which He is most love ? . . . Where before Christ, or where now otherwise than in Christ and in the cross of the divine suffering together with and for man, where in all the story of the universe was or is love so love, or God so God? "[2] But the difficulty is that, at first sight, the Incarnation and Atonement seem to be merely partial and temporary episodes in the life of God : it seems as though time was when they were not. The Christian doctrine of the Trinity therefore, by projecting these relations of God to Man into the eternal being of the Absolute, is meeting a real religious need.

---

[1] This view is also expressed in Essays V. and VI. in this volume.
[2] *The Gospel in the Gospels*, pp. 265, 272-273.

We have said [1] that a belief in the divinity of Christ is necessary to the Christian scheme of salvation. The life and death of Jesus Christ can only become the ruling force in the lives of all men, if they are a real expression of the character of the Godhead, and if the life of God is really implicated in them. Now Christian theology does not shrink from the startling assertion that Jesus lives in the life of the Church, and that the life of human fellowship and love at its highest is the life of God on earth. It is by partaking fully in this common life, that men may become partakers in the divine life and "put on immortality"; and nothing short of this is truly human. It is self-surrender to the common good which is self-surrender to God : duty to our neighbour and duty to God are, in essence, indistinguishable. This seems strange and paradoxical. But it is familiar to the highest religious experience. "If a man say, I love God, and hateth his brother, he is a liar." "God is love ; and he that dwelleth in love, dwelleth in God, and God in him." [2] But the apparent strangeness is due partly to that superstition about personality which we have tried to combat, and which can only see, in the artist's self-expression through the products of his mind, something outside him. And, to the Christian, God is Love. He is more than *a* person, for He is tripersonal. And this has come to be perceived through reflection on His presence in the Church and His identity with the life of humanity.

Further, the belief that the Incarnation and the Atonement are permanent elements in the life of God is necessary, not only to the efficacy of the Christian religion, but to the vindication of God. World-history is not something at which God looks on as a spectator or which He directs from above, but something in which He genuinely partakes. It is sometimes suggested that Creation, Incarnation, and Atonement spring from

---

[1] In Essay VI. pp. 314-315, 321-322.
[2] 1 John iv. 16, 20.

the *will* rather than the *nature* of God.   If this means
that there is anything arbitrary about them, and that,
if they had not been, God could still have been God,
we must unhesitatingly reject the suggestion.[1]   " With
reverence be it said, the very being and blessedness of
God are implicated in the existence, the perfection, the
salvation of finite souls." [2]

If Man is bound to God, and only comes to himself
by throwing himself on God, this relation must be
grounded in the very nature of God Himself.   And is
not this asserted in the doctrine of the Trinity?   The
true life of man, the Christian holds, consists in filial
love of God ; and belief in the divinity of God the
Son implies that filial love is a quality of God Himself.[3]
We are always in danger of leaving out of our conception of God some of the most precious things in human
experience, in deference to some false idea of divine
dignity.   Thus it is only with difficulty that we can
persuade ourselves to think of God as loving men with
the particularity with which one man loves another.
Such love seems too small a thing for the attention of
God.   But we should by now have learnt to distrust
our canons of greatness.   The waters of Jordan may
have properties of greater value than those of Abana
and Pharphar.   To deny love to God is to belittle
Him : it is to make man superior to God.[4]

In the same way, if religious experience is the
highest thing in the life of man, we must not make
this foreign to the life and experience of God Himself.[5]

---

[1] But see the reconciliation of " nature " and " will " in Essay V. pp. 247-248.
[2] John Caird, *The Fundamental Ideas of Christianity*, p. 155.
[3] Cf. Essay V. p. 251.
[4] Cf. Browning's *Saul* :

> I refrain lest I worst
> E'en the Giver in one gift.   Behold I could love if I durst.

[5] The opposite view would make God incapable of sharing in some of the best
things in human life ; as the popular hymn deprives the angels of the experience of
redemption :

> A song which even angels can never, never sing ;
> They know not Christ as Saviour, but worship Him as King.

God Himself must be religious ; and this is implied by the doctrine of the Trinity, which means that God can " know God."

The " hard saying "—that the love of man for God is part of the love wherewith God loves Himself— would then contain a profound truth. The union of God and man is necessary to the full reality of either. Christian theism differs from other theism largely by its emphasis on immanence ; and this is not nearly enough realized.

III. This View is not " Pantheistic "

At this point, we may probably feel considerable uneasiness. Our argument so far seems to be, that the intellectual foundations of religion should be stated rather as the philosopher than as the man of religion is accustomed to state them ; that this is really borne out by experience and even—or, perhaps, most of all—by religious experience ; that, in short, popular theology has a good deal to learn from philosophy, and that philosophy takes us nearer than the accepted theology to a true expression of the religious consciousness. But if so, we shall have to meet two grave difficulties.

(1) It will be said that our conclusion, even if true, is certainly revolutionary ; and that, disguise it as we may, it is Pantheism not Theism. And, though Pantheism may take a Christian form, there is really something pagan and aristocratic about it. It certainly does away with the individual, personal God of ordinary religion. But if Christianity, when it comes to full consciousness of its own meaning and implications, becomes pantheistic, at least let us have the fact clearly stated and emphasized and not glossed over !

(2) We have claimed to base our argument on experience. But it may be said that the experience on which we have drawn is too partial ; and that we have treated mysticism as though it were the true norm of

spiritual excellence, whereas it is really a one-sided and specialized development. Hence we have travelled in our search for evidence away altogether from our concrete world of buying and selling, of loving and suffering, of ordinary human life and human interests ; away from will and character, and from the Western world of striving and achieving, to the quietism of the shadowy East ;[1] away above all from the historical development of religion and of Christianity, with which the rest of this volume deals, and which we are professing to justify. Thus the mystic and the saint are not identical. And even about the term "saint" there is something a little hectic and sickly. The average man agrees with William James in treating "saintliness" as an abnormal development of particular excellences, admirable in many ways, but with distinct limitations, and far from being a model which all men should imitate.

These difficulties are formidable, but not final. We need not be too much afraid of labels. If we are accused of "pantheism" we need not be in too great a hurry to exculpate ourselves, but should rather ask what exactly are the objectionable features of pantheism. These appear to be, a tendency to antinomianism and the fact that it springs from a partial and one-sided experience. But it is necessary to distinguish. It *is* true of some mysticisms and some monisms that they leave out much and reduce all human interests and human distinctions to illusion. But this is not true of all. There is a mysticism which is not specialized, but is that to which all our higher experiences point. In the fine words of Mr. McTaggart : "A mysticism which ignored the claims of the understanding would no doubt be doomed. None ever went about to break logic but in the end logic broke him. But there is a mysticism which starts from the standpoint of the understanding and only transcends that standpoint, in

1 But Christianity is not a European religion in origin.

so far as it shows itself not to be ultimate. To transcend the lower is not to ignore it." [1]

The vital question then is not, "Is our conclusion mystical and 'pantheistic'?" but "Is it continuous with ordinary life and ordinary morality? Does the optimism, which we proclaim, in fact make the issue of goodness and evil unreal? Does the union of man with God, which is the centre of our philosophy, in fact make human selfhood unreal?" The appeal here is to actual experience. The philosophy which we are advocating admittedly rests on *some* experience, though the value of that experience is questioned. And, in experience, it is where the sense of union with God is greatest that individuality is strongest. It is where the sense of redemption is so strong as to break out into the address, *O felix culpa quae talem et tantum meruit habere Redemptorem*, that the practical antipathy to sin is greatest. If it is only by the way of repentance that sin itself becomes an element in good, the danger of antinomianism is unreal.[2] To Pantheism, in the objectionable sense, all specific finitude and all moral distinctions are lost. But this is not so, on our view. For, first, our contention is, that the kind of experience on which we are building is central and not specialized, that it is not merely one path of ascent, but the upland to which *all* such paths lead. And, secondly, experience seems to show that the seeming contradictions in such a view are not to be pressed. For it is the man who is most wholly possessed by God who is the man of richest and most effective individuality; and it is the saint, in whom the experience of redemption is the centre of bliss, who is actually the least sinful of

---

[1] *Studies in Hegelian Cosmology*, p. 292.

[2] Cf. Webb, *op. cit.* pp. 274-275. "The condition of *atonement* is *repentance*; except where there is repentance, sin is not done away. Now repentance excludes the antinomian attitude which regards sin as no sin. It presupposes a realization of its character as sin. . . . A man could not be at once in the attitude of making light of sin by treating it as the proper and inevitable means to something better, and in the attitude of condemning sin as sin must be condemned in any repentance which could bring the forgiveness by which the sin is taken away." Cf. also Essay VI.

men. Development is continuous ; the later steps do
not reverse the earlier ; nothing that is of value at the
lower stages is simply lost at the higher.

We are here involved in the wider issue of the
proper relation of philosophy to common sense. On
the one hand, philosophy must start from common
sense.[1] Unless it can establish its continuity with the
ordinary experience of the mass of men, it is simply in
the air. And it is the failure to do this sufficiently that
is the chief weakness of the philosophies generally, as
compared with the religions. But, because it must
start from common sense, it does not follow that it
must end there. The conclusions of science as to the
ultimate nature of the physical universe carry us very
far indeed from first appearances'; but we accept them,
because the scientist is able to demonstrate the continuity
of his conclusions with ordinary sense-experience. To
say that the language of some great mystic about
absorption in God is very remote from popular
experience, is not to say that it may not be of supreme
philosophical importance. Our Jacob's ladder must be
firmly planted on earth, but it may lead to the heaven
of heavens.

IV. This Philosophy is not Inconsistent with Orthodox Christianity

Our sincerity and consistency may be questioned
from the other side ; from the camp, not of the theologians, but of the philosophers. We have followed
the general line of thought of Dr. Bosanquet and Mr.
Bradley. Does not this really carry us altogether
beyond orthodox theology, as in the opinion of these
distinguished thinkers it certainly does? Thus Dr.
Bosanquet finds room in his system for Christianity as
"a great world-experience," one of the highest, higher

[1] See above, p. 435.

and truer than mere morality, but partial and inadequate
in various assignable ways. Christian theology is, from
this point of view, a piece of anthropomorphic picture-
thinking. The Absolute is something bigger and
wider than any personal or quasi-personal God, something more like Swinburne's "Hertha" :

> I am that which began ;
> Out of me the years roll ;
> Out of me God and man ;
> I am equal and whole.
> God changes, and man, and the form of them bodily ; I am the soul.

Christian optimism, with its "heaven" in the future,
is too naïve, too much like a fairy story. The true
optimism is of sterner stuff, and is from a human point
of view more austere ; having more of the spirit of the
great Shakespearean tragedies, promising no "happy
endings," but only leaving us with the feeling, "nothing
is here for tears."

If this is the conclusion of the masters, does it not
imply a want of intellectual courage on our part to stop
short of it ? Will not a future generation look on a
position such as ours as we look on the "harmonies"
of Genesis and Science which abounded in the maga-
zines of the "'seventies" and "'eighties"? Are we
not attempting an insecure combination of thought and
sentiment, and refusing to face fully the logic of our
own argument ? And should we not do better boldly
to face the facts, even if it means moving far from our
moorings and putting out to the open sea ? There is
a spiritual cowardice which begins to count the cost of
truth and takes refuge in a very subtle insincerity. It
is difficult to be sure that one has sufficiently discounted
the influence of a particular tradition and environment.
For such reasons as these, the professed Christian hardly
gets a hearing in the world of philosophy ; and the
esoteric Christian is rather a humbug.

It is difficult to argue here, for the issue is not

so much a matter of logic[1] as of the estimate of relative values and proportions in experience. For this is the way in which we arrive at the premisses of our philosophy. What is wanted here is judicial capacity as distinct from dialectical acuteness; the power, as Dr. Bosanquet says, to grasp the "higher obvious" and put the central things in the centre, or, as he finely calls it, the "penetrative imagination." It is in this region that we have to meet our philosophical critics; and we cannot hope to argue and convince, but only to indicate the grounds on which we believe it possible with honesty to adopt a different view from theirs.

(a) *Our view gives a more central place in experience to Religion.*—We look on Christianity not as "*a* great world-experience," but as *the* great world-experience; the leaven with expansive power to leaven the whole lump. The message of Christianity is the supremacy of love; and this is confirmed by a philosophical examination of experience.

> For life with all it yields of joy or woe
> Is just our chance o' the prize of learning love.

This is not only the secret of human life, but the clue to the inner meaning of the whole universe.

We give, then, more place to humanity and to human interests in the Absolute, because we give to religion—and to Christianity—a more inclusive and interpretative position in world-experience.

(b) *We wish to insist more on the difference in truth of different categories and the superiority of the highest.*—The fetish of size contributes to a negative result. We need to insist on the importance of quality as against quantity, and (in Mr. Illingworth's words) of "spiritual intensity against material immensity." We must inter-

---

[1] I do not in the least mean to question Dr. Bosanquet's view (*op. cit.* chap. viii.) that the judgment of values is in the last resort a rational judgment. But the element of reason is here deeply imbedded and not easily producible for controversial purposes.

pret the Whole in terms of the highest thing in it
rather than insist on its quasi-spatial vastness. Otherwise, we inevitably use a lower category where we might
use a higher.

> For the loving worm within its clod
> Were diviner than a loveless God
> Amid all his worlds, I will dare to say.

The measure of anthropomorphism in the Christian
doctrine of Incarnation is on the line of the philosophical development from Spinoza to Hegel and of
the increase of readiness to see perfection in what is
determinate and, in that sense, limited.

(c) *We can emphasize the continuity between popular
and " esoteric " theology, because we are aware of development within experience.*—If the greatness of the gulf
between the finite and the Infinite is urged against
us—as when Mr. Bradley says, " For me a person is
finite or is meaningless "[1]—we may reassure ourselves by
the recollection that we are familiar in experience with
growth in inclusiveness and in identity with others ;
and that this, so far from being inconsistent with the
individuality and richness which is characteristic of
personality, actually tends to keep pace with it.[2]

(d) *The recognition of an element of metaphor in all
theology need not debar it from a philosophical status.*—
We must admit that there is an element of picture-
thinking in all theology. We have to use symbols or
metaphors in which a more advanced intelligence would
no doubt see crudities. But this admission is robbed of
its sting, if it is not suggested that the philosopher is
initiated into something better. Until we have better
categories at our disposal it is idle to throw stones. If,
then, it is said that the Absolute contains self-conscious
beings, but is not itself a self-conscious being, we shall

---

[1] *Appearance and Reality* (2nd Edition), p. 532.

[2] Cf. Bosanquet, *op. cit.* p. 223. " It is facile but dangerous, simply to drop the
higher characters of experience, when we endeavour to conceive the Absolute. It is
a more trustworthy plan to indicate, if possible, the line of their transmutation."

reply that this is to think too exclusively in spatial terms. It would only be sound, if we could find a unity which was higher than the unity of self-consciousness. "Man, once descried, imprints for ever his presence on all lifeless things." We must not relapse to a lower level of thought.

We shall, then, scarcely be content with the language of Dr. Inge: "The God of religion is not the Absolute, but the highest form under which the Absolute can manifest Himself to finite creatures in various stages of imperfection."[1] We shall prefer to say with Mr. Webb: "God is more (not less) than the Absolute in so far as in religion I know (or at least feel) the Absolute to be in this respect—worshipfulness—more than by itself the abstract term Absolute expresses."[2]

We must expect to be told that, in the view here taken, we are attempting to combine inconsistencies, and so are showing a want of intellectual grasp. But such logic is too narrow for life, in which we are continually finding that the truth can only be expressed in the form of paradoxes. Thus Knowledge, on the one hand, as recent philosophers have insisted, is in its very nature an awareness of an object which is independent of the act of awareness ; on the other hand, when knowledge of the universe is in question, the knowing must make a difference to the object known, for the universe includes the knowing mind and its knowledge and would be incomplete without it. In Choice again, as Green and other moralists have insisted, there must be a disinterested desire for the object apart from any effect that it is to produce on the chooser ; otherwise, as with the mere pleasure-seeker, the effect is not forthcoming. And yet, as Green also points out, to "choose" an object is to conceive of it as in some way tending to the personal good or satisfaction of the chooser. Thus, in love, the object of desire is at once the loved one and communion with him.

---

[1] *Personal Idealism and Mysticism*, p. 13.   [2] *Op. cit.* p. 254.

So, when we come to Religion, the object of worship is at once God as transcendent—as real and complete in Himself; and the union of man with God, without which, in the last resort, God Himself is incomplete. This is suggested by Dr. Inge: "During a philosophical discussion not long ago, one of the speakers observed, ' I could not worship what is part of myself '; to which the other replied, ' And I could not worship what is *not* part of myself.' " [1] The paradoxes of Christian morals are familiar. And Mr. Webb reminds us that the chief characteristic of the Christian attitude to Sin is the combination of an insistence on the need of repentance, which by itself might appear morbid, with an optimistic assurance of forgiveness, which by itself might appear immoral.

These paradoxes, by their presence at all points of the compass, support one another. No doubt the contradictions are not ultimate ; but, at our level of thought, the inclusion of an element of contradiction seems to be a sign of reality and of largeness of view rather than of error. A criticism, then, which merely points to superficial contradictions, is adapted to the schools rather than to real life. [2]

But, at this point, we may again feel uneasy. "Is not " we may be asked, "your contrast of logic and life simply a cheap appeal *ad populum* ? At least, if you adopt this line, do not pretend to offer a philosophical defence of religion ! You cannot eat your cake and have it ; use logic up to a point, and then, when it becomes a nuisance, dismiss it ; assume the truth of the Law of Contradiction as long as you are refuting rival theories, and treat it as obsolete when it seems likely to be used against your own view. Does not honesty demand that you should define your terms, and

---

[1] *Contentio Veritatis*, p. 61.

[2] This appeal to life is the nerve of the whole dialectic process in the Hegelian system. The mind is driven on, through contradictions, from one category to another, because real experience is always proving itself too large to be contained in the categories so far arrived at.

that, if, for instance, you are going to discuss personality, you should use the term in a clear and consistent sense all through ? When it becomes clear that personality, as we ordinarily understand it, is not attributable to God, you must not turn round and say : ' When we speak of divine "personality," we must be understood to use the term in a Pickwickian sense.' Our hearts warm to J. S. Mill, when he rejects any such conjuring and proclaims : ' I will call no being " good " who is not what I mean when I apply the term to my fellow-creatures.' You may, indeed, save yourselves from refutation by such manœuvres ; but only because honest men will retire from the argument. But when theologians indulge in this kind of apologetics, they are viewed by persons of the type of Leslie Stephen with a certain robust contempt."

Here, again, we must admit that theologians have sometimes given cause for complaint. But the edge of the accusation is partly turned if we recognize that there is an element of paradox in *all* experience, and that it is not merely invented *ad hoc* by the slippery theologian. And we can but appeal to experience, and ask which is the farthest from truth in other walks of life, the Paradox or the Dilemma ? It always sounds plausible to demand a plain answer (yes or no) to a plain question. Yet the dilemma is the familiar device of bullying counsel with a bad case. " The plain man and the practical judge expect a plain answer, yes or no, to a plain question. But the investigator and the criminologist have learned that plain questions and plain answers are only possible for those of hurried and blunted senses, guilty and not guilty are terms of a limited province and are conditioned in their application by a social convention." [1] Hence it is just dislike of mere verbiage and determination to see things as they are which should carry us beyond such sharp antinomies.

[1] Wallace, *Lectures and Essays*, p. 556.

Under these circumstances, it is natural to demand a criterion ; as when Henry Sidgwick remarked that he had never been able to distinguish between those contradictions which were a mark of error, and those which were supposed to be a sign of the higher truth. But it is not possible to give any clear answer to this natural demand : it is impossible to lay down any *a priori* criterion. We can only appeal to "the penetrative imagination" as exercised upon the individual case. And here the contradictions with which we are dealing are contradictions which have been actually, to some extent, transcended in actual experience.

We have raised a very ambitious problem ; and our suggestions towards a solution are, at the best, fragmentary and unsatisfying. The reader can hardly avoid feeling this, for the writer himself feels it strongly. Yet we need not therefore end on a pessimistic note.

(1) It is of the greatest importance, for truth's sake, to understate rather than to overstate the results of argument ; and we should not be too much disappointed, if we end with questions rather than with answers, for it is half the battle to ask the right questions. Moreover, as was suggested in the Introduction to this Essay, the present situation is transitional. We can only expect, therefore, tentative results, and to present something of the nature of "an interim report."

(2) Though in Part Three there is nothing like a complete answer to the difficulties raised in Parts One and Two, I believe that the suggestions towards an answer rest on a sufficiently secure basis to give a real intellectual support to the religious life. We have tried to vindicate our right to hold a position, which, from opposite sides, is denounced as an inconsistent and impossible compromise. Hence we have been obliged, in Part Three, to defend ourselves on two sides at once. To the religious critic, who argues that, though the

personality of God is vital to religion, the Absolute is plainly impersonal, we have said : " Revise your conception of personality ! The conception on which your difficulty is based is intellectually crude, and is not borne out by the highest religious experience." To the philosopher, who says that our reasoned formulation of experience should be carried to its logical conclusion, and that, if this is done, religion will be left behind, we have ventured to reply : " Pay greater attention to the experience of the religious man ; it may be that you will find that the answer to its riddles, and to all the riddles of life, is to be learned, not by leaving this particular experience on one side, but by pushing further and further into its heart."

If we are dissatisfied with this conclusion, may it not be partly because we are inclined to ask more of philosophy than it can possibly give, and so to underrate what may be really gained ? Philosophy can offer no pocket-answer to infidelity. It cannot outrun experience, or put into experience what is not as yet there. It cannot make an irreligious man religious. The task of philosophy is to enable us to make coherent and intelligible to ourselves such experience, religious or otherwise, as we have. To say that you cannot make men religious by logical argument is about as true and about as false as it is to say that you cannot make them moral by Act of Parliament. In each case, it is possible to remove some difficulties, and so to contribute a little to the desired result. Furthermore, it cannot be fairly expected that philosophy, working in abstraction, should construct *ex vacuo* the whole of Christian belief. What it may do, is to provide a framework, into which the religion of the Incarnation fits, and which that religion welds together.

Such being the state of the case, it may be that some will feel that we have talked too glibly of " development," and have taken up too patronising an attitude towards the theology of the saints. Our reply to these is that, if, in any points, we would develop or modify the theology of the saints, it is only by a more consistent appeal to the implications of their own religious experience. The understanding of that experience is the whole task of the theologian. The experience itself is the foundation from which all our theorizings start and the tribunal by which, in their turn, our theories must themselves be judged.

EPILOGUE

EPILOGUE

ALL who try to mould into new forms of expression the elements of the spiritual life must end with a sense of failure. What they cast into the crucible is so precious, and what comes out of it is so disappointing.

The writers of this book have tried to find ways of saying to the men of their own time what they believe and why they believe it. They are convinced that it was right to try, that they have done their best, and that they have not succeeded. The expression of faith in words can never be accomplished; only life can express it. The Word must become flesh if it is to redeem the world; it is the Life which is the Light of men.

The kingdom of God is not yet come; the world-rulers of this darkness have not fallen. The dumb need of the heathen world is still unsatisfied; the nations, whose citizens profess allegiance to Christ, show but few traces of His Spirit's influence either in their own condition or in their dealings with one another.

Jesus of Nazareth claimed that He was the Founder of the kingdom of God. That claim will never be admitted as a consequence of reasoning, however

cogent ; it will be admitted when men again see His
followers conquering the world for Him by His own
methods in the power of His Spirit.

> O that the armies indeed were arrayed ! O joy of the onset !
> Sound, thou Trumpet of God, come forth, Great Cause, to
> array us,
> King and leader appear, thy soldiers sorrowing seek Thee.

So we are tempted to exclaim, as we see men's hearts
failing them for fear and for looking after those things
which are coming on the earth.   But it is at such times
that we are bidden to look up, for our redemption
draweth nigh.

And indeed the hour is come ; already the armies are
arrayed ; the battle is begun.   For all the world is in
transformation.   Europe and America seethe with
social movement ; India toils in the birth-pangs of
an unknown future ; Japan has leapt to the van of
civilisation ; China is awake from age-long sleep and
plunging into new life.   Even the Dark Continent is
astir as Mohammedanism surges across it.   Now is the
opportunity and the test of faith ; and even now in the
vision of faith the Captain of the Armies of Salvation
goes forth conquering and to conquer.

INDEX

INDEX

Abelard, 239, 240-43, 255, 257
Absolutism. *See* God
Adoptionist position, 248
Advent Hope, the, 45, 170
Agape. *See* Eucharist
Agnosticism—
philosophical. *See* God
rise of popular, 4-11
Allen—
Archdeacon, 113
A. V. G., 422
Allin, T., 237
Anselm, St., 239-40, 241, 257, 301
Anthropomorphism, 40, 291, 447-8,
452, 454, 475, 493, 498, 506,
508, 516, 518
Anti-Christ, 89, 121, 169, 200
Apocalypse, the, 89, 198-201
Apocalyptic Eschatology—
Anti-Christ, the, 89, 121, 169,
200
attitude of our Lord towards, 14,
94, 101-2, 107-10, 111-19,
127, 156-7, 246, 260
cosmology of, 111-12
development of, 87-92
eschatological interpretation of
Gospels, 76-8
interimsethik, 14, 107-10
John the Baptist, influence on,
92-3
materialistic symbolism of, 112,
136, 137, 156, 200, 201
Messiah, conception of, in, 89-
91, 92, 173-4, 246
Messiah, pre-existence of, 91,
174, 207
Messianic Kingdom. *See* Kingdom of God

Apocalyptic Eschatology (*contd.*)—
New Jerusalem, 89, 200
permanent value of, 119-21,
170
pseudonymity of, 89, 102, 199
resurrection of the dead in, 89,
130-31, 136
Son of Man, 90-91, 101-2, 116-
119, 173-4
transvaluation of, in New Testa-
ment, Essay IV. *passim*
Apollinarianism, 75, 229-30, 248
Apologetic, true and false, 78, 140,
377, 490
Apostolic succession, 370, 382-7,
393, 409, 418-22
Canons, 420
Church Order, 420
Aquinas, St. Thomas, 390, 430
Archdeacon, office of, 415
Arianism, 227-8
Aristotle, 222, 223, 224, 232, 277,
367, 434, 471, 499, 503
Ascension, the, 131 f., 155, 322, 343
Athanasius, St., 228-9, 238, 413
Atonement, 46, 124-7, 172-5, 193-8,
229, 234, 237-42, 254-5, 262,
266-335, 344, 509, 510-11,
514
Augustine, St., 202, 235-8, 256, 292,
365, 373, 388
Authority—
and Church Order, 381-402,
408-22
and reason, 62-3, 352, 365-80,
469, 475-6
and reunion, 403-7
and truth, 365-80
of Church, 66, 351-3, VIII. *passim*

Authority (*contd.*)—
of Scripture, 60, 62-7, 70
principle of, 362-422

Babylon, 65, 89, 200
Balfour, Right Hon. A. J., 468
Baptism, 98, 156, 161-2, 183, 185,
237, 388, 409
of Christ, 94, 98, 117, 260
Bartlet, J. V., 387
Batiffol, P., 383
Bender, W., 506
Bergson, H., 480, 481
Berkeley, Bishop, 454
Bernard, St., 235, 240, 257
Bible, the, 27-71
attitude of Reformers to, 372
authority of, Essay II. *passim*
cosmology of, 10 f., 111-12,
131 f.
degrees of inspiration in, 36,
69
development of theology and
ethics in, 39-45, Essay IV.
passim
historical value of, 67-8. *See
also* Gospels
infallibility of, 29-30, 372
Binyon, Laurence, 309
Bishops, 370-71, 394-400, 410-22
Blatchford, R., 428
Bosanquet, B., 280, 296, 431, 445,
453, 481, 489, 502, 515, 517,
518
Bradley, A. C., 451
Bradley, F. H., 442, 449, 452, 453,
469, 475, 477, 485, 489, 515,
518
Bright, W., 391
Brontë, Emily, 479
Browning, 7, 24, 47, 51, 61, 64,
216, 249, 252, 284, 288, 307,
473, 488, 491, 502, 507, 511
Burke, 281
Burkitt, F. C., 76, 113, 117
Bury, F. B., 68
Bushnell, H., 319
Butler, Bishop, 483

Caird, E., 429, 479
Caird, J., 505, 511
Caldecott, A., 483, 491
Calvinism, 390
Carlyle, Thomas, 5, 7, 31

Catholicism, 381-6, 391-407
Roman, one-sided development
of authority in, 371, 375
Charism, 370, 400, 409, 410, 421
Chesterton, G. K., 284, 305, 437, 441
Choice, act of, 277, 519
Christ—
Adoptionist view of, 248
Apollinarian view of, 75, 229 f.,
248
Arian view of, 227-8
as Prophet, 94-9, 102, 103, 385
Ascension of, 131 f., 155, 322,
343
Baptism of, 94, 98, 117, 260
Call of, 94-9
concealment of Messiahship, 117,
156
death of, 121-7, 174-9, 194-8,
216, 237-42, 262, 298-316,
509
descent into Hades, 332
Divinity of, 46, 79, Essays IV.
and V. *passim*, 314-16, 379,
509-11
Dynamic Monarchian view of,
225
Eutychian view of, 230
fellowship in, 357 f.
Historic, the, 73-145
human knowledge of, 75-6, 213,
250, 368, 385, 408
Humanity, real, of, 75, 229-30,
316
mediation of, in Creation, 188,
192, 227
Messianic consciousness of, 98-
102, 121-7, 153, 208, 385,
408
Monophysite view of, 75, 230
Nestorian view of, 230, 234
new creation in, 176, 188
New Testament interpretation of,
147-210
originality of, 101-2, 104, 113, 125
pre-existence of, 174-5, 187-8,
207, 249
Priesthood of, 193-8, 322, 393
Resurrection of, 17, 21, 81, 127-
141, 151-5, 168, 178, 315-16,
339, 379
sinlessness of, 153-4, 248, 259,
305, 313-14, 368
teaching of, 103-18

Christ (*contd.*)—
  Temptation of, 99-102, 248, 260, 313-14
  vindication in history of, 22, 141-5
  " Warrior " conception of, 91-2, 101, 260
Church, 339-59, 322-3
  and sacraments, 343 etc., 391 etc. *See also* Sacraments
  authority of, 66, 365-80, 351-3
  infallibility of, 368-71
  influence of secular environment on, 355-8
  inspiration of, 367 etc.
  institutionalism in, 391 etc., 401, 404, 408-22
  laity in, 399, 400
  orders, 381-402, 408-22
  primitive, 151-64, 340-41, 409 *sqq.*
Cicero, 351
Civilization, modern, 15-18
Class-divisions, 357
Clement of Rome, 398, 412, 416, 419, 420
Clericalism, 396, 398
Cobden, Richard, 8
Coleridge, S. T., 29, 70-71, 281
Communion—
  of Saints, 332, 343, 344-59, 404
  spiritual, 402
  the Holy. *See* Eucharist
  with God, 32-4, 42, 46, 55, 56, 61, 65, 128, 184, 215-17, 238, 253, 275, 287, 305-6, 314, 372, 392
Communism, 348
Comte, 440
Confession, practice of, 396-7, 404
Congregationalism, 394
Continuity, principle of, x, 395
Conversion, 95-9, 292-3, 302, 326-7, 328, 358
  of St. Paul, 98, 165-8
Copernicus, 11, 436, 438, 460
Corporate witness. *See* Authority
Cosmology, Biblical, 10 f., 112, 131 f.
Covenant, the New, 44, 193-6
Creation, 227-8
  the New, 176
Creed, of Union, 231
  the Nicene, 68
Creighton, Bishop, 65

Criticism, duty of, 375, 378
Crucifixion, the, 17, 21, 49, 51, 121-7, 141, 151-2, 153-4, 164, 171-6, 238-42, 255, 257, 269-335, 341-2
Cumont, F., 182
Cyprian, St., 371

Dale, R. W., 271
Damien, Father, 310
Darwin, C., 6
Darwinism, 6, 11, 24, 433, 439
David Copperfield, 296, 308-10
Deacons, office of, 411-22
Dead, Prayers for the, 346-7, 404
Deism, 5, 244
Descartes, 427, 432, 433, 458, 489
Development, intellectual, 373-80, 428, 472
  of theology, 39-41, 45-6, 428, 430
Didache, 369, 383, 388, 396, 412, 415-16, 419
Dinsmore, C. A., 297, 298, 322
Diocese, size of, 399, 415
Divinity of Christ. *See* Christ
Dobschütz, E. von, 45
Du Bose, W. P., 320, 330, 509
Duchesne, L., 383
Du Maurier, G., 436

Eliot, George, 5, 298
Emerson, R. W., 275, 276, 490
Episcopacy. *See* Bishops
Eschatology. *See* Apocalyptic Eschatology
Eucharist, 162-3, 183-7, 196, 254-5, 343-7, 388, 391-2, 410, etc.
  and ministry in primitive Church, 410 etc.
  and mystery religions, 183, 401
  as sacrifice, 184, 196, 254-5, 344-6, 392
  Catholic view of, 391-3
  original significance of, 162-3
  Pauline doctrine of, 184-7
  Protestant view of, 388
Eucken, R., 480
Eutyches, 230-31
Evangelicalism, strength and weakness of, 4, 13, 303, 304, 318-319, 324, 327, 328, 330, 405
Evil, problem of, 9, 47, 48, 50, 215, 218-23, 228, 246, 274-85, 464, 483-4

Experience, religious, 27-71, 152-71, 203-9, 287-311, 321-33, 352, 376, 378-80, 386, 391-2

Fairbairn, A. M., 303

Faith—
and freedom, 7
and reason, 373-80
and the sacraments, 343-5, 388, 391-2
as interpreted by St. Paul, 178-9
as interpreted in Epistle to the Hebrews, 192
individual and corporate, 351-3
mediated through Christ and His acts, 20-23, 154
mediated through the Scriptures, 36-9
paradox of, 48 etc.

Fall, the, 282-3

Fellowship in Christ, 357-8

Forgiveness, 110-11, 235, 269, 293, 325, 329, 354, 387, 397, 520

Forsyth, P. T., 303

Forsyth, T. M., 445

Friends, Society of, 388, 402

Gairdner, W. H. J., 508

German Protestantism, 372, 389
theology, 76, 78

Gibson, Munro, 69

Glover, T. R., 105, 160

God—
and the Absolute, 424-524
Agnostic attitude towards, 214, 438-46
anger of, 41, 241, 278, 279-80, 287, 302
Deistic view of, 5, 139, 244
experienced need of, 478-9
" humanity " of, 249, 251, 252
influence of political ideas on conception of, 244
love of, 48, 111, 159, 183, 208-9, 240-42, 254-7, 262, 287, 296-300, 341, 347, 358, 387, 509, 510
Marcion's conception of, 241
moral attributes of, 213-14, 245, 251, 461-77
Old Testament conception of, 39-41, 218-19, 241
Personality of, 244-5, 248-51, 431, 488-512. See also Trinity

God (contd.)—
" proofs " of existence of, 427, 432-4
relation to the world and to man, 190-91, 192, 218, 240, 246, 348, 359, 478-80, 487-8, 503-7, 509-12, 514
vindication of rule of, 22, 43, 129, 140-41, 510
" God-fearers," 164

Goethe, 502

Gore, C. (Bishop of Oxford), 75, 383, 399, 400

Gospel of St. John—
general characteristics of, 82-3, 202-8
Logos doctrine of, 203-4, 207, 214, 227, 243-5

Gospels, Synoptic—
development of eschatology in, 112
historical value of, 67-8, 80-82, 83-7
" humour " in, 105
originality of St. Mark, 81, 86, 98, 117
" Q," 82, 93, 99, 101, 112, 152, 155
sources of, 80-82
Synoptic problem, 80-82
title Son of God in, 103, 119

Gosse, E., 10, 269

Grace—
as moulding character, 326
Augustinian doctrine of, 237
of orders, 399-400, 421
Protestant view of, 387
sacramental view of, 391 etc.
See also Eucharist

Greek Fathers, theology of, 223-33, 238, 253, 255, 281, 327

Green, T. H., 277, 280, 480, 499, 501, 519

Gregory of Nyssa, 231

Guilt. See Sin

Gunkel, H., 186, 187

Hamilton, H. F., 383

Harnack, A., 226, 230, 234, 238, 413, 420

Harris, Rendel, 160

Hatch, E., 422

Hawkins, Sir J. C., 86

Heathen religions, 181-3, 218, 331, 341, 401

Heaven, 112, 196-7, 219, 222, 245, 323, 339, 343, 344, 345, 392, 484, 516
Hebrew prophets, psychology of, 37, 94-8, 118
Hebrews, Epistle to the, 191-8, 322
Hegel, 56, 480, 483, 485, 490, 518, 520
Heine, 29
Hellenism, 163, 165, 193, 207
Hellenist attitude, the, 164-6, 253-255, 484
Henley, W. E., 285
Heraclitus, 214
Herrmann, W., 372, 389
Holland, H. Scott, 279, 483
Holmes, C. J., 278
Hood, Thomas, 285
Hooker, 482
Hort, F. J. A., 422
Hügel, Baron B. von, 53, 389
Hume, 441, 454, 455, 470, 484
Huxley, 463

Ignatius, St., 412-19
Illingworth, J. R., 517
Immortality, 89, 115, 127-37, 510. See Life, eternal
Incarnation, 212-63, 299, 388, 509-512, 518. See also Christ
Individualism, 177, 234, 253, 284-5, 307-9, 349-50
Individuality, 225, 480, 500, 505
Individuals, interdependence of, 253-254, 501
Inge, W. R., 207, 332, 519, 520
Inspiration. See Bible and Church
Institutionalism. See Church
Intellectual unsettlement, 4-11
Interimsethik. See Apocalyptic
Interpretation of Christ in New Testament, 147-210
Invocation of Saints, 346-7
Irenaeus, St., 370, 421

Jacks, L. P., 496, 497, 498
James, William, 58, 96, 97, 271, 272, 274, 276, 289, 427, 469, 470, 471, 480, 481, 485, 489, 490, 492, 506, 513
Jerome, St., 412-19
Jewish history, traditional view of, 67
Johannine Epistle, first, 202-10

John, St.—
the Apostle, 198-9, 202-3, 208-9, 214, 243, 245, 246, 257, 427
the Baptist, 92-4, 161
Jones, Sir Henry, 50, 437, 501
Joseph, H. W. B., 459
Josephus, 94
Judaism, 65, 151, 196, 201, 409, 507-8
Liberal, 163-5, 169, 191-3, 195-6. See also Hellenism
Judgment, 112, 142, 161-2, 270-71, 334-5
Juristic mode of thought, 233, 239, 240, 301-2
Justice, 124, 241, 270-71, 281, 302, 305
Justification, 107, 318-20, 325-6

Kant, 288, 427, 434-5, 439, 489
Khayyám, Omar, 241, 279, 440
Kingdom of God, 89, 108, 111-15, 127, 130, 142, 143, 170, 180, 184, 185, 189, 190-91, 262, 306, 310, 316, 357, 358, 359, 385

Laity. See Church
Lake, Kirsopp, 92, 158, 163, 185, 401
Laplaee, 243
Law, William, 57
Law—
our Lord's estimate of, 106-7, 164-5
St. Paul's estimate of, 105-6, 169-171, 273
St. Stephen's estimate of, 164-5
in relation to prophecy, 40, 409
sacrificial—
our Lord as fulfilling, 125-6
in Hebrews, 193
Laying on of hands, 162, 399, 411, 422
Lay-preaching, 400
Legalism, 365-6, 386, 409
Leo's Tome, 230
Leuba, J. H., 506
Life, eternal, 112, 207, 343-5. See also Immortality
Lightfoot, Bishop, 412, 413
Lincoln, Abraham, 307
Lindsay, T. M., 422
Literalism, 102, 131

Locke, 427, 439, 445, 456, 462, 471
Lodge, Sir Oliver, 274, 282, 287, 294, 297
Logic and life, 513, 515-18, 520
Logical realism, 224, 226, 229
Logos, doctrine of the, 203-4, 207, 214-15, 227, 232, 243-5, 249, 332, 480
Lotze, 480, 482, 504
Lowrie, Walter, 413, 417
Luther, 57, 59, 372

Maccunn, J., 8
Maine, Sir Henry, 280, 283
Manichaeism, 237
Mansel, H. L., 440
Marcionism, 241
Martineau, J., 464
Martyrdom, subjective value of, 312
Mass, the, 396, 403, 404
McTaggart, J. E., 277, 278
Messiahship. See Christ
Messianic Hope. See Apocalyptic
Metaphysics, importance of, 217, 389-90, Essay IX. passim
Mill, J. S., 5, 12, 328, 434, 463, 521
Ministry, the Christian, 381-402, 408-22
Miracle, 17, 129-41, 166-8, 186, 243, 258-9, 492
Missions, 354, 358-9, 410-11
Moberly, R. C., 242, 247, 291, 294, 301, 308, 315, 319, 330, 398, 422, 474, 500
Modernism, 16, 459
Mohammedanism, 65, 508
Mommsen, 68
Monasticism, 16, 356
Monism, 513
Monolatry, 39
Monophysitism, 75, 230
Monothelite heresy, the, 248
Montgomery, Bishop, 358
Moore, Aubrey, 427, 431, 476, 492, 493
Morality, modern criticism of, Essay I.
Moralization of religion, 40-41, 317, 328, 487
Morley, Lord, 276, 437
Mystery religions, 181-3, 401
Mysticism, 83, 235, 512, 513-15
Mythologies, early, 290

"Natural Theology, 5, 427, 428, 470
Neo-Platonism, 228, 235
Nestorius, 230, 234
Nettleship, R. L., 311, 321, 327, 501
Newman, J. H., 33, 330, 440, 469
Nicaea, Synod of, 421
Nicene Creed, the, 68
Nietzsche, 77
Nominalism, 224

"Once-born" and "twice-born," 97, 274-6, 333
Orders. See Church
Origen, 232, 237, 359

Pain, problem of, 47-8, 124, 220-23, 246, 464
Paley, 462
Pantheism, 489, 512-15
Paul, St., 98, 166-191, 219, 245, 272-3, 320, 326, 328, 339, 343, 349, 350, 427, 474, 499
Paul of Samosata, 226-7, 247
Paulinism, 168-91, 272-3
Pelagian controversy, 234-7
Penance, 397
Penitence, 125, 293-8, 303, 307-9, 514
Pentecost, 151-3, 155, 158-60, 323
Personality, 98-9, 248-50, 326-7, 487-512, 523
Pharisaism, 106-7, 261, 305, 328
Philo, 163, 193, 207
Philosophy and religion, 389-90, Essay IX. passim
Pigou, A. C., 457, 469
Plato, 207, 222-4, 232, 277, 434, 483, 485
Platonism, Christian, 328
Neo-, 228, 235
Plutarch, 68
Poincaré, H., 96
Political development, effect of, 244
Polybius, 68
Positivism, 485
Prayer, 139, 294, 306, 318, 324, 354, 355
Presbyters, 411-22
Priesthood—
and sacrifice. See Sacrifice

Priesthood (*contd.*)—
ministerial, 381-400
of Christ. *See* Christ
of Church, 393, 397-8
Pringle-Pattison, A., 448, 480, 495
Private judgment, 375
Progress, 6, 139
Prophecy—
Christian, 158, 198-9, 203, 369, 370, 380, 400, 405, 410, etc.
false, in primitive Church, 416
fulfilment of, 124-7, 142-5, 157
Hebrew, 28, 38, 57, 87-8, 93, 94-9, 122, 124-7
Messianic. *See* Apocalyptic
Prophet, Christ as. *See* Christ
Prophetic theory of ministry, 381, 387-8, 400
Propitiation, 175
Protestantism, 371-3, 375, 386, 387-8, 390-92, 395, 401-7
German, 372
Prothero, R. E., 29
Psychology of conversion and vocation, 95-8

"Q." *See* Gospels
Quietism, 487, 513

Rackham, R. B., 399
Rashdall, H., 430
Redemption, 170-78, 222, 226, 227-228, 232, 237, 256, Essay VI. *passim*
Religious and aesthetic senses, analogy of, 51-3
Renan, E., 77
Resurrection, the, 17, 21, 81, 127-141, 151-5, 168, 178, 315-316, 339, 379
Retribution, Essay VI. *passim*
Reunion, 355, 385, 403-7
Revelation, 32-57, 70, 159-60, 206-208, 217, 223, 345-6
Reynolds, J., 476
Richmond, W., 457
Ritschlianism, 372, 389, 390
Robinson, J. Armitage, 190, 340, 359
Romanes, G. J., 471
Roscellinus, 224
Ross, Johnston, 276
Russell, Bertrand, 10, 16

Sabatier, Auguste, 372
Sabellian heresy, 248, 251
Sacraments, 162-4, 183-5, 231, 323, 343-7, 382-3, 387-8, 391-422. *See also* Church, Baptism, Eucharist, Laying on of hands, Penance
Sacrifice—
our Lord as fulfilling, 124-7, 193-8, 306, 322
Eucharistic, 184, 196, 254-5, 344-6, 392. *See also* Atonement *and* Christ
Saint-Beuve, 41
Saints, invocation of, 346-7
Salvation, 43, 114, 171, 238, 295, 300, 304, 307-20, 325, 329, 330-335, 353, 387, 409, 510, 511
Sanctification, 107, 318, 319, 325
Sanday, W., 85, 300, 303
Scepticism, 435, 459, 470, 472, 489
Schmiedel, P., 185
Schweitzer, A., 76, 77, 78, 117, 120
Selbie, W. B., 387
Semi-Arianism, 228
Sense, religious, 57-63
Shorthouse, J. H., 503
Sidgwick, Henry, 6, 441, 522
Simpson, J. G., 301, 311, 328, 330
Sin, 34, 35, 44, 257, 272, 274-85, 289, 303, 309, 310, 312-15, 316, 319, 324, 327, 328, 333, 514, 520
original, 282-5, 313
Smith, Robertson, 32
Socialism, 17, 349
Socrates, 464
Sohm, R., 413
Son of Man. *See* Apocalyptic Eschatology
Spencer, H., 434
Spinoza, 351, 454, 489, 518
Spirit, Holy, 56, 59, 60, 66, 151-2, 158-9, 162, 179-80, 185-8, 198, 203, 206, 209, 237, 253-256, 263, 322-3, 341, 347, 350-51, 355-9, 365-70, 382, 388, 390, 400, 403-4
in experience of primitive community, 151-2, 158-9, 162
in theology of atonement, 322-3
Johannine doctrine of, 201, 203, 206-9
mediated by institutions, 382, 404

Spirit, Holy (*contd.*)—
 operative in the Church, 341, 347, 350-51, 355-9, 365-70
 Pauline doctrine of, 179-80, 185-8
Spirit and matter, false antithesis of, 258, 390
Spiritual gifts, 186, 400
Stephen, Leslie, 281, 428, 440, 445, 469, 471, 482
Stephen, St., 164-5, 166, 169
Streeter, B. H., 85, 86, 101, 107, 112, 113
Student Movement, 325
Substance, philosophy of, 223-34, 246-57, 489, 495-6
Suffering, glory of, 208, 245
 problem of. *See* Pain
 vicarious. *See* Vicarious suffering
Swinburne, 516
Symbolism, 118, 163, 176, 196, 197, 201, 271, 287, 306, 411, 507
Synoptic problem. *See* Gospels

Taylor, A. E., 446, 448, 449, 453, 475
Temple, Archbishop, 105, 226, 233, 259-60
 W., 236, 292
Temptation, the, 99-102, 260, 313
Tennant, F. R., 283
Tennyson, 6, 132, 136, 445, 466, 488
Thackeray, H. St. J., 131
Theology—
 and metaphysics, 217, 389-90, Essay IX. *passim*
 and religion, 38-9, 374, 379
 development of—
  in Old Testament, 39-41
  in New Testament, 45, 151-210
  in Eastern Church, 223-33
  in Western Church, 233-42

Theology (*contd.*)—
 influence of politics on, 244
 no finality in, x
Thompson, Francis, 318
Thucydides, 68
Tiberius, 142
Tolstoy, 486
Tradition, 27, 84-7, 197, 270, 370, 374, 375, 377, 378, 392, 427-430
Trinity, the Holy, 159-60, 248-51, 508-12
Turner, C. H., 412, 413
Tyrrell, Father, 29, 47, 71, 76, 409

Ultramontanism, 371

Vicarious penitence, 296-7, 307-10
 suffering, 121-7, 157, 172-3, 177, 195, 220-22, 287, 297, 310, 324, 326
Visions, 95-9, 134, 136, 166-8, 200-201, 252

Wallace, W., 477, 500, 504, 508, 521
Walpole, G. H. S., 55
Ward, J., 480
Webb, C. C. J., 58, 341, 379, 426, 431, 433, 499, 503-4, 514, 519, 520
Weinel, P., 185, 203
Weiss, J., 76, 153-4
Wells, H. G., 10, 349, 436
Wesley, 275
Whitman, Walt, 275-6
Wilberforce, S., 70
Wilson, J. M., 57, 300
Wordsworth, J., 399
 W., 452

Xenophon, 205

THE END